Optiminity and Pecuniary Perfusion Protographia of Adglutinated Curatorium Concrescence and Accretions

Felix Boyd

Optiminity and Pecuniary Perfusion Protographia of Adglutinated Curatorium Concrescence and Accretions

First Edition December 2025

Written by Felix Boyd

TABLE OF CONTENTS

CHAPTER 1: INTRODUCTION

CHAPTER 1: INTRODUCTION

Preview

The effects of mergers and acquisitions on the economy profoundly affect the business world, which is undergoing profound change as a result. This chapter explains the scenario of mergers and acquisitions that took place in India and elsewhere around the globe. This chapter will address the history of mergers and acquisitions, the different types of these deals, as well as the various characteristics of these deals. The legal structure of mergers and acquisitions was covered in a cursory manner in this article. The implications of mergers and acquisitions are discussed further in this chapter.

1.1 Background of Corporate Mergers and Acquisitions

The economy has undergone significant transformations since the implementation of accelerated structural reforms. Facing various macro and micro-level challenges common to developing economies, the government introduced a comprehensive strategy addressing economic, social, political, legal, and financial aspects. This approach aims to improve competitiveness in the short term while ensuring long-term sustainability. To adapt to the constantly changing business environment, organizations have increasingly recognized the need for corporate restructuring, which is essential for survival, growth, efficiency, and competitiveness amid both opportunities and challenges.

In recent years, many companies have announced restructuring initiatives to achieve rapid growth. Corporate restructuring can take many forms, but mergers and acquisitions (M&As) have emerged as the most popular method. This strategy has become a vital component of long-term growth plans for corporate. Since 1992, there has been a notable rise in the number of M&As in the market, accompanied by a significant increase in their market value. Mergers and acquisitions involve changes to an organization's corporate structure, including substantial modifications to its business or financial framework, with the goal of enhancing value for stakeholders.

A merger is a comprehensive procedure through which a company can integrate its business operations, enhancing its position in order to achieve corporate objectives, synergies, and maintain competitiveness. This can be achieved through various means such as mergers and acquisitions, takeovers, split-ups, leveraged buy-outs, spin-offs, joint ventures, employee stock option plans, divestitures, strategic alliances, franchising, disinvestment, and share buybacks.

Mergers and acquisitions (M&A) is a strategy in which two or more corporate organizations enter into a sequence of financial transactions in which the relevant entities are amalgamated or taken over for a number of reasons. These became increasingly popular in the late 19th century and are still performed in large numbers today.

1.1.1 History of Corporate Mergers and Acquisitions

There have been six periods of strong merger activity in the history of the United States, known as "merger waves." According to studies, merger waves are typically triggered by a combination of economic, regulatory, and technical shocks. The first four waves occurred between 1897 and 1904, 1916 and 1929, 1965 and 1969, and 1984 and 1989. The first merger wave began during the 1883 slump, peaked between 1898 and 1902, and came to a close in 1904. Several industries were merged during the second merger wave. During the third merger wave, there was a historically high level of merger activity. Following the third merger wave, a historic merger created the framework for the widespread hostile takeover of large established firms in the fourth merger wave. Evidently, the transaction value in the sixth merger wave, which spanned the four years from 2004 to 2007, was on par with the fifth wave and more than the deal value in the fourth wave.

Overall macroeconomic environment, growth in the GDP, rising interest rates, and financial policies are some of the decent financial variables that lead to the majority of mergers and acquisitions. These elements not only initiate the M&A process but also actively contribute to the development of merger and acquisition strategies between the bidder and target companies.

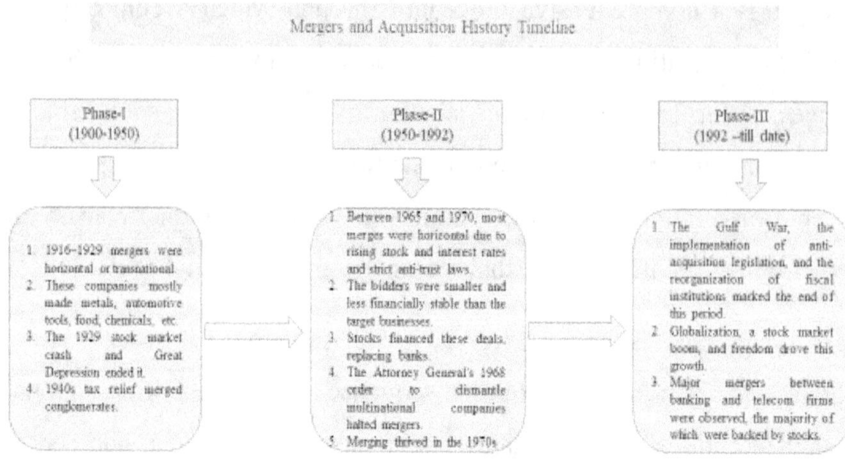

Figure 1.1: Timeline of Mergers and Acquisitions History

Source: *Compiled by Author from Various Sources*

The history of mergers and acquisitions dates back to the 19th century and has gone through the following stages:

Phase-I (1900 to 1950)

Mergers between companies that were anti-competitive and had market domination based on their productivity in industries like power, railroads, etc. occurred during this time. The majority of the horizontal mergers that took place during this time frame included the steel, metal, and construction sectors.

The majority of mergers that occurred during the first phase were deemed failed because they were not effective enough to achieve the necessary competency. The slowing of the global financial system in 1903, which was followed by the fall of the stock market in 1904, served as the catalyst for the catastrophe. The permitted structure was also uninspiring throughout this time. Later, the Supreme Court's direction on anti-competitive mergers said that the Sherman Act might be used to dissolve them.

This phase, in contrast to the one before it, focused on mergers between oligopolies rather than rival businesses. The financial boom that followed World War I served as the impetus for mergers and acquisitions. The rise also sparked technological and scientific advances as well as the establishment of infrastructure companies that provided the support needed for the expansion of railroads and car transportation. Government policies put in place in the 1920s created an environment in which businesses could coexist peacefully. Government and commercial banks and other financial institutions made a substantial contribution to the process of mergers and acquisitions.

The mergers that took place between 1916 and 1929 were either horizontal or transnational in scope. The majority of these businesses produced metals, automotive tools, food products, chemicals, etc.

The great depression and a sharp collapse in the stock market marked the end of this period in 1929. The tax breaks granted in the 1940s, however, encouraged conglomerates to engage in M&A activity.

Phase-II (1950 to 1992)

The majority of mergers between 1965 and 1970 were horizontal mergers, which were brought on by rising stock and interest rates as well as the strict enforcement of anti-trust laws and regulations. The target corporations were larger and more financially stable than the bidding companies at this time. These mergers' sponsorship by stocks eliminated the roles that banks had previously actively played in investing operations.

The Attorney General made the decision to dismantle the multinational corporations in 1968, which put a halt to subsequent merger activity. The decision was made as a result of the corporations' poor performance. But in the 1970s, mergers started to take off and built a name for themselves by working well. Some of these included the mergers of Colt Industries and Garlock Industries, OTIS Elevator and United Technologies, and INCO and ESB.

Phase-III (1992 to till date)

In this phase, businesses that were far larger than those in earlier rounds were acquired. Industries including oil and gas, pharmaceuticals, finance, and aviation merged their operations with those of their domestic and foreign competitors. Cross-border buyouts became commonplace, with the majority being hostile in character. The Gulf War, the implementation of anti-acquisition legislation, and the reorganization of fiscal institutions marked the end of this period.

Globalization, an increase in the stock market boom, and deregulation legislation all contributed to this period's growth. Major mergers between banking and telecom firms were observed, the majority of which were backed by stocks.

Industrialists' perspectives changed, and they now prioritize long-term profitability over transient gains via choosing mergers and acquisitions. Many companies joined the acquisition trend as a result of encouraging economic developments, business investments, and updated governmental regulations. Consequently, the trend of mergers and acquisitions will persist as long as corporate entities exist and the economic environment is favorable.

1.2 Role of Mergers and Acquisitions

1.2.1 Company perspective of mergers and acquisitions

1.2.1.1 Operating Synergies

When the activities of the acquirer and the target are combined, operational synergies result. Revenue growth is one sort of operating synergy. It involves obtaining price power in a certain market or having the ability to boost sales volume by breaking into other markets, such as by utilizing one business's sales force or distribution network or by marketing to the clients of another company. Cost savings are a second sort of operating synergy. As was already noted, many businesses see M&As as a strategy to grow to a certain size and, as a result, be able to take advantage of economies of scale and decrease production costs. Additionally, a purchase may result in cost reductions in marketing, advertising, or R&D. Revenue growth and cost-cutting are more likely in situations where firms want to acquire new businesses and expand their business to new competitors.

1.2.1.2 Financial Synergies

The decrease in borrowing expenses results in the realization of financial synergies. Big firms generally have access to larger and more cost-effective sources of capital compared to smaller enterprises. The third wave of mergers and acquisitions (M&As)

was driven by the rationale that diversifying into unrelated industries may effectively mitigate risk, enhance firms' ability to get loans, and lower their pre-tax borrowing costs. The differential tax treatment between debt and equity amplifies the benefits associated with risk mitigation. Consequently, the cost of financing for a corporation, adjusted for taxes, diminishes as the proportion of debt in its capital structure increases. Nevertheless, based on historical data, it may be argued that corporations often tend to overstate the extent to which mergers and acquisitions (M&As) can mitigate risks and provide tax benefits. Although financial synergies have the potential to create value, especially in the context of leveraged acquisitions.

1.2.1.3 Managerial Synergies

A strong management team can replace a low-performing one, creating managerial synergy. One benefit of acquisition is that they provide the chance for the acquirer to fire ineffective management, perhaps improving the performance of the target.

1.2.2 Expansion of business

Mergers and acquisitions play an important role in the expansion of businesses in the economy; it is a natural process to acquire small and other businesses to capture the market in particular segments. However, we occasionally see that the growth of specific segments is also dependent on other complementary and intermediary goods, which is why we must focus on related products and materials for final goods. Instability in the business compels the investor to diversify his or her investment. Due to that, a large segment is trying to become the market influencer and has established a strong position. In any case, one of the inherent characteristics of most merger and acquisition transactions is the goal of business expansion.

1.2.3 Power to capture market positions in the economy

Companies always prefer to carve out a niche for themselves in a certain market and economy. The majority of corporate mergers and acquisitions refer to the consolidation of companies in an effort to establish their own niche or place in the market and reduce the danger of being overtaken by rivals in this area. M&A aids in the acquisition of power in marketplaces and certain business sectors, however, we may argue that here as well. A company's perspective indicates that it is likely to outgrow its capital and other resource limitations.

1.2.4 Price stability of the particular product

Price stability is another reason for market consolidation, both horizontally and vertically, if related products and services are produced in that economy. The merger and acquisition shared the most business similarities because the combined company would become a price maker for the goods and services it manufactures. Although it will happen at some point, it may not happen because another competitor stands up and creates a new trend in the specific segments and businesses with new distinct services and goods. After globalization, developed economies were also interested in investing in developing economies due to the large scalability of the products and services.

1.2.5 Economic Perspective of Mergers and Acquisitions

It has been seen that developed economies have more mergers and acquisition deals in comparison to developing and underdeveloped economies. It means that small businesses with similar types of products and services are more focused on merging so that they can consolidate their specific businesses and establish market positions in the particular products and services related to that industry. Developing economies have more opportunities to scale their businesses with higher margin profits than developed economies.

1.2.6 Scale to production and services

Depending on the size of the market and the number of customers, produce goods and services. The demands of the economy in terms of consumption, however, also influence the size of the firm. Otherwise, if more goods and services are created, scalable manufacturing might lead to corporate losses. Forecasting future demand and ensuring economic viability.

1.2.7 Stability of Businesses

The stability of businesses depends on multiple factors, but it is a requirement of business activities to change their perspective on the market, industries, and economy. However, mergers and acquisitions enable large businesses to grow through small or large consolidation executions with financial decisions to relate all such parameters to our goals in this regard.

1.3 Types of Mergers and Acquisitions

Mergers and Acquisitions are classified into different sections as described below.

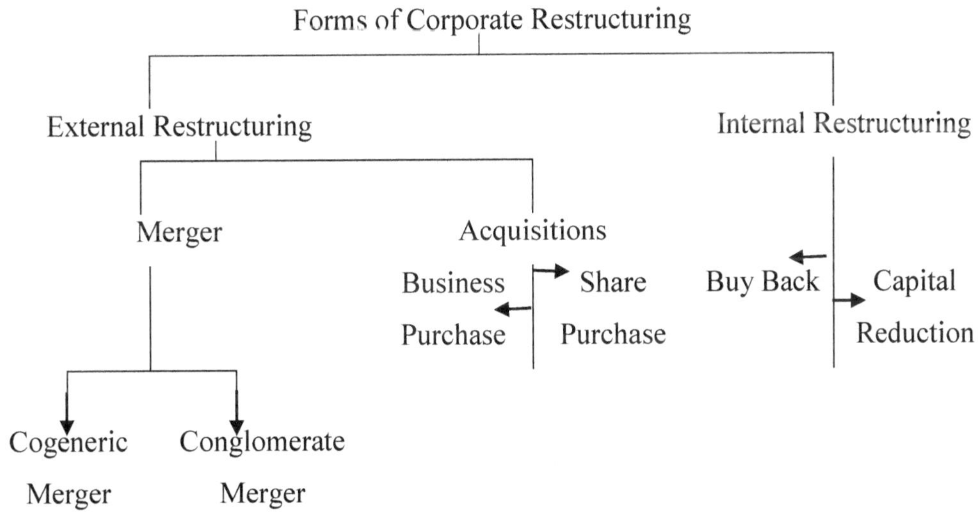

Figure 1.2: Conceptual model of Corporate Restructuring

Source: *Compiled by Author from Various Sources*

Horizontal, vertical, and conglomerate mergers are the three types of mergers. The characteristics of these forms vary, as do their impact on corporate success.

1.3.1 Horizontal Mergers and Acquisitions

Such pairs are commonly observed among competitors. This form of merger and acquisition occurs between firms that were previously competitors and offer products that customers see as substitutes, with the aim of attaining horizontal integration.

In India, horizontal mergers have been the most common and important form of merger. Horizontal mergers are described as mergers of companies with similar or related product lines. A recent example of horizontal mergers in the market is the online streaming industry. Disney+ and Hotstar are an example of horizontal mergers.

According to the findings of a number of studies, since liberalization, sixty percent of mergers have been of the horizontal kind (as noted in). In the last several years, there have been a number of significant mergers of this kind in the telecommunications industry in India, including ones involving Vodafone and Idea. The financial services industry has seen quite a few mergers of this kind, including the recent combination of Canara Bank and Syndicate Bank. A merger occurred between IBM and Red Hat in the domain of information technology.

1.3.2 Vertical Mergers and Acquisitions

During this kind of merger and acquisition, the buyer and seller have previously established relationships between the two firms. It might take the shape of a merger of businesses operating at various stages of the same manufacturing chain or that provide complementary goods and services. Forward mergers are when one firm acquires one of its customers, while backward mergers are when one company acquires one of its suppliers. Vertical mergers occur when two or more firms working on separate but related phases of production of the same products or services combine their resources. The primary goal of these sorts of mergers is to ensure continuous and reliable supply networks. The combination of Hutch and Essar may be indicative of vertical consolidation.

1.3.3 Conglomerate Mergers

This form of corporate consolidation, characterised by a corporation's acquisition or merger with another business operating in a distinct industry, does not fall within the category of vertical integration or horizontal integration. During the 1960s, there was a notable prevalence of conglomerate mergers and acquisitions due to the constraints imposed by antitrust enforcement, which prohibited corporations from engaging in simultaneous vertical and horizontal corporate consolidations.

In 2002, eBay and PayPal were merged which is another example of a vertical merger. E bay is an e-commerce platform that facilitates online shopping and auctions, whereas Paypal offers financial services for money transfers and online payment processing. Both entities were engaged in distinct industries.

Conglomerate mergers occur when two companies with no value chain or peer rivals combine. Conglomerate mergers are described as a combination of companies that are not rivals and do not have a buyer-seller relationship. The merger between L&T and

Voltas Ltd., Walt Disney, and American Broadcasting Co. are examples of conglomerate mergers.

Mergers and acquisitions, abbreviated as M&A, are two words that, while having distinct legal meanings, are sometimes used synonymously with one another. When two firms of around the same size come together to form a bigger organization, this process is known as a merger. In contrast, an acquisition is when a larger corporation pays for and takes over the activities of a smaller business. This process is known as "absorption." The board of directors of the company that will be acquired makes the decision as to whether a merger and acquisition agreement will be friendly or hostile.

1.4 Indian Corporate Mergers and Acquisitions

1.4.1 Indian Corporate Mergers and Acquisitions deals

Different patterns of mergers and acquisitions have emerged in India over the course of many decades. Diverse segments of India's economy have had distinct initial effects from mergers and acquisitions. Business mergers and acquisitions have led to these changes. The practice of merging two companies is ancient. Their prominence in the marketplace has risen and fallen throughout time, but they remain an important part of the present day. They have also increased their overseas operations, which might be a reaction to the fierce global competition. There has been a rise in the number of cross-border mergers and acquisitions (M&As), making it important to have a global perspective on these transactions.

Table -1.1: Number of Mergers and Acquisitions during the financial year (FY) 2010-11 to 2020-21 last eleven years in India.

Year	Numbers of Acquisitions	Numbers of Mergers	Total
2010-11	642	445	1087
2011-12	1208	462	1670
2012-13	972	387	1359
2013-14	928	404	1332
2014-15	965	413	1378

Year	Numbers of Acquisitions	Numbers of Mergers	Total
2015-16	953	472	1425
2016-17	849	430	1279
2017-18	917	447	1364
2018-19	676	325	1001
2019-20	633	287	920
2020-21	838	396	1234
2021-22	898	637	1535

Source: *CMIE database*

As we can see from the above table the number of mergers and acquisitions have reduced proportionately in 2018- 2019 and 2019-2020. And if we analyse the above data, it has been observed that the acquisitions have reduced at a greater percentage in comparison to mergers in 2018-19 and 2019-20.

Corporate executives confront the need to show that their actions are backed by shareholders' wealth maximization objectives. These strategic decisions exercise benefits that could be realized and become evident after a substantial time has passed. Managers are also instigated to keep in line with the immediate demands so as to maximize shareholders' wealth. Hence, a trade-off between long-term wealth maximization and short-term wealth maximization has to be undertaken. This may be one of the causes of information asymmetry which can be corrected through dissemination and exposition of information signals.

To a greater extent, the short-term success of any financial restructuring decision depends upon its adaptability by various stakeholders. Every restructuring decision carry with itself a strong signal to various interest groups and buyback is one of them among them. Such decisions fetch strong reactions based on the differential between the current market price and the buyback price as declared by the company.

1.4.2 Relative Performance of Indian Companies

Renneboog & Vansteenkiste, (2019) stated failure or success of the firm depends upon the performance of the company after and around M & A. It has been established that post-takeover deal performance was affected due to intervention in the form of voting or activism, CEO overconfidence, acquirer target relatedness, and complementarily. The research was done on the basis of geographical area or country-wise analysis.

1.5 Legal framework in India

The Indian Companies Act, which was passed in 2013, the Income Tax Act, which was passed in 1961, the Securities and Exchange Board of India Act (SEBI), which was passed in 1992, the SEBI (Substantial Acquisitions of Shares and Takeovers) Regulations, which were passed in 2011, the Reserve Bank of India Act, which was passed in 1935, the Competition Act, which was passed in 2002, and the Foreign Exchange Management Act, which was passed in 1999 are the primary examples of these controlling legislations.

2013 Act Relating to Corporations

In accordance with Indian law, a merger of two or more businesses is regulated by sections 230 to 235 of the Companies Act, which are together referred to as the "Merger Provisions." The Consolidation Provisions are in fact worded in such a broad manner that they would provide for and regulate all types of corporate restructuring that a company may possibly undertake; this includes mergers, amalgamations, demergers, spin-offs/hive-offs, and any other compromise, agreement, settlement or arrangement between a company and its members and/or its creditors. This includes mergers, amalgamations, demergers, spin-offs/hive-offs, and so on.

A merger is essentially a contractual arrangement between the merging entities and their respective shareholders. In order to initiate a merger, each firm seeking to merge with one or more other firms must file an application with the National Company Law Tribunal (referred to as the "tribunal") that has jurisdiction over the company. This application is necessary to convene meetings of the shareholders and/or creditors associated with each respective firm involved in the merger. A merger involves a contractual agreement between the firms involved in the merger and their respective owners. Subsequently, the tribunal possesses the authority to mandate the convening of a meeting including the company's creditors and shareholders. If a merger is approved by a majority representing 9/10th in value of the creditors/shareholders present and voting at a meeting, and afterwards sanctioned by the tribunal, it becomes legally obligatory on all creditors/shareholders of the firm. If a merger is met with disagreement from the majority, which constitutes 9/10th in value, of the creditors/shareholders present and voting at the meeting, the merger will not be implemented. The court will not give its approval to a merger or any other kind of corporate reorganization unless it is certain that the firm has given all of the pertinent information. Once a company submits a certified copy of the order that approves the merger to the Registrar of Companies, the approval of the merger by the tribunal will become official and effective.

Act of 2002 Relating to Competition

The Competition Act of 2002 has four key sections, which include anti-competitive dealings, abuse of authority, mixed control, and market advocacy. Mergers, a kind of combination, are often employed as a tactic by corporations to grow their operations, combine with other businesses, and get rid of their rivals. (Shapiro, 2019)

SEBI Guidelines

Companies that are traded on Indian stock exchanges are overseen by the Securities and Exchange Board of India (often known as "SEBI"), which is a regulatory organization. The Securities and Exchange Board of India (Substantial Acquisition of Shares and Takeovers) Regulations, 1997 (also known as the "Takeovers") have been repealed as a result of the Securities and Exchange Board of India (Substantial Acquisition of Shares and Takeovers) Regulations, 2011, which came into effect in 2011. (the "Takeovers").

Act Concerning Income Tax, 1961

The Indian Income Tax Act has provisions for tax exemptions for the merger or de-merger of two business identities. These provisions may be found in the act. In order to be eligible for the allocation, it is necessary for certain mergers or demergers to comply with the requirements of sections 2(19AA) and section 2(1B) of the Indian Income Tax Act, as applicable.

Foreign Exchange Management Act, 1999

The regulatory framework governing the transfer and issuance of shares to non-resident corporations is encapsulated in the Foreign Exchange Management (Transfer or Issue of Security by a Person Resident Outside India) Regulations, 2000. These regulations were promulgated by the Reserve Bank of India through Government Notification GSR no. 406(E) on the 3rd of May, 2000. The aforementioned laws are specified in the Foreign Exchange Management (Transfer or Issue of Protection by a Person Residing Outside of India) Regulation of 2000. The regulations delineated under this particular framework govern the allocation of shares or securities by an Indian corporate entity to people who are residing in India. These regulations provide overarching principles that guide the procedures involved in this process.

Legal Procedure for the Initiation and Completion of Company Mergers:

i. Review of object provisions: The articles of association of both firms need to be reviewed to see whether or not they have the authority to merge into one entity. In addition, the main clause of the company that is merging should stipulate that it is allowed to continue operating the business of the combined firm. In the event that such terms do not exist, the company law board, the board of directors, and the shareholders will be needed to provide their permission.

ii. Notification of stock exchanges: The stock exchanges where the firms that are merging or being combined are listed need to be notified about the merger plan. Copies of all notifications, resolutions, and orders should be sent through regular mail to the stock exchanges that are relevant to the situation.

iii. Approval of the draught merger proposal by the respective boards. The respective boards of directors (BODs) should provide their approval to the proposed merger proposal. Each company's board of directors needs to vote on and approve a resolution that gives the company's directors and management permission to investigate the subject further.

iv. Application to the National Company Law Tribunal is necessary following the approval of the merger proposal draughts by the respective boards. Each company is required to submit an application to the tribunal located in the state where its registered office is situated. This application enables the tribunal to facilitate the convening of meetings for shareholders and creditors, with the purpose of obtaining approval for the merger proposal.

v. Dissemination of notifications to shareholders and creditors: To facilitate the organisation of meetings involving shareholders and creditors, it is necessary for each firm to send a notice and an explanatory statement of the meeting, as authorised by the tribunal, to its respective shareholders and creditors. This communication should be despatched in a timely manner, ensuring that recipients are provided with a 21-day advance notice. The convening of meetings for shareholders and creditors is a necessary need. Additionally, it is advised that notification of the meetings be disseminated by the publication of notices in two distinct newspapers.

vi. The convening of meetings for shareholders and creditors: It is imperative for every company to convene a shareholders' meeting in order to obtain approval for the proposed merger strategy. In order for the merger to be successfully ratified, it is necessary that a minimum of 75% of shareholders, who cast their votes either in person or by a proxy, support the proposed merger scheme. The aforementioned notion is also applicable to those who owe debts.

vii. Request for Tribunal approval and Implementation of Orders: Following the acceptance of the merger proposal by both shareholders and creditors, the merging entities are required to formally submit a petition to the tribunal seeking approval of the proposed merger scheme. It is imperative that this task be completed expeditiously. It is necessary to ensure that a notification pertaining to the identical matter is disseminated through two distinct publications.

viii. The process of submitting the order to the registrar involves providing certified authentic copies of the Tribunal order within the timeframe specified by the court.

The primary legislations that govern the aforementioned aspects consist of the Indian Companies Act of 2013, the Income Tax Act of 1961, the Securities and Exchange Board of India Act (SEBI) of 1992, the SEBI (Substantial Acquisitions of Shares and Takeovers) Regulations of 2011, the Reserve Bank of India Act of 1935, the Competition Act of 2002, and the Foreign Exchange Management Act of 1999.

1.6 Scope of Merger and Acquisition

The phenomenon of mergers and acquisitions has experienced a surge in global prominence in recent years. The rise in popularity of these factors may be attributed to the processes of globalisation, liberalisation, advancements in technology, and the highly competitive nature of the corporate environment. Mergers and acquisitions constitute a significant component within the realm of corporate finance. The utilisation of this approach is often employed in the reconfiguration of commercial organisations. The initiation of mergers and acquisitions in India can be attributed to governmental entities. The economic reform implemented in India since 1991 has presented several obstacles in both the local and international arenas. The escalation of competitiveness in the international market has compelled Indian corporations to go for mergers and acquisitions as a significant strategic decision.

The year 2020 has seen a number of noteworthy and important mergers and acquisitions. These agreements have a major effect not only on the corporate environment but also on market competition. One of the major acquisitions was made by Reliance as they have acquired Future Group for approximately Rs. 24,713 crores. The Group's separately listed divisions, including clothing, supply chain, and grocery, would be combined into Future Enterprises Ltd. (FEL) and eventually absorbed by Reliance Industries Ltd. as part of the transaction (RIL). (Source: EMIS database).

Reliance Industries Limited has also entered into Home Décor as it bought Urban Ladder Home Decor Solutions Pvt. Ltd for Rs. 182.12 crore, giving it a foothold in the online furniture market. RIL's retail unit, Reliance Retail Ventures Ltd. (RRVL), now controls 96 percent of Urban Ladder as a result of this transaction. Another major acquisition was made between ITC and Sunrise Foods. ITC (India Tobacco Brand), a well-known diversified business brand, has acquired Kolkata-based spices manufacturer Sunrise Foods Pvt. Ltd. in order to expand its spice business. Via the contract, ITC acquired 100 percent of SFPL's equity share capital for an all-cash price of Rs 2,150 crore.

Social networking services have also seen some big mergers and acquisitions like Facebook's USD 5.7 billion investment in Jio Platforms was the largest M & A deal in the first half of 2020. Along with this, the food delivery sector has also grown in the field of mergers and acquisitions. Zomato, an online food delivery service, has purchased Uber's food delivery service, Uber Eats, for about USD 350 million. Uber acquired 9.99 percent equity in Zomato in this all-stock deal to move the entire Uber Eats Company. The health sector has also seen growth with Reliance Retail Ventures Limited, RIL acquiring a controlling equity interest in Vitalic Health Pvt. Ltd. and its subsidiaries (collectively known as' Netmeds'). The transaction was estimated to be worth around Rs. 60 crores. Reliance Industries Limited (RIL) acquired a majority equity position of 60% in Vitalic Health, together with complete ownership of the equity share capital of its subsidiaries, namely Dadha Pharma Pvt. Ltd., Tresara Health Pvt. Ltd., and Netmeds Market Place Limited. This acquisition was executed in accordance with the terms outlined in the investment agreement. (Source: IIFL securities website).

Hindustan Unilever Limited (HUL) one of India's largest consumer goods companies, has also finalized a Rs. 31,700 crore merger with GlaxoSmithKline (GSK) Consumer Limited. The merger between these two consumer giants would affect the competition in the market. This amalgamation will mainly help HUL as it gets a new range of renowned products.

Minda Industries Ltd. acquired the German counterpart Delvis for a value of USD 23.03 million in the year 2019. This acquisition was settled through a combination of equity and debt which means affecting the financing pattern of the company. In 2020, Urban Ladder Home Décor Solutions Pvt Ltd.'s 96% has been acquired by Reliance Retail Ventures Limited for a total consideration of USD 24.41 million. Another deal which has influenced the company's market price and improved operational performance is the acquisition of Indian e-commerce company Gabbardeals, run by PNR Commerce Services Pvt Ltd by Instaone Software Pvt Ltd in 2020.The acquisition of beverage maker Rakyan Beverages Pvt Ltd by Wingreens Farms Pvt Ltd for a total consideration of USD 15 million.

Recently, a merger between Canara Bank and Syndicate Bank took place. This merger would enable Canara Bank to become the fourth largest public sector bank. This merger was made to consolidate the banking sector. The merged organisation would own aggregate assets amounting to around 10.248 trillion rupees, with a total net loan portfolio valued at approximately 6.332 trillion rupees. (Source: Canara Bank Official website)

Mergers and acquisitions have become a prevalent phenomenon in global corporate restructuring. The Vodafone Mobile Services Ltd. and Idea Cellular Ltd. Was merged on 31st August 2018. The merger between these two companies had expected to generate Rs. 140 billion annual synergies out of which Rs. 84 billion relates to the OPEX synergy, equivalent to NPV of approx. Rs 700 billion. (Source: Vodafone official website)

There has been a change in the frequency with which businesses in India merge their operations or purchase one another. In a similar vein, the direct effects of the mergers and acquisitions that have taken place in various parts of the Indian economy have led to a variety of distinct outcomes. Even though mergers and acquisitions (M&A) have been around for a long time and have had ebbs and flows of popularity over the course of the years, they continue to play an important part in the business world today. They have also expanded their operations around the globe, which may be a reaction to the rising competition coming from other nations. The importance of doing research on mergers and acquisitions that include many countries cannot be overstated.

***

CHAPTER 2:
LITERATURE REVIEW

CHAPTER 2: LITERATURE REVIEW

Overview

This chapter examines the parameters and dimensions of mergers and acquisitions with rigour. It has systematized the existing methodological approaches to mergers and acquisitions concept analysis. A comprehensive literature review is conducted, beginning with an introduction to mergers and acquisitions and their theories. It discusses numerous factors and dimensions that influence mergers and acquisitions. It provides an overview of the study's dimensions and the gaps that prompted its execution.

Consideration is given to bibliometric analysis in order to provide the perspective and contemporary issues associated with mergers and acquisitions deals. In addition, this chapter examines a structured literature review based on the objectives. The overall literature review assisted in identifying various research gaps and appropriate research methods for this study. Finally, it contributes to the literature on the financing pattern, financial performance, and operating performance of mergers and acquisitions.

2.1 Introduction

Both theoretical and empirical basis for mergers and acquisitions is provided in this chapter. It is separated into two major sections. The first comprises a systematic literature review (SLR), second is a bibliometric examination of mergers and acquisitions. In SLR, 153 research articles regarding mergers and acquisitions are referenced and discussed. Furthermore, the bibliometric study relied heavily on RStudio, with some network graphs acquired from Vos-viewer and data pulled from the Scopus database. The study of bibliometric evaluation of mergers and acquisitions is evaluated and detailed based on the author's, publications, country, and organization. Finally, for 8328 and 153, a thorough literature study and bibliometric analysis of mergers and acquisitions are explored.

2.1.1 Definition of Mergers and Acquisitions

A merger strategy is one in which two or more businesses combine their operations to form a single, legally-binding entity. In the case of an acquisition, two or more companies come together to form a new entity, but the target company does not become an integral part of the acquiring company; rather, it continues to function as the acquiring company's subsidiary while maintaining its independent existence. A transaction known as a merger or acquisition is any business arrangement in which two or more companies come together to form a single entity. It is necessary for both groups of shareholders to give their assent in order for a merger, which is combining the interests of two firms to form a new business.

Section 2(1B) of the Income Tax Act of 1961 provides a definition for the term "amalgamation" in the context of companies. According to this definition, amalgamation refers to the process of combining one or more companies with another company, or the merging of two or more companies to form a single entity. The companies involved in this process are referred to as the amalgamating company or companies, while the company resulting from the merger is known as the amalgamated company. This amalgamation is carried out in a manner that:

i) By virtue of the amalgamation, all the assets of the merging entities become the property of the resulting corporation.

ii) All of the obligations of the merging companies just prior to the merger become the liabilities of the merged company.

iii) As a result of the amalgamation, shareholders who hold at least three-fourths of the entire value of the amalgamating firm or companies' shares (excluding shares owned by the merged company or its subsidiary prior to the merger) will become shareholders of the amalgamated company.

2.1.2 Theories of Mergers and Acquisitions

There exist several theories within the realm of mergers and acquisitions (M&A) that elucidate the motivations for firms' involvement in such deals. M&A value creation theories show that mergers of firms make every effort to raise the firm's worth and protect the interests of shareholders.

According to Coase (1937), mergers are value-adding activities since M&A provides new technology that aids in lowering transaction costs in the market and within the firm, such as production costs. It has also been discovered that M and A create synergy. Bradley et al. (1983) explain this by claiming that synergies emerge due to economies of scale, the involvement of effective management, advancements in production techniques, and the usage of complementary resources together.

Motis (2007) has grouped together many different reasons for mergers and acquisitions into two different ideas. The first category, known as industrial organization theories, discusses motivations such as expanding market power, enhancing operational efficacy, and acting defensively or preemptively. These motivations focus on value-enhancing actions carried out by the company, with the end goal being an increase in future profits and, consequently, an increase in shareholder value. Motives such as resolving agency difficulties, internal inefficiencies, and capital market defects are included in the second set of theories labeled corporate governance theories. These reasons do not take into account the best interests of the company's shareholders; rather, they focus on the interests of the company's managers. Therefore, mergers that are carried out with such motivations are not activities that raise the value of the company; rather, they increase the wealth of management. Gorton et al. (2009) proposed a merger theory that explains three aspects of size. These aspects are as follows: (1) mergers occur in specific industries when organisations attempt to expand their size.; (2) the key catalyst for the occurrence of mergers in waves is the magnitude of the industry.; and (3) large acquirers overpay for the transaction. Large acquirers generate more money, whereas medium acquirers sign more contracts.. Weston et al. (2011) have shown that theories of mergers and acquisitions may be broken down into three distinct categories. These categories are as follows: (1) mergers as a source of added value; (2) mergers are operations that reduce value.; and (3) mergers with very less impact on value.

2.1.2.1 Efficiency Theory

According to the efficiency theory, mergers occur because two organisations have unique benefits and drawbacks, as well as varied degrees of production. The differential efficiency theory is the name given to this sort of theory. The merging of a firm with inefficient management by a company with efficient management facilitates the transfer of managerial efficiency, leading to both private and social gains. This is because the merger not only improves the performance of the company that has been performing poorly, but it also saves the resources of the economy. The phenomenon referred to as the managerial synergy hypothesis is characterised by the allocation of surplus management ability inside an organisation that lacks sufficient effective managerial resources.

2.1.2.2 Synergy Theory

The purpose of mergers and acquisitions is to combine two companies' resources to reap the combined entity's synergistic benefits. It is expected that the valuation of the merged entity would surpass the individual valuations of both the acquiring firm and the target firm.The advantages arise from the attainment of financial or operational synergies, which are realised by leveraging economies of scale in the management of the enterprise. This indicates that when the two companies unite, their fixed costs will be divided throughout a larger production scale, resulting in a lower overall fixed cost. In addition to economies of scale, there is another type of this phenomenon that is referred to as economies of scope. This form of economy arises when the acquiring firm and the target company combine their complementary resources in order to generate synergistic benefits.

2.1.2.3 Diversification

The term "diversification" refers to the process of expanding either geographically or in terms of the variety of products offered, or both. The advantages of diversification encompass reputational gains, the safeguarding of reputational capital, and the inclination towards diversification shown by both employees and managers. It aids in boosting a company's capacity to take on debt and decreases the present value of the company's future tax liability. In spite of the inherent instability introduced by mergers, this ultimately leads to a stable flow of capital into the business.

2.1.2.4 Information and Signaling Theory

According to this concept, when two separate investors access distinct pieces of information, their subsequent behaviours should be distinct. The announcement of the merger serves as a valuable source of information and acts as a signal to market players, providing insights into the anticipated effects of the agreement on the overall value of the involved firms. The disclosure of a merger event suggests that the valuation of the target entity may experience an increase or a twofold rise, or alternatively, that the new ownership would potentially displace the existing management team. Additionally, it can sometimes be interpreted as a hint that there will be a growth in the cash flows and future values (Weston et al., 2010).

2.1.2.5 Agency Problems and Managerial Theory

The phenomenon referred to as an agency dilemma arises when a conflict of interest emerges between the shareholders, who assume the role of principals, and the management, who assume the role of agents, inside a corporation. Weston et al. (2010) said that Jensen and Meckling (1976) have examined the potential consequences of agency issues. This was mentioned in the article. For instance, a manager is regarded as the agent of the firm as a whole as well as the shareholders individually. Managers with a lesser ownership stake in the firm tend to allocate less time towards activities that generate money for the organisation. Due to the substantial allocation of resources required in the form of incentives for overseeing managerial operations, it is unfeasible for all organisations to effectively monitor those activities.As a result, businesses incur additional expenses as a result of the agency problem. The aforementioned expenditures encompass the fees associated with contract structure, the expenses incurred in monitoring agent actions, the costs related to the preparation of bonds with agents to facilitate optimal decision-making for the firm, and the residual costs arising from disparities in decision-making between agents and principals.

2.2 Structured Literature Review

Going to begin with the early years and focusing on the literature that was ultimately shortlisted. A few studies, such as Chudamani and Shalini's (1983) comparison of some of the existing journal acquisition models and discussion of their significance in library acquisitions, are examples. Although Todd (1984) focused on the diversification and growth of shipbuilding, few of the research, accordingly, Balasubramanian and Bhattacharyya (1986) described the automated environment for online acquisition systems to consider various factors for establishing database structure. Nevertheless, Foster (1986) calculated a rush over the past five years to switch from equity to debt and use cash to lower number of shares outstanding a significant portion of its capital from one of it has gotten . In addition, Barnhart (1987) focused on "critical success factors" and how it is a challenge for management in a merger and acquisition. At the same time, however, Adler and Sneath (1987) described the five important characteristics for the ideal acquisition candidate in the United States, which added a different dimension to the discussion. In this decade, the majority of the studies came from different areas and aspects to provide significance; in this regard, Tse and Crawford (1989) examined the merger and acquisition activity in the hospitality industry for the period of time between 1970 and 1988. On the other hand, Love (1989) presented two significant critical evaluations on external control, and its technique, which was based on existing merger economics literature, was proven to give an inappropriate framework for regional analysis. Both of these reviews focused on the effectiveness of external control. It was also noted that, whereas external control had got a lot of attention, there had been very little systematic study done to measure the economic implications of inward acquisition. In this sequence, Chakrabarti (1990) considered 31 acquisitions for which data had been obtained through structured interviews and questionnaires from executives in the acquired divisions as well as from corporate officers. Executives completed these interviews and questionnaires in the acquired divisions and by corporate officers. The research looked at achievement in terms of sales, profits, return on investments, expanding the customer base, and growing market share. It also looked at innovative strategies and expanding the customer base.

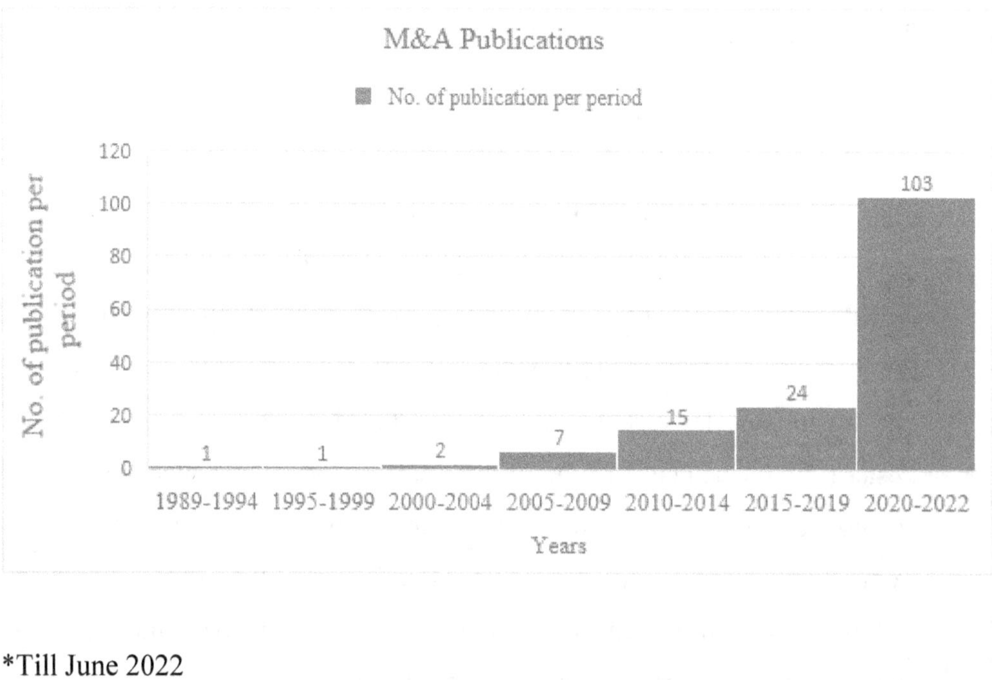

*Till June 2022

Figure-2.1 M&A publications

Source: *Compiled by Author from Scopus data*

An SLR is an articulated strategy for systematically identifying, examining and criticizing the condition of research and literature. A three-step procedure identifies and reviews publications (i.e., journal articles, conference papers, papers in press, and book chapters) relating to stakeholders and M&A for inclusion in the SLR. First, keywords were searched in bibliometric data. Second, data was cleansed using other discipline publications that were unrelated to our research topic. Third, data filters use terms that are more focused on M&A. The dataset was limited to the years 1983 to June 2022. Furthermore, a synopsis of the literature from 153 research publications is taken into the study.

SLRs evaluate articles using coding to look for a unit of the analysis indicated in the analytical framework. Themes were found, classified, and aggregated from thc SLR's 153 articles. A timeline was made, and four groups were assigned identifiers. The timeline and identified groups are represented in Figure 2.1 and Table 2.1.

Table 2.1
SLR results (1983 to 2022)

		Publications	% of 153 publications
A	**Key Components**		
	Financial Performance	32	20.92
	Cross-border M&A	20	13.07
	Operating Efficiency	3	1.96
	Value of the firm	3	1.96
	Shareholders	4	2.61
	Financing Pattern	3	1.96
	Gender diversity	1	0.65
	Culture	3	1.96
B	**Sector/Industry**		
	Banking Sector	11	7.19
	Manufacturing Sector	3	1.96
C	**Research Methods**		
	Regression, OLS,	81	52.94
	DEA	7	4.58
	ANOVA	2	1.31
	GARCH	1	0.65
	Fama Fench model	4	2.61

Table 2.1
SLR results (1983 to 2022)

		Publications	% of 153 publications
D	**Contribution of Publishers**		
	Journal of Corporate Finance	10	6.54
	Strategic Management Journal	5	3.27
	International Review of Financial Analysis	4	2.61

* Manufacturing sector consist all other industry like steel industry, etc.
Source: *Compiled by Author*

After that, the subsequent decade saw a greater emphasis placed on research concerning corporate mergers and acquisitions. Datta and Yu (1991) examined the human side in merger and acquisition and emphasized issues related to the habitual domains of the two organizations, and the potential costs associated thereon. In this sequence, Olden (1992) focused on engineering firms where to consider their component "finders", "minders", and "grinders" among its owners and managers who became successors of the acquired company. Although Bhat (1992) focused his analysis of manufacturing unit acquisition on acquiring or producing advanced manufacturing technologies while taking into account the firm's strategic and operational repercussions, this does not negate the fact that Bhat's research has a different emphasis. Datta et al. (1992) was one of the few studies that examined the empirical literature that looked at the effect of multiple factors on the growth of shareholder wealth in the context of mergers and acquisitions. According to the findings, mergers and acquisitions benefit the shareholders of the target business but not the shareholders of the company bidding. The findings also indicate that the use of stock financing has a substantial impact on the wealth of shareholders of the target enterprise as well as shareholders of the bidding enterprise. Chatterjee et al., (1992) examined the congruence of the top management cultures inside the merging organisations, with the correlation between shareholder benefits and the level of relatedness. The results suggest a notable negative correlation between perceptions of cultural disparities and shareholder advantages, even when controlling for factors such as the acquiring company's attitudes towards diversity and the respective magnitudes of the merging organisations. In addition, Jordan (1992) performed an analysis of the strategic drivers that are responsible for this trend before moving on to investigate the ways in which R&D strategy and human resource management practices interact in a global context. Jordan (1992) focused primarily on agricultural research and development locations. Examples of U.S. companies beginning research and development in Japan and Japanese companies building R&D facilities in the United States offer an essential perspective. This is because human resources policies and the historical nature of research and technology development in the two countries are vastly different. Two different case studies have been selected to demonstrate the various stages of strategic development.

Furthermore, Kang (1993) described the foreign direct investments in cross-border mergers and acquisitions in relation to Japanese bids and to the portfolio of Japanese bidders and U.S. targets as improving with bidder leverage, bidder linkages to financial institutions through borrowings, and the devaluation of the dollar relative to the value of the Japanese yen. On the other hand, not a lot of research has been done to elucidate. Despite this, Kaplan (1994) evaluated the value of Federated Department Stores after the company had filed for bankruptcy and contrasted it to the value of the company before Campeau Corporation acquired it. The post-bankruptcy valuation took into account all of the costs, both direct and secondary, associated with the bankruptcy and the financial difficulties. The valuation of Federated's assets increased by $3.1 billion in 1992 dollars, equivalent to an increase of $1.6 billion in 1987 dollars. This increase is only marginally lower than that reported by Kaplan (1989), suggesting that net bankruptcy expenditures were extremely low or nonexistent. The acquisition of Federated demonstrates that a highly leveraged deal can increase value while failing to satisfy debt obligations; as a result, bankruptcy (and financial crisis) does not necessarily have to be expensive.

The topics of discussion for the research are "Financing Pattern," "Operating Efficiency," "Financial Performance," and "Value of the Company." propose new research avenues and discover opportunities to merge different clusters in order to evaluate mergers and acquisitions from the perspective of a number of different academic disciplines for each cluster. Using co-citation and cluster analysis, major research streams in the mergers and acquisitions (M&A) literature are discovered. Each of the newly discovered clusters focuses on a different problem, which makes it easier for researchers in the academic world to identify fundamental questions, findings that are at odds with one another, and fresh paths worthy of further investigation.

Further, the literature review has been categorized into five broad areas in that four have related to our research objectives, and the fifth is considering others and further has been classified into respective segments.

2.2.1 Literature Related to Financing Pattern

The financial health of SMEs in transitioning economies was assessed by Barth et al. (2011). This framework identifies monetary roadblocks, and their impact on funding practices is investigated further. Despite these variations, it is defined by Renneboog and Szilagyi, (2008) as any transaction that alters the underlying capital structure of the organization in a way that increases or decreases risk. Feng et al. (2017), Davies et al. (2018), Yan, (2018), Jory et al., (2020), and Levine & Wu (2021) are some examples of studies that have looked at the impact of merger law on M&A deals that span cross-borders, the connection between the method of payment in M&A deals and the subsequent change in firm-specific stock price crash risk, and the nature of public-private partnerships. Meanwhile, Davies et al. (2018) highlight the importance of foreign direct investment (FDI), which is also common in developing countries, in shaping the capital structure of businesses and fostering the growth of technology-based infrastructure.

Moreover, Greenfield investments and cross-border mergers & acquisitions are two types of FDI. The fundamental difference between GF investment and other types of investments is that GF investment is reliant on the MNE's internal resources. As a further addition, Yan (2018) looked into the effects of merger law on cross-border mergers and acquisitions.

Jory et al. (2020) looked into how the method of payment used in mergers and acquisitions affected the likelihood of a stock price drop for the acquired company. The researchers looked into how this type of compensation affected the probability of a stock market meltdown. An increase in risk is seen in proportion to the use of stock as a funding source for the deal. The likelihood of a stock price crash is largest for overvalued acquirers, defined as those with a positive market-to-book ratio after adjusting for the industry. This is due to the fact that an overvaluation implies that the buyer is parting with cash in excess of what the target company is worth.

On the other hand, Masulis & Simsir (2018) have studied the effects of mergers as a direct result of target firms' decisions to sell control and the factors that impact those decisions. Targets in M&A transactions are distinct from targets in bidder-initiated deals in terms of their attributes. In addition to the financial constraints imposed by contracts, target enterprises often show signs of financial and economic trouble before the start of a contract.

Barth et al., (2011) examined the funding pattern of SMEs in mergers and acquisitions. This study explored the direct relationship between mergers and acquisitions and their impact on financing patterns. Despite the fact that few studies have been conducted, Feng et al., (2017), Devies et al., (2018), Yan (2018), Jory et al., (2020), and Levine & Wu, (2021) have been linked to the impact of mergers on capital structure, foreign direct investment on financing patterns, the impact of merger law on cross-border merger and acquisitions, and the relationship between the form of payment used in mergers and acquisitions and the resulting shift in firm-specific stock.

2.2.2 Literature Related to Operating Efficiency

Earlier Operating efficiency was based primarily on labor efficiency in the manufacturing sector. In this regard, target company labor effectiveness has a negative correlation with M&A activity (O'Shaughnessy & Flanagan,1998). After a long time, many research studies started appearing in the service sector to evaluate the operating efficiency, for example – the banking sector, hospitality, etc. Halkos and Tzeremes (2013) conducted research in the Greek banking industry to determine the degree to which 45 possible bank mergers and acquisitions improved the operating efficiency of the combined institutions. Although, McCarthy and Dolfsma (2015) found that since the introduction of the euro, there has been a significant increase in the number of transactions that have been publicly declared due to operational activity. This finding lends credence to the theories that policy can influence firm geography and that introducing the euro has led to increased business activity within the Eurozone. Yet, Moatti et al., (2015) highlighted how mergers and acquisitions increase bargaining leverage in the short term, whereas organic expansion increases operating efficiency over time, and Kiselakova & Sofrankova (2015) projected increase in net operating profit when the merger/acquisition was implemented. However, Noles et al., (2015) suggested that operating margins declined after the merger. Although Akpan et al., (2018) focused on efficiency in addition to value creation in horizontal mergers and acquisitions in the context of Nigeria.

Further, Yang (2019) investigated the connections between the amount of money spent, the number of target hotels acquired in acquisitions, and the acquirer hotel groups' subsequent financial success following the purchase. During that time, a regression study discovered that the magnitude of the rise in acquirer hotel groups' EBITDA and operating efficiency ratio was more dependent on the number of target hotels purchased by the acquirer hotel groups than on the amount of money invested in the acquisitions. This was the case despite the fact that the amount of money invested in the acquisitions was significantly higher. In this regard, when analyzed according to best-practice regimens, the behavior of the merged companies and the companies that resulted from the merger will eliminate the missed incentives observed in average-cost yardstick competition (Teusch, 2019). In addition, Bernile and Lyandres (2019) focused on the operational efficiencies resulting from mergers. The idea of industrial organization predicts that related businesses will experience the following benefits due to increased operational efficiencies. To begin, the merged business have a competitive edge over its rivals due to increased operational efficiencies, which will result in the competitors' stock prices falling. Second, the merged company's production costs are reduced due to enhanced operational efficiency, which also results in lower equilibrium output rates, which benefit the merged company's customers. Finally, increasing operational efficiencies while decreasing costs can help to merge companies achieve equilibrium, optimal production levels, and subsequent demand for inputs, all of which are to the advantage of the suppliers of the merged company. However, Ferris et al. (2019) investigated how acquiring companies in stock-for-stock mergers artificially inflate earnings by reducing discretionary expenses, manipulating sales to raise revenue, and overproducing items in order to minimize costs.

The behavior of the corporation as well as its performance following the acquisition was analyzed by Oberts (2020). In stock-for-stock mergers, the corporations doing the acquiring have the chance to control earnings before signing a merger agreement. This allows them to boost their stock price and reduce the cost of acquiring the company that they are merging with. Despite this, Fasipe and Sun (2020) used post-SOX data from mergers and acquisitions that occurred between 2003 and 2013 to evaluate whether stock-for-stock acquirers used more real-activity manipulation to inflate earnings in the fiscal year prior to the merger announcement than cash acquirers did. This evaluation determined whether stock-for-stock acquirers used more real-activity manipulation to inflate earnings (Fasipe & Sun, 2020). Further, he looked into the question of whether or not purchasing companies in stock-for-stock mergers participated in real-world activity manipulation in the year leading up to the announcement of the merger. Specifically, the researchers were interested in determining whether or not these companies did so. In a stock-for-stock merger, there are typically three phases: negotiation, reaching an agreement, and a stock swap between the acquiring and target firms using a fixed stock swap ratio. Liu et al., (2022) examined the effect of the uniqueness of the bidder-target relationship, also known as the number of firms that share the bidder-target relationship, on merger synergies.

When considering all of the aforementioned literature that pertains to specific operating efficiency, only limited number of the literature, including Halkos and Tzeremes, (2013), Moatti at el., (2015), Akpan et al., (2018), Yang (2019), and Bernile & Lyandres, (2019), are directly associated with fundamental aspects of operating efficiency. Additionally, McCarthy and Dolfsma (2015), Stephen P.Ferris et al., (2019), Oberts, (2020), Fasipe and Sun, (2020), and Liu et al., (2022) are the bulk of the studies that take into consideration the indirect impact that mergers and acquisitions have on efficiency. Nevertheless, for the sake of this study, operating efficiency was evaluated using the revised timeline and methodology. Most studies were more concerned with the business aspects of mergers and acquisitions than with the economics of day-to-day operations. Only a few of them were connected to the industrial processes that went on in the realm of heavy parts and commodities manufacturing units. Having said that, this study considers the firm's financial aspects and operational efficiency.

2.2.3 Literature Related to Financial Performance

The financial performance and future prospects of M&A deals are the subjects of discussion in this section of the study. The effectiveness of mergers and acquisitions has been a contentious topic for several decades. Singh and Montgomery (1987) explored the impact the acquisition techniques have on economic performance, whereas Richards and Manfredo (2003) analyzed the post-merger performance of agricultural cooperatives, while Mei & Sun (2008) investigated the financial performance of the United States forest products industry. Although Kumar (2009) evaluated the corporate performance of Indian companies, but Siegel & Simons (2010) emphasized on plant productivity. Based on the method, Francoeur (2006) used the fama french three-factor model to evaluate the long-run performance of cross-border mergers and acquisitions. Few of them, for example, Palmer et. al., (2007) focused on the performance of top insurance companies. However, J. Yang and Gon Kim, (2010) have considered hospitality firms to evaluate post-merger stock performance. Furthermore, Shim, (2011) has placed an emphasis on diversification and performance in the insurance industry, and Huian (2011) has analyzed the post-merger accounting performance of Romanian banks. Another diversified study was conducted by Huian (2011). As a result of advances in technology, Chen (2012) has focused his research on the effects of IT-enabled resources on organizational capacities and company performance. Although only a small number of Indian research (Reddy, 2014; Srinivasa Reddy et al., 2013; A. Srinivasan & Thampy, 2017; S. Srinivasan, 2020) have concentrated on issues such as international competition, diversification, and state-owned banks. The constraint shared by all studies is that their focus is on the performance of companies in relation to a particular event or industry. In addition to that, the majority of them do not restrict the area geographically. Further, Hsueh & Wang (2014); Du et al., (2014), Aureli (2015); Cho et al., (2016); P. H. Hsu et al., (2021); Moatti et al., (2015); Rashid & Naeem, (2017) looked at R &D partnership network and correlated with firm performance, research, and development (R&D) influence, unlisted Italian companies acquired by emerging markets of multinationals, the global retail industry, the impact of CEO celebrity on managerial risk, and corporate performance respectively.

Whereas few studies were also conducted in emerging markets, such as Abdou et al., (2016) assessed the impact of M & A on the financial performance of the Nigerian market, Zhu et al., (2017) evaluated counterproductive to its market reaction and Kumaraswamy et al., (2019) focused on the influence of restructuring on the financial performance of Gulf Cooperation Council enterprises. However, Y. Yang (2019) studied the implications that the size of the acquisition had on the financial performance of a hotel company. Although, Mingwei et al., (2020) increased the scale of the company; yet, this does not mean that he has significantly increased strength, and Ocieszak, (2020) focused on deals involving sector diversification and found that changing the CEO of a company after purchasing it has a negative impact on the financial performance of the acquired business.

In addition to this, support the idea of conducting additional research on the topic of performance outcomes. Few of the studies showed targeted firms have lower revenue and liquidity (Desyllas & Hughes, 2009), Unfavorable merger news returns increase the likelihood of M&A firms misstating their financial statements (Bens et al., 2012), Bouzgarrou (2014) did not find evidence to support the synergistic hypothesis of mergers and acquisitions. Moreover, Oyna et al., (2018) investigated that the use of M&A leads to better financial performance. However, Borodin et al., (2020) considered different aspects to discernible impact on the profitability index of the chosen firms. Few of the studies, for example (Caiazza et al., 2021) sustainability performance, (Liu et al., 2021) country resources and cross-border M&A, (Caiazza et al., 2021) cross-border M&A, (Y. Li & Singal, 2021) deal characteristics, (J. Hsu et al., 2021) long-run performance of cross-border acquirers, (D. H. Zhu & Westphal, 2021) corporate strategy and performance, have considered performance-based analysis in their study on the relationship between structural power and corporate strategy, knowledge diversity of key managerial and its innovation performance in reverse cross-border mergers and acquisitions. Further, Duan et al. (2022), ESG performance (Barros et al., 2022), justification for adopting experience learning as a functional method of obtaining greater M&A performance (Schweizer et al., 2022), and cultural differences and cross-border (Korzeb et al., 2022) are all topics that are covered in this study. Moreover, Ferris & Sainani (2021) identified the role of the chief financial officer in the M&A process, and Wang et al., (2021) focused on the excessive spending of corporate social responsibility funds in mergers and acquisitions, although, Srinivasa Reddy et al., (2013) considered an event study to evaluate the average abnormal return (AAR), and accounting ratios have been considered to explore the long-run financial performance for which t-stat had been applied. Most of these things were done to investigate long-term financial performance. The research looked at performance in terms of sales, profits, return on investments, expanding the customer base, and growing market share. It also looked at innovative strategies and expanding the client base.

The fact that every merger and acquisition is unique (as well as every company) is a crucial factor that adds to the ongoing argument on whether or not M&A activities improve performance. Because there are a number of moderating elements that influence the performance of mergers and acquisitions (for example, the attributes of the acquirer, the characteristics of the target firm, and expectations), individual agreements are not necessarily similar. As a consequence of this, we recommend that future research be predicated on industry-specific business performance in order to gain a deeper comprehension of the evaluation of subsequent businesses.

2.2.4 Literature Related to the Value of the firm

This section contains a large number of research articles that were read to give the particular technique to be evaluated, as well as a comprehensive assessment of major and minor factors of the factor or component of market behavior. Born at al., (1999) focused on executive severance arrangements that are commonly referred to as golden parachutes. These arrangements are made contingent on a change in management of the company. During a power battle for control of a corporation, considerable agency costs can accumulate, but these contracts have the ability to bring those costs down. Past studies on golden parachute contracts have shown that these types of contracts have little impact on shareholder value, with the exception of signaling an increased likelihood of a control struggle. They devised a more efficient executive severance agreement that will strike a balance between the interests of shareholders and target business managers in the event that managers are required to sell the company. They devised a prototype for the perfect contract by incorporating a modest one-time payment as well as a payment that was proportional to the increase in the value of the company that was realized as a result of the sale.

In the year 2000, there was a considerable increase in the number of businesses whose value is mostly derived from intangible assets, with little or no value linked with tangible assets. This trend continued throughout the decade. Conventional valuation approaches, which are based on accounting principles and assume that the value of the company's assets equals a percentage of the total value, have invariably resulted in an underestimate of the value of businesses such as these. Further, Sullivan (2000) investigated the problem of assigning a monetary value to intangible assets held by businesses and provided two methods for doing so. In addition to this, it discussed two common scenarios in which company value is required and investigates the ways in which value might be appraised by employing non-traditional perspectives on companies in addition to conventional approaches for valuation. The worth of the company as a going concern and the value of the company under the conditions of a merger or acquisition are the two scenarios that are being considered. According to Delaney and Wamuziri (2004), linked takeovers typically result in substantial and favorable benefits for the target company's owners. Although Wang (2005) discovered that acquiring companies had a higher level of business success than the companies they acquired and that target companies have a higher level of business success than non-target organizations. However, between 1987 and 2004, Antoniou et al. (2007) investigated the wealth effects for shareholders (both short and long term) of UK frequent bidders acquiring public, private, and/or subsidiary targets with alternate ways of payment.

Furthermore, Bates et al. (2008) examined the relationship between board composition, takeover activity, and transaction outcomes for a group of enterprises. The classification of a company by the target board has minimal impact on the likelihood that the company will be acquired if it is targeted. Furthermore, shareholders of targets with a classified board earn bid returns comparable to those of targets with a single class of directors, but they receive a larger portion of the overall bid excess. However, although board classification reduces the possibility of obtaining a takeover offer, the monetary impact on the company's worth is quite minor. The research generally refutes the widely held belief that board classification is an anti-takeover strategy that supports management entrenchment.

The typical justification for mergers and acquisitions is the creation of additional value or an increase in operational efficacy. The facts, however, do not indicate the presence of advantages in terms of the enterprises' costs, productivity, profitability, or market value. The current body of research is unique in that it focuses on evaluating the effects of mergers during the time that they are being carried out. As a result, the possibility of observing total integration between the combined businesses is reduced. Few other different dimensions, consider for example, Bernad et al., (2010) investigated the effect that mergers and acquisitions had on the overall productivity of Spanish savings banks over the long run, but Evripidou (2012) evaluated the influence of mergers on the systemic risk of bidder enterprises in the airline industry and identified the motivations that lead to mergers in the industry. In which further, Bernad et al. (2013) concentrated their research on the effects that mergers have on the profitability of Spanish savings banks again.

Further, Akpan et al. (2018) examined the impact that voluntary horizontal mergers and acquisitions had on operating performance in Nigeria between 1995 and 2012 using various complementary research methods. The efficient market hypothesis was utilized by Ding et al. (2018) in order to predict the short-term influence that a particular occurrence would have on the shareholder value of a corporation. According to Larkin and Lyandres (2019), found-related frictions can result in inefficient mergers. These types of mergers are characterized by the fact that the complementarity gains resulting from bringing the acquirer's products and technologies and the target under one roof are lower than the gains that could have been realized if a different bidder had acquired the target. Although, Laurion (2020) found that focusing on non-GAAP financial data can assist investors in better understanding the performance of a firm as well as its value. Companies need to exercise extreme caution when it comes to the presentation of non-GAAP earnings per share (EPS), despite the fact that no regulations govern this statistic.

2.2.5 Other related literature

The other relevant literature pertaining to M&A in the field of finance, management, economic and machine learning is presented. Further we have categorized the literature into five broad areas (1) merger and acquisition deals analysis, (2) purely related to the theory or concept of mergers and acquisitions, (3) valuation of particular M&A deals, (4) M&A deals impact the market price of the share and (5) different dimension of cross-border mergers and acquisitions.

Firstly, I had my sights set on investigating M&A transactions in detail. The labor efficiency of the acquired company tends to go down after an M&A, according to the research by O'Shaughnessy and Flanagan (1998). Targets are larger than non-acquired enterprises and are more likely to be unprofitable and have insufficient liquidity, according to the research by Desyllas and Hughes (2009). Also, targets are frequently involved in M&A deals. Moreover, Majumdar et al. (2012) found that the telecoms industry saw a positive cash flow after a merger. Both Hsueh and Wang (2014) and Du et al. (2014) focused on the connections between R&D collaboration networks and commercial success. Having more public backing allowed SOEs to do larger deals, buy more companies or stakes with cash, and acquire corporations with higher debt loads, as shown by Tavares Lehmann & Lehmann (2017). On the other hand, Tripathi & Lamba (2015) focus on the positive effects of a merger on the stakeholders' and employees' well-being.

Moreover, Fernald et al., 2015 looked into methods of commercializing biotechnology. Oyna et al. (2018) observed that using mergers and acquisitions leads to increased financial performance, while Mishra (2018) concluded that growing previously existing markets should be given priority. These two research articles both appeared in print in 2018. Boubaker and Naoui (2020) analyzed the post-merger performance of the acquiring firms; Trejo et al., (2021) examined if company M&A experience is related to the likelihood of acquisition completion; Li et al., (2021) explain the story of M&A in Chinese banking over the past 15 years; and Lee et al., (2021) show positive and strong correlations between M&A transactions, indicating progress in the theory. On the other hand, Zheng et al. (2021) focused on enhancing environmental sustainability from an M&A perspective. Researchers Yang and Wu found that in 2021, bad press about a potential M&A deal increased the likelihood that the deal would be scrapped. Wan et al. (2021) show that in high-information-asymmetry transactions, such as mergers, the presence of expert knowledge improves the outcome. The consequences of mergers on the American labor market and the aviation industry were analysed by Kim et al. (2021). Yet, De Sousa et al. (2021) showed that firms with more board interlocks are more likely to combine or acquire other firms. Choi et al. (2021) examined healthcare industry mergers and acquisitions, whereas Leschik et al., (2022) evaluated M&As in Germany.

Further, Kirjavainen et al. (2021) found that operational activities are more directly related to interruption planning. Burns et al. (2021) discovered that the greater the number of DSCs on a board of directors, the greater the value of an acquisition. Tampakoudis et al. (2022) studied the link between gender diversity and shareholder wealth. This study by Ju et al. (2022) looked into why fewer municipal gas companies are now due to mergers and acquisitions. The study by Ahluwalia and Kassicieh from 2022 showed that financial clusters had an impact on M&A activity between startups. Findings from 2022 research conducted by Alimov suggest that lowering trade barriers improves the quality of business acquisition decisions generally. When controlling for acquisition experience, Irwin et al. (2022) find that acquisitions made by firms outside of the acquiring firm's industry perform better over the long run in a complicated environment. As part of the post-merger integration process, Karamustafa et al., (2022) found that a number of identities rose to prominence. As an additional point, Stefko et al. (2022) determined that civil rights are not a key factor leading to the expansion of mergers and acquisitions in EU nations. According to the findings of Raithatha and Ladkani (2022), it would appear that family firms are hesitant to participate in mergers and acquisitions.

Second, new theory or a deeper conceptual understanding was developed as a result of the research. In particular, Maroof et al. (2017) adjusted the company's valuation and assessed the effectiveness of vertical integration in M&As in Pakistan. Yen and Andre (2019) found that the effectiveness of legal enforcement varies from nation to country, which in turn affects the effectiveness with which agency difficulties are mitigated, and the results of M&A deals are realized. They reached this verdict after thinking about various other aspects that are relevant. Maroof and Jawad (2019) showed that vertical integration was the most successful among the three Integration techniques chosen by firms to conclude merger discussions. However, Shao et al. (2021) focused their study on categorizing M&A deals. Research by Cipollina et al. (2021) suggests that the institutional features of the countries where the firms are based influence the beneficial link between M&As and GVCs participation. Acero et al. (2021) 's research suggest that lowering the board of directors size and splitting the chairman and CEO's responsibilities can boost acquirer profits. It has been found by Calcagno et al. (2021) that the correlation between deal premium and length of negotiation is nonlinear. Using this equation, global computation is possible. Bathelt and Henn (2021) showed that information transfers in M&A procedures rely heavily on professional trust development, while Fang et al. (2021) find that businesses show a higher probability of bid announcements after the law's implementation. However, Institutional macroeconomic considerations matter in IT company M&As, as Bhasin et al. explained (2021). CSR scores are inversely related to M&A activity, as per Krishnamurti et al., (2021). Gu et al., (2022) found that companies' exposure to the M&A peer impact hindered their long-term success. Krishna and Jain (2022) rehash prior research by highlighting the value of open innovation for non-residents. Bauer et al., (2022) studied the acquisition pattern shifts that occurred during the 2009 COVID-19 pandemic. The results of using a variety of marketing materials were found to be statistically significant, as shown by Lv et al., (2022). Cotei et al. (2022) investigated how policy uncertainty affects M&A, whereas Pereira et al. (2022) zeroed in on sustainable energy systems. Using M&A's "case-to-theory transformation approach," Niederman and Baker (2022) analyzed it.

Third, the valuation of the specific M&A deal initially suggested that operating margins declined after the merger (Noles et al., 2015). Financial synergies from mergers and acquisitions were also studied by Mihaiu (2018). Notwithstanding Ma & Xu's (2020) assertion that incorporating the target's segments greatly boosts the acquirer's performance, Kiisk & Rungi's (2020) research indicated that adopting a strategy of internal knowledge production negatively affected financial results. According to Jang and Yehuda (2021), deal synergies are inversely related to the target's adjustment costs, while Chu et al. (2021) found that acquisitions considerably raised consumers' intrinsic preferences or valuations. Gregoriou et al., (2021) studied the unpredictability of economic policy. Based on their research, Chatterjee et al., (2021) concluded that a bidder with greater stock liquidity had a greater chance of acquiring a public target. Gregori Loureiro & Silva (2021) state that acquirers who look for companies in countries with more vital investor protection legislation find beneficial acquisition synergy. Takeover premiums are found to be higher when litigation is pending prior to an M&A announcement, as shown by Basnet et al. (2021). Cash-rich enterprises engaging in ESOs-induced M&A operations Huang et al. (2021), would benefit financially. According to Ho et al. (2021), analysts' target price estimates might be a useful means of communication. Information on the quality of purchases is accurately included in loan pricing, as demonstrated by Gao et al., (2021). Bugeja et al. (2021) showed that acquirers are more likely to employ equity financing to acquire targets with a higher likelihood of informed trading. Although, Zhu et al. (2021) found that organizations with controlling shareholders who make commitments are more likely to engage in mergers and acquisitions than companies whose owners do not make pledges. Gao et al. (2022) found that having financial advisors around moderated the negative correlation between an aggressive green marketing strategy and the completion of an M&A transaction. Filip et al. (2022) discovered that growth, synergies, human capital, and brands are all negatively correlated with acquirer stock returns after the announcement of an acquisition. Following an acquisition, Shafique and Hagedoorn (2022) claimed that acquiring companies increases their R&D output. In their study of M&A activity, Li et al., (2022) found that financialization had effects. Boo and Kim (2022) provided evidence linking poor merger announcement returns to sudden cuts in marketing and research and development spending, using numerous studies in their argument. Chen et al. (2022) found that the relative level of CSR between the acquiring and acquired companies was significantly connected with the extent of the acquirer's earnings and the synergy benefits realized as a result of the purchase.

Fourth, Kolari et al. (2021) found that abnormal returns for the business actions they studied were significant in subperiods both before and after 2002, M&A businesses with higher unfavourable merger announcement returns were shown to be more likely to misstate their financial statements after the merger., according to research conducted by Bens et al. (2012). While Abdou et al. (2016) analyzed the impact of M & A on the financial performance of the Nigerian market, Kiselakova & Sofrankova (2015) conducted an analysis on the projected growth estimates of net operating profit subsequent to the implementation of the merger and acquisition. These two studies were both released to the public in 2015 & 2016. After their research, Sahu and Agarwal (2017) concluded that mergers and acquisitions improve the profit margin. Yet, Syukur and Bungkilo (2020) discovered that deciding to pursue an acquisition agreement can have an adverse effect on profitability, debt, and efficiency.

Moreover, Dennis et al. (2021) have demonstrated that companies issuing bank funding before M&As experience abnormal return patterns. Findings from the study by Wang et al. (2021) showed that acquirers have a lower cost of financing than non-acquirers and that the effect of acquisitions is more evident for companies based in provinces with less established markets. Carline and Gogineni's (2021) research showed that a lower propensity to spend in mergers and acquisitions is associated with higher instrumented ATPs. According to research, acquisition firms that purchase businesses backed by a syndicate have lower announcement returns (Nguyen and Vu, 2021).

The fifth and final set of M&As from throughout the globe tackles the sensitive issue of cultural sensitivity. An important focus for Smimou (2015) was the reaction of markets to news of cross-border mergers and acquisitions. According to Mishra and Jaiswal's (2017) research, mergers and acquisitions boost export competitiveness in both the short and long term. Findings from the study by Gregori and Nardo (2021) showed that the introduction of a formal screening process does not negatively affect FDI from other countries. The acquiring firms in the sub-sample of cross-border mergers also had much more acquisition experience and financial leverage, according to an analysis by Gada et al. (2021). According to Shen et al. (2021) there is a positive correlation between the size of M&A deals and the level of geopolitical risk, which remains stable over time and declines.

Nevertheless, Da Costa et al. (2021) explored the cultural, managerial, and organizational ramifications of M and A outcomes, and they discovered that, based on their research, Alcalde and Powell (2022) found that foreign mergers and acquisitions by Chinese companies have a significant positive effect on their CSR. Cross-border acquisitions, as determined by Yang et al. (2022), have a significant and positive effect on the CSR practices of Chinese acquirers. The machine learning models were applied by Hong et al. (2022) in order to produce predictions on judgments regarding cross-border mergers and acquisitions. Li et al. (2022) found that the extent to which economic policy uncertainty in the host country affected cross-border mergers and acquisitions of state-owned enterprises was small. As part of their study of the global financial system, Wójcik et al. (2022) examined mergers and acquisitions that crossed national boundaries. According to Chan and Zheng (2022)'s research, migrant networks have a favorable and considerable impact on mergers and acquisitions that take place across international borders (M&A), Shi et al. (2022) discovered that CSR has an impact on how the market responds to news of cross-border mergers and acquisitions.

Researchers Yang et al. (2022) discovered that corruption has a strong, negative relationship with the firm's acquisitiveness while accounting for cultural differences. Nevertheless, Umashankar et al. (2022) discovered that M&As negatively affect customers' happiness. In their article, Huang et al. (2022) explored the potential for shareholder lawsuits, and the decision businesses must make regarding whether or not to pursue international expansion. Expanding the factor market in a home nation may have a negative link with EMF investments made in more developed countries, as Reddy et al. (2022) stated.

Our research makes a substantial contribution to the existing body of scholarly work and ought to be acknowledged for this fact. This graph analysis, which is extensive, up-to-date, and distinct from the academic literature that was mentioned earlier, was created by using the stock price of the listed businesses that were the results of mergers and acquisitions. Previous researchers have looked at a variety of factors, including operating performance (Yeh & Hoshino, 2002), firm efficiency (Labban, 2010), risk associated with the international exchange market (Crude Oil Market) (Comment & Schwert, 1995), business combination (Anwar et al., 2015), and stock return volatility (Clarke et al., 2019). Elnahas et al. (2017) highlighted a particular reference regarding the influence of religious beliefs on M&A behavior. Our primary concern was a specific factor connected to the stock market.

Since the introduction of the euro, there has been a tremendous increase in the number of business transactions that are made public. The conclusion is that the location of enterprises is influenced by policy is given more weight as a consequence of these findings. Although, Bernile & Lyandres (2019) investigated how the organizational improvements gained by acquirers through horizontal acquisitions impacted the businesses that they competed with McCarthy & Dolfsma (2015). In order to determine how acquisitions affect the PERs of steelmakers that have been purchased, both the financial organization and the steelmaker under consideration are analyzed. Comparison and contrast of the acquired steelmaker's pre-acquisition and post-acquisition success measures are carried out using a variety of methodologies (Huh, 2015). Further, Yeh and Hoshino (2002) researched companies' performance. In addition to this, they also analyzed the productivity of the merging companies, which is measured by the total productivity factor (TPF), also known as output per unit of total input. This allowed them to investigate the role that the Keiretsu played in the changes in efficiency brought about by mergers, whether those changes were for the better or, the worse. Utilizing the TPF method, he analyzes the level of technical efficiency exhibited by the business.

In order to provide evidence of changes in bidder wealth in bancassurance mergers, Fields et al. (2007) investigated combinations of insurance companies and commercial banks in both the United States and internationally. Specifically, the researchers focused on the United States (primarily Europe). In addition, they used standard techniques for event studies to determine whether or not the announcement of a merger between a bank and an insurance company affects the shareholders' wealth.

However, Anwar et al., (2015) conducted research to investigate the significance of risk in relation to the variability of output. Although Martin and Sayrak's (2003) primary areas of research focused on the effects of diversification on business value as well as the long-term tendency of diversification, but Cai et al. (2016) investigated merger and acquisition (M&A) situations where the acquiring company and the acquired company shared an auditor. In addition to this, they calculated the total abnormal returns of the combined portfolios of the purchaser and the targets that were relatively close to the announcement date.

Moreover, Hu et al. (2020) researched how managers' access to trade credit has impacted their judgments regarding mergers and acquisitions. They investigated the impact of trade credit on the anomalous returns of mergers and acquisitions in the near term by using mean-adjusted returns, value-weighted market-adjusted returns, and value-weighted market-model-adjusted returns. All of these return measures were weighted by market capitalization. In addition, they discussed the ways in which trade credit boosts acquirers' negotiating strength and creates synergies in the wake of mergers and acquisitions.

The capital asset pricing model (CAPM) takes into account not only market risk but also size and value concerns. As a consequence, the model considers the fact that value stocks and small-cap stocks have traditionally outperformed the market overall.

Adjustments to the model for these two additional factors are what are responsible for explaining this propensity towards outperformance. Furthermore, the pricing approach for assets known as the three-factor model was developed by Fama and French in the year 1992. The the Carhart four-factor model and value-weighted Fama-French three-factor model were utilized to compute long-term anomalous results. In a few studies, Hunter and Ali (2014) utilized two distinct iterations of the monetary model to reassess the dollar-to-yen exchange rate. In this regard, Reddy (2019) presented a new conceptual framework for gaining a comprehension of growth strategies by comparing organic and artificial growth.

Adjusting for the efficiency and profitability of local banking markets, Colombo and Turati (2014) employed probit and zero-inflated Poisson (ZIP) models to evaluate the direct influence of economic and social factors at the regional level on the probability of seeing a bank in a merger and acquisition (M&A) transaction, as well as the count of acquiring banks. The aforementioned models were employed to assess the direct influence of economic and social factors at the regional level on the probability of witnessing a bank in a merger and acquisition (M&A) transaction, as well as the quantity of acquiring banks involved. Further, Beccalli and Frantz (2013) conducted research in order to determine the variables that contribute to the decision of a bank to either merge with another institution or be acquired.

According to the findings of Aghion et al., (2021), centralised businesses and organisations are subject to a greater degree of damage as a result of adverse events in comparison to their decentralised counterparts. When negative shocks are anticipated by using exogenous variables, such as the age of a commodity, exports by nation, or the number of businesses that are operational, this is the scenario that plays out. Swidler et al. (2019) investigated the anomalous findings further by focusing on whether the activist is a board member.

In this section, Tamosiuniene and Duksaite (2009) established a connection between the activity of mergers and acquisitions (M&A) and economic development as well as foreign direct investment. They came to the conclusion that the general value of mergers and acquisitions (M&A), a country's gross domestic product (GDP), a country's inward foreign direct investment (FDI), and a country's outward FDI all play a part in determining the volume of mergers and acquisitions activity. It is imperative that the growth of the companies participating in the mergers and acquisitions be brought to light to maximize the potential benefits to the combined company.

Fong et al. (2019) investigated the significance of a company's culture in U.S. mergers and acquisitions (M&A), which were the subject of their research. Our research is primarily focussed on the businesses' achievements, both in terms of their operational and financial success. We have looked at a number of important metrics in order to determine the impact that a merger or acquisition will have on a business's bottom line.

Overvaluation of the businesses that were investigated by Vagenas-Nanos (2020) who utilized a difference-in-differences estimator within a regression framework to determine BHAR for various holding durations. In the same vein, research has been done on the impacts of voluntary horizontal mergers and acquisitions on the success of the acquirer, the business that was acquired, and the business that was created as a result of the combination of the two businesses. Akpan et al. (2020) researched the value creation of businesses that merged in Nigeria between the years 1995 and 2012 to determine whether there is a correlation between technological efficiency and value creation.

Last but not least, this section has been concluding the systematic literature portion, which is an essential part of the section.

2.3 Bibliometric Analysis

Using literature analysis to hone in on a specific area and broaden the scope of a particular research dimension is a novel and scientific method for refining large documents (such as research papers, articles, book chapters, books, etc.). For this reason, I plan to assess everything that could influence the current direction of M&A studies.

In this respect, I have culled bibliometric information from the Scopus database in order to search for the following keywords:

"Mergers and Acquisitions", "Mergers", "Acquisitions", "M&A", "M&As", "Corporate Restructuring", "Amalgamation".

The above-mentioned keywords are limited to the social science, economics, finance area of journals, and found 8285 numbers of documents from the period from 1983 to 2022. These documents are categorized as articles, articles in the press, books, book chapters, conference papers, editorials, notes, review papers, and short surveys. Most of the documents are articles, conference papers, review papers, and notes, contributing 94.49% to the particular research domain. 58.78% contributed through the articles, 15.17% through the conference papers, 10.64% through the review papers, and 9.90% through the notes. However, 5.51% comes through short surveys, book chapters, books, editorials, and articles in the press.

A bibliometric strategy is used to identify on the basis of the main information, average citation per year, annual scientific production, most relevant sources, most locally cited sources (from reference lists), source clustering through Bradford's Law, source dynamics, and so on. The most relevant authors, the authors who are most locally cited, the author's local effect, the most relevant affiliations, and the most cited countries. In light of this, sections have organized the portions of this chapter.

Table 2.2: Summary of literature review

Total articles	8328
Eliminated articles that are not related	7284
Industry-based journal (particulars events and news)	65
Other disciplines (e.g., engineering, science etc.)	826
Articles that are used to review further (SLR)	153

Source: *Compiled by Author from Scopus data*

Total publications, as mentioned in table-2.2, were extracted from the Scopus database and eliminated publications that are not related to academics or the M&A core concern with finance and analytical perspectives. Otherwise, I keep all such relevant publications to review further with the package of RStudio to evaluate the impact of research papers and publications

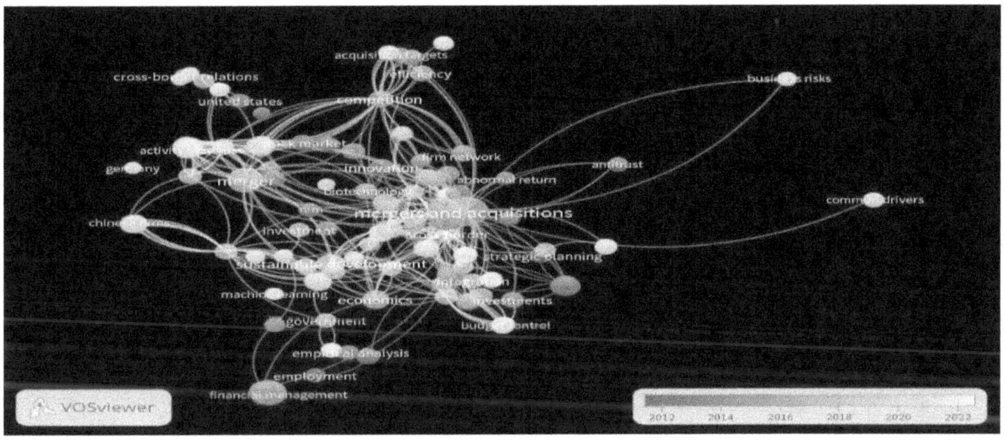

Figure-2.2: Keywords Overlays

Source: *Compiled by Author from VOSviewer*

2.3.1 Main information

Using R tools based on the graphical user interface (GUI), biblioshiny is a package of R in which bibliometric data extracted from the Scopus database is put into getting a result with stabilizing different aspects considered. The following main information on the bibliometric data and document characteristics is given in Table-2.3.

Table: 2.3 Information Summary of bibliometric data

Timespan	**1983-20**	**2000-03**	**2004-06**	**2007-12**	**2013-17**	**2018-22**
Sources (Journals, Books, etc)	98	188	273	760	689	715
Documents	231	1172	1563	1870	1716	1733
Annual Growth Rate %	30.04	18.37	-27.28	3.94	11.32	-16.08
Document Average Age	24.5	19.9	17.2	12.4	6.78	2.18
Average citations per doc	38.21	11.59	13.71	22.79	15.55	5.017
References	4054	6526	13259	54761	70677	85330
DOCUMENT CONTENTS						
Keywords Plus (ID)	926	2866	6127	9076	6136	5556
Author's Keywords (DE)	380	599	1056	4349	4661	4996
AUTHORS						
Authors	350	732	1172	3502	3568	3937
Authors of single-authored docs	77	298	386	457	315	233
AUTHORS COLLABORATION						
Single-authored docs	117	994	1224	531	347	258
Co-Authors per Doc	1.78	1.25	1.35	2.27	2.54	2.86

Table: 2.3 Information Summary of bibliometric data

Timespan	1983-20	2000-03	2004-06	2007-12	2013-17	2018-22
International co-authorships %	7.359	2.218	3.135	13.58	23.72	29.37
DOCUMENT TYPES						
Article	161	412	444	1138	1261	1412
Article in press	0	0	0	0	0	1
Book	0	0	1	8	2	5
Book chapter	0	0	1	35	46	43
Conference paper	29	0	94	568	340	215
Editorial	0	4	0	3	4	2
Note	12	455	325	10	7	4
Review	29	239	450	61	46	49
Short survey	0	19	248	19	10	2

The table-2.3 shows all data into six timespans, and it has been segregated for running the CSV file on RStudio. All these results have been combined to give an overall view of the publications. It is reflected that 2007-2012 have more publications across all six timespans. However, the average growth rate was high during 2013-2017.

2.3.2 Annual scientific production

Combining all data into one dataset to represent the annual scientific production from 1983 to June, 2022. The figure-2.3 shows the graphical presentation of the year-wise publications.

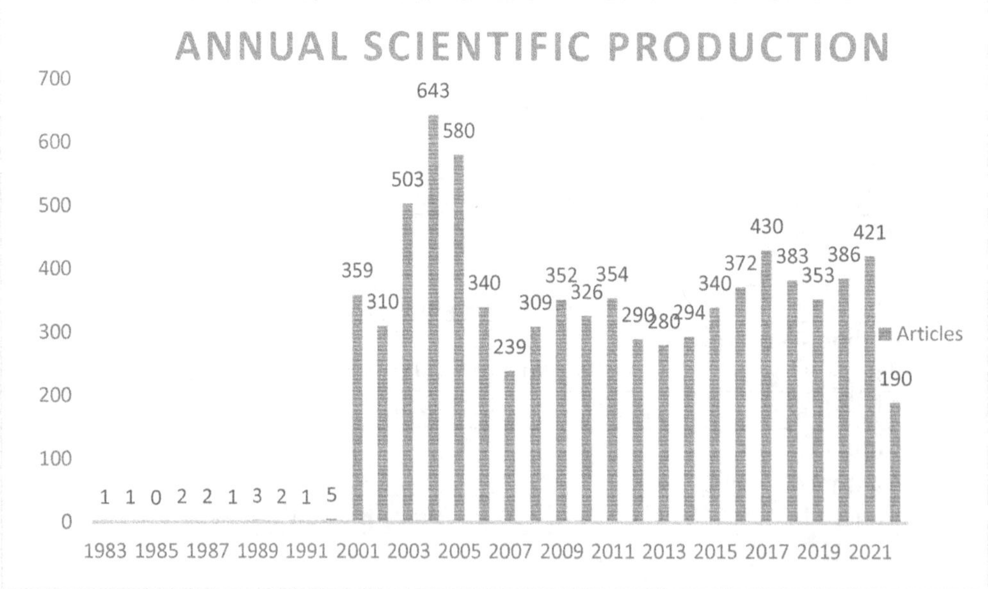

Figure-2.3: Annual scientific production

Source: *Compiled by Author from Scopus data*

2.3.3 Average citation per year

Table 2.4: Average citation per year based on bibliometric data

Year	N	MeanTCperArt	MeanTCperYear	CitableYears
1983	1	2.00	0.05	39
1984	1	3.00	0.08	38
1985	0	0.00	0.00	0
1986	2	0.00	0.00	36
1987	2	2.00	0.06	35
1988	1	0.00	0.00	34
1989	3	6.33	0.19	33
1990	2	29.00	0.91	32
1991	1	6.00	0.19	31
1992	5	155.60	5.19	30
1993	9	43.44	1.50	29
1994	7	38.57	1.38	28
1995	6	28.83	1.07	27
1996	13	127.54	4.91	26
1997	33	32.42	1.30	25
1998	41	27.66	1.15	24
1999	17	110.76	4.82	23
2000	87	15.83	0.72	22
2001	359	7.61	0.36	21
2002	310	22.71	1.14	20
2003	503	7.58	0.40	19
2004	643	15.15	0.84	18
2005	580	12.84	0.76	17
2006	340	12.48	0.78	16
2007	239	22.86	1.52	15
2008	309	28.33	2.02	14
2009	352	27.77	2.14	13
2010	326	24.06	2.01	12
2011	354	15.38	1.40	11
2012	290	18.37	1.84	10
2013	280	19.41	2.16	9
2014	294	17.65	2.21	8
2015	340	18.91	2.70	7
2016	372	12.82	2.14	6
2017	430	11.30	2.26	5
2018	383	9.98	2.49	4
2019	353	6.81	2.27	3
2020	386	4.44	2.22	2
2021	421	1.62	1.62	1
2022	190	0.39		0

Source: *Compiled by Author from Scopus data*

From 2001 to 2004, the average number of citations per year increased, then decreased until 2007. However, it increased from 2007 to 2011, and then increased again from 2012 to 2022.

2.3.4 Most relevant sources

Based on the number of articles published in journals and through other mode of publication, we have listed the top 15 sources that are most preferable toe publication related to Mergers and Acquisition research. In which Chemical Market Reporter, Jane's Defence Weekly, Official Board Markets, Pulp and Paper, Strategic Management Journal, PPI Pulp and Paper International, Journal of Corporate Finance, International Journal of Industrial Organization, Printing World, Journal of Cleaner Production, Total Telecom, Management Science and Journal of Banking and Finance. However, one of the conference proceedings related to Advances in Public –Private Partnerships.

Table 2.5: Most Relevant Sources based on the number of articles

Sources	**Articles**
CHEMICAL MARKET REPORTER	370
JANE'S DEFENCE WEEKLY	307
OFFICIAL BOARD MARKETS	228
PULP AND PAPER	185
STRATEGIC MANAGEMENT JOURNAL	170
PPI PULP AND PAPER INTERNATIONAL	127
JOURNAL OF CORPORATE FINANCE	105
INTERNATIONAL JOURNAL OF INDUSTRIAL ORGANIZATION	103
JOURNAL OF FINANCIAL ECONOMICS	72
PRINTING WORLD	68
JOURNAL OF CLEANER PRODUCTION	62
TOTAL TELECOM	57
MANAGEMENT SCIENCE	50
JOURNAL OF BANKING AND FINANCE	43
ADVANCES IN PUBLIC-PRIVATE PARTNERSHIPS - PROCEEDINGS OF THE 2ND INTERNATIONAL CONFERENCE ON PUBLIC-PRIVATE PARTNERSHIPS	41

Source: *Compiled by Author from Scopus data*

2.3.5 Most local cited sources

Table -2.6: Most cited sources based on bibliometric data from the Scopus database

Sources	Articles
JOURNAL OF FINANCIAL ECONOMICS	11133
STRATEGIC MANAGEMENT JOURNAL	9389
JOURNAL OF FINANCE	7748
ACADEMY OF MANAGEMENT JOURNAL	3800
JOURNAL OF INTERNATIONAL BUSINESS STUDIES	2969
ORGANIZATION SCIENCE	2504
ACADEMY OF MANAGEMENT REVIEW	2349
ADMINISTRATIVE SCIENCE QUARTERLY	2218
JOURNAL OF MANAGEMENT	1872
THE JOURNAL OF FINANCE	1752
MANAGEMENT SCIENCE	1536
JOURNAL OF CORPORATE FINANCE	1502
JOURNAL OF MANAGEMENT STUDIES	1433
HARVARD BUSINESS REVIEW	1423
AMERICAN ECONOMIC REVIEW	1362
RESEARCH POLICY	1288
REVIEW OF FINANCIAL STUDIES	1273
JOURNAL OF BANKING AND FINANCE	1169

Source: *Compiled by Author from Scopus data*

In Table 2.6, the most cited sources from 1983 to 2022 have been mentioned, in the field of mergers and acquisitions-related research. The total cited articles are around 1,45,529. However, 56,720 cited articles from 18 sources, which is around 38.98%. The top five cited articles as the Journal of Financial Economics, Strategic Management Journal, Journal of Finance, Academy of Management Journal, and Journal of International Business Studies, with cited articles are 11133, 9389, 7748, 3800, and 2969 respectively.

2.3.6 Bradford's Law

Although Bradford developed an argument in his book Documentation that he felt may affect the distribution of articles in publications, a slew of studies has been written nearly two decades after he released the "law." Most of these papers are focused on how the law is applied to various areas of library operations and journal dissemination. More than 75% of the papers examined demonstrated that their implementations followed Bradford's law, with only a handful exhibiting minor variations. Bradford's law, as it originally proposed, asserts that "if the journals having articles on a particular subject are organized in decreasing order of the number of articles they contained on the subject, then consecutive zones of periodicals containing the same number of articles on the subject create the simple geometric series."

Bradford referred to the first zone as the core of publications explicitly devoted to the subject. For example, under the law, it was possible to determine the extent to which articles on a specific subject appear in journals devoted to other subjects. However, from Bradford's perspective, it is to be anticipated that a magazine devoted to a certain subject may incorporate an item of interest intended for any other issue.

Based on Bradford's Law, the Most reliable source of articles has been considered the all-data summarizing into descending order to evaluate.

Table 2.7: Source clustering through Bradford's Law

Source	Rank	Freq	CumFreq	Zone
CHEMICAL MARKET REPORTER	1	370	370	Zone 1
JANE'S DEFENCE WEEKLY	2	307	677	Zone 1
OFFICIAL BOARD MARKETS	3	142	819	Zone 1
PPI PULP AND PAPER INTERNATIONAL	4	93	912	Zone 1
PULP AND PAPER WEEK	5	87	999	Zone 1
OFFICIAL BOARD MARKETS	6	86	1085	Zone 1
PRINTING WORLD	7	68	1153	Zone 1
PULP AND PAPER WEEK	8	67	1220	Zone 1
STRATEGIC MANAGEMENT JOURNAL	9	53	1273	Zone 1

Source: *Compiled by Author from Scopus data*

2.3.7 Most relevant authors

Table 2.8: Most relevant authors based on bibliometric data

Name of Authors	Sum of Articles
CHANG J	49
VAN ARNUM P	34
ZHANG Y	33
LEWIS JAC	26
WANG Y	26
JARVIS L	24
LI J	22
LIU Y	22
DE GUZMAN D	20
LI H	20
LERNER I	19

Name of Authors	Sum of Articles
LI Y	17
LIU H	17
MIRASOL F	17
CHAN APC	16
MULHOLLAND D	16
ANDERSON G	15
MADURA J	14
SCHIERECK D	14
ZHANG W	14

Source: *Compiled by Author from Scopus data*

In Table 2.8, more than nine thousand authors have contributed articled. Chang, Van, Zhang, Lewis, and Wang are the top five authors whose contribution is 168 research papers, around 2% of the total contribution.

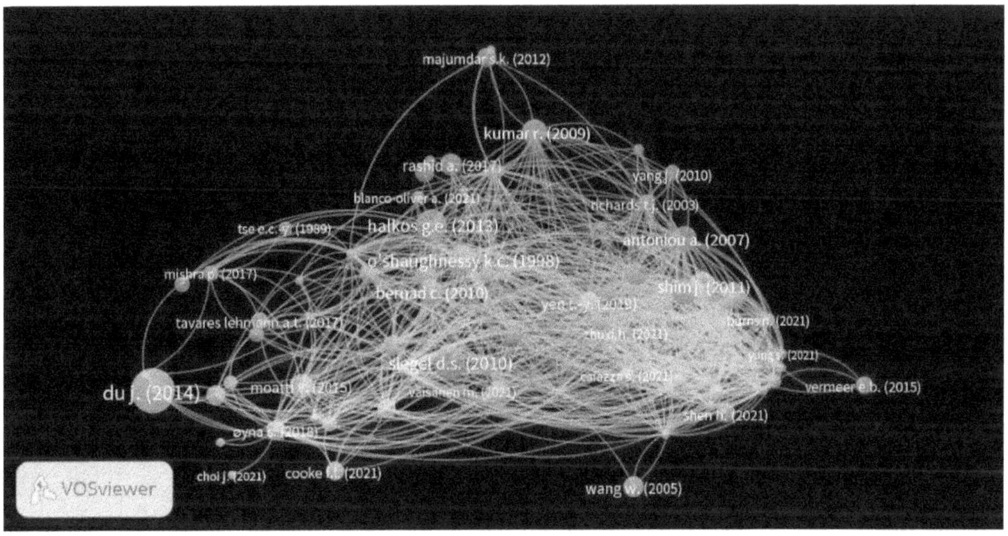

Figure-2.4: Author's Co-occurrence

Source: *Compiled by Author from Vosviewer*

2.3.8 Most relevant affiliations

Table 2.9: Top 20 Institution list based on bibliometric data analysis

Institutions	No. of Articles
CONCORDIA UNIVERSITY	57
UNIVERSITY OF CAMBRIDGE	50
UNIVERSITY OF CALIFORNIA	48
INDIANA UNIVERSITY	41
BEIJING JIAOTONG UNIVERSITY	40
WUHAN UNIVERSITY	37
TILBURG UNIVERSITY	34

Institutions	No. of Articles
FLORIDA ATLANTIC UNIVERSITY	31
MICHIGAN STATE UNIVERSITY	31
NATIONAL TAIWAN UNIVERSITY	31
TSINGHUA UNIVERSITY	31
UNIVERSITY OF MARYLAND	30
CITY UNIVERSITY OF HONG KONG	29
PEKING UNIVERSITY	28
UNIVERSITY OF BIRMINGHAM	27
UNIVERSITY OF READING	27
CALIFORNIA STATE UNIVERSITY	26
NANYANG TECHNOLOGICAL UNIVERSITY	26
UNIVERSITY OF GRONINGEN	26
UNIVERSITY OF MACEDONIA	26

Source: *Compiled by Author from Scopus data*

The most relevant affiliations are Concordia University, University of Cambridge, University of California, Indian University, Beijing Jiaotong University, and Wuhan University. However, few of the institution has more impact than the top five affiliations.

2.3.9 Most cited countries

Table 2.10: Most cited countries based on bibliometric data

Countries	Average Article Citations	Total Contribution (TC)
USA	45.22	48402
UNITED KINGDOM	25.14	8878
CHINA	14.45	7232
NETHERLANDS	44.68	4619
FRANCE	107.83	4336
CANADA	40.24	3787
GERMANY	13.66	2824
HONG KONG	28.51	2816
AUSTRALIA	37.54	2337
FINLAND	29.37	2110
ISRAEL	57.52	1846
ITALY	41.09	1817
SPAIN	26.25	1675
SWEDEN	34.18	1389
AUSTRIA	64.13	1312
BELGIUM	38.16	1093
INDIA	5.79	1046

Source: *Compiled by Author from Scopus data*

USA, United Kingdom, China, Netherlands, and France are the top five countries, contributing 69.24% to the total contribution. However, India is in the 20th position in the country-wise most cited countries.

2.4 Research Gap

While reviewing research papers, it has been found that regression analysis used in the previous studies are 52.94 percent with different variables, data envelopment analysis (DEA) (M. N. U. Akpan et al., 2018; Blanco-Oliver, 2021; Duan et al., 2022; Halkos & Tzeremes, 2013; Lang, 2021; J. Li et al., 2021; Rahman et al., 2016) are used around 4.58 percent and Fama-French Models (Antoniou et al., 2007; Cho et al., 2016; Francoeur, 2006; J. Hsu et al., 2021) are near to 2.61 percent as statistical tools. Few of the studies have dealt with the financing decision or payment techniques of M&A deals, and most of the studies are event-based analyses (Delaney & Wamuziri, 2004; Francoeur, 2006; Klitzka et al., 2022; C. Li et al., 2022; Mei & Sun, 2008; Monteiro & Silva, 2022). Though some studies do have relevance to the Indian context, the vast majority are rooted in either the United States or China. N. Zhang (2016) aims to analyse post-SOX data in order to examine the phenomenon known as the "anticipation effect." This effect refers to the incorporation of investors' expectations regarding the profitability of corporations' future acquisitions and their subsequent impact on the long-term valuation of acquiring firms into forward-looking pricing. Acquiring businesses in stock-for-stock mergers employ various strategies such as curtailing discretionary spending, manipulating sales to augment income, and engaging in overproduction of goods to mitigate the cost of goods sold. (Fasipe & Sun, 2020) have been able to artificially inflate profits in the past. After a merger or purchase, a company's operational efficiency can be compared to the acquirer's using a method called stochastic frontier analysis. Since this is the case, the stochastic frontier analysis (SFA) offers a new angle from which to evaluate productivity. Greenfield and merger and acquisition are defined in terms of finance by Davies et al. (2018). Financial success, financing structure, shareholder wealth, and operational efficacy can all be examined in the context of mergers and acquisitions. Efficiency, capital structure, and shareholder riches are just some possible investigation areas. Competition among businesses is heating up, so businesses need to evaluate novel methods to give investors a better return. There is a need for this research in the current scenario because of the increasing competition between businesses. There is scope in this field to analyze variables related to efficiency, capital structure, and shareholder wealth. With the enhancement of the competition between the companies, the present need to assess new approaches to provide better results for investors. This study filled the time gap for M& A deals during the present scenario due to the growing competitive business environment between firms in the economy.

This study analyzes the impact of financing patterns, operating efficiency, shareholder wealth, and firm financial performance pre and post-merger and acquisition.

2.5 Objective of the Study

The study's objective is the comparative analysis of corporate mergers and acquisitions efficiency and financing patterns. More precisely, we write it in the pointwise fashion as follows:

1. To analyze the financing pattern of the resulting companies pre and post-M&As.
2. To compare the operating efficiency of the merged company based on pre and post-M&As.
3. To study the impact of mergers and acquisitions on the financial performance of resulting listed companies.
4. To analyze the impact of M&As on the shareholders' wealth of the listed companies in the short-run.

The significance of carrying out this research is to find out the effect of merger and acquisition in various sectors, not just limited to one sector. This study will help us know how the merger and acquisition impact the sectors before and after the acquisition. It will provide stakeholders with a broader and more analysed perspective of the impact of M&As on different dimensions in the short and long run.

Secondly, it will help the **financial market players** to make better decisions about whether or not to invest in the desired entity, and it will also let them know about the actual impact on the Indian economy. It will also provide the scope of further research work.

Last but not least, it will help determine the firm's efficiency after mergers and acquisitions occur.

2.6 Conclusion

The M&A literature has risen rapidly, notably since the early 1990s, but especially after 1992 in India. The objectives of this paper were to identify significant moments and persons in the M&A literature, highlight major study streams, and indicate future research prospects. A bibliometric analysis was done on 8328 papers published between 1983 and 2022, with 145529 citations noted across time.

First, we detected research activities across time and listed the most significant M&A published papers to provide researchers with convenience and help them comprehend and examine the core literature of M&A research, as indicated in Appendix B. Second, this chapter provides the development of authors, organisations, and attributes within the M&A research society, which is a valuable perspective in the context of author-specific publication activities, identification, and funding, as well as M&A recognition for joint efforts or scholarly self.

The results of our investigation indicate that M&A research often engages in container thinking. We provide important recommendations for future research within each of the six research streams, as well as suggestions for how to better connect different clusters and expand the field of M&A study, based on our exhaustive investigation. Furthermore, we recommend that future bibliometric studies assess M&A from a multidisciplinary viewpoint, highlight country and regional-specific differences (such as the differences in research themes between India and other parts of the world), or concentrate on a wide variety of publications to advance M&A studies.

***

CHAPTER 3:

RESEARCH METHODOLOGY

CHAPTER 3: RESEARCH METHODOLOGY

Preview

This chapter provides an overview of the research methods employed in the present study. The research technique has undergone comprehensive analysis, considering the procedures utilised by other researchers in the area or studies with similar aims and objectives. The chapter provides validation for the chosen research methodology by showing that the selected approaches and techniques are well-suited to the study aims and yield results that are both valid and reliable.

After conducting a comprehensive analysis of current techniques, the author was able to formalize the methodology for achieving the research objectives. A comprehensive review of the literature on mergers and acquisitions financing patterns, financial performance, operating efficiency, and shareholder wealth was conducted in order to identify research gaps.

3.1 Introduction

The definition of research is an investigation into a subject. A methodical and empirical approach to discovering information about a specific topic. We conduct research to learn more about something that piques our interest or causes us concern. This is a systematic and scientific technique for gathering, analyzing, and interpreting data. As per Clifford Woody's perspective, the process of research encompasses the identification and refinement of problems, formulation of hypotheses or proposed solutions, collection, organisation, and evaluation of data, derivation of deductions and conclusions, and rigorous testing of these deductions and conclusions to ascertain their validity in relation to the formulated hypothesis. Thus, study constitutes a novel and valuable contribution to human knowledge.

When attempting to solve a research problem, you must employ a research methodology. It could be considered a field of study that examines the methods used in scientific investigation. This article discusses the various steps and justifications involved in conducting research on a specific topic. What matters most is that we meticulously planned this research in order to generate trustworthy results that will help us achieve our objectives. This chapter's objective is to explain the choices made in the study design, including the techniques employed for the collecting and analysis of data., as well as the overall scope of the project, and to fill in the voids identified in the previous chapter.

We stated the same thing in the previous section of the literature review when we discussed how we had narrowed down the available literature to determine the research's objectives.

In the conceptual framework, the models are discussed, and an introduction to the formulation of the hypothesis that will be investigated in this research is provided. The empirical literature review serves as the foundation for the conceptual framework, which provides a summary of the topics that are being studied in this research study.

3.2 Research Study Variables

The formulation of the variables that is used in this study project was grounded in both an analysis of existing empirical research on mergers and acquisitions as well as strategies that have been successfully applied in the real world. The use of panel data may be seen as a direct result of this factor in the study. The information for the panel data is obtained from the Bloomberg database, and after that, the information is organized into something comparable. In order to finish the analysis of the missing data, the moving average method, together with interpolation and extrapolation, was used. In addition to this, the Z-score is used so that it may be normalized. In light of this, we relied on a variety of statistical approaches during the course of the study to ensure that we satisfy the requirements of a number of our objectives. Examination of the efficiency of corporate mergers and acquisitions, as well as comparisons of the financing patterns of the organizations that were created as a consequence of these activities. In this regard, we make use of regression and stochastic frontier analysis in order to increase the effectiveness as well as the performance of the research analysis. On the other hand, in order to determine the wealth of shareholders and the pattern of financing, applied event research that was based on a regression model for either the shareholders wealth or the firm's value was used.

3.3 Data Description and Sample Size

Our sample was derived from a single database, namely the Bloomberg database, which contains information on mergers as well as accounting data and ratios. The strategies that were used in order for the mergers to be included in the preliminary sample.

- The acquirer's listing status is specified, whereas there are no restrictions imposed on the listing status of the target.
- Mergers took place during the financial year 2016-17 and 2017-18.

Table 3.3.1: List of variables

Variable	Description
OPM	Operating profit margin
ROCE	Return on capital employed
DER	Debt equity ratio
RSQ_SALES	R squared sales
NROCE	Normalized return on capital employed
RWTA	Return on capital employed with total assets
OROA	Operating return on assets
SALES	Turnover
FAT	Five years average turnover
IT	Inventory turnover
ROA	Return on assets
NI	Net income
EBITDA	Earnings before interest, tax, depreciation and amortization
EBIT	Earnings before interest and taxes
ROC	Return of capital
FL	Financial leverage
DFL	Degree of financial leverage

Variable	Description
DOL	Degree of operating leverage
CFNI	Cash flow net income
MA_5D	5 days moving average
MA_20D	20 days moving average
MA_30D	30 days moving average
RSI_30D	Relative strength index based on 30 days
TA	Total Assets

Note: PR denotes pre-mergers and acquisitions, PO indicates post-mergers and acquisitions

Source: *Compiled by Author*

3.4 Financing Pattern of Resulting Companies

The debt-equity ratio is a combination of capital structure in the broader aspect. This ratio can be changed as per their methods of acquisition such as intrinsic value, swap ratio, payment consideration, and different approaches to acquire the business entity that leads to change in their capital proportion before and after merger and acquisition. That proportion may also influence the financing pattern. In this objective, the financing pattern of the resulting companies is analyzed before and after mergers and acquisitions by using the debt-equity ratio. In the next segment, the source of the data collected for this objective is discussed.

3.4.1 Source of financial data and variables

This research focuses on the links between debt and equity while also taking mergers and acquisitions into account. Whereas the Bloomberg database offers information on the financing structure in the form of percentages of debt equity as well as other measures. However, the data of mergers and acquisitions that took place during the fiscal year 2016–2017 and 2017-18 is taken i.e., the data of 593 companies have been analyzed, only 368 of those companies have been taken into consideration because the data of other companies is unavailable . In addition, as part of my analysis of the company's performance, certain ratios are compared before and after the merger. Textual concepts are used to inform the creation of variables that relate to the many sources of finance that are involved. In the subsequent phase, these factors are divided into two distinct categories: pre-mergers and post-mergers as well as acquisitions. Accounting measures that, following a merger, define the amount of debt-equity.

Table-3.4.1: Sample restrictions

Criteria	Merger	Acquisition
Initial Sample	93	500
Sufficient Information of companies	60	308
Information regarding debt-equity proportion	60	308
Non-availability of merged companies' information	33	192
Manual screening and mergers-related variables	60	308
Covered by Bloomberg database	60	308
Sufficient data by Bloomberg database	60	308

Source: *Compiled by Author from Bloomberg database*

In addition, we have constructed a single global variable called the Debt Equity Ratio to comprehensively describe the influence of financing. This global variable was constructed in accordance to the theoretical considerations that were taken into account. It has a base case, which has a zero value, the issuing of new common stock is represented by negative numbers, whereas bank funding is represented by positive values. All of these values are relative to the overall variable. By using financial ratios, a significant element of the present research is capturing the potential for high profits brought by the synergy of the organizations that are created as a consequence.

3.4.2 Method

Chen et al. (2018) used a two-stage discrete choice Heckman correction model to compensate for endogeneity. They discovered that as these accounting standards and the incentives associated with them change, so does bidder behavior. Yajie (2020) ,Fischer (2017) employed OLS regression, Logit, and Probit regression to assess the various hypotheses. In this objective, a regression model has been used, accordingly as Fischer, (2017) and Yajie, (2020) used the regression model as given:

$$y = \alpha + \beta_1 x_1 + \beta_2 x_2 + \beta_3 x_3 \dots + \beta_t x_t + e \quad (1)$$

Further, we modified the following equations:

$$PR\_DER_{it} = \alpha + \beta_1 PR\_RSQ\_Sales_{it} + \beta_2 PR\_NROCE_{it} + \beta_3 PR\_RWTA_{it} + e \quad (2)$$

$$PO\_DER_{it} = \alpha + \beta_1 PO\_RSQ\_Sales_{it} + \beta_2 PO\_NROCE_{it} + \beta_3 PO\_RWTA_{it} + e \quad (3)$$

Where, y = dependent variable as debt-equity ratio (DER)

x = independent variable as RSQ_Sales, NROCE, RWTA, etc.

α = the intercept.

β = the slope.

e= residual

Based on the above two equations, a comparison of impacting factors of mergers and acquisitions.

Further, considered the fixed effect on the year and run this with the same variables. Accordingly, equations (2) and (3) are used.

Due to that, Let us consider with eliminating the RWTA to get the impact of the debt-equity ratio pre and post-mergers and acquisitions.

$$PR\_DER_{it} = \alpha + \beta_1 PR\_RSQ\_SALES_{it} + \beta_2 PR\_ROCE_{it} + e \quad (4)$$

$$PO\_DER_{it} = \alpha + \beta_1 PO\_RSQ\_SALES_{it} + \beta_2 PO\_ROCE_{it} + e \quad (5)$$

Where, y = dependent variable as debt-equity ratio (DER)

x = independent variable as r squared sales and return on capital employed.

α = the intercept.

β = the slope.

e= residual

Further, equation (4) and (5) is modified by eliminating r squared sales and return on capital employed to see the impact of return on capital employed with total assets on debt equity ratio before and after the mergers and acquistions. The new equations are as follows:

$$PR\_DER_{it} = \alpha + \beta_1 PR\_RWTA_{it} + e \quad (6)$$

$$PO\_DER_{it} = \alpha + \beta_1 PO\_RWTA_{it} + e \quad (7)$$

The equations are further taken during the year of merger and acquisition. Firstly, r squared sales and return on capital employed is taken to see the impact of these variables on debt-equity ratio of the company during the year of merger and acquisition. The equation is as follows:

$$DER_{it} = \alpha + \beta_1 RSQ\_SALES_{it} + \beta_2 ROCE_{it} + e \quad (8)$$

Further, the equation is modified and only return on capital employed with total assets is taken into consideration to see the impact of it on debt-equity ratio during the year of merger and acquisition. The equation is as follows:

$$DER_{it} = \alpha + \beta_1 RWTA_{it} + e \quad (9)$$

Lastly, all the variables are taken together to evaluate the impact of them on debt-equity ratio during the year of merger and acquisition. The equation is as follows:

$$DER_{it} = \alpha + RSQ\_Sales_{it} + \beta_2 ROCE_{it} + \beta_3 RWTA_{it} + e \quad (10)$$

Further, equation (4) , (5) , (6) and (7) taken into consider with overall impact of debt-equity ratio considering all the years, as equation reset with following variables:

$$DER_{it} = \alpha + \beta_1 RSQ\_SALES_{it} + \beta_2 ROCE_{it} + e \quad (11)$$

$$DER_{it} = \alpha + \beta_1 RWTA_{it} + e \quad (12)$$

$$DER_{it} = \alpha + \beta_1 RSQ\_Sales_{it} + \beta_2 ROCE_{it} + \beta_3 RWTA_{it} + e \quad (13)$$

3.4.3 Hypotheses

Based on the objective of the study, the following hypotheses are formulated as follows:

Ho1: There is no significant change in financing pattern in the pre and post M&As of the resulting companies.

Table 3.4.2 Hypotheses for the financing pattern

Null Hypotheses	Description
$Ho_{1.1}$	There is no impact of R squared Sales on DER before the merger
$Ho_{1.2}$	There is no impact of ROCE on DER before the merger
$Ho_{1.3}$	There is no impact of RWTA on DER before the merger
$Ho_{1.4}$	There is no impact of R squared Sales on DER after the merger
$Ho_{1.5}$	There is no impact of ROCE on DER after the merger
$Ho_{1.6}$	There is no impact of RWTA on DER after the merger
$Ho_{1.7}$	There is no impact of R squared Sales on DER during the merger
$Ho_{1.8}$	There is no impact of ROCE on DER during the merger
$Ho_{1.9}$	There is no impact of RWTA on DER during the merger
$Ho_{1.10}$	There is no impact of R squared Sales on DER on the overall merger
$Ho_{1.11}$	There is no impact of ROCE on DER on the overall merger
$Ho_{1.12}$	There is no impact of RWTA on DER on the overall merger
$Ho_{1.13}$	There is no impact of R squared Sales on DER before acquisition
$Ho_{1.14}$	There is no impact of ROCE on DER before acquisition
$Ho_{1.15}$	There is no impact of RWTA on DER before acquisition
$Ho_{1.16}$	There is no impact of R squared Sales on DER after acquisition
$Ho_{1.17}$	There is no impact of ROCE on DER after acquisition
$Ho_{1.18}$	There is no impact of RWTA on DER after acquisition

Null Hypotheses	Description
$Ho_{1.19}$	There is no impact of R squared Sales on DER during acquisition
$Ho_{1.20}$	There is no impact of ROCE on DER during acquisition
$Ho_{1.21}$	There is no impact of RWTA on DER during acquisition
$Ho_{1.22}$	There is no impact of R squared Sales on DER on overall acquisition
$Ho_{1.23}$	There is no impact of ROCE on DER on overall acquisition
$Ho_{1.24}$	There is no impact of RWTA on DER on overall acquisition

3.5 Operating Efficiency of Resulting Companies

Operational efficiency is a key performance indicator that quantifies the effectiveness of generating profit related to the expenses incurred in day-to-day business operations. The level of operational efficiencies directly correlates with the profitability of the corporations or investment. This phenomenon occurs when the entity demonstrates the capacity to create higher revenues or achieve bigger returns at a comparable or reduced cost compared to an alternative option. The operating efficiency of the companies pre- and post-merger as well as acquisition is evaluated using different accounting ratios. The stochastic frontier analysis model is used for analyzing the impact of different ratios on the operating efficiency of the companies. Sources of financial data and variables are discussed in the next segment.

3.5.1 Source of financial data and variables

This objective centers on examining the influence of various ratios on operational performance, with a concurrent consideration of mergers and acquisitions. The Bloomberg database provides statistics on operational efficiency by utilizing several accounting ratios. The data pertaining to mergers and acquisitions during the fiscal year 2016-2018 has been examined, specifically the data of 593 companies. However, only 454 of these companies have been included in the analysis as the data of the few companies is unavailable so they are excluded. Furthermore, as a component of the assessment of the corporation's operating performance, certain ratios are taken prior to and subsequent to the amalgamation. Textual notions are employed to facilitate the formulation of variables that pertain to the several sources of operating efficiency that are implicated. In the succeeding phase, the aforementioned elements are categorized into two separate groups: pre-merger and post-merger. The accounting metrics that ascertain the operational effectiveness of organizations subsequent to a merger.

Table-3.5.1: Sample restrictions

Criteria	Merger	Acquisition
Initial Sample	93	500
Sufficient Information of companies	73	381
Information regarding operating profit	73	381
Non-availability of merged companies information	20	119
Manual screening and mergers related variables	73	381
Covered by Bloomberg database	73	381
Sufficient data by Bloomberg database	73	381

Source: *Compiled by Author*

3.5.2 Method

The data is taken from the Bloomberg database of listed resulting companies from 2013 to 2022, compiling data from 593 companies for analysis. The separate analysis of the companies merged and acquired is undertaken to see the impact of operating efficiency on the companies pre- and post-merger as well as acquisition. The methodology which is used to evaluate the impact is stochastic frontier analysis. Additionally, the subsequent section will go into the definition of stochastic frontier analysis and elucidate its intended objectives.

3.5.2.1 Using stochastic frontier analysis

Stochastic frontier analysis (SFA) use econometric models to estimate production frontiers, cost frontiers, or profit frontiers, while also assessing efficiency in relation to these frontiers. The concept of production efficiency may be described as the ratio between the actual output and the maximum possible output. Production efficiency is a concept that establishes a connection between the actual output of a production process and the maximum output that might theoretically be achieved. In a more expansive context, the framework of counterfactual analysis may be employed to examine any scenario in which the actual result deviates from the anticipated result in one of two ways: either the actual result falls short of or exceeds the expected outcome. Stated differently, the observed result has the ability to diverge from the predicted outcome in either a positive or negative manner. However, this study has taken into consideration this model to analyze the operating efficiency of the resulting companies in both cases, mergers as well as acquisitions. Different stochastic frontier models analysis are used which are the maximum likelihood estimator, technological inefficiency, time-varying model and time-invariant inefficiency model. Further, these models are explained in detail in the next segment.

3.5.2.2 Estimation Method: Maximum Likelihood Estimator

Fixed-effects and random-effects models are attractive because they can be used to estimate waste without making any assumptions about distributions. In spite of the fact that the COLS model for cross-sectional data presented in the preceding chapter is also distribution-free, the cross-sectional COLS model does not account for statistical error. However, this is not the situation with models that include both fixed and random effects, where both terms are present. MLE can be used to estimate even if the distribution-free premise is not met by simply making assumptions about the distributions of and, as in Pitt and Lee (1981). Parameters are estimated by maximising the loglikelihood function, which is obtained from the likelihood function of the model using the distributional assumptions. Last but not least, a JLMS version can be used to quantify wastefulness (Kumbhakar 1987). The Battese and Coelli (1988) formula can be used to calculate efficiency values. For the MLE, the model is written as:

$$\begin{aligned} y_{it} &= f(\boldsymbol{x}_{it};\boldsymbol{\beta}) + \epsilon_{it}, \\ \epsilon_{it} &= v_{it} - u_i, \\ v_{it} &\sim N(0,\sigma_v^2), \\ u_i &\sim N^+(\mu,\sigma_u^2). \end{aligned} \tag{14}$$

The likelihood function for the i th observation.

$$\ln L_i = \text{constant} + \ln \Phi\left(\frac{\mu_{i*}}{\sigma_*}\right) + \frac{1}{2}\ln(\sigma_*^2) - \frac{1}{2}\left\{\frac{\sum_t \epsilon_{it}^2}{\sigma_v^2} + \left(\frac{\mu}{\sigma_u}\right)^2 - \left(\frac{\mu_{i*}}{\sigma_*}\right)^2\right\} - T\ln(\sigma_v) - \ln(\sigma_u) - \ln \Phi\left(\frac{\mu}{\sigma_u}\right) \quad (15)$$

where

$$\mu_{i*} = \frac{\mu\sigma_v^2 - \sigma_u^2 \sum_t \epsilon_{it}}{\sigma_v^2 + T\sigma_u^2}$$

$$\sigma_*^2 = \frac{\sigma_v^2\sigma_u^2}{\sigma_v^2 + T\sigma_u^2}.$$

In order to calculate the model's log-likelihood function, we simply add lnLi, over i, i =1,.....,N.

Log-likelihood maximisation yields the minimum mean squared error (MLE) of the values.

3.5.2.3 Conceptualizations of Technical Inefficiency

Although Lee and Schmidt examined both fixed- and random-effects models; however, we offer their model in a significantly modified manner in this study. The purpose of this is to establish a basis for comparison with other time-varying efficiency models, such as Kumbhakar (1990), Battese and Coelli (1992), and Kumbhakar and Wang (2005). In this context, we have used the assumption that u_i follows a random distribution and λ_t represents fixed parameters. The Lee-Schmidt model is considered to be more comprehensive than the Kumbhakar (1990), Battese and Coelli (1992), and Kumbhakar and Wang (2005) models due to the inclusion of λ_t as parameters. These parameters represent the coefficients of time dummies, TD_t ,which have been normalised with one coefficient set to unity for identification purposes. All of these models may be obtained as a specific instance of the Lee-Schmidt model by applying suitable constraints on λ_t. One limitation of this model is the excessive number of parameters in λ_t, which may render it unsuitable for high values of T.

3.5.2.4 Time-invariant Inefficiency Model

The time-invariant inefficiency model may be developed as a special case from the aforementioned models. In the case where the parameter λ_t is equal to 1 for all time periods, the model simplifies to the time-invariant inefficiency model.

Once the parameters λ_t and u_i have been calculated, it is possible to evaluate the level of technical inefficiency.

$$\hat{u}_{it} = \max_i\{\hat{u}_i\hat{\lambda}_t\} - \{\hat{u}_i\hat{\lambda}_t\} \quad (16)$$

Battese and Coelli (1992) model assumes

$$G(t) = \exp[\gamma(t - T)], \quad (17)$$

where T is the terminal period of the sample. The requirements proposed by Kumbhakar (1990) and Battese and Coelli (1992) may be effectively compared by expressing the Kumbhakar formulation as

$$G(t) = 2 \times [1 + \exp(\gamma_1(t - T) + \gamma_2(t - T)^2)]^{-1} \quad (18)$$

Then, at the terminal point $u_{iT} = u_i$.

Finally, Kumbhakar and Wang (2005) use the following specification

$$G(t) = \exp[\gamma(t - \underline{t})], \quad (19)$$

where $\underline{t}$ is the starting period of the sample. Both (17) and (19) are equivalent analytically, but their interpretations are different. The study conducted by Battese and Coelli (1992) and the modified specification proposed by Kumbhakar (1990), $u_i \sim N^+(\mu, \sigma_u^2)$ indicates the distribution of inefficiency at the final point, that is, $u_{it} = u_i$ when $t = T$. With (19), $u_i \sim N^+(\mu, \sigma_u^2)$ defines the baseline distribution of inefficiency. The preference for one specification over the other may vary depending on the individual uses. It is to be noted that the Kumbhakar and Wang (2005) model controlled for fixed firm effects which is not done in any of the models discussed so far.

Because the conditional distribution of variable u is known, it is possible to calculate moments of any continuous function of $u \mid \epsilon$. Similarly, the aforementioned methodology may be employed to get observation-specific estimates of the efficiency index , $\exp(-u_i)$. Following Battese and Coelli (1988), it can be shown that

$$E[\exp(-u_i) \mid \epsilon_i] = \exp\left(-\mu_{*i} + \frac{1}{2}\sigma_*^2\right)\frac{\Phi\left(\frac{\mu_{*i}}{\sigma_*} - \sigma_*\right)}{\Phi\left(\frac{\mu_{*i}}{\sigma_*}\right)} \tag{20}$$

where μ_{*i} and σ_* are defined in (21). Point estimates of $\exp(-u_i)$ are obtained by substituting maximum likelihood estimates of the parameters into the equation. The estimate possesses a numerical value ranging from 0 to 1, where a value of 1 signifies complete efficiency.

The log likelihood function based on (22) for each observation i is [10]

$$L_i = -\ln\left(\frac{1}{2}\right) - \frac{1}{2}\ln(\sigma_v^2 + \sigma_u^2) + \ln\phi\left(\frac{\epsilon_i}{\sqrt{\sigma_v^2 + \sigma_u^2}}\right) + \ln\Phi\left(\frac{\mu_{*i}}{\sigma_*}\right), \tag{21}$$

where

$$\mu_{*i} = \frac{-\sigma_u^2 \epsilon_i}{\sigma_v^2 + \sigma_u^2}$$
$$\sigma_*^2 = \frac{\sigma_v^2 \sigma_u^2}{\sigma_v^2 + \sigma_u^2}$$

The technical inefficiency of an output-focused stochastic production frontier model may be stated as

$$\ln y_i = \ln y_i^* - u_i,\ u_i \geq 0,$$
$$\ln y_i^* = f(\boldsymbol{x}_i; \boldsymbol{\beta}) + v_i,$$

where y_i is a scalar representing the observed output, $\boldsymbol{X}_i$ is a $\boldsymbol{J} \times 1$ vector representing the input variables, is a $\boldsymbol{J} \times 1$ vector representing the associated coefficient vector, V_i is a zero-mean random error, and $u_i \geq 0$ represents production inefficiency, where i specifies the number of observations (companies, persons, etc.). The function representing the stochastic production frontier is given by equation (21). Stochastic as a result of v_i, the frontier identifies the highest potential level of output for a given $\boldsymbol{x}$. The output (y_i) is constrained below the frontier output level (y_i^*) because $u_i \geq 0$.

The subsequent version of a model may be more convenient:

$$\begin{aligned} \ln y_i &= f(\boldsymbol{x}_i; \boldsymbol{\beta}) + \epsilon_i \\ \epsilon_i &= v_i - u_i \end{aligned} \tag{22}$$

where ϵ_i represents the error term which, also known as the composed error term.

3.5.2.5 Time-varying Model

The models that we have already examined, which fluctuate over time, incorporate inefficiency by means of certain parametric functions. In the Lee-Schmidt model, it is seen that both the components of u_i and λ_t exhibit determinism. The model may be estimated on the assumption that u_i is a random variable, whereas λ_t is a deterministic function of time, such as time dummies. While Lee and Schmidt conducted their estimation of this model without imposing any distributional assumptions on $\boldsymbol{u}_i$, we will now explore these models by including distributional assumptions on $\boldsymbol{u}_i$. The subsequent generic formulation is employed to examine the many models within a cohesive framework.

$$\begin{aligned} y_{it} &= f(\boldsymbol{x}_{it}; \boldsymbol{\beta}) + \epsilon_{it}, \\ \epsilon_{it} &= v_{it} - u_{it}, \\ u_{it} &= G(t)u_i, \\ v_{it} &\sim N(0, \sigma_v^2), \\ u_i &\sim N^+(\mu, \sigma_u^2), \end{aligned} \tag{23}$$

where the function of time (t) is $G(t) > 0$. In the present model, the level of inefficiency (u_{it}) is not constant for a certain individual; rather, it exhibits temporal variability and also varies among different people. The inefficiency present in this particular model may be broken down into two separate elements: a deterministic temporal component denoted as $G(t)$, and a random individual component referred to as $\boldsymbol{U}_i$. The use of the panel structure of the data in this model is facilitated by the stochastic component, denoted as $\boldsymbol{U}_i$. The component $\boldsymbol{U}_i$ represents individual-specific characteristics, whereas the component $G(t)$ represents time-varying factors that are shared among all individuals.

Time-invariant inefficiency model (where inefficiency is fixed or random)

$$
\begin{aligned}
y_{it} &= \beta_0 + \boldsymbol{x}'_{it}\boldsymbol{\beta} + v_{it} - u_i \\
&= \alpha_i + \boldsymbol{x}'_{it}\boldsymbol{\beta} + v_{it} \qquad (24)\\
\alpha_i &\equiv \beta_0 - u_i
\end{aligned}
$$

The model employed in this study is a conventional panel data model, whereby α_i represents the latent individual effect. In this study, the researchers employ conventional panel data fixed- and random-effects estimators to estimate the model parameters, which include α_i. The sole distinction lies in the conversion of the estimated value of $\hat{\alpha}_i$ to derive the estimated value of $\boldsymbol{U}_i, \hat{u}_i$.

One significant limitation of this methodology is the inability to differentiate between individual variation and inefficiency. To clarify, the presence of time-invariant heterogeneity is intertwined with inefficiency, leading to potential ambiguity in the estimation of $\hat{u}_i$. It is plausible that $\hat{u}_i$ captures not just inefficiency but also heterogeneity, maybe even replacing inefficiency altogether.

Another possible concern regarding the model is to the assumption of inefficiency being time-invariant. If the value of T is very high, it is unlikely that a business's inefficiency would remain constant over a prolonged duration, and it is unusual that an entity exhibiting persistent inefficiency would be able to sustain itself in the market.

3.5.3 Hypotheses

Based on the objective of the study, the following hypotheses are formulated as follows:

Ho2: There is no statistically significant change in operating efficiency in pre and post-M & A.

Table 3.5.2 Hypotheses for the operating efficiency

Null Hypotheses	**Description**
$Ho_{2.1}$	There is no impact of OROA and FAT on OPM before the merger
$Ho_{2.2}$	There is no impact of Sales on OPM before the merger
$Ho_{2.3}$	There is no impact of IT and ROA on OPM before the merger
$Ho_{2.4}$	There is no impact of OROA and FAT on OPM after the merger
$Ho_{2.5}$	There is no impact of Sales on OPM after the merger

Null Hypotheses	Description
$Ho_{2.6}$	There is no impact of IT and ROA on OPM after the merger
$Ho_{2.7}$	There is no impact of OROA and FAT on OPM during the merger
$Ho_{2.8}$	There is no impact of Sales on OPM during the merger
$Ho_{2.9}$	There is no impact of IT and ROA on OPM during the merger
$Ho_{2.10}$	There is no impact of OROA and FAT on OPM on overall merger
$Ho_{2.11}$	There is no impact of Sales on OPM on overall merger
$Ho_{2.12}$	There is no impact of IT and ROA on OPM on overall merger
$Ho_{2.13}$	There is no impact of OROA and FAT on OPM before acquisition
$Ho_{2.14}$	There is no impact of Sales on OPM before acquisition
$Ho_{2.15}$	There is no impact of IT and ROA on OPM before acquisition
$Ho_{2.16}$	There is no impact of OROA and FAT on OPM after acquisition
$Ho_{2.17}$	There is no impact of Sales on OPM after acquisition
$Ho_{2.18}$	There is no impact of IT and ROA on OPM after acquisition
$Ho_{2.19}$	There is no impact of OROA and FAT on OPM during acquisition
$Ho_{2.20}$	There is no impact of Sales on OPM during acquisition
$Ho_{2.21}$	There is no impact of IT and ROA on OPM during acquisition
$Ho_{2.22}$	There is no impact of OROA and FAT on OPM on overall acquisition
$Ho_{2.23}$	There is no impact of Sales on OPM on overall acquisition
$Ho_{2.24}$	There is no impact of IT and ROA on OPM on overall acquisition

3.6 Financial Performance of Resulting Companies

The financial performance of the resulting companies is a key indicator to determine their success or failure. Different parameters are used by the companies to analyze their financial performance such as different financial ratios. The major decisions of the companies are based upon the financial performance of the companies. Even the decision of merger and acquisition is also somehow dependent upon this. In this study, the financial performance of the companies is analyzed pre- and post-merger as well as acquisition. The financial performance is analyzed using different accounting ratios. In the next segment, the sample taken for the purpose of this objective is discussed.

3.6.1 Source of financial data and variables

This objective focuses on analyzing the impact of different ratios on financial performance, while also taking into account mergers and acquisitions. The Bloomberg database offers comprehensive financial performance information through the use of several accounting ratios. The analysis focused on the data on mergers and acquisitions throughout the financial year 2016-2018, especially encompassing a sample of 593 firms. However, the research only includes 458 firms, as the insufficient data of other companies has been omitted. Moreover, as part of the evaluation of the company's financial performance, certain ratios are compared before and after the merger. Textual concepts are utilized to aid in the development of variables that relate to the many factors influencing financial success. In the subsequent stage, the aforementioned components are classified into two distinct categories: pre-merger and post-merger. The accounting parameters that determine the financial success of businesses following a merger.

Table-3.6.1: Sample restrictions

Criteria	Merger	Acquisition
Initial Sample	93	500
Sufficient Information of companies	93	385
Information regarding financial performance	93	385
Non-availability of merged companies' information	20	115
Manual screening and mergers-related variables	73	385
Covered by Bloomberg database	73	385
Sufficient data by Bloomberg database	73	385

Source: *Compiled by Author from Bloomberg data*

3.6.2 Method

The data is taken from the Bloomberg database of listed resulting companies from 2013 to 2022, compiling data from 593 companies for analysis. As a result, we entered the data into the regression model shown below:

$$\gamma = \alpha + \beta_1 x_1 + \beta_2 x_2 + \beta_3 x_3 + \beta_4 x_4 \dots \beta_t x_t + e \quad (25)$$

Further, we modified with variable and data comparison, as follows:

$$Pre\_Income_{it} = \alpha + \beta_1 Pre\_ROCE_{it} + \beta_2 Pre\_DFL_{it} + \beta_3 Pre\_EBIT_{it} + \beta_4 Pre\_DOL_{it} + \beta_5 Pre\_EBITDA_{it} + \beta_6 Pre\_ROC_{it} + \beta_7 Pre\_ROA_{it} + \beta_8 Pre\_FL_{it} + \beta_9 Pre\_cfNI_{it} + e \quad (26)$$

$$Post\_Income_{it} = \alpha + \beta_1 Post\_ROCE_{it} + \beta_2 Post\_DFL_{it} + \beta_3 Post\_EBIT_{it} + \beta_4 Post\_DOL_{it} + \beta_5 Post\_EBITDA_{it} + \beta_6 Post\_ROC_{it} + \beta_7 Post\_ROA_{it} + \beta_8 Post\_FL_{it} + \beta_9 Post\_cfNI_{it} + e \quad (27)$$

$$Pre\_Income_{it} = \alpha + \beta_1 Pre\_EBITDA_{it} + \beta_2 Pre\_EBIT_{it} + e \quad (28)$$

$$Post\_Income_{it} = \alpha + \beta_1 Post\_EBITDA_{it} + \beta_2 Post\_EBIT_{it} + e \quad (29)$$

$$Pre\_Income_{it} = \alpha + \beta_1 Pre\_ROA_{it} + \beta_2 Pre\_ROC_{it} + e \quad (30)$$

$$Post\_Income_{it} = \alpha + \beta_1 Post\_ROA_{it} + \beta_2 Post\_ROC_{it} + e \quad (31)$$

$$Pre\_Income_{it} = \alpha + \beta_1 Pre\_ROCE_{it} + \beta_2 Pre\_FL_{it} + e \quad (32)$$

$$Post\_Income_{it} = \alpha + \beta_1 Post\_ROCE_{it} + \beta_2 Post\_FL_{it} + e \quad (33)$$

$$Pre\_Income_{it} = \alpha + \beta_1 Pre\_DFL_{it} + \beta_2 Pre\_DOL_{it} + e \quad (34)$$

$$Post\_Income_{it} = \alpha + \beta_1 Post\_DFL_{it} + \beta_2 Post\_DOL_{it} + e \quad (35)$$

$$Pre\_Income_{it} = \alpha + \beta_1 Pre\_CFNI_{it} + e \quad (36)$$

$$Post\_Income_{it} = \alpha + \beta_1 Post\_CFNI_{it} + e \quad (37)$$

Adding some other variables to understand the impact of the overall performance of the companies

Getting results of equations (26), (27), (28), (29), (30) ,(31), (32), (33), (34), (35), (36) and (37) put to use in the below equation:

$$Overall\_FinPerf_{it} = \alpha + \beta_1 Pre\_Finperf_{it} + \beta_2 Post\_Finperf_{it} + e \quad (38)$$

3.6.3 Hypotheses

Based on the objective of the study, the following hypotheses are formulated as follows:

Ho3: There is no statistical significant change in their financial performance in pre and post M &A.

Table 3.6.2 Hypotheses for the financial performance

Null Hypotheses	Description
$Ho_{3.1}$	There is no impact of EBITDA and EBIT on financial performance before the merger
$Ho_{3.2}$	There is no impact of ROA and ROC on financial performance before the merger
$Ho_{3.3}$	There is no impact of ROCE and FL on financial performance before the merger
$Ho_{3.4}$	There is no impact of DFL and DOL on financial performance before the merger
$Ho_{3.5}$	There is no impact of CFNI on financial performance before the merger
$Ho_{3.6}$	There is no impact of EBITDA and EBIT on financial performance after the merger
$Ho_{3.7}$	There is no impact of ROA and ROC on financial performance after the merger
$Ho_{3.8}$	There is no impact of ROCE and FL on financial performance after the merger

Null Hypotheses	**Description**
$Ho_{3.9}$	There is no impact of DFL and DOL on financial performance after the merger
$Ho_{3.10}$	There is no impact of CFNI on financial performance after the merger
$Ho_{3.11}$	There is no impact of EBITDA and EBIT on financial performance during the merger
$Ho_{3.12}$	There is no impact of ROA and ROC on financial performance during the merger
$Ho_{3.13}$	There is no impact of ROCE and FL on financial performance during the merger
$Ho_{3.14}$	There is no impact of DFL and DOL on financial performance during the merger
$Ho_{3.15}$	There is no impact of CFNI on financial performance during the merger
$Ho_{3.16}$	There is no impact of EBITDA and EBIT on financial performance considering overall merger
$Ho_{3.17}$	There is no impact of ROA and ROC on financial performance considering overall merger
$Ho_{3.18}$	There is no impact of ROCE and FL on financial performance considering overall merger
$Ho_{3.19}$	There is no impact of DFL and DOL on financial performance considering overall merger
$Ho_{3.20}$	There is no impact of CFNI on financial performance considering overall merger
$Ho_{3.21}$	There is no impact of EBITDA and EBIT on financial performance before the acquisition
$Ho_{3.22}$	There is no impact of ROA and ROC on financial performance before the acquisition
$Ho_{3.23}$	There is no impact of ROCE and FL on financial performance before the acquisition

Null Hypotheses	Description
$Ho_{3.24}$	There is no impact of DFL and DOL on financial performance before the acquisition
$Ho_{3.25}$	There is no impact of CFNI on financial performance before the acquisition
$Ho_{3.26}$	There is no impact of EBITDA and EBIT on financial performance after the acquisition
$Ho_{3.27}$	There is no impact of ROA and ROC on financial performance after the acquisition
$Ho_{3.28}$	There is no impact of ROCE and FL on financial performance after the acquisition
$Ho_{3.29}$	There is no impact of DFL and DOL on financial performance after the acquisition
$Ho_{3.30}$	There is no impact of CFNI on financial performance after the acquisition
$Ho_{3.31}$	There is no impact of EBITDA and EBIT on financial performance during the acquisition
$Ho_{3.32}$	There is no impact of ROA and ROC on financial performance during the acquisition
$Ho_{3.33}$	There is no impact of ROCE and FL on financial performance during the acquisition
$Ho_{3.34}$	There is no impact of DFL and DOL on financial performance during the acquisition
$Ho_{3.35}$	There is no impact of CFNI on financial performance during the acquisition
$Ho_{3.36}$	There is no impact of EBITDA and EBIT on financial performance considering overall acquisition
$Ho_{3.37}$	There is no impact of ROA and ROC on financial performance considering overall acquisition
$Ho_{3.38}$	There is no impact of ROCE and FL on financial performance considering overall acquisition

Null Hypotheses	Description
$Ho_{3.39}$	There is no impact of DFL and DOL on financial performance considering overall acquisition
$Ho_{3.40}$	There is no impact of CFNI on financial performance considering overall acquisition

3.7 Shareholder's Wealth

The valuation component of mergers and acquisitions transactions consistently addresses the worth of the business or the wealth of its shareholders. Nevertheless, the authenticity of the appraisal at that particular level is limited. Investors employ their own assumptions to do calculations. In this study, two factors have been taken into consideration: the regression model and the event study based on the Capital Asset Pricing Model (CAPM). In the regression model, we have included the influence of many factors on the last traded stock price, such as the relative strength index (RSI), the 30-day, 20-day, and 5-day moving averages, as well as the total assets.

3.7.1 Source of financial data and variables

This objective is on the analysis of the influence of moving averages of stock price on owners' wealth, with consideration given to mergers and acquisitions. The Bloomberg database provides extensive stock price data by means of graphical representations. The investigation primarily concentrated on the data pertaining to mergers and acquisitions during the fiscal years 2016-2018, with particular emphasis on a sample of 593 organizations. Nevertheless, the scope of the study is limited to a sample size of 380 organizations, as the dataset excludes information of those companies whose sufficient information is unavailable. Additionally, as a component of my assessment of the company's shareholders' worth, specific averages are compared prior to and subsequent to the merger. Textual notions are employed to facilitate the formulation of variables that pertain to the diverse elements that impact the stock price of a firm. In the second phase, the aforementioned elements are categorized into two unique classifications: pre-merger and post-merger. The accounting variables that influence the financial value of shareholders in corporations subsequent to a merger.

Table-3.7.1: Sample restrictions

Criteria	Merger	Acquisition
Initial Sample of Mergers	93	500
Sufficient Information of companies	63	317
Information regarding the last traded stock price	63	317
Non-availability of merged companies' information	30	183
Manual screening and mergers-related variables	63	317
Covered by Bloomberg database	63	317
Sufficient data by Bloomberg database	63	317

Source: *Compiled by Author from Bloomberg data*

3.7.2 Method

The data is taken from the Bloomberg database of listed resulting companies from 2013 to 2022, compiling data from 593 companies for analysis. As a result, we entered the data into the regression model shown below:

$$\gamma = \alpha + \beta_1 x_1 + \beta_2 x_2 + \beta_3 x_3 + \beta_4 x_4 \ldots \beta_t x_t + e \qquad (39)$$

Further, we modified with variable and data comparison, as follows:

$$Pre\_last\ Price_{it} = \alpha + \beta_1 Pre\_MA\_30D_{it} + \beta_2 Pre\_MA\_20D_{it} + \beta_3 Pre\_MA\_5D_{it} + \beta_4 Pre\_RSI\_30D_{it} + \beta_5 Pre\_TA_{it} + e \qquad (40)$$

$$Post\_last\ Price_{it} = \alpha + \beta_1 Post\_MA\_30D_{it} + \beta_2 Post\_MA\_20D_{it} + \beta_3 Post\_MA\_5D_{it} + \beta_4 Post\_RSI\_30D_{it} + \beta_5 Post\_TA_{it} + e \qquad (41)$$

Further, the equations are modified by eliminating moving average of 5 days , relative strength index of 30 days and total assets to see the impact of other two variables on stock price.

$$Pre\_last\ Price_{it} = \alpha + \beta_1 Pre\_MA\_30D_{it} + \beta_2 Pre\_MA\_20D_{it} + e \qquad (42)$$

$$Post\_last\ Price_{it} = \alpha + \beta_1 Post\_MA\_30D_{it} + \beta_2 Post\_MA\_20D_{it} + e \qquad (43)$$

The equations are again modified by taking only moving average of 5 days and relative strength index of 30 days to check the impact of these variables on stock price.

$$Pre\_last\ Price_{it} = \alpha + \beta_1 Pre\_MA\_5D_{it} + \beta_2 Pre\_RSI\_20D_{it} + e \qquad (44)$$

$$Post\_last\ Price_{it} = \alpha + \beta_1 Post\_MA\_5D_{it} + \beta_2 Post\_RSI\_20D_{it} + e \qquad (45)$$

Lastly, the equations are run taking only total assets as the variable to see the impact of it on stock price.

$$Pre\_last\ Price_{it} = \alpha + \beta_1 Pre\_TA_{it} + e \qquad (46)$$

$$Post\_last\ Price_{it} = \alpha + \beta_1 Post\_TA_{it} + e \qquad (47)$$

Getting results of equations (42), (43), (44), (45), (46) and (47) put to use in the below equation:

$$last\ Price_{it} = \alpha + \beta_1 MA\_30D_{it} + \beta_2 MA\_20D_{it} + \beta_3 MA\_5D_{it} + \beta_4 RSI\_30D_{it} + \beta_5 TA_{it} + e \qquad (48)$$

3.7.2.1 Event analysis

We describe one initial sample of all acquisitions and mergers of resulting companies using data from the National Stock Exchange (NSE). The M &As in the final sample must satisfy the following requirements: (1) listed public limited companies, which are publicly traded firms with data available on the NSE; (2) financial institutions that do not own a controlling interest in the target prior to the merger announcement.

While hundreds of mergers and acquisitions have taken place in the current context, the size of our sample has been greatly decreased due to our requirements that the transaction constitutes a change in ownership and that stock price data be accessible for the study.

There were 3,155 mergers and acquisitions announced in the last three years out of which we have randomly selected a sample of 593 companies listed with NSE. This study is based on secondary data collected from the NSE database. The 593 listed companies incorporated in the data relates to the manufacturing, service, and infrastructure sector broadly. This is further categorized into industry types such as steel, sugar, textile, information technology, fertilizers, automotive, locomotive, power, coal, chemical, real estate, and constructive industry.

The stock price impacts were studied using the event study methodology. This strategy has proven to be quite effective in a wide range of finance-related subjects, including corporate finance, accounting, and management. It's also commonly used to analyze the effects of mergers and acquisitions, stock splits, new legislation, earnings announcements, and other financial events on the stock market(Anwar et al., 2015).

The abnormal return is defined as the difference between the actual and expected returns on a given day, as calculated by the market model using the following equation:

$$R\,i,t \;=\; \alpha\, i \;+\; \beta i\, R\, m,t \;+\; E\, i,t \qquad (49)$$

Where $R\; i,t$ is the expected return on stock i at time t, $R\; m,t$ is the corresponding return on the NSE and Ei,t is the error term. Equation 2 is used to calculate the abnormal return (AR) for each firm on each day:

$$ARi,t \;=\; Ri,t - (\alpha i \;+\; \beta i\; Rm,t\,) \qquad (50)$$

The event window evaluated was 61 days, which included 30 days prior to the date of date, 30 days following the date of the announcement, and the day of the announcement. Day zero was designated as the day of the announcement of the merger and acquisition.

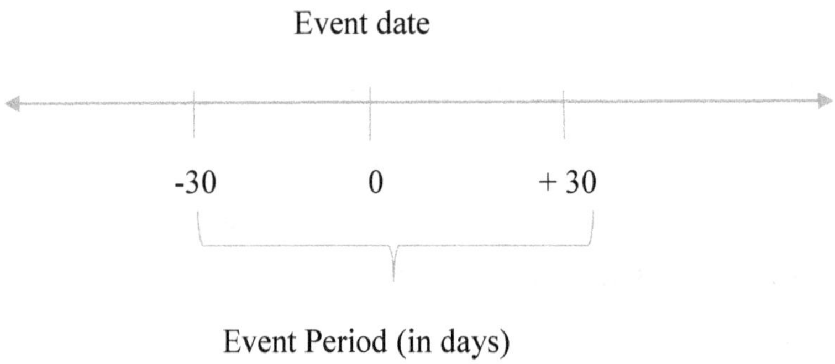

3.7.2.2 Analysis of Variance

Variance was chosen as the risk metric because it is a good predictor of risk and includes both uncertainty and changes in systematic risk. As a result, it has an impact on the correctness of our statistical inferences (Anwar et al., 2015). Variance is denoted as σ_2

which was calculated for each event i, i.e. merger and acquisition announcement using Equation (iii):

$$\sigma 2 = \sum_{i=1}^{N} \frac{(R_t - AR)^2}{N} \quad (51)$$

Where, R_t represents returns over time t, AR represents the average return over time t (provided by Ri/N), and N represents the number of observations.

3.7.2.3 Conceptual Framework

In developing the conceptual framework for this research study, the author linked a specific event, namely a merger and acquisition announcement, to the abnormal returns gained by shareholders. According to the empirical literature, the best model for this type of study is:

ARit= Rit- E(Rit) (52)

Where ARit is the abnormal return at day t, Rit is the discrete actual return on day t, and E(Rit) is the discrete expected return on day t.

The data will be analyzed by using accounting ratios and stochastic frontier analysis. The ratios would be presented in the form of absolute mean, and standard deviation of the companies in two groups of periods (e.g. pre and post-M&As). The t-test would be applied to examine the significance of the difference in mean ratio between two groups of M & A deals. Analysis of variance (ANOVA) will be used to determine the significance of variation in operating leverage ratios and other variables under reference in this study.

Regression and mean of the variable were used by Fong et al., (2019). The various other techniques used by him were the tightness–looseness index, and the score of the individualism–collectivism index. Regression analysis has been used by Ranganathan & Singh, (2021). The Dif-in-difs estimator was used by Vagenas-Nanos (2020). Whereas Sichong Chen et al., (2020) used a binary logit model and a panel data model. CAR has been used by Alhenawl and Stllwell (2018). The OLS regression is often used to see whether mergers in high-tech industries trigger a secondary positive market reaction. Zhang et al. (2019) in order to control for firm and year heterogeneities, fixed-effects panel regressions were used with a variety of control variables.

3.7.3 Hypotheses

Based on the objective of the study, the following hypotheses are formulated as follows:

Ho4: There is no statistical significant change in their financial performance in pre and post M &A.

Table 3.7.2 Hypotheses for the value of the firm

Null Hypotheses	**Description**
$Ho_{4.1}$	There is no impact of moving average of 30 days and 20 days on the value of the firm before the merger
$Ho_{4.2}$	There is no impact of the moving average of 5 days and relative strength index of 30 days on the value of the firm before the merger
$Ho_{4.3}$	There is no impact of total assets on the value of the firm before the merger
$Ho_{4.4}$	There is no impact of moving average of 30 days and 20 days on the value of the firm after the merger
$Ho_{4.5}$	There is no impact of the moving average of 5 days and relative strength index of 30 days on the value of the firm after the merger
$Ho_{4.6}$	There is no impact of total assets on the value of the firm after the merger
$Ho_{4.7}$	There is no impact of moving average of 30 days and 20 days on the value of the firm during the merger
$Ho_{4.8}$	There is no impact of the moving average of 5 days and relative strength index of 30 days on the value of the firm during the merger
$Ho_{4.9}$	There is no impact of total assets on the value of the firm during the merger
$Ho_{4.10}$	There is no impact of moving average of 30 days and 20 days on the value of the firm considering the overall merger
$Ho_{4.11}$	There is no impact of the moving average of 5 days and relative strength index of 30 days on the value of the firm considering the overall merger

Null Hypotheses	Description
$Ho_{4.12}$	There is no impact of total assets on the value of the firm considering the overall merger
$Ho_{4.13}$	There is no impact of moving average of 30 days and 20 days on the value of the firm before acquisition
$Ho_{4.14}$	There is no impact of the moving average of 5 days and relative strength index of 30 days on the value of the firm before acquisition
$Ho_{4.15}$	There is no impact of total assets on the value of the firm before acquisition
$Ho_{4.16}$	There is no impact of moving average of 30 days and 20 days on the value of the firm after acquisition
$Ho_{4.17}$	There is no impact of the moving average of 5 days and relative strength index of 30 days on the value of the firm after acquisition
$Ho_{4.18}$	There is no impact of total assets on the value of the firm after acquisition
$Ho_{4.19}$	There is no impact of moving average of 30 days and 20 days on the value of the firm during acquisition
$Ho_{4.20}$	There is no impact of the moving average of 5 days and relative strength index of 30 days on the value of the firm during acquisition
$Ho_{4.21}$	There is no impact of total assets on the value of the firm during acquisition
$Ho_{4.22}$	There is no impact of moving average of 30 days and 20 days on the value of the firm considering overall acquisition
$Ho_{4.23}$	There is no impact of the moving average of 5 days and relative strength index of 30 days on the value of the firm considering overall acquisition
$Ho_{4.24}$	There is no impact of total assets on the value of the firm considering overall acquisition

3.8 Statistical Tools

Techniques are used to collect data or evidence for analysis in order to identify new knowledge or achieve a positive perspective on an issue. Mean, median, graphs, chart and correlation, regression, and ANOVA can be used in the descriptive as well as inferential techniques respectively to analyze financing patterns, operating efficiency, financial performance, and shareholders' wealth. If we look into variables, we will find interesting things to compare the data of selected companies or firms during the study period.

3.9 Conclusion

This chapter discussed the research methodology that will be utilized for the current investigation. The research methodology has been thoroughly analyzed, taking into consideration the methodologies employed by other researchers in the field or area with comparable aims and objectives. The chapter validates the research design and approach choices by demonstrating that the methodologies and techniques selected are ideal for achieving the research objectives and will produce valid and reliable results.

After conducting a comprehensive analysis of current techniques, the authors were able to formalize the methodology for achieving the research objectives. A comprehensive literature evaluation on mergers and acquisitions is conducted to identify the gaps in the field of study.

***

CHAPTER 4: DATA ANALYSIS AND INTERPRETATION

CHAPTER 4: DATA ANALYSIS AND INTERPRETATION

Preview

The study is divided into four objectives. In this chapter, all four objectives have been analyzed and interpreted for the selected dataset consisting of 593 companies that have been merged or acquired during the financial year 2016-17 & and 2017-18.

4.1 Introduction

This chapter of the study considers the implementation of the models, methodology, and approach described in chapter three. The collected data is summarized and presented in the form of numerical figures, tables, charts, and figures, as well as an explanation and interpretation of the processed data. A description discernment of the processed data is provided using the regression, stochastic frontier analysis, and event study approach.

During the estimation window, STATA and R were used to calculate the regression and stochastic frontier analysis, etc. parameters, as well as the coefficients of correlation and determination between cumulative abnormal stock returns and the expected returns. Microsoft Excel2013 was used to enumerate the event study methodology and establish the abnormal returns, t-test statistics, and chart building. Further, the chapter has been categorized into four objectives which first objective deals with financing patterns, the second objective relates to operating efficiency, the third provides the financial performance of the resulting companies, and the fourth deals with shareholders' wealth and value of the firm.

4.2 Regression results of the objective one

The relationship between return on capital employed (ROCE) and debt-equity ratio (DER) is being analyzed by using the linear regression model. However, Barth et al., (2011); and Tavares Lehmann & Lehmann, (2017) used ordered logit regression and t-tests respectively to analyze the financing pattern. Although Cheng & Yu, (2010) use the principal-agent model of Public-private partnership (PPP).

Table 4.1.1 -Descriptive Statistics of Financing Pattern – Merger

Statistic	N	Mean	St. Dev.	Min	Max
PR_RSQ_SALES	240	0.30733	0.831917	-2.615068	1.890066
PR_ROCE	240	0.012242	0.987964	-2.687259	2.75874
PR_DER	240	0.01681	1.047069	-2.0608	2.674128
PR_RWTA	240	0.135069	0.98454	-1.873919	2.801635
PO_RSQ_SALES	240	-0.321738	0.937922	-2.391082	1.937827
PO_ROCE	240	-0.118228	0.907829	-2.508336	2.276865
PO_DER	240	-0.026887	0.916394	-2.384163	2.842034
PO_RWTA	240	-0.132135	0.930072	-2.348011	2.48081

Note: The dependent variable is total debt to total equity

Source: *Compiled by Author from R output sheet*

Table 4.1.1 depicts the descriptive statistics of the dependent as well as independent variables used in this study in the case of pre-merger and post-merger. The mean of r squared sales is 0.30733 before the merger which has become negative 0.321738 after the merger. Similarly, other variables ROCE, DER, and RWTA had a positive mean before the merger which has become negative post-merger thereby depicting that before the merger all the variables performed relatively better to improve the debt-equity ratio of the company as compared to post-merger. The standard deviation defines the risk, in this case, the standard deviation of r-squared sales is high in the post-merger scenario thereby indicating that r-squared sales have more risk involved after a merger. However, in the case of ROCE and RWTA, the risk is reduced if compared to the pre-merger scenario. Further, the impact of all the variables on the debt-equity ratio is analyzed before and after the merger using regression in the next segment.

Table 4.1.2 displays the regression outcomes incorporating both random and fixed effects. Prior to the merger, the coefficient of R-squared sales exhibited a value of 0.122 under the random effect model, while it reached 0.163 under the fixed effect model. This indicates that an increase in the value of R-squared sales will result in a corresponding increase of 12.2% and 16.3% in the debt-equity ratio under the random effect and fixed effect models, respectively. Similarly, with an increase in the value of ROCE, the mean of DER also increases. But in this case, the value of ROCE is negative in both fixed and random effect models which means an increase in the value of ROCE

Table 4.1.2 -Impact of R-Squared Sales and ROCE on DER Before Merger

	Dependent variable:			
	der			
	(1)	(2)	(3)	(4)
rsq_sales	0.122	0.163*		
	(0.087)	(0.098)		
roce			−0.058	−0.060
			(0.069)	(0.078)
Constant	0.012		0.018	
	(0.096)		(0.087)	
Observations	216	216	236	236
R^2	0.009	0.017	0.003	0.003
Adjusted R^2	0.004	−0.313	−0.001	−0.331
F Statistic	1.938	2.788* (df = 1; 161)	0.713	0.587 (df = 1; 176)
Note:			*p<0.1; **p<0.05; ***p<0.01	

Source: *Compiled by Author from R output sheet*

will reduce the debt-equity ratio. As a result, R-squared sales, and normalized ROCE have affected the DER at a greater rate under the fixed effect regression model. In the next table, the impact of RWTA on DER is analyzed using a regression model.

Table 4.1.3 -Impact of RWTA on DER Before Merger

	Dependent variable:	
	der	
	(1)	(2)
rwta	−0.122*	−0.155*
	(0.069)	(0.080)
Constant	0.035	
	(0.088)	
Observations	236	236
R^2	0.013	0.021
Adjusted R^2	0.009	−0.307
F Statistic	3.093*	3.767* (df = 1; 176)
Note:	*p<0.1; **p<0.05; ***p<0.01	

Source: *Compiled by Author from R output sheet*

The regression outcomes, which incorporate both random and fixed effects, are presented in Table 4.1.3. Before the merger took place, the coefficient of RWTA demonstrated a value of 0.122 when analyzed using the random effect model. However, when the fixed effect model was employed, the coefficient of RWTA increased to 0.155. This indicates that an increase in the value of RWTA will result in a corresponding decrease of 12.2% and 15.5% in the debt-equity ratio under the random effect and fixed effect models, respectively. Consequently, RWTA has exerted a more pronounced impact on the DER when analyzed using a fixed-effect regression model. Further, the regression results of all the variables showing the impact on DER based on the Hausman test are reported in the next table.

Table 4.1.4 -Regression Results of Financing Pattern Before Merger

	Dependent variable:		
	der		
	(1)	(2)	(3)
rsq_sales	0.122		
	(0.087)		
roce		−0.058	
		(0.069)	
rwta			−0.122*
			(0.069)
Constant	0.012	0.018	0.035
	(0.096)	(0.087)	(0.088)
Observations	216	236	236
R^2	0.009	0.003	0.013
Adjusted R^2	0.004	−0.001	0.009
F Statistic	1.938	0.713	3.093*
Note:	*p<0.1; **p<0.05; ***p<0.01		

Source: *Compiled by Author from R output sheet*

Table 4.1.4 presents the regression results that incorporate either random or fixed effects, based on the outcomes obtained after conducting the Hausman test. Specifically, if the p-value is less than 0.05, fixed effects are employed, whereas if the p-value is greater than 0.05, random effects are used. When considering the random effect, the observed values are found to be statistically insignificant. The table presents results that indicate a random effect, leading to the conclusion that the relationships between a dependent variable (DER) and independent variables (R squared sales, ROCE, and RWTA) are not statistically significant prior to the merger. Now, the impact of all the variables on DER is evaluated in the case of post-merger as well in the next segment.

Table 4.1.5 -Impact of R-Squared Sales and ROCE on DER After Merger

	Dependent variable:			
	der			
	(1)	(2)	(3)	(4)
rsq_sales	−0.019	−0.007		
	(0.063)	(0.071)		
roce			−0.064	−0.077
			(0.066)	(0.076)
Constant	−0.048		−0.036	
	(0.087)		(0.081)	
Observations	216	216	236	236
R^2	0.0004	0.0001	0.004	0.006
Adjusted R^2	−0.004	−0.335	−0.0003	−0.328
F Statistic	0.091	0.009 (df = 1; 161)	0.923	1.024 (df = 1; 176)
Note:			*p<0.1; **p<0.05; ***p<0.01	

Source: *Compiled by Author from R output sheet*

The regression outcomes, which incorporate both random and fixed effects, are presented in Table 4.1.5 after the merger. Following the merger, the R-squared coefficient for sales demonstrated a value of 0.019 within the framework of the random effect model, whereas it attained a value of 0.007 within the fixed effect model. These findings suggest that a rise in the R-squared sales value is associated with a reduction of 1.9% and 0.7% in the debt-equity ratio when employing the random effect and fixed effect models, respectively. Nevertheless, before the merger, there existed a positive correlation between the R-squared values of sales and the debt-to-equity ratio (DER). The correlation between Return on Capital Employed (ROCE) and Debt-to-Equity Ratio (DER) exhibits a negative association, both prior to and subsequent to the merger. Consequently, Post-merger has a more negative impact on the Debt-to-Equity Ratio (DER) in relation to the R-squared sales. Next, the impact of RWTA on DER is evaluated using a regression model after the merger in Table 4.1.6.

Table 4.1.6 displays the regression results that encompass both random and fixed effects. Following the merger, the coefficient of RWTA exhibits values of 0.080 and

Table 4.1.6 -Impact of RWTA on DER After Merger

	Dependent variable:	
	der	
	(1)	(2)
rwta	−0.080	−0.138*
	(0.065)	(0.075)
Constant	−0.039	
	(0.081)	
Observations	236	236
R^2	0.006	0.019
Adjusted R^2	0.002	−0.310
F Statistic	1.491	3.364* (df = 1; 176)
Note:	*p<0.1; **p<0.05; ***p<0.01	

Source: *Compiled by Author from R output sheet*

0.138 under the random effect and fixed effect models, respectively. Prior to the occurrence of the merger, the coefficient of RWTA exhibited a value of 0.122 when assessed using the random effect model, and 0.155 under the fixed effect model. This finding suggests that downward trend in the negative value of RWTA will lead to a corresponding improvement in the debt-equity ratio when considering both the random effect and fixed effect models, respectively. There exists a negative correlation between the Return on capital employed with Total Assets (RWTA) and the Debt-to-Equity Ratio (DER) in both the pre-merger and post-merger scenarios. However, the impact of RWTA on the DER was more negatively correlated prior to the merger, as evidenced by the higher value of the coefficient in the pre-merger period compared to the post-merger period. Further, the regression results of all the variables showing the impact on DER after the merger on the basis of the Hausman test are reported in the next table.

Table 4.1.7 presents the regression results that incorporate either random or fixed effects, based on the outcomes obtained after conducting the Hausman test. Specifically, if the p-value is less than 0.05, fixed effects are employed, whereas if the p-value is greater than 0.05, random effects are used. When considering the random effect, the observed values are found to be statistically insignificant. The table presents results that indicate a random effect, leading to the conclusion that the relationships between a

Table 4.1.7 -Regression Results of Financing Pattern After Merger

	Dependent variable:		
	der		
	(1)	(2)	(3)
rsq_sales	−0.019		
	(0.063)		
roce		−0.064	
		(0.066)	
rwta			−0.080
			(0.065)
Constant	−0.048	−0.036	−0.039
	(0.087)	(0.081)	(0.081)
Observations	216	236	236
R^2	0.0004	0.004	0.006
Adjusted R^2	−0.004	−0.0003	0.002
F Statistic	0.091	0.923	1.491
Note:	*p<0.1; **p<0.05; ***p<0.01		

Source: *Compiled by Author from R output sheet*

dependent variable (DER) and independent variables (R squared sales, ROCE, and RWTA) are not statistically significant before and after the merger. Next, the impact of all the variables on DER is analyzed in the year of the merger using a regression model.

Table 4.1.8 displays the regression results, which encompass both random and fixed effects. During the year of the merger, the R-squared coefficient for sales exhibited a value of 0.134 when analyzed within the context of the random effect model, while it achieved a value of 0.159 within the fixed effect model. The results of this study indicate that an increase in the R-squared sales value is linked to a decrease of 13.4% and 15.9% in the debt-equity ratio when using the random effect and fixed effect models, respectively. However, prior to the merger, a positive correlation was observed between the R-squared values of sales and the debt-to-equity ratio (DER). There is a negative correlation observed between the Return on Capital Employed (ROCE) and Debt-to-Equity Ratio (DER) during the periods leading up to, during, and following a merger. Consequently, it can be posited that the R-squared sales variable exerted a more pronounced influence on the debt-to-equity ratio (DER) prior to the merger, whereas

Table 4.1.8 -Impact of R-Squared Sales and ROCE on DER During Merger

	Dependent variable:			
	der			
	(1)	(2)	(3)	(4)
rsq_sales	−0.134*	−0.159		
	(0.075)	(0.104)		
roce			−0.153*	−0.120
			(0.079)	(0.133)
Constant	0.005		−0.062	
	(0.085)		(0.081)	
Observations	108	108	118	118
R^2	0.029	0.042	0.031	0.014
Adjusted R^2	0.020	−0.934	0.023	−0.989
F Statistic	3.175*	2.324 (df = 1; 53)	3.711*	0.818 (df = 1; 58)
Note:				*p<0.1; **p<0.05; ***p<0.01

Source: *Compiled by Author from R output sheet*

the return on capital employed (ROCE) variable exhibited a greater negative impact in the year of the merger. Further, the impact of RWTA on DER after the merger is analyzed in Table 4.1.9.

Table 4.1.9 -Impact of RWTA on DER During Merger

	Dependent variable:	
	der	
	(1)	(2)
rwta	−0.075	−0.194
	(0.086)	(0.127)
Constant	−0.070	
	(0.084)	
Observations	118	118
R^2	0.007	0.038
Adjusted R^2	−0.002	−0.940
F Statistic	0.763	2.316 (df = 1; 58)
Note:		*p<0.1; **p<0.05; ***p<0.01

Source: *Compiled by Author from R output sheet*

Table 4.1.9 displays the regression results that encompass both random and fixed effects. In the year of the merger, the coefficient of RWTA exhibits values of 0.075 and 0.194 under the random effect and fixed effect models, respectively. Following the merger, the coefficient of RWTA exhibits values of 0.080 and 0.138 under the random effect and fixed effect models, respectively. Prior to the occurrence of the merger, the coefficient of RWTA exhibited a value of 0.122 when assessed using the random effect model, and 0.155 under the fixed effect model. This finding suggests that an increase in the negative value of RWTA will lead to a corresponding decline in the debt-equity ratio when considering both the random effect and fixed effect models, respectively. There exists a negative correlation between the Return on capital employed with Total Assets (RWTA) and the Debt-to-Equity Ratio (DER) in both the pre-merger and post-merger scenarios. However, the impact of RWTA on the DER was more negative prior to the merger, as evidenced by the higher value of the coefficient in the post-merger period under the random effect model and in the year of the merger under the fixed effect model. In the next segment, the results of the regression are reported on the basis of the Hausman test in the year of the merger.

Table 4.1.10 -Regression Results of Financing Pattern During Merger

	Dependent variable:		
	der		
	(1)	(2)	(3)
rsq_sales	−0.134*		
	(0.075)		
roce		−0.153*	
		(0.079)	
rwta			−0.075
			(0.086)
Constant	0.005	−0.062	−0.070
	(0.085)	(0.081)	(0.084)
Observations	108	118	118
R^2	0.029	0.031	0.007
Adjusted R^2	0.020	0.023	−0.002
F Statistic	3.175*	3.711*	0.763
Note:	*p<0.1; **p<0.05; ***p<0.01		

Source: *Compiled by Author from R output sheet*

Table 4.1.10 presents the regression results that incorporate either random or fixed effects, based on the outcomes obtained after conducting the Hausman test. Specifically, if the p-value is less than 0.05, fixed effects are employed, whereas if the p-value is greater than 0.05, random effects are used. When considering the random effect, the observed values are found to be statistically insignificant. The table presents results that indicate a random effect, leading to the conclusion that the relationships between a dependent variable (DER) and independent variables (R squared sales, ROCE, and RWTA) are not statistically significant before, during, and after the merger. Until now, the impact of all the variables on the debt-equity ratio is discussed before, during, and after the merger. Now, the impact of all the variables on the debt-equity ratio is discussed in the case of the overall merger in the next segment.

Table 4.1.11 -Impact of R-Squared Sales and ROCE on DER considering Overall Merger

	Dependent variable:			
	der			
	(1)	(2)	(3)	(4)
rsq_sales	0.001	0.001		
	(0.043)	(0.046)		
roce			−0.074*	−0.077*
			(0.041)	(0.044)
Constant	−0.00001		−0.020	
	(0.041)		(0.039)	
Observations	540	540	590	590
R^2	0.00000	0.00000	0.005	0.006
Adjusted R^2	−0.002	−0.111	0.004	−0.105
F Statistic	0.0004	0.0003 (df = 1; 485)	3.218*	3.024* (df = 1; 530)
Note:				*p<0.1; **p<0.05; ***p<0.01

Source: *Compiled by Author from R output sheet*

Table 4.1.11 displays the regression results, which encompass both random and fixed effects. Considering all the years i.e., before, during, and after the merger the coefficient of R-squared sales is 0.001 under both random and fixed effect models. During the year of the merger, the R-squared coefficient for sales exhibited a value of 0.134 under the random effect model, and 0.159 under the fixed effect model. There is a negative correlation between the R-squared Sales and DER post and during the merger. However, prior to the merger and in the overall merger a positive correlation was observed between the R-squared values of sales and the debt-to-equity ratio (DER). There is a negative correlation observed between the Return on Capital Employed (ROCE) and Debt-to-Equity Ratio (DER) during the periods leading up to, during, and following a merger as well as in the overall merger. Consequently, it can be posited that the R-squared sales variable exerted a more pronounced influence on the debt-to-equity ratio (DER) prior to the merger, whereas the return on capital employed (ROCE) variable exhibited a greater negative impact in the year of the merger. Further, the impact of RWTA on DER is evaluated using a regression model considering the overall merger in Table 4.1.12.

Table 4.1.12 -Impact of RWTA on DER considering Overall Merger

	Dependent variable:	
	der	
	(1)	(2)
rwta	−0.059	−0.060
	(0.041)	(0.044)
Constant	−0.018	
	(0.039)	
Observations	590	590
R^2	0.004	0.004
Adjusted R^2	0.002	−0.107
F Statistic	2.070	1.912 (df = 1; 530)
Note:	*p<0.1; **p<0.05; ***p<0.01	

Source: *Compiled by Author from R output sheet*

Table 4.1.12 displays the regression results that encompass both random and fixed effects. In the overall merger, the coefficient of RWTA is 0.059 and 0.060 under the random and fixed effect model. In the year of the merger, the coefficient of RWTA exhibits values of 0.075 and 0.194 under the random effect and fixed effect models, respectively. Following the merger, the coefficient of RWTA exhibits values of 0.080 and 0.138 under the random effect and fixed effect models, respectively. Prior to the occurrence of the merger, the coefficient of RWTA exhibited a value of 0.122 when assessed using the random effect model, and 0.155 under the fixed effect model. This finding suggests that an increase in the value of RWTA will lead to a corresponding decline in the debt-equity ratio when considering both the random effect and fixed effect models, respectively. There exists a negative correlation between the Return on capital employed with Total Assets (RWTA) and the Debt-to-Equity Ratio (DER) in all scenarios. However, the impact of RWTA on the DER was more negative prior to the merger, as evidenced by the higher value of the coefficient in the post-merger period under the random effect model and in the year of the merger under the fixed effect model. Next, the regression results are reported considering the overall merger on the basis of the Hausman test in Table 4.1.13.

Table 4.1.13 -Regression Results of Financing Pattern considering Overall Merger

	Dependent variable:		
	der		
	(1)	(2)	(3)
rsq_sales	0.001		
	(0.043)		
roce		−0.074*	
		(0.041)	
rwta			−0.059
			(0.041)
Constant	−0.00001	−0.020	−0.018
	(0.041)	(0.039)	(0.039)
Observations	540	590	590
R^2	0.00000	0.005	0.004
Adjusted R^2	−0.002	0.004	0.002
F Statistic	0.0004	3.218*	2.070
Note:	*p<0.1; **p<0.05; ***p<0.01		

Source: *Compiled by Author from R output sheet*

Table 4.1.13 presents the regression results that incorporate either random or fixed effects, based on the outcomes obtained after conducting the Hausman test. Specifically, if the p-value is less than 0.05, fixed effects are employed, whereas if the p-value is greater than 0.05, random effects are used. When considering the random effect, the observed values are found to be statistically insignificant. The table presents results that indicate a random effect, leading to the conclusion that the relationships between a dependent variable (DER) and independent variables (R squared sales, ROCE, and

RWTA) are not statistically significant before, during, and after the merger. However, in the case of the overall merger, the relationship between R-squared sales and DER is statistically significant. Next, the correlation of all the variables with each other in case of merger is reported in Table 4.1.14. Further, the impact of all the variables on debt-equity in pre- and post-acquisition is discussed in the next segments.

Table 4.1.14 -Correlation Matrix of Financing Pattern-Merger

	rsq_sales	roce	der	rwta
rsq_sales	1			
roce	0.004	1		
der	0.001	-0.089	1	
rwta	0.004	0.699	-0.063	1

Source: *Compiled by Author from R output sheet*

Table 4.1.14 shows the correlation between the variables in the case of a merger. The R-squared Sales and all the variables (DER, RWTA, and ROCE) are positively correlated. However, DER and ROCE as well as DER and RWTA are negatively correlated. In all the tables above, the impact of all the variables on the financing pattern is analyzed in the merger. Similarly, in the next segment, the impact of all the variables on the financing pattern is evaluated in the case of acquisition starting with the descriptive statistics.

Table 4.1.15 -Comparison of Pre-and Post-Merger of DER

S.No.	Company Name	Pre-Mergers				Post-Mergers			
		2013	2014	2015	2016	2019	2020	2021	2022
1	Crystal Crop Protection Ltd	-0.7171	0.6266	-2.0608	-0.2029	0.5665	-0.3893	0.0886	-0.3893
2	Sterlite Power Transmission Ltd	-0.2790	-0.2790	-0.2790	-0.2790	2.8420	-0.3674	-0.4114	-0.3894
3	Olive Bar & Kitchen Pvt Ltd	-0.6471	-1.1918	-1.0768	-0.6137	0.8676	1.5246	-0.2990	-0.2990
4	Hero Future Energies Pvt Ltd	0.3261	-1.6853	2.3375	-0.0211	-0.5985	0.0764	-0.2611	0.0764
5	ECap Equities Ltd	-1.5812	-1.7364	-0.1262	-0.3976	0.8087	0.8087	0.8087	-0.2022
6	Ashok Leyland Ltd	-0.9417	-0.7728	-0.6589	-0.8063	0.7612	1.0509	1.4805	1.2657
7	AMJ Land Holdings Ltd	2.3832	1.2498	-0.3452	-0.3587	-0.2861	-0.5133	-0.5499	-0.5316
8	Anup Engineering Limited/The	-0.9487	-0.9487	-0.9487	-0.9487	-0.9487	-0.9487	-0.9487	-0.9487
9	Arvind Ltd	0.6848	1.3957	1.6611	-0.5843	0.1616	-0.6740	-1.3263	-1.0002
10	Astral Ltd	1.9206	0.9077	0.5005	0.5181	-0.5396	-1.1725	-1.0216	-1.0970
11	Adani Total Gas Ltd	-0.2256	0.1199	-0.5711	-1.0138	0.1584	1.6744	-0.2296	-0.2296
12	Bharti Airtel Ltd	-1.0169	-1.6171	-0.3844	-0.2186	-0.1936	1.5243	1.0318	1.2780
13	Balaji Amines Ltd	1.9438	1.5361	0.3252	-0.4853	-0.1255	-0.8105	-0.9573	-0.8839

S.No.	Company Name	Pre-Mergers				Post-Mergers			
		2013	2014	2015	2016	2019	2020	2021	2022
14	Borosil Renewables Ltd	-1.3500	-0.9873	0.1556	-0.6361	1.9508	0.1417	0.9851	0.5634
15	Berger Paints India Ltd	1.7764	1.8813	-0.4590	-0.5802	0.0953	-0.8209	-0.1780	-0.4994
16	Birlasoft Ltd	1.6375	1.6485	0.1393	0.5999	-0.6117	-0.7407	-0.8217	-0.7812
17	Chordia Food Products Ltd	-0.5346	0.0705	0.0476	-0.7946	1.6704	0.2843	1.6704	-0.2443
18	Chalet Hotels Ltd	-0.1927	0.0440	1.0144	1.6183	-0.9524	-0.7990	-0.4777	-0.6384
19	CL Educate Ltd	0.0462	0.2057	0.0459	0.2057	1.1521	1.2336	-2.3842	-0.5753
20	DiGiSPICE Technologies Ltd	-1.4685	-1.2680	0.7783	-1.2280	-0.0525	0.2921	1.2404	0.7663
21	Dr Lal PathLabs Ltd	-1.6532	-0.0345	-0.0345	-0.0345	-0.3256	-0.3807	2.2214	0.9204
22	Elpro International Ltd	-0.4877	-0.4820	-0.4820	1.8968	-0.4291	-0.4473	-0.5208	-0.4840
23	Foods & Inns Ltd	1.7108	0.4683	1.0889	0.5652	-0.9714	-0.8867	-0.7001	-0.7934
24	Future Market Networks Ltd	0.1455	0.7771	-0.4861	-0.6093	-0.6519	-0.3934	2.1674	0.8870
25	Godrej Industries Ltd	-0.2159	0.4580	1.1046	1.9181	-1.2816	-1.1741	-0.1805	-0.6773
26	Godrej Agrovet Ltd	-0.2537	2.5100	0.0620	-0.8753	-0.2915	0.3010	0.0047	0.3010
27	Havells India Ltd	2.6741	0.5286	-0.4876	0.3835	-0.5727	-0.1799	-0.1724	-0.1761
28	HealthCare Global Enterprises Ltd	-0.3286	-0.0589	-0.6891	-0.7505	2.6746	0.2134	-0.2156	-0.0011
29	Hexaware Technologies Ltd	0.0613	0.0613	0.0613	0.0613	-1.4879	1.9340	-0.2623	0.8359
30	Indiabulls Real Estate Ltd	-0.8062	-0.0063	1.5672	1.7935	-0.2442	-0.9446	-0.8811	-0.9129
31	Indo Amines Ltd	1.8516	0.4744	-0.6254	-1.7148	0.3084	-0.7978	1.0611	0.1316
32	Indus Towers Ltd	-0.4743	-0.5437	-0.8201	-0.8201	-0.1510	1.7961	0.9834	1.3897
33	Infibeam Avenues Ltd	1.0571	-0.2391	-0.5575	2.4809	-0.4883	-0.4956	-0.6126	-0.5541
34	Inox Leisure Ltd	-0.6785	-0.8057	-0.7596	-0.7007	1.2164	1.1968	1.0822	1.1395
35	JSW Steel Ltd	0.0390	0.2815	1.9742	1.0516	0.3773	-0.2750	-1.5361	-0.9055
36	LTIMindtree Ltd	-0.8091	0.0509	-1.7483	-0.8487	1.4037	0.0932	-0.2269	-0.0669
37	Morganite Crucible India Ltd	-0.1540	0.2546	1.1046	1.9181	-1.2846	-1.1654	-0.1545	-0.6564
38	Minda Corp Ltd	2.0718	0.8764	0.3969	0.4534	-0.2916	-0.8256	-1.0635	-0.9446
39	Modern India Ltd	0.6114	0.1571	-0.9344	-1.1071	1.5097	0.3502	1.5097	-0.2325
40	Mukund Ltd	-0.9722	-0.8763	-0.8334	2.3612	0.3470	0.5618	0.0222	0.2920
41	Narayana Hrudayalaya Ltd	0.1027	-0.4507	-1.4229	-1.7788	1.1108	0.9846	-0.3705	0.3071
42	Nath Industries Ltd	1.4815	-0.2276	0.0508	-0.9672	-0.0443	-1.5704	1.5474	-0.0115
43	National Fittings Ltd	-1.3395	-0.6773	-0.2170	-1.4279	0.8095	-0.1271	0.1730	0.0230
44	Optiemus Infracom Ltd	1.7215	0.8709	0.0359	0.4437	0.1436	-1.0606	-1.3918	-1.2262
45	Piramal Enterprises Ltd	-0.7418	-1.8502	-0.5504	1.0786	0.1137	-0.4997	0.4267	-0.0365
46	Reliance Industries Ltd	0.4231	0.5784	0.7928	0.6345	0.6866	-1.4224	-1.4634	-1.4429
47	RPSG Ventures Ltd	0.1493	0.1493	0.1493	0.1493	-0.6661	-1.2060	2.3200	0.5570
48	S Chand & Co Ltd	2.5910	0.4546	0.1649	-1.0031	-0.2327	-0.6172	-0.4249	-0.6172
49	Schaeffler India Ltd	-0.0935	-0.0935	1.6025	0.6674	-0.8544	-0.4019	-1.3069	-0.8544
50	Sundram Fasteners Ltd	1.5509	1.8458	0.3950	-0.1178	-0.2843	-0.9186	-0.9528	-0.9357
51	Solara Active Pharma Sciences Ltd	0.0554	0.0554	0.0554	-0.4988	0.5966	-1.9534	2.0773	0.0619
52	Somany Ceramics Ltd	0.7031	0.4144	-1.8934	0.3868	0.7818	-0.9150	-0.4804	-0.6977
53	Strides Pharma Science Ltd	-1.8633	-1.4095	1.1834	0.4528	-0.2397	-0.3748	1.0750	0.3501
54	Thomas Cook India Ltd	-0.4839	1.8432	1.1641	-1.3606	-0.1610	0.0248	-0.0681	0.0248
55	Tech Mahindra Ltd	-1.5673	-1.0795	-0.5947	-0.3982	1.9585	0.5527	0.0147	0.2837
56	Timken India Ltd	-1.0651	-1.4564	-1.1133	-0.3309	-0.1297	1.4912	0.4654	0.9783
57	TV18 Broadcast Ltd	-0.5127	-0.3805	-1.1009	-0.8961	1.8258	-0.1524	-0.5358	-0.3441
58	TV Today Network Ltd	0.5046	-0.5933	2.2954	0.9763	-0.3238	-0.5512	-0.1923	-0.3718
59	Uniply Industries Ltd	1.4540	1.7832	-0.0581	0.5521	-0.9333	-0.8795	-0.9333	0.2266

S.No.	Company Name	Pre-Mergers				Post-Mergers			
		2013	2014	2015	2016	2019	2020	2021	2022
60	Wipro Ltd	-1.4074	-0.5455	0.9615	1.0523	-0.9218	-0.6294	0.9450	0.1578

Source: *Compiled by Author*

Table 4.1.15 presents a comparative analysis of the debt and equity ratios prior to and after to the merger. The years 2013, 2014, 2015, and 2016 may be classified as pre-merger years, whereas the years 2019, 2020, 2021, and 2022 can be categorised as post-merger years. It is commonly asserted that a lower debt equity ratio is indicative of a more favourable financial position. Based on the aforementioned analysis, it can be inferred that the merger has demonstrated advantageous outcomes for the firms involved, as seen by the consistent drop in this ratio subsequent to the merger. Nevertheless, in certain instances, it has merely been augmented, but still seen as a favourable ratio if it reaches a value of 1 or 1.5. Based on the prevailing trend seen among firms, where the majority exhibit a ratio below 1 or up to 1.5, the merger undertaken by the companies is regarded as a favourable option. This strategic move has effectively enhanced the financial structure of the organisation.

Table 4.1.16 - Descriptive Statistics of Financing Pattern- Acquisition

Statistic	N	Mean	St. Dev.	Min	Max
PR_RSQ_SALES	1232	0.199984	0.861335	-2.669273	2.375092
PR_ROCE	1232	0.062979	0.940779	-2.49317	2.845819
PR_DER	1232	0.086309	1.019642	-1.987841	2.769727
PR_RWTA	1232	0.114628	0.969073	-2.637952	2.84605
PO_RSQ_SALES	1232	-0.247511	0.967653	-2.645404	2.252804
PO_ROCE	1232	-0.09758	0.953035	-2.51871	2.700659
PO_DER	1232	-0.021894	0.893153	-2.365267	2.651419
PO_RWTA	1232	-0.136678	0.924944	-2.711481	2.682052

Source: *Compiled by Author from R output sheet*

Table 4.1.16 depicts the descriptive statistics of the dependent as well as independent variables used in this study in the case of pre-acquisition and post-acquisition. The mean of r squared sales is 0.199984 before acquisition which has become negative 0.247511 after acquisition. Similarly, other variables ROCE, DER, and RWTA have a positive mean before acquisition which has become negative post-acquisition thereby depicting that before acquisition all the variables performed relatively better to improve the debt-equity ratio of the company as compared to post-acquisition. The standard deviation defines the risk, in this case, the standard deviation of r-squared sales and ROCE is high in the post-acquisition scenario thereby indicating r-squared sales have more risk involved after acquisition. However, in the case of RWTA, the risk is reduced if compared to the pre-acquisition scenario. In the next table, the impact of r-squared sales and return on capital employed on the debt-equity ratio is discussed.

Table 4.1.17 displays the regression outcomes incorporating both random and fixed effects. Prior to the acquisition, the coefficient of R-squared sales exhibited a value of 0.051 under the random effect model, while it reached 0.052 under the fixed effect model. This indicates that an increase in the value of R-squared sales will result in a corresponding increase of 5.1% and 5.2% in the debt-equity ratio under the random effect and fixed effect models, respectively. Similarly, with an increase in the value of ROCE, the mean of DER also increases. But in this case, the value of ROCE is negative in both fixed and random effect models which means an increase in the value of ROCE will reduce the debt-equity ratio. As a result, R-squared sales, and normalized ROCE

Table 4.1.17 -Impact of R-Squared Sales and ROCE on DER Before Acquisition

	Dependent variable:			
	der			
	(1)	(2)	(3)	(4)
rsq_sales	0.051 (0.036)	0.052 (0.041)		
roce			−0.045 (0.033)	−0.057 (0.038)
Constant	0.077* (0.044)		0.101** (0.041)	
Observations	1,044	1,044	1,124	1,124
R^2	0.002	0.002	0.002	0.003
Adjusted R^2	0.001	−0.331	0.001	−0.330
F Statistic	2.035	1.606 (df = 1; 782)	1.923	2.291 (df = 1; 842)
Note:			*p<0.1; **p<0.05; ***p<0.01	

Source: *Compiled by Author from R output sheet*

have affected the DER at a greater rate under the fixed effect regression model. Further, the impact of return with total assets on the debt-equity ratio is shown in Table 4.1.18.

The regression outcomes, which incorporate both random and fixed effects, are presented in Table 4.1.18. Before the acquisition took place, the coefficient of RWTA demonstrated a value of 0.073 when analyzed using the random effect model. However, when the fixed effect model was employed, the coefficient of RWTA increased to 0.097. This indicates that an increase in the value of RWTA will result in a corresponding decrease of 7.3% and 9.7% in the debt-equity ratio under the random effect and fixed

Table 4.1.18 -Impact of RWTA on DER Before Acquisition

	Dependent variable:	
	der	
	(1)	(2)
rwta	−0.073**	−0.097***
	(0.031)	(0.036)
Constant	0.103***	
	(0.040)	
Observations	1,192	1,192
R^2	0.005	0.008
Adjusted R^2	0.004	−0.323
F Statistic	5.605**	7.152*** (df = 1; 893)
Note:	*p<0.1; **p<0.05; ***p<0.01	

Source: *Compiled by Author from R output sheet*

effect models, respectively. Consequently, RWTA has exerted a more pronounced impact on the DER when analyzed using a fixed-effect regression model. In the next segment, the regression results of the impact of all the variables on the debt-equity ratio before acquisition are analyzed on the basis of the Hausman test.

Table 4.1.19 presents the regression results that incorporate either random or fixed effects, based on the outcomes obtained after conducting the Hausman test. Specifically, if the p-value is less than 0.05, fixed effects are employed, whereas if the p-value is greater than 0.05, random effects are used. When considering the random effect, the observed values are found to be statistically insignificant. The table presents results that indicate a random effect, leading to the conclusion that the relationships between the dependent variable (DER) and independent variables (R squared sales, ROCE, and RWTA) were not statistically significant prior to the acquisition. In this table the results of the variables' impact on the debt-equity ratio are discussed before the acquisition, however in the next segment the effect of these variables on the debt-equity ratio after

Table 4.1.19 -Regression Results of Financing Pattern Before Acquisition

	Dependent variable:		
	der		
	(1)	(2)	(3)
rsq_sales	0.051		
	(0.036)		
roce		−0.045	
		(0.033)	
rwta			−0.073**
			(0.031)
Constant	0.077*	0.101**	0.103***
	(0.044)	(0.041)	(0.040)
Observations	1,044	1,124	1,192
R^2	0.002	0.002	0.005
Adjusted R^2	0.001	0.001	0.004
F Statistic	2.035	1.923	5.605**
Note:	*p<0.1; **p<0.05; ***p<0.01		

Source: *Compiled by Author from R output sheet*

the acquisition is discussed in order to compare the change in the financing pattern of the companies pre- and post-acquisition.

Table 4.1.20 -Impact of R-Squared Sales and ROCE on DER After Acquisition

	Dependent variable:			
	der			
	(1)	(2)	(3)	(4)
rsq_sales	0.045*	0.057**		
	(0.025)	(0.027)		
roce			−0.133***	−0.138***
			(0.025)	(0.027)
Constant	−0.013		−0.051	
	(0.044)		(0.041)	
Observations	1,044	1,044	1,124	1,124
R^2	0.003	0.005	0.024	0.030
Adjusted R^2	0.002	−0.326	0.024	−0.294
F Statistic	3.141*	4.324** (df = 1; 782)	28.177***	25.777*** (df = 1; 842)
Note:				*p<0.1; **p<0.05; ***p<0.01

Source: *Compiled by Author from R output sheet*

The regression outcomes, which incorporate both random and fixed effects, are presented in Table 4.1.20. Following the acquisition, the R-squared coefficient for sales demonstrated a value of 0.045 within the framework of the random effect model, whereas it attained a value of 0.057 within the fixed effect model. These findings suggest that a rise in the R-squared sales value will increase the DER by 4.5% and 5.7% when employing the random effect and fixed effect models, respectively. Before the acquisition, there existed a positive correlation between the R-squared values of sales and the debt-to-equity ratio (DER). The correlation between Return on Capital Employed (ROCE) and Debt-to-Equity Ratio (DER) exhibits a negative association, both prior to and subsequent to the acquisition. Consequently, Prior to the acquisition has had a more pronounced impact on the Debt-to-Equity Ratio (DER) in relation to the R-squared sales under the random model. However, under fixed effect, R-squared sales have a more profound effect in post-acquisition. The impact of return with total assets on the debt-equity ratio is analyzed in Table 4.1.21 after acquisition.

Table 4.1.21 -Impact of RWTA on DER After Acquisition

	Dependent variable:	
	der	
	(1)	(2)
rwta	−0.131***	−0.143***
	(0.026)	(0.029)
Constant	−0.052	
	(0.039)	
Observations	1,192	1,192
R^2	0.021	0.027
Adjusted R^2	0.020	−0.298
F Statistic	25.282***	24.747*** (df = 1; 893)
Note:	*p<0.1; **p<0.05; ***p<0.01	

Source: *Compiled by Author from R output sheet*

Table 4.1.21 displays the regression results that encompass both random and fixed effects. Following the acquisition, the coefficient of RWTA exhibits values of 0.131 and 0.143 under the random effect and fixed effect models, respectively. Prior to the occurrence of the acquisition, the coefficient of RWTA exhibited a value of 0.073 when assessed using the random effect model, and 0.097 under the fixed effect model. This finding suggests that an upward trend in the value of RWTA will lead to a corresponding decline in the debt-equity ratio when considering both the random effect and fixed effect models, respectively. There exists a negative correlation between the Return on capital employed with Total Assets (RWTA) and the Debt-to-Equity Ratio (DER) in pre and post-acquisition. However, the impact of RWTA on the DER was more negative prior to the merger, as evidenced by the higher value of the coefficient in the post-acquisition period compared to the pre-acquisition period. The regression results of the variables on the debt-equity ratio after acquisition are presented in Table 4.1.22 on the basis of the Hausman test.

Table 4.1.22 presents the regression results that incorporate either random or fixed effects, based on the outcomes obtained after conducting the Hausman test. Specifically, if the p-value is less than 0.05, fixed effects are employed, whereas if the p-value is

Table 4.1.22 -Regression Results of Financing Pattern After Acquisition

	Dependent variable:		
	der		
	(1)	(2)	(3)
rsq_sales	0.045* (0.025)		
roce		−0.133*** (0.025)	
rwta			−0.131*** (0.026)
Constant	−0.013 (0.044)	−0.051 (0.041)	−0.052 (0.039)
Observations	1,044	1,124	1,192
R^2	0.003	0.024	0.021
Adjusted R^2	0.002	0.024	0.020
F Statistic	3.141*	28.177***	25.282***
Note:	*p<0.1; **p<0.05; ***p<0.01		

Source: *Compiled by Author from R output sheet*

greater than 0.05, random effects are used. When considering the random effect, the observed values are found to be statistically insignificant. The table presents results that indicate a random effect, leading to the conclusion that the relationships between the dependent variable (DER) and independent variables (R squared sales, ROCE, and RWTA) are not statistically significant before and after the acquisition. The impact of r squared sales, return on capital employed, and return with total assets on debt-equity ratio is analyzed pre- and post-acquisition. Further, the same is analyzed in the year of acquisition as well in the next table.

Table 4.1.23 displays the regression results, which encompass both random and fixed effects. During the year of the acquisition, the R-squared coefficient for sales exhibited a value of 0.028 when analyzed within the context of the random effect model, while it achieved a value of 0.012 within the fixed effect model. The results of this study indicate that an increase in the R-squared sales value is linked to a decrease of 2.8% and 1.2% in the debt-equity ratio when using the random effect and fixed effect models, respectively. However, before and after the acquisition, a positive correlation was observed between the R-squared values of sales and the debt-to-equity ratio (DER).

Table 4.1.23 -Impact of R-Squared Sales and ROCE on DER During Acquisition

	Dependent variable:			
	der			
	(1)	(2)	(3)	(4)
rsq_sales	−0.028	−0.012		
	(0.040)	(0.059)		
roce			−0.066*	−0.041
			(0.039)	(0.054)
Constant	−0.104**		−0.099**	
	(0.043)		(0.042)	
Observations	522	522	562	562
R^2	0.001	0.0001	0.005	0.002
Adjusted R^2	−0.001	−1.004	0.003	−1.000
F Statistic	0.491	0.039 (df = 1; 260)	2.848*	0.567 (df = 1; 280)
Note:			*p<0.1; **p<0.05; ***p<0.01	

Source: *Compiled by Author from R output sheet*

There is a negative correlation observed between the Return on Capital Employed (ROCE) and Debt-to-Equity Ratio (DER) during the periods leading up to, during, and following a merger. Consequently, it can be posited that the R-squared sales variable exerted a more pronounced influence on the debt-to-equity ratio (DER) prior to the acquisition under the random effect model and after the acquisition under the fixed effect model, whereas the return on capital employed (ROCE) variable exhibited a greater negative impact after acquisition. In the next segment, the impact of return with total assets on the debt-equity ratio is analyzed in the year of acquisition.

Table 4.1.24 displays the regression results that encompass both random and fixed effects. In the year of acquisition, the coefficient of RWTA exhibits values of 0.104 and 0.090 under the random effect and fixed effect models, respectively. Following the acquisition, the coefficient of RWTA exhibits values of 0.131 and 0.143 under the random effect and fixed effect models, respectively. Prior to the occurrence of the acquisition, the coefficient of RWTA exhibited a value of 0.073 when assessed using the random effect model, and 0.097 under the fixed effect model. This finding suggests that an increase in the negative value of RWTA will lead to a corresponding decline in

Table 4.1.24 -Impact of RWTA on DER During Acquisition

	Dependent variable:	
	der	
	(1)	(2)
rwta	−0.104***	−0.090*
	(0.039)	(0.054)
Constant	−0.103**	
	(0.041)	
Observations	596	596
R^2	0.012	0.009
Adjusted R^2	0.010	−0.985
F Statistic	7.023***	2.820* (df = 1; 297)
Note:	*p<0.1; **p<0.05; ***p<0.01	

Source: *Compiled by Author from R output sheet*

the debt-equity ratio when considering both the random effect and fixed effect models, respectively. There exists a negative correlation between the Return on capital employed with Total Assets (RWTA) and the Debt-to-Equity Ratio (DER) in all the situations. However, the impact of RWTA on the DER was more negative post-acquisition, as evidenced by the higher value of the coefficient. Further, in the next table, the regression results are discussed on the basis of the Hausman test in the year of acquisition.

Table 4.1.25 presents the regression results that incorporate either random or fixed effects, based on the outcomes obtained after conducting the Hausman test. Specifically, if the p-value is less than 0.05, fixed effects are employed, whereas if the p-value is greater than 0.05, random effects are used. When considering the random effect, the observed values are found to be statistically insignificant. The table presents results that indicate a random effect, leading to the conclusion that the relationships between the dependent variable (DER) and independent variables (R squared sales, ROCE, and RWTA) are not statistically significant before, during, and after the acquisition. Now, the impact of all the variables on the debt-equity ratio considering overall acquisition

Table 4.1.25 -Regression Results of Financing Pattern During Acquisition

	Dependent variable:		
	der		
	(1)	(2)	(3)
rsales	−0.028 (0.040)		
roce		−0.066* (0.039)	
roceta			−0.104*** (0.039)
Constant	−0.104** (0.043)	−0.099** (0.042)	−0.103** (0.041)
Observations	522	562	596
R^2	0.001	0.005	0.012
Adjusted R^2	−0.001	0.003	0.010
F Statistic	0.491	2.848*	7.023***
Note:	*p<0.1; **p<0.05; ***p<0.01		

Source: *Compiled by Author from R output sheet*

is also analyzed in the next segment.

Table 4.1.26 displays the regression results, which encompass both random and fixed effects. Considering all the years i.e., before, during, and after the acquisition the coefficient of R squared sales is 0.027 and 0.028 under the random and fixed effect model, respectively. During the year of the acquisition, the R-squared coefficient for sales exhibited a value of 0.028 under the random effect model, and 0.012 under the fixed effect model. There is a negative correlation between the R squared Sales and DER in the year of acquisition However, prior to the acquisition, post-acquisition, and in overall acquisition a positive correlation was observed between the R-squared values

Table 4.1.26 -Impact of R-Squared Sales and ROCE on DER considering Overall Acquisition

	Dependent variable:			
	der			
	(1)	(2)	(3)	(4)
rsq_sales	0.027	0.028		
	(0.020)	(0.021)		
roce			−0.075***	−0.078***
			(0.019)	(0.020)
Constant	0.004		0.003	
	(0.019)		(0.018)	
Observations	2,610	2,610	2,810	2,810
R^2	0.001	0.001	0.006	0.006
Adjusted R^2	0.0003	−0.110	0.005	−0.105
F Statistic	1.859	1.761 (df = 1; 2348)	16.006***	14.999*** (df = 1; 2528)
Note:				*p<0.1; **p<0.05; ***p<0.01

Source: *Compiled by Author from R output sheet*

of sales and the debt-to-equity ratio (DER). There is a negative correlation observed between the Return on Capital Employed (ROCE) and Debt-to-Equity Ratio (DER) during the periods leading up to, during, and following an acquisition as well as in overall acquisition. Consequently, it can be posited that the R-squared sales variable exerted a more pronounced influence on the debt-to-equity ratio (DER) prior to the acquisition under the random effect and post-acquisition under the fixed effect, whereas the return on capital employed (ROCE) variable exhibited a greater negative impact in post-acquisition. In the next table, the impact of return with total assets on debt-equity ratio considering overall acquisition is discussed.

Table 4.1.27 displays the regression results that encompass both random and fixed effects. In the overall merger, the coefficient of RWTA is 0.079 and 0.083 under the random and fixed effect model. In the year of acquisition, the coefficient of RWTA exhibits values of 0.104 and 0.090 under the random effect and fixed effect models, respectively. Following the acquisition, the coefficient of RWTA exhibits values of 0.131 and 0.143 under the random effect and fixed effect models, respectively. Prior to the occurrence of the acquisition, the coefficient of RWTA exhibited a value of 0.073 when assessed using the random effect model, and 0.097 under the fixed effect model.

Table 4.1.27 -Impact of RWTA on DER considering Overall Acquisition

	Dependent variable:	
	der	
	(1)	(2)
rwta	−0.079***	−0.083***
	(0.018)	(0.020)
Constant	0.003	
	(0.017)	
Observations	2,980	2,980
R^2	0.006	0.007
Adjusted R^2	0.006	−0.104
F Statistic	18.684***	17.850*** (df = 1; 2681)
Note:		*p<0.1; **p<0.05; ***p<0.01

Source: *Compiled by Author from R output sheet*

This finding suggests that an increase in the value of RWTA will lead to a corresponding decline in the debt-equity ratio when considering both the random effect and fixed effect models, respectively. There exists a negative correlation between the Return on capital employed with Total Assets (RWTA) and the Debt-to-Equity Ratio (DER) in all scenarios. However, the impact of RWTA on the DER was more negative after the acquisition, as evidenced by the higher value of the coefficient in the post-acquisition period. Finally, the regression results of the impact of variables on financing patterns are discussed in Table 4.1.28 considering overall acquisition.

Table 4.1.28 presents the regression results that incorporate either random or fixed effects, based on the outcomes obtained after conducting the Hausman test. Specifically, if the p-value is less than 0.05, fixed effects are employed, whereas if the p-value is greater than 0.05, random effects are used. When considering the random effect, the observed values are found to be statistically insignificant. The table presents results that indicate a random effect, leading to the conclusion that the relationships between the dependent variable (DER) and independent variables (R squared sales, ROCE, and RWTA) are not statistically significant before, during, after, and overall acquisition. In the next segment, the correlation of all the variables with each other is presented in Table 4.1.29 in case of an acquisition.

Table 4.1.28 -Regression Results of Financing Pattern considering Overall Acquisition

	Dependent variable:		
	der		
	(1)	(2)	(3)
rsq_sales	0.027 (0.020)		
roce		−0.075*** (0.019)	
rwta			−0.079*** (0.018)
Constant	0.004 (0.019)	0.003 (0.018)	0.003 (0.017)
Observations	2,610	2,810	2,980
R^2	0.001	0.006	0.006
Adjusted R^2	0.0003	0.005	0.006
F Statistic	1.859	16.006***	18.684***
Note:	*p<0.1; **p<0.05; ***p<0.01		

Source: *Compiled by Author from R output sheet*

Table 4.1.29 -Correlation Matrix of Financing Pattern-Acquisition

	rsq_sales	roce	der	rwta
rsq_sales	1			
roce	0.067	1		
der	0.032	-0.074	1	
rwta	0.104	0.797	-0.082	1

Source: *Compiled by Author from R output sheet*

Table 4.1.29 shows the correlation between the variables in the case of acquisition. The R-squared Sales and all the variables (DER, RWTA, and ROCE) are positively correlated. However, DER and ROCE as well as DER and RWTA are negatively correlated. In the next table, the null hypotheses are formed to evaluate the acceptance or rejection of the impact of variables on the debt-equity ratio.

Table 4.1.30 -Comparison of Pre-and Post-Acquisition of DER

S.No.	Company Name	Pre-Acquisition				Post-Acquisition			
		2013	2014	2015	2016	2019	2020	2021	2022
1	Virtusa Consulting Services Pvt Ltd	-1.1632	-1.1629	-1.1629	0.5922	0.6538	-0.2676	0.1931	-0.2676
2	Haldia Energy Ltd	2.0841	1.0976	0.4907	0.3269	-0.7193	-0.9094	-0.8144	-0.9094
3	Tata Power Renewable Energy Ltd	1.9934	0.0476	1.4840	-1.1509	-0.2174	-0.1684	-0.1929	-0.1684
4	Casagrand Builder Pvt Ltd	0.2240	0.0996	0.3484	2.3252	-0.7892	-1.1075	0.2390	0.2390
5	Valuefirst Digital Media Pvt Ltd	-0.1200	-0.5386	-0.1200	-0.9572	0.6019	1.3061	0.9540	1.3061

S.No.	Company Name	Pre-Acquisition				Post-Acquisition			
		2013	2014	2015	2016	2019	2020	2021	2022
6	JM Financial Asset Reconstruction Co Ltd	-0.2404	0.7373	-0.4822	0.7373	0.9756	0.4662	0.7209	0.4662
7	Srei Equipment Finance Ltd	-1.4392	-0.9779	1.6643	0.3432	-0.2509	-0.2509	-0.2509	-0.2509
8	ReNew Power Pvt Ltd	-1.2745	-1.0905	-0.9939	-0.5972	1.3483	0.9264	1.3483	-0.2843
9	Shriji Polymers India Ltd	1.7139	1.6636	0.1750	0.2597	-0.7057	-0.9831	-0.8444	-0.9831
10	Lalitpur Power Generation Co Ltd	-0.9184	1.3146	1.3865	1.2427	-0.2096	-0.1604	-0.7334	-0.9691
11	Assets Care & Reconstruction Enterprise Ltd	-	-	-	-	1.5000	-1.5000	-	-1.5000
12	HomeShop18	-0.8305	-0.9607	1.2772	1.6386	-0.3504	0.0459	-0.1522	0.0459
13	GMR Airports Ltd	1.7126	1.4801	0.4384	-0.8743	-0.8767	-0.4613	0.1672	0.1672
14	SVP Builders India Ltd	-0.0333	-1.2380	1.1715	1.3752	-0.6880	-0.8161	-0.7520	-0.8161
15	Jain Farm Fresh Foods Ltd	-1.3388	-1.0202	-1.3388	-0.7015	1.3709	0.5035	0.9372	0.5035
16	Salzer Magnet Wires Ltd	1.4665	1.0800	0.1412	-1.5560	0.2829	0.2829	0.2829	0.2829
17	Choicest Enterprises Ltd	0.0249	0.0249	-1.3073	-0.9578	0.9070	1.1081	1.0076	1.1081
18	MRC Logistics India Pvt Ltd	0.4415	-0.3649	-0.1630	-1.3440	-0.2980	-0.6086	-0.4533	-0.6086
19	World Resorts Ltd	1.1187	1.7811	-0.3481	0.1013	-1.3856	0.2535	0.2535	0.2535
20	Escorts Heart Institute and Research Centre Ltd	0.0522	-0.7811	0.8854	0.9238	1.3369	-1.3751	-0.0191	-1.3751
21	Alivira Animal Health Ltd	-1.1514	0.5936	-1.1514	2.3386	-0.4416	-0.0782	-0.4416	0.1796
22	Biocon Biologics Ltd/India	-0.1165	-0.1165	-0.1165	-0.1165	0.1128	1.7548	-2.2171	-0.2311
23	Nowrosjee Wadia & Sons Ltd	-0.1479	1.7159	0.6501	1.7159	-0.6454	-0.7707	-0.7081	-0.7707
24	Telesonic Networks Ltd	0.0995	0.0995	-0.5080	0.7912	-1.2837	0.4033	-1.2837	0.0995
25	Amtek Auto Ltd	0.4078	0.9350	1.1640	1.8535	-0.7267	-0.7267	-0.7267	-0.7267
26	Takasago Thermal Engineering Co Ltd	-1.2202	-0.9008	-0.6530	-1.1958	0.4524	1.1038	1.3679	1.2358
27	20 Microns Ltd	1.6280	1.5425	0.9628	-0.0019	-0.6992	-0.8887	-0.7832	-0.8359
28	Smartchem Technologies Ltd	0.7454	-0.8637	2.3545	-0.1113	-0.9550	0.1061	0.1061	0.1061
29	Lotte Confectionery Co Ltd	-0.1740	-0.1740	1.6594	0.2062	0.0136	-0.1114	-1.1844	-0.6479
30	Jasper Industries Pvt Ltd	-0.2813	0.9811	1.2646	1.7823	-1.0496	-0.7803	-0.9150	-0.7803
31	CavinKare Pvt Ltd	-1.2642	2.1251	0.9061	-0.3087	-0.2781	-0.9249	0.1504	0.1504
32	Reliance Jio Infocomm Ltd	-0.3686	-0.3686	-0.3686	1.7143	-1.0444	0.3332	-1.0444	0.0889
33	ProConnect Supply Chain Solutions Ltd	-0.9542	-1.0744	-0.8856	-0.9325	1.1586	1.0894	1.1240	1.0894
34	Ebixcash Ltd	0.2846	-0.0060	0.7060	0.1331	-1.4974	-0.5744	-1.4974	0.2590
35	TATA Advanced Systems Ltd	-0.7688	-0.9273	-0.7856	-0.5944	0.6534	1.7057	-0.2949	-0.2949
36	Tata Sons Pvt Ltd	-0.8211	-1.6356	-0.9872	1.1279	1.0134	-0.2605	-0.2605	-0.2605
37	Indian Farmers Fertilizer Cooperative Ltd	0.8322	1.0269	1.6619	0.7885	-0.2931	-1.1133	-1.0102	-1.0618
38	Inditrade Business Consultants Ltd	2.4114	0.1423	0.0169	-0.5082	0.0435	0.4123	-0.2906	0.0609
39	Jaquar & Co Pvt Ltd	-1.3021	0.2881	-1.3021	1.8783	-0.4293	-0.2588	-0.3441	-0.2588
40	Minda SAI Ltd	1.5000	-	1.5000	-1.5000	-	-	-	-
41	Tata Capital Ltd	-1.6804	-1.1899	0.1030	-0.6986	1.0716	0.0767	0.2936	0.1852
42	SFO Technologies Pvt Ltd	1.5090	0.1152	1.5090	-1.2786	0.3746	-0.6272	-0.1263	-0.6272
43	EbixCash World Money Ltd	-1.4804	0.0322	-1.4804	1.5448	0.1071	0.9234	0.0696	0.0696
44	Indian Seamless Enterprises Ltd	2.7611	-0.0890	-0.4901	0.0048	-0.5493	-0.4834	-0.5493	0.1291
45	Avana Logistek Ltd	1.1033	0.5755	2.2604	-0.6764	-0.5802	-0.5251	-0.5527	-0.5251
46	Royal Highland Distilleries Ltd	-0.8094	2.4377	-0.7124	-0.7124	0.3053	0.3053	0.3053	0.3053
47	Poly Hose India Rubber Pvt Ltd	-1.2193	-1.8293	-0.6093	-0.2731	1.0561	0.3513	0.7037	0.3513
48	Minda Rinder Pvt Ltd	-0.1429	-0.9254	-0.1429	-1.7079	1.6068	-0.0813	-0.0813	-0.0813
49	Olive Commercial Co Ltd	-0.5926	-0.5379	-0.6445	-0.7011	-0.4320	1.5542	1.3290	1.4416
50	BCL Secure Premises Pvt Ltd	-0.3096	-0.3172	-0.3020	-0.2386	-0.3323	-0.3602	-0.3463	-0.3602
51	JSW Cement Ltd	0.2008	0.6958	0.2008	1.1908	-0.3224	-1.6944	0.1867	0.1867
52	Carysil Ltd	0.9779	2.4438	0.0323	-0.3127	-0.5373	-0.7788	-0.6683	-0.7236
53	Adani Power Ltd	-0.3434	-0.2707	-0.3141	0.3092	-0.2159	-0.4743	-0.5621	-0.5182
54	Adani Green Energy Ltd	-1.0333	-0.7910	-1.0333	-0.5488	-0.1737	0.5962	1.9620	1.2791
55	Adani Transmission Ltd	1.0899	2.4535	-0.2737	-0.2885	-0.4723	-0.3960	-0.3898	-0.3929
56	Redribbon Modulex Buildings Ltd	-1.1721	-1.4158	-0.8931	-0.6316	0.6449	1.0095	1.2294	1.1194
57	Adani Enterprises Ltd	1.4967	1.8382	0.0689	0.0597	-1.0983	-0.8563	0.2660	-0.2951
58	Advanced Enzyme Technologies Ltd	2.4597	1.0167	0.0866	-0.3337	-0.5697	-0.6066	-0.5957	-0.6012
59	Allcargo Logistics Ltd	0.4901	-0.7206	-0.8757	-0.6961	1.1547	1.2401	0.7218	0.9810
60	Veecon Media & Television Ltd	1.0854	1.0840	0.2411	-1.0057	0.0070	0.1070	0.9189	0.5129
61	Asian Hotels East Ltd	1.9182	1.7816	-0.1684	-0.3776	-0.8311	-0.6783	-0.1187	-0.3985
62	Asahi India Glass Ltd	1.8750	1.4994	0.8112	-0.4713	-0.6018	-0.5903	-0.7914	-0.6909
63	AJR Infra and Tolling Ltd	-0.3128	-0.6431	-0.1151	0.8715	0.4239	0.4239	0.4239	0.4239
64	Amarjothi Spinning Mills Ltd	2.0744	0.8551	0.3481	-0.1566	-1.0721	-0.9124	-0.6277	-0.7700
65	Alankit Ltd	0.1647	-0.6085	-1.1571	-0.6085	0.4476	0.5686	0.6572	0.6129
66	Altran Technologies SASU	-1.8212	-1.0589	-0.2258	-0.3900	0.9917	1.0318	0.9917	-0.2529

S.No.	Company Name	Pre-Acquisition				Post-Acquisition			
		2013	2014	2015	2016	2019	2020	2021	2022
67	Amber Enterprises India Ltd	1.2821	1.4341	1.1301	0.5669	-0.7810	-0.9001	-0.2226	-0.5613
68	Nettle Infrastructure Investments Ltd	-0.0963	1.8156	1.1898	-0.5613	-0.8950	-0.8950	-0.8950	-0.8950
69	Asian Paints Ltd	-0.9170	0.2482	-1.4376	-0.3625	1.2876	0.2068	1.5435	0.8751
70	Apollo Tyres Ltd	-1.2286	-1.5064	-1.1491	0.0037	1.5194	0.8268	0.6017	0.7143
71	Aurobindo Pharma Ltd	1.8131	1.3383	0.7673	-0.3669	-0.4156	-0.7522	-1.1950	-0.9736
72	Anant Raj Ltd	-1.0165	-1.1374	-0.9118	-0.6183	1.2742	1.1774	-0.8170	0.1802
73	Ajmera Realty & Infra India Ltd	-0.1322	-0.9261	-0.6039	-0.0773	1.6626	0.5921	-1.5333	-0.4706
74	Adani Power Mundra Ltd	-1.7457	-0.6122	1.5825	0.4852	-0.2585	-0.2585	-0.2585	-0.2585
75	Aarvee Denims & Exports Ltd	-0.6358	-0.7887	-0.7391	-0.7990	-0.1155	0.8639	1.8866	1.3752
76	IndusInd Media & Communications Ltd	-0.6265	-1.1847	-0.0213	0.6810	1.4176	-1.1523	-0.5022	-0.8273
77	Ashapura Minechem Ltd	0.7745	0.7745	0.7745	0.7745	-1.1799	-1.1187	-1.1925	-1.1556
78	Vipani Hotels & Resorts Ltd	2.0966	0.8984	-0.1729	-0.8404	0.2549	0.0712	-1.4058	-0.6673
79	Asya Infosoft Ltd	-0.0883	-1.1553	-0.5137	-1.1553	0.5829	1.2716	0.9273	1.2716
80	AXISCADES Technologies Ltd	0.1071	-0.9178	-1.1968	-0.3614	1.3993	-0.3086	-0.8183	-0.5635
81	BCL Industries Ltd	1.0794	0.9510	0.8973	1.1942	-0.8355	-1.1229	-1.0679	-1.0954
82	Birla Corp Ltd	-1.1404	-0.9658	-1.0981	2.1385	0.2073	-0.1810	-0.0510	-0.1160
83	Bharat Forge Ltd	0.9600	-0.7764	0.3922	-1.5957	0.3103	1.0809	0.6414	0.8611
84	Bhagyanagar India Ltd	-0.7234	-0.6765	-0.9489	-0.2453	-0.5640	1.1489	1.4430	1.2960
85	Bio Green Papers Ltd	0.6171	0.7190	1.1030	1.2975	0.7126	0.5358	0.6212	0.5358
86	Bajaj Electricals Ltd	-0.3273	-0.1472	1.0947	0.0183	-0.0012	-0.6799	-1.3447	-1.0123
87	Bal Pharma Ltd	-1.4082	-1.6377	-0.0961	-0.4195	1.8044	0.6789	0.0937	0.3863
88	Balasore Alloys Ltd	2.0250	-1.5620	-1.1949	0.4062	0.5308	0.0969	0.5308	-0.0785
89	Heritage Nutrivet Ltd	1.3327	0.9135	1.2543	0.5420	-0.0216	-1.6585	-0.3492	-1.0038
90	Bodal Chemicals Ltd	2.7697	0.2375	-0.2208	-0.3905	-0.5046	-0.3471	-0.1929	-0.2700
91	Balrampur Chini Mills Ltd	0.9566	1.5284	1.2035	0.6876	-0.6183	-0.9621	-1.0516	-1.0069
92	Bharat Road Network Ltd	0.4944	1.7873	1.7873	-0.5901	-0.5846	-0.5807	-0.5573	-0.5690
93	BSE Ltd	0.9070	0.0713	1.7428	-0.3979	-0.7929	-0.7894	-0.7894	-0.7980
94	Infutec Healthcare Ltd	-0.1730	-0.6948	-0.1730	-1.2167	0.3163	1.6872	-0.1893	-0.1893
95	Indigrid 2 Ltd	-0.3288	-0.4618	-0.6015	-0.8753	1.9611	0.6599	-0.7143	-0.0272
96	Byke Hospitality Ltd/The	-0.3892	-0.6160	-0.8956	-1.0084	0.2350	1.0419	1.6568	1.3493
97	Future Speciality Retail Ltd	-0.2951	0.0443	2.1739	-1.4095	0.1284	0.1284	0.1284	0.1284
98	Calcom Vision Ltd	0.0477	0.0477	0.0477	-0.4293	2.3064	-0.4614	-1.2249	-0.8432
99	Cartrade Tech Ltd	0.1604	0.1604	0.1604	-1.4440	0.2136	0.0143	1.8579	0.9361
100	Chembond Chemicals Ltd	2.2203	1.4784	-0.2125	-0.3327	-0.5518	-0.6070	-0.6204	-0.6137
101	Coffee Day Enterprises Ltd	1.5689	1.7343	-0.1945	-0.0398	-0.8628	-1.0234	-0.7980	-0.9107
102	Ceat Ltd	2.3094	-0.3370	-0.9616	-0.6577	0.5784	-0.3740	0.5770	0.1015
103	California Software Co Ltd	0.1060	0.1060	-1.0350	-0.9083	-0.0561	0.4711	1.9316	1.2013
104	Chemfab Alkalis Ltd	0.0673	0.0673	0.0203	0.2924	1.3194	0.7975	-2.3653	-0.7839
105	Cholamandalam Financial Holdings Ltd	0.6338	0.2861	-1.9878	-1.6781	0.8127	0.6090	0.3865	0.4978
106	Cian Agro Industries & Infrastructure Ltd	2.5473	-0.7183	0.0943	-0.1443	-0.8949	0.1768	0.1768	0.1768
107	Spice Money Ltd	-1.7331	-1.0811	-0.6097	-0.3690	0.1398	1.2088	0.6743	1.2088
108	Colorchips New Media Ltd	2.1525	0.6520	-0.1042	0.3561	-0.9421	-0.9421	-0.9421	-0.9421
109	Confidence Petroleum India Ltd	0.2157	0.2346	0.1019	2.4696	-0.6520	-0.6640	-0.9420	-0.8030
110	Century Plyboards India Ltd	2.0974	1.0538	0.2829	0.2995	-0.7415	-0.9951	-0.9122	-0.9537
111	Cravatex Ltd	-0.9840	-1.0054	-0.8533	0.4612	-0.7597	-0.4438	0.9037	0.2300
112	Coromandel International Ltd	0.1977	2.0807	0.5572	0.1467	-0.4030	-1.1154	-1.1383	-1.1268
113	CRISIL Ltd	0.1069	0.1069	0.1069	-0.9624	-0.9624	1.9214	0.4311	1.1762
114	Cyient Ltd	-1.7434	-0.7545	-0.3361	-0.4889	1.8413	0.7614	0.6141	0.6877
115	Dalmia Bharat Ltd	1.2941	1.0476	1.2941	0.8010	-0.6603	-0.9246	-1.0861	-1.0053
116	Datamatics Global Services Ltd	1.4247	1.1682	0.8564	-0.8701	0.8813	-1.2345	-0.5380	-0.8863
117	Dilip Buildcon Ltd	-0.1544	1.9438	1.6689	-0.5382	-0.4357	-0.0235	-0.5034	-0.2634
118	Deep Industries Ltd	0.1762	0.1762	0.1762	0.1762	0.1762	-1.5855	1.9378	0.1762
119	DEN Networks Ltd	0.2230	0.1551	2.2050	0.3147	-1.0087	-0.9129	-1.0087	0.2402
120	Deepak Fertilisers & Petrochemicals Corp Ltd	-1.1180	-0.3242	0.6798	-0.6491	0.8915	-0.3546	-1.1159	-0.7353
121	Digicontent Ltd	0.1170	0.1170	0.1170	-1.0530	-0.3663	-0.3663	2.2536	0.9437
122	Avenue Supermarts Ltd	1.1605	1.4188	1.5121	0.2883	-0.8273	-0.8206	-0.7739	-0.7972
123	Donear Industries Ltd	1.8661	1.4873	0.4085	0.0288	-0.8943	-0.9811	-0.7202	-0.8506
124	Dr Reddy's Laboratories Ltd	1.6615	0.8066	-0.2194	0.8800	-1.1820	-0.9335	-0.8975	-0.9155
125	Synegra EMS Ltd	-1.5732	-1.2886	-0.7363	-0.4549	1.1531	0.7225	0.3776	0.5500
126	ABM Knowledgeware Ltd	-0.1124	-0.1120	-0.1020	0.9161	0.8695	-0.0548	-2.2541	-1.0934
127	Emami Realty Ltd	-0.3526	-0.1994	2.2915	1.2581	0.1274	-0.5055	-0.6724	-0.5890

S.No.	Company Name	Pre-Acquisition				Post-Acquisition			
		2013	2014	2015	2016	2019	2020	2021	2022
128	Eurofins Scientific SE	1.8065	0.0236	1.4032	-0.7323	0.4341	-0.5682	-1.2666	-0.9174
129	Eris Lifesciences Ltd	-0.5212	-0.5132	0.9870	-0.5416	-0.4507	-0.5073	-0.1117	-0.3095
130	ESAB India Ltd	-0.1659	-0.1659	-0.1659	-0.1659	1.2387	0.3430	-2.0794	-0.8682
131	Fermenta Biotech Ltd	-0.8551	-1.2748	-0.9094	-0.4129	0.3748	0.0451	0.0368	0.0409
132	Fortis Healthcare Ltd	0.8104	1.2976	0.1304	0.5046	-0.7602	-0.9275	-1.3587	-1.1431
133	Future Retail Ltd	-0.0957	-0.0957	-0.8879	-0.8517	-0.3328	1.6534	0.6603	1.6534
134	Future Supply Chain Solutions Ltd	0.1723	0.1723	-1.2826	-1.0138	0.7091	1.0901	1.0901	1.0901
135	Gallantt Ispat Ltd/Old	2.6617	-0.8265	-0.3024	0.0148	-0.4082	0.0270	-0.8226	-0.3978
136	Garnet International Ltd	-0.7148	-0.7148	-0.7045	-0.7467	-0.4784	0.1545	0.8950	0.5248
137	Godrej Consumer Products Ltd	0.6398	0.7071	0.7429	1.3967	-0.0188	-1.2147	-1.4490	-1.3319
138	Goodricke Group Ltd	-1.2218	-1.2235	-1.2235	0.1113	1.3642	0.5937	0.7202	0.6569
139	Genesis IBRC India Ltd	0.1762	1.9378	-1.5855	0.1762	0.1762	0.1762	0.1762	0.1762
140	Gillanders Arbuthnot & Co Ltd	0.2454	1.9868	1.1312	0.2624	-0.7022	-1.0827	-0.8924	-1.0827
141	Gloster Ltd	-0.0655	-0.0655	-0.0655	0.5896	1.2183	0.1433	-2.2133	-1.0350
142	JK Investors Bombay Ltd	-0.1547	-0.4020	-0.5825	-0.9689	0.3370	1.4002	1.2089	1.3045
143	Grandeur Products Ltd	-0.5140	-1.0985	-0.5140	-1.6830	1.0885	0.5542	-0.0050	-0.0050
144	Grasim Industries Ltd	-0.9406	-0.7681	-1.2625	-1.3536	1.1920	0.6123	0.1477	0.3800
145	Greenpanel Industries Ltd	-0.1029	-0.1029	-0.1029	0.9261	0.8491	-0.0548	-2.1320	-1.0934
146	Greatship India Ltd	-0.4830	0.6299	1.9378	0.6912	-0.3018	-1.1796	-0.7407	-1.1796
147	GTPL Hathway Ltd	0.7555	1.0182	0.4929	0.9038	-0.5927	-0.9975	-1.1188	-1.2993
148	Gujarat State Petronet Ltd	-0.1557	-0.3836	-0.4360	-0.6887	0.1844	-0.4980	-0.8374	-0.6677
149	Happiest Minds Technologies Ltd	-0.0502	-0.0502	-0.0502	-0.0502	1.4289	-2.0047	0.4252	-0.7897
150	Harish Textile Engineers Ltd	0.0097	0.0097	0.0097	-1.4951	0.2031	1.3210	0.7621	1.3210
151	Hester Biosciences Ltd	0.4013	0.4098	-0.2470	-0.4520	-0.1928	-0.9218	2.2700	0.6741
152	HCL Technologies Ltd	-0.4858	-0.7266	-0.7835	-1.1843	1.7382	0.7089	0.6575	0.6832
153	Hindustan Foods Ltd	1.4491	1.4491	1.4491	-0.6259	-0.6216	-0.6212	-0.6192	-0.6202
154	Hindware Home Innovation Ltd	-0.1375	-0.1375	-0.1375	-0.1375	1.6677	-0.9973	-1.0830	-1.0402
155	HFCL Ltd	0.6868	-0.8691	1.9604	0.9707	0.0393	0.1688	-1.4334	-0.6323
156	Hindustan Media Ventures Ltd	-1.3012	0.9738	2.2584	0.2233	-0.8004	-0.3422	-0.5713	-0.3422
157	Himatsingka Seide Ltd	-1.1160	-1.5695	-1.1132	-0.6695	1.0371	0.4178	0.9201	0.6690
158	Hi-Tech Gears Ltd/The	-1.4143	-1.4035	-1.4640	0.8526	0.3459	0.4415	0.5957	0.5186
159	HT Media Ltd	-0.8312	-1.6098	1.6626	1.0926	-0.4620	-0.8223	0.1408	-0.3407
160	Huhtamaki India Ltd	-1.4037	-1.5541	1.1821	1.5387	0.0109	-0.1994	0.0109	0.0236
161	IFB Industries Ltd	-0.4415	-0.6718	-0.8898	-0.7489	1.2941	0.7796	1.3893	1.0844
162	Sintex Prefab & Infra Ltd	1.5646	0.7763	1.5646	-0.0119	-0.9340	-0.9340	-0.0788	-0.0788
163	India Motor Parts and Accessories Ltd	1.5921	1.5989	1.0144	-0.4329	-0.4898	-0.8404	-0.8404	-0.8404
164	India Grid Trust	0.0812	0.0812	-0.9945	-0.8964	-0.4468	1.5668	1.0787	1.3228
165	Infosys Ltd	0.1273	0.1273	0.1273	0.1273	-0.2731	-1.6180	2.2730	0.3275
166	Info Edge India Ltd	-0.4390	-0.5189	-0.5309	-0.5323	2.6514	0.5314	-0.2308	0.1503
167	Scott Edil Pharmacia Ltd	-0.3371	-0.0121	-0.3371	0.3129	-1.1591	0.8958	1.5664	1.2311
168	Indian Oil Corp Ltd	1.5512	-0.0034	-1.0072	-1.1195	1.4612	0.3541	0.1665	0.2603
169	Ipca Laboratories Ltd	-0.3639	1.7918	1.0354	0.9908	-0.6468	-1.2615	-0.4125	-0.8370
170	IRB Infrastructure Developers Ltd	1.0972	0.7489	1.0993	0.1333	-1.5926	0.3728	-1.6635	-0.6453
171	IRB InvIT Fund	0.1161	0.1161	-1.1931	-0.8931	-0.1809	1.0776	1.4698	1.2737
172	Raymond Apparel Ltd	-0.8526	-0.4592	0.6740	-1.0694	0.0175	0.6813	1.6792	1.1803
173	Bharti Hexacom Ltd	-1.1938	-1.2335	-0.9325	-0.8681	1.2113	0.6184	0.6721	0.6453
174	Jaykay Enterprises Ltd	0.2154	0.1542	-1.4570	-0.4283	1.0274	0.5291	0.4883	0.5087
175	Jiya Eco-Products Ltd	1.2805	1.2805	0.3087	1.0642	-1.0559	-1.0502	-1.0559	0.2633
176	Jindal Worldwide Ltd	1.6069	1.1359	0.4423	-0.3601	-0.9650	-1.0905	-0.9470	-1.0187
177	Josts Engineering Co Ltd	-1.3039	-1.0569	0.0349	1.9184	0.7547	-0.7673	-0.0063	-0.7673
178	Jaiprakash Associates Ltd	-0.4639	-0.4712	-0.4718	-0.4587	-0.4422	-0.4127	2.5112	1.0493
179	Jindal Saw Ltd	1.6491	1.0904	0.9600	0.2877	-0.7691	-1.0750	-0.8346	-0.9548
180	JSW Energy Ltd	1.0572	0.6565	1.4525	1.0658	-0.3338	-1.0450	-1.2124	-1.1287
181	Jayshree Chemicals Ltd	0.1179	2.7584	-0.4318	-0.4291	-0.4426	-0.4421	-0.4426	0.1881
182	Kalyan Jewellers India Ltd	0.1947	0.3998	0.1947	0.6050	-1.4136	-0.7953	-1.0343	-0.9148
183	KDDL Ltd	1.7651	1.5124	-0.2986	-0.8823	0.6932	0.0585	-0.7205	-0.3310
184	Khemani Distributors & Marketing Ltd	2.5874	0.2971	0.2971	0.2971	-0.5843	-0.6091	-0.5850	-0.5971
185	Karma Energy Ltd	-0.2901	-0.4832	0.7403	-0.6256	0.9582	1.9066	-1.0599	0.4233
186	Kajaria Ceramics Ltd	2.1232	1.1956	0.6801	-0.1907	-0.5481	-0.7826	-0.6977	-0.7401
187	Kirloskar Oil Engines Ltd	-0.6099	-0.6609	-0.6604	-0.6837	-0.4355	0.6048	2.0969	1.3509
188	KPIT Technologies Ltd	0.1770	0.1770	0.1770	-1.5932	0.2545	1.3191	0.7277	1.0234

S.No.	Company Name	Pre-Acquisition				Post-Acquisition			
		2013	2014	2015	2016	2019	2020	2021	2022
189	Kalpataru Power Transmission Ltd	0.5769	1.9076	1.0311	0.0416	-0.0837	-1.2789	-0.4940	-0.8865
190	Kridhan Infra Ltd	0.7625	0.7014	0.4241	0.2129	-0.9965	-0.8982	-0.8982	-0.8982
191	Kemistar Corp Ltd	0.9582	1.8546	0.2548	-1.4852	0.1618	0.1618	0.1618	0.1618
192	Kothari Products Ltd	-0.6107	-0.9478	-0.5756	-0.9907	1.2451	1.3294	-0.9180	0.2057
193	Kothari Petrochemicals	0.7540	1.2097	0.5467	1.3116	-1.1340	-0.9379	0.2590	0.2590
194	Dishnet Wireless Ltd	-0.4234	1.9231	1.8705	-0.4956	-0.4713	-0.4716	-0.4785	-0.4751
195	Larsen & Toubro Ltd	1.0478	1.0417	0.6048	0.0750	0.6281	-0.8370	-1.8360	-1.3365
196	Lloyds Metals & Energy Ltd	-0.7063	-0.2685	1.6563	1.2692	-0.3496	-1.3193	0.2086	0.2086
197	Mahesh Developers Ltd	-0.0611	2.6566	-0.6071	-0.6025	-0.6181	0.1536	0.1536	0.1536
198	Maithan Alloys Ltd	2.1654	1.3614	0.4354	-0.4450	-0.6118	-0.5388	-0.6296	-0.5842
199	CE Info Systems Ltd	-0.1463	-0.1463	-0.1463	1.3163	0.4004	-0.6033	-1.6985	-1.1509
200	Matrimony.com Ltd	0.2377	0.2377	-1.7440	-0.4283	1.0274	0.5291	0.4883	0.5087
201	Kosmo One Business Park Ltd	0.2498	-0.0058	0.5054	1.9738	0.2425	-0.7428	0.4497	-0.1465
202	Megri Soft Ltd	0.9487	0.9487	0.9487	0.9487	0.9487	0.9487	0.9487	0.9487
203	Mahindra Lifespace Developers Ltd	1.6350	0.9925	1.6241	-0.3053	-0.6521	-0.6261	-0.6024	-0.6143
204	Mahindra & Mahindra Ltd	0.4573	0.3479	-1.7191	-0.3745	0.8093	-0.2253	1.6247	0.6997
205	MM Forgings Ltd	-1.2605	2.6144	-0.3008	-0.2062	-0.4038	0.0886	0.0886	0.0886
206	Mega Nirman and Industries Ltd	0.9853	1.7506	0.2199	-1.4852	0.1618	0.1618	0.1618	0.1618
207	Marathon Nextgen Realty Ltd	-0.9684	-0.9424	-0.7883	-0.9424	0.4070	0.8783	1.6497	1.2640
208	Moschip Technologies Ltd	-0.0013	-0.8826	0.2515	-0.8826	0.2070	0.9471	0.3341	0.6406
209	Marico Ltd	2.5249	0.7089	-0.1369	-0.9991	-0.1194	-0.3120	-0.5038	-0.4079
210	Majestic Research Services and Solutions Ltd	-0.9677	-0.0927	-0.7038	-0.9625	-0.3435	1.6746	0.6655	1.6746
211	Mirza International Ltd	1.3951	1.1337	-0.3009	-1.3776	1.2852	-0.2497	-1.1930	-0.7213
212	HCL Comnet Ltd	-0.2347	1.7561	0.5595	1.7561	-0.5636	-0.6517	-0.6931	-0.6724
213	Mawana Sugars Ltd	-0.2180	1.7052	0.2553	1.7052	0.0166	-0.7034	-0.1655	-0.4344
214	Mayur Leather Products Ltd	-1.3992	-0.9145	-0.8511	-0.8778	0.7557	1.6996	-0.2722	0.7137
215	Nazara Technologies Ltd	1.4313	0.9092	1.4313	0.3871	-0.9321	-1.0034	-0.9321	-0.0675
216	NBCC India Ltd	0.9486	0.9486	0.9486	0.9486	-0.9517	-0.9366	-0.9667	-0.9517
217	Satchmo Holdings Ltd	-1.8371	-1.7543	-0.4556	0.5782	0.5782	0.5782	0.5782	0.5782
218	Nettlinx Ltd	-1.7700	-1.0120	-0.6547	-0.0581	1.2567	0.1913	-0.1926	-0.0007
219	Nila Spaces Ltd	0.0886	0.0886	0.5056	1.1143	-0.6598	-1.2144	-0.9371	-1.2144
220	Nila Infrastructures Ltd	-0.8888	0.2089	-0.6941	1.4467	-0.4023	1.3922	-1.0003	0.1960
221	Natco Pharma Ltd	1.5527	2.0872	-0.5945	0.0677	-0.5059	-0.7166	-0.3472	-0.5319
222	Orient Beverages Ltd	-1.2596	-0.8173	-0.6434	-0.3654	-0.3251	1.2486	1.5228	1.3857
223	Orient Bell Ltd	1.8173	1.0178	0.6460	0.4983	-0.6464	-0.8849	-1.2638	-1.0744
224	Oracle Financial Services Software Ltd	-1.0976	-1.1001	-1.1001	-1.1001	1.2520	0.2723	0.4823	0.3773
225	Om Infra Ltd	1.5604	1.6811	1.0000	-0.4996	-0.6434	-0.4574	-0.4979	-0.4776
226	Oil & Natural Gas Corp Ltd	-1.1689	-1.0320	-1.7249	-0.1696	1.1731	1.1176	0.2613	0.6894
227	Oriental Rail Infrastructure Ltd	-1.0715	-0.7910	0.3410	0.8049	0.4984	-0.7594	-0.9677	-0.8635
228	Padmanabh Industries Ltd	-0.9671	-0.9041	-0.1132	-1.0056	1.1264	1.1264	1.1264	1.1264
229	Palco Metals Ltd	0.7486	-0.9548	0.0854	-0.4374	-1.1354	-0.1430	2.2450	0.9698
230	Parsvnath Developers Ltd	-0.7664	-0.7631	-0.7635	-0.7190	-0.1948	1.4244	1.4244	1.4244
231	Shree Pushkar Chemicals & Fertilisers Ltd	2.7430	0.0905	-0.6162	-0.7416	-0.3911	-0.3976	-0.1085	-0.2531
232	Pervasive Commodities Ltd	0.1296	0.1296	-1.1122	-1.0224	0.2377	1.2276	1.2276	1.2276
233	Peninsula Land Ltd	-0.7826	-0.7792	-0.7809	-0.7782	1.1619	1.1619	1.1619	1.1619
234	Prestige Estates Projects Ltd	-0.6867	-0.5622	0.1188	0.1501	1.4494	-1.0445	-0.8583	-0.9514
235	Phoenix Mills Ltd/The	0.7781	0.9786	1.4343	1.0001	-0.6969	-0.8579	-1.3495	-1.1037
236	Pidilite Industries Ltd	-0.9966	-0.8646	-0.6137	-0.7786	1.2037	0.9142	1.3306	1.1224
237	Pil Italica Lifestyle Ltd	0.1655	0.1655	0.1655	0.1655	-1.1850	-0.4434	2.1249	0.8408
238	Panacea Biotec Ltd	-0.1849	0.1965	0.3945	0.5044	1.1496	1.1496	-1.8019	-0.3261
239	Prakash Pipes Ltd	-0.0869	-0.0869	-0.0869	-0.0869	1.5994	-1.7223	-0.1377	-0.9300
240	Praxis Home Retail Ltd	0.0387	0.0387	-0.6223	-0.6191	-0.5089	-0.5089	2.4496	0.9703
241	Precision Camshafts Ltd	2.2132	1.4703	-0.2271	-0.7432	-0.3203	-0.3293	-0.5074	-0.4184
242	Pricol Ltd	-0.9102	0.0194	-0.1163	-1.1948	2.2821	-0.0234	-0.7771	-0.4002
243	Prime Urban Development India Ltd	-0.9704	-0.9715	-0.9368	-0.8800	0.6745	1.2603	1.2603	1.2603
244	Power Grid Corp of India Ltd	0.6733	0.9490	0.8223	0.5256	-0.8631	-0.6914	-1.7046	-1.1980
245	Reliance Communications Ltd	-1.1614	-1.2212	-1.1463	-1.1172	0.7743	0.7743	0.7743	0.7743
246	Rane Holdings Ltd	0.6115	0.1998	0.5918	-1.1553	-0.0507	-0.5757	1.9047	0.6645
247	Rain Industries Ltd	1.1888	1.2767	1.2729	0.6673	-0.7422	-0.6830	-1.2568	-0.9699
248	Rajapalayam Mills Ltd	1.8695	1.5188	0.7690	-0.7683	-0.4964	-0.4943	-0.4552	-0.4747
249	Royal Orchid Hotels Ltd	-0.5030	-0.9282	-1.0148	-0.5172	0.3111	1.2216	1.4775	1.3495

S.No.	Company Name	Pre-Acquisition				Post-Acquisition			
		2013	2014	2015	2016	2019	2020	2021	2022
250	Raymond Ltd	1.9256	1.1356	-0.6532	-0.5395	0.4436	0.4887	-1.1942	-0.3527
251	Saksoft Ltd	1.1160	0.6624	0.4438	1.2300	-0.8087	-0.9536	-1.4216	-1.1876
252	Samvardhana Motherson International Ltd/IN	1.1609	0.8715	1.1023	0.9080	-1.0687	-1.1004	-1.0687	0.2711
253	Sat Industries Ltd	0.1340	0.4277	2.4781	-1.2899	-0.2501	-0.4057	-0.1649	-0.2853
254	Sembcorp Industries Ltd	-1.6033	-1.0407	-0.7394	-0.3062	0.1655	1.4853	0.9658	1.2256
255	SEAMEC Ltd	-0.8784	-1.1768	-0.5800	-0.6591	0.2127	0.8811	1.2908	1.0860
256	Steel Exchange India Ltd	-0.6702	-0.4844	-0.6096	-0.1146	0.7662	-0.6404	-0.8165	-0.7284
257	Setubandhan Infrastructure Ltd	-0.6872	-0.5740	-0.7688	-0.6674	0.5004	1.1447	1.4868	1.3157
258	Sagar Cements Ltd	0.7486	-0.9471	0.0625	-0.4374	-1.1543	-0.1430	2.0825	0.9698
259	Smartlink Holdings Ltd	-0.9643	-0.9587	-0.9650	-0.9343	1.1447	0.7984	1.2578	1.0281
260	SH Kelkar & Co Ltd	0.2517	0.4412	-1.3734	-1.5900	0.2458	0.7784	1.2664	1.0224
261	Sical Logistics Ltd	0.2899	0.4205	0.6000	1.5218	-1.0975	-1.0975	-1.0975	-1.0975
262	Shristi Infrastructure Development Corp Ltd	-0.9019	-0.8541	-0.8010	-0.6362	-0.0754	1.4032	1.4032	1.4032
263	Singer India Ltd	-0.9110	-0.9110	-0.4787	0.1861	1.8279	1.3318	-0.7542	-0.6630
264	Alkem Laboratories Ltd	-0.9010	-1.1832	-0.3039	-0.3308	-0.9866	1.1947	0.9960	1.0953
265	Sobha Ltd	-1.6783	-0.6064	-0.4766	-0.6872	1.4664	1.3235	0.0441	0.6838
266	Span Divergent Ltd	0.4444	-1.1534	-1.1525	-0.8817	0.1822	1.2250	1.2250	1.2250
267	SRF Ltd	1.2735	1.6169	0.3233	-0.3446	-0.0823	-1.1602	-1.2139	-1.1871
268	TVS Srichakra Ltd	2.5430	0.6739	-0.7237	-0.1653	-0.4053	-0.9929	0.0174	-0.4878
269	Sonata Software Ltd	-0.8507	-0.4544	2.5487	-0.4276	0.2227	-0.0553	0.3801	0.1624
270	S&S Power Switchgear Ltd	-0.8237	-0.8205	-0.8242	-0.7503	1.1608	1.1608	1.1608	1.1608
271	Sunil Hitech Engineers Ltd	2.3384	0.4610	-0.5313	-0.0650	-1.1266	0.2153	0.2153	0.2153
272	Sun Pharmaceutical Industries Ltd	-0.4788	1.4762	0.5881	0.7313	-0.0272	-0.9617	-1.5047	-1.2332
273	Swan Energy Ltd	-0.5132	0.0270	0.4564	0.4183	-1.3526	0.9149	1.2963	1.1056
274	Surya Roshni Ltd	1.3777	0.8495	0.4300	0.7202	-0.1780	-1.0873	-1.5528	-1.3200
275	Talwalkars Better Value Fitness Ltd	-0.6305	0.5394	-1.0941	-1.7028	0.6834	1.3451	-0.2536	-0.2536
276	Tata Steel Ltd	0.7626	1.4337	0.5999	1.0884	0.0179	-0.8264	-1.6145	-1.2204
277	TeamLease Services Ltd	-0.7462	-0.3284	0.1518	-0.8085	2.5825	-0.3022	0.4922	0.0950
278	Tube Investments of India Ltd	-0.2010	0.9044	0.6244	0.9044	-1.5491	1.2804	-1.5240	-0.1218
279	Thermax Ltd	2.0081	1.7122	-0.2059	-0.8082	-0.6465	-0.3411	-0.2973	-0.3192
280	Ramco Cements Ltd/The	1.3207	1.8572	0.3633	-0.9070	0.0338	-0.2249	0.0011	-0.1119
281	Trejhara Solutions Ltd	-0.1888	-0.1888	-0.1888	1.6989	-0.6810	-0.7447	-1.0283	-0.8865
282	Trent Ltd	-0.5138	-0.8817	-0.9025	-0.7272	0.5489	0.6497	1.8640	1.2569
283	Torrent Pharmaceuticals Ltd	-1.0438	0.6217	-0.7781	-1.0967	0.9787	-0.2323	-0.7380	-0.4852
284	Tata Chemicals Ltd	1.7369	1.7295	0.6179	-0.4540	-0.2484	-0.5165	-0.7470	-0.6317
285	TVS Motor Co Ltd	-1.1657	-0.9810	-1.1882	-1.2238	1.0291	0.7517	0.9572	0.8545
286	Universal Autofoundry Ltd	-0.2174	0.4933	-0.9282	-1.5071	-0.1958	0.2836	1.8050	1.0443
287	Uniply Decor Ltd	0.4542	2.2504	0.1406	0.4043	-0.9382	-0.8928	0.2289	0.2289
288	UFO Moviez India Ltd	0.8717	0.2748	-0.9626	-1.1428	-0.0578	1.2443	0.8514	1.0478
289	Umiya Tubes Ltd	1.7793	1.2269	-0.9307	-1.0530	0.2556	0.2556	0.2556	0.2556
290	UNO Minda Ltd	2.0917	0.3037	0.6865	-0.6468	0.7170	-0.1946	-1.3402	-0.7674
291	UPL Ltd	-1.1193	-1.2864	-0.3073	-0.2744	1.1518	0.2473	0.0077	0.1275
292	Varroc Engineering Ltd	0.1523	0.2286	-0.7359	-1.7039	0.3122	0.3331	0.3227	0.3331
293	Varun Beverages Ltd	2.3480	1.2411	0.0835	-0.4893	-0.5198	-0.5561	-0.5844	-0.5702
294	Vikas Lifecare Ltd	-0.1762	-0.1762	-0.1762	-0.1762	-0.1762	1.5855	-1.9378	-0.1762
295	Hemisphere Properties India Ltd	-1.2685	-0.9373	-0.6736	-0.7962	1.0915	1.0185	1.1925	1.1055
296	Vidhi Specialty Food Ingredients Ltd	1.3695	1.5217	1.2173	0.0083	-1.1454	-0.4217	-0.7835	-0.4217
297	Vardhman Textiles Ltd	2.1758	1.0083	0.7840	-0.2265	-0.6145	-0.6221	-0.9320	-0.7771
298	Vinayak Vanijya Ltd	-0.9179	-0.9122	-0.9235	1.0472	-0.9933	0.8971	0.8618	0.8794
299	White Organic Agro Ltd	2.2735	1.4489	-0.4680	-0.4679	-0.4658	-0.4623	-0.4640	-0.4623
300	Windsor Machines Ltd	-1.3480	1.7779	1.0947	0.6569	-0.2524	-0.4303	-1.1714	-0.8008
301	WPIL Ltd	1.4008	-1.1114	1.4591	1.0417	0.4091	-0.4154	-0.6526	-0.5340
302	Yaari Digital Integrated Services Ltd	-1.1507	-0.8382	-0.6584	1.1466	1.8803	-0.4903	0.6814	0.0956
303	Zee Entertainment Enterprises Ltd	-0.8427	-0.8343	1.7764	1.5715	-0.2781	-0.5482	-0.8415	-0.6949
304	Zee Media Corp Ltd	-0.2433	2.2560	0.3701	-1.1223	-0.1216	0.5456	0.0189	0.2822
305	Zensar Technologies Ltd	0.3856	0.0665	-0.3188	-0.6522	2.3747	0.0192	-0.2377	-0.1092
306	Zee Learn Ltd	1.1690	1.6591	1.4491	-0.3245	-0.7725	-0.5660	-0.5570	-0.5615
307	Zuari Agro Chemicals Ltd	0.9193	0.3135	-0.0301	-1.0854	1.7527	-1.3220	0.4658	-0.4281
308	Zydus Lifesciences Ltd	1.3319	0.5271	-0.7211	1.0250	0.5350	-0.9959	-1.4515	-1.2237

Source: *Compiled by Author*

Table 4.1.30 illustrates a comprehensive examination of the debt and equity ratios both before and after the acquisition. The years 2013, 2014, 2015, and 2016 may be characterised as pre-acquisition years, whereas the years 2019, 2020, 2021, and 2022 can be defined as post-acquisition years. It is a widely held belief that a lower debt equity ratio is indicative of a more advantageous financial condition. Based on the aforementioned analysis, it can be deduced that prior to acquisition, a majority of the companies exhibited a negative ratio, indicating negative shareholder equity. This implies that the liabilities of the company exceeded its assets, and subsequently, this ratio either decreased negatively or became positive following the acquisition. The alteration in the debt-equity ratio yields a favourable influence on the financial performance of the firms subsequent to the acquisition.

Table 4.1.31 -Comparison of Pre- and Post-Merger and Acquisition

Variable	Merger		Acquisition	
	Pre	**Post**	**Pre**	**Post**
Objective 1: Financing Pattern				
R squared Sales	0.122	-0.019	0.051	0.045*
Return on Capital Employed	-0.058	-0.064	-0.045	-0.133***
Return with Total Assets	-0.122*	-0.080	-0.073**	-0.131***

Note: *p<0.1, **p<0.05, ***p<0.01

Table 4.1.31 presents a comparative analysis of the influence of the R-squared sales and return on capital employed on the debt-equity ratio before and after a merger and acquisition event. The analysis reveals that the variable of R-squared sales exhibited a favourable influence on the debt equity ratio prior to the merger, but subsequently displayed a negative impact following the merger. However, following an acquisition, the coefficient of the r-squared sales variable has decreased, indicating a positive influence on the debt-equity ratio. The return on capital employed and return on total assets have negative values both before and after the merger and acquisition, indicating a detrimental effect on the debt-equity ratio.

Table 4.1.32 -Regression Analysis of Financing Pattern on DER

Null Hypotheses	Description	Accept/Reject
$Ho_{1.1}$	There is no impact of R squared Sales on DER before the merger	Fail to Reject
$Ho_{1.2}$	There is no impact of ROCE on DER before the merger	Fail to Reject
$Ho_{1.3}$	There is no impact of RWTA on DER before the merger	Rejected
$Ho_{1.4}$	There is no impact of R squared Sales on DER after the merger	Fail to Reject
$Ho_{1.5}$	There is no impact of ROCE on DER after the merger	Fail to Reject
$Ho_{1.6}$	There is no impact of RWTA on DER after the merger	Fail to Reject
$Ho_{1.7}$	There is no impact of R squared Sales on DER during the merger	Rejected
$Ho_{1.8}$	There is no impact of ROCE on DER during the merger	Rejected
$Ho_{1.9}$	There is no impact of RWTA on DER during the merger	Fail to Reject
$Ho_{1.10}$	There is no impact of R squared Sales on DER on the overall merger	Fail to Reject
$Ho_{1.11}$	There is no impact of ROCE on DER on the overall merger	Rejected
$Ho_{1.12}$	There is no impact of RWTA on DER on the overall merger	Fail to Reject
$Ho_{1.13}$	There is no impact of R squared Sales on DER before acquisition	Fail to Reject
$Ho_{1.14}$	There is no impact of ROCE on DER before acquisition	Fail to Reject
$Ho_{1.15}$	There is no impact of RWTA on DER before acquisition	Rejected

Null Hypotheses	Description	Accept/Reject
$Ho_{1.16}$	There is no impact of R squared Sales on DER after acquisition	Rejected
$Ho_{1.17}$	There is no impact of ROCE on DER after acquisition	Rejected
$Ho_{1.18}$	There is no impact of RWTA on DER after acquisition	Rejected
$Ho_{1.19}$	There is no impact of R squared Sales on DER during acquisition	Fail to Reject
$Ho_{1.20}$	There is no impact of ROCE on DER during acquisition	Rejected
$Ho_{1.21}$	There is no impact of RWTA on DER during acquisition	Rejected
$Ho_{1.22}$	There is no impact of R squared Sales on DER on overall acquisition	Fail to Reject
$Ho_{1.23}$	There is no impact of ROCE on DER on overall acquisition	Rejected
$Ho_{1.24}$	There is no impact of RWTA on DER on overall acquisition	Rejected

Source: *Compiled by Author from R output sheet*

It may be concluded from the above regression analysis in the case of the merger there is a more negative effect after the merger in the case of return on capital employed and r-squared sales. However, the negative impact of return with total assets has reduced after the merger which shows a positive impact of this variable on the debt-equity ratio. Although, in the case of an acquisition the coefficient of r squared sales is positive pre- and post-acquisition. But this coefficient has reduced after acquisition which means post-acquisition the impact of this variable has declined on the debt-equity ratio of the company. Similarly, the negative effect of the other two variables has increased post-acquisition on the debt-equity ratio.

4.3 Stochastic Frontier results of the objective two

The operating efficiency of the firm is determined by the success or failure of the business. Few of the studies (Halkos & Tzeremes, 2013; Liu et al., 2022; Moatti et al., 2015) have considered operating performance or efficiency. However, this study is different in various aspects such as method, variables, time frame, and geographical area. In this study, stochastic frontier analysis is taken into consideration to get the technical inefficiency and time-invariant model.

Table 4.2.1 -Descriptive Statistics of Operating Efficiency - Merger

Statistic	N	Mean	St. Dev.	Min	Max
PR_OPM	292	0.101833	0.710503	-2.268302	2.425858
PR_OROA	292	0.481128	1.962816	-2.513585	15.798385
PR_SALES	292	-0.256637	0.525931	-1.197058	2.81252
PR_FAT	292	0.258665	0.722424	-1.606139	2.585211
PR_IT	292	0.145465	0.666665	-2.020318	2.741206
PR_ROA	292	2.20826	2.909007	-2.653158	11.826394
PO_OPM	292	0.191927	1.256827	-2.556054	3.116862
PO_OROA	292	0.257923	2.205555	-2.401824	15.798385
PO_SALES	292	0.707036	1.166132	-2.279127	3.093781
PO_FAT	292	0.040614	1.179321	-2.187202	3.046673
PO_IT	292	0.40758	1.279767	-2.092871	3.145719
PO_ROA	292	1.970498	2.947757	-3.245817	13.350071

Source: *Compiled by Author from Stata output sheet*

Table 4.2.1 depicts the descriptive statistics of the dependent as well as independent variables used in this study in the case of pre-merger and post-merger. The mean of operating return on assets, five-year average turnover, inventory turnover, and return on assets is 0.481128, 0.258665, 0.145465, and 2.20826 respectively before the merger which has become 0.257923, 0.040614, 0.40758, and 1.970498 after the merger. The mean of only five-year average turnover and inventory turnover has increased post-merger, thereby indicating a positive impact of the inventory turnover and five-year average turnover post-merger. However, the mean of Sales was negative before the merger which has become positive after the merger. Thereby indicating a positive impact of sales on the operating performance of the companies after the merger. The standard deviation defines the risk, in this case, the standard deviation of operating return on assets, sales, five-year average turnover, inventory turnover, and return on assets is high in the post-merger scenario thereby indicating more risk is involved after the merger. In the next table, the impact of operating return on assets and five-year average turnover on the operating efficiency or profit margin of the company is analyzed before the merger in different models of stochastic frontier analysis.

Table 4.2.2 -Impact of OROA and FAT on Operating Efficiency Before Merger

	Dependent variable		
	Operating Profit Margin		
	(1)	(2)	(3)
oroa	0.8014927***	0.8010874***	0.8014919***
	(0.0339247)	(0.0337054)	(0.0338701)
fat	-0.1143965***	-0.1174498***	-0.1143941***
	(0.0376212)	(0.036847)	(0.0374015)
constant	0.0893244**	0.088227***	0.089313***
	(0.0452509)	(0.031371)	(0.0354902)
lnsigma2	3.158029	3.278282***	3.140437***
	(6.463653)	(0.0066405)	(0.006649)
ilgtgamma	5.000421	5.119537***	4.9827***
	(6.508752)	(0.0934642)	(0.0942744)
mu	-181.364	-191.2398	-178.2766
	(1180.71)		
eta	0.0540818		0.0541157
	(0.1221278)		(0.1025063)
sigma2	23.52419	26.53014	23.11396
	(152.0522)	(0.1761742)	(0.1536846)
gamma	0.9933099	0.9940567	0.9931912
	(0.0432526)	(0.0005522)	(0.0006375)
sigma_u2	23.36682	26.37247	22.95658
	(152.0524)	(0.1756323)	(0.1530228)
sigma_v2	0.1573782	0.1576755	0.1573794
	(0.0150745)	(0.146944)	(0.014796)
Note:			*p<0.1; **p<0.05; ***p<0.01

Source: *Compiled by Author from Stata output sheet*

Table 4.2.2 presents the different models of Stochastic Frontier analysis before the merger. The first model relates to the Time-varying decay model (truncated – normal), the second model relates to the Time invariant inefficiency model, and the third model relates to the Time-varying decay inefficiency model. In the time-varying decay model (truncated -normal), the coefficient of mu i.e., -181.364 implies that a one percent increase in operating ROA and a five-year average turnover of pre-merger will result in a decline of the growth rate. From the z value, it can be said that pre-operating return on assets and pre-five-year average turnover have a significant impact on operating margin.

In the Time invariant inefficiency model, the coefficient of operating ROA is 0.8010874 which indicates that the operating performance in pre-merger has improved across all companies. Pre-operating return on assets, and pre-five-year average turnover significant values in influencing pre-operating margin at 1% level. In time-varying decay inefficiency, the operating ROA positively influences the operating margin before the merger. However, the five-year average turnover is negatively influencing the operating margin. The coefficient value of OROA and five-year average annual turnover is significant in pre-merger at the 1% level.

Further, the impact of inventory turnover and return on assets on operating efficiency is evaluated using three different models of stochastic frontier analysis before the merger.

Table 4.2.3 -Impact of IT and ROA on Operating Efficiency Before Merger

	Dependent variable		
	Operating Profit Margin		
	(1)	(2)	(3)
it	-0.0146971	-0.0245142	-0.0146971
	(0.063624)	(0.0702975)	(0.063624)
roa	-0.0093162	0.00705	-0.0093161
	(0.0223278)	(0.0190437)	(0.0223279)
constant	0.5159532***	1.098567	0.5159536***
	(0.2092374)	(2.240585)	(0.2092384)
lnsigma2	-1.029742***	-0.8719139***	-1.029742***
	(0.1629329)	(0.1013601)	(0.1629325)
ilgtgamma	-1.722538*	-1.466137***	-1.722539*
	(0.901036)	(0.5199197)	(0.9010341)
mu	0.0767474	1.010723	0.0767487
	(0.5807492)	(2.24603)	(0.5807492)
eta	0.3481527		0.3481523*
	(0.2178607)		(0.2178612)
sigma2	0.3570992	0.4181505	0.3570991
	(0.0581832)	(0.0423838)	(0.0581831)
gamma	0.1515445	0.1875305	0.1515444
	(0.1158541)	(0.0792164)	(0.1158538)
sigma_u2	0.0541164	0.078416	0.0541164
	(0.0482697)	(0.0367117)	(0.0482695)
sigma_v2	0.3029828	0.3397345	0.3029827
	(0.0334928)	(0.0383582)	(0.0334928)
Note:	*p<0.1; **p<0.05; ***p<0.01		

Source: *Compiled by Author from Stata output sheet*

Table 4.2.3 presents the different models of Stochastic Frontier analysis before the merger. The first model relates to the Time-varying decay model (truncated – normal), the second model relates to the Time invariant inefficiency model and the third model relates to the Time-varying decay inefficiency model.

In the time-varying decay model (truncated -normal), the coefficient of *mu* i.e., 0.0767474 implies that for a one percent increase in ROA and inventory turnover of pre-merger, the growth rate will rise by 7.67 percent. From the z value, it can be said that return on assets and inventory turnover have an insignificant impact on operating margin. In the Time invariant inefficiency model, the coefficient of ROA is 0.00705 which indicates that the operating performance in pre-merger has improved across all companies. ROA, inventory turnover has an insignificant value in influencing pre-operating margin.

In time-varying decay inefficiency, the ROA and inventory turnover negatively influence the operating margin before the merger. The coefficient value of ROA and inventory turnover are also insignificant like in other models. Further, the impact of sales on operating efficiency is also analyzed before the merger in Table 4.2.4.

Table 4.2.4 -Impact of Sales on Operating Efficiency Before Merger

	Dependent variable		
	Operating Profit Margin		
	(1)	(2)	(3)
Sales	0.1270964*	0.1629605**	0.1270964*
	(0.0867172)	(0.0801089)	(0.0867172)
constant	0.7704284*	1.381229*	0.770428*
	(0.477068)	(21.18621)	(0.4770678)
lnsigma2	-0.7328432***	-0.7027942***	-0.7328432***
	(0.0879531)	(0.0847187)	(0.0879531)
ilgtgamma	-2.062577***	-1.934321***	-2.062577***
	(0.5701076)	(0.5219889)	(0.5701077)
mu	0.55635	1.237603	0.5563495
	(0.5169583)	(21.18631)	(0.5169583)
eta	0.0800819		0.080082
	(0.0987212)		(0.0987213)
sigma2	0.4805408	0.4951997	0.4805408
	(0.042265)	(0.0419527)	(0.0422651)
gamma	0.1127877	0.126273	0.1127877
	(0.0570488)	(0.0575901)	(0.0570488)
sigma_u2	0.0541991	0.0625304	0.0541991
	(0.0289305)	(0.0300994)	(0.0289305)
sigma_v2	0.4263417	0.4326693	0.4263417
	(0.0407966)	(0.041351)	(0.0407966)
Note:		*p<0.1; **p<0.05; ***p<0.01	

Source: *Compiled by Author from Stata output sheet*

Table 4.2.4 displays the various models used in Stochastic Frontier analysis before the occurrence of a merger. The initial model pertains to the Time-Varying Decay Model (Truncated-Normal), while the second model pertains to the Time Invariant Inefficiency Model. Lastly, the third model pertains to the Time-Varying Decay Inefficiency Model.

The time-varying decay model, specifically the truncated-normal variant, indicates that the coefficient of mu, denoted as 0.55635, signifies that a one percent increase in turnover will result in a growth rate increase of 55.63 percent. Based on the calculated z value, it can be concluded that Sales exert a statistically significant influence on the operating margin at a significance level of 10%.

According to the Time Invariant Inefficiency Model, the Coefficient of Sales is determined to be 0.1629605. This value suggests that the operating performance of all companies involved in the merger has exhibited improvement. The sales variable demonstrates a substantial impact on the pre-operating margin, with statistical significance observed at a 5% level.

In the context of a time-varying decay inefficiency model, it is observed that the turnover has a positive influence on the operating margin before the merger. The significance of the coefficient value of turnover is consistent with that observed in other models. Finally, the results of all the variables are analyzed together before the merger to show its effect on the operating efficiency of the company.

Table 4.2.5 displays the various models used in stochastic frontier analysis before the occurrence of a merger. The initial model pertains to the Time-Varying Decay Model (Truncated-Normal), while the second model pertains to the Time Invariant Inefficiency Model. Lastly, the third model pertains to the Time-Varying Decay Inefficiency Model.

The time-varying decay model, particularly the truncated-normal variant, suggests that the coefficient of Mu, represented as β, indicates that an increase in OROA and Sales will lead to a decrease in the growth rate, as the coefficient of Mu is negative. Based on the computed z value, it can be inferred that, except for Sales, all other variables demonstrate a statistically significant impact on the operating margin at significance levels of 1% and 5%. According to the Time Invariant Inefficiency Model, the Coefficient of OROA and Sales is determined to be 0.7705649 and 0.0272069 respectively. This value suggests that the operating performance of all companies

Table 4.2.5 -Stochastic Frontier Results of Operating Efficiency Before Merger

	Dependent variable		
	Operating Profit Margin		
	(1)	(2)	(3)
roa	-0.0355318***	-0.0333951***	-0.035735***
	(0.0104611)	(0.0100065)	(0.009897)
oroa	0.7676655***	0.7705649***	0.7662328***
	(0.0390413)	(0.0381558)	(0.0376089)
sales	0.0055321	0.0272069	-0.0031624
	(0.0526142)	(0.0499066)	(0.0506374)
fat	-0.1128918***	-0.1248448***	-0.0977033***
	(0.0381228)	(0.0373545)	(0.0383682)
it	-0.0854208**	-0.0828405**	-0.0755222**
	(0.0387517)	(0.0382555)	(0.0377816)
constant	0.1555872***	0.0835573**	34.55969
	(0.0599961)	(0.0369137)	(393.4399)
lnsigma2	-1.603217***	-1.927589***	-2.028031***
	(0.4164183)	(0.0935088)	(0.101063)
ilgtgamma	-0.5504535	-2.631423***	-13.59954
	(1.204459)	(0.1005187)	
mu	-2.163775	-3.697175	34.39617
			(393.4381)
eta	0.4754548*		0.0017919
	(0.3212053)		(0.0204286)
sigma2	0.2012481	0.1454985	0.1315944
	(0.0838034)	(0.0136054)	(0.0132932)
gamma	0.3657592	0.0671433	0.00000124
	(0.2794097)	(0.006296)	
sigma_u2	0.0736084	0.0097692	0.000000163
	(0.0862518)	(0.0000746)	
sigma_v2	0.1276398	0.1357293	0.1315942
	(0.0141017)	(0.0136051)	
Note:		*p<0.1; **p<0.05; ***p<0.01	

Source: *Compiled by Author from Stata output sheet*

before the merger has exhibited improvement. The OROA, ROA, FAT, and IT demonstrate a substantial impact on the pre-operating margin, with statistical significance observed at a 1% and 5% level. ROA, five-year average annual turnover, and inventory are negatively influencing the operating performance of the companies before the merger.

In the context of a model that accounts for time-varying decay inefficiency, empirical evidence suggests that the operating return on assets (ROA) exerts a positive impact on the operating margin in the period preceding the merger. Nevertheless, it is worth noting that all other variables exhibit a detrimental impact on the operational performance of the companies before the merger. With the exception of turnover, all other variables exhibit a statistically significant impact at a significance level of 1%. Further, the impact of operating return on assets and five-year average turnover is discussed in the case of after-merger using three different models of stochastic frontier analysis.

Table 4.2.6 -Impact of OROA and FAT on Operating Efficiency After Merger

	Dependent variable		
	Operating Profit Margin		
	(1)	(2)	(3)
oroa	0.9151801***	0.9142983***	0.906867***
	(0.0311758)	(0.0297752)	(0.0308345)
fat	0.0537782*	0.0525538*	0.0445523*
	(0.0340955)	(0.0315005)	(0.0326475)
constant	1.164421	1.386223	315.6581
	(1.082942)	(5.704662)	
lnsigma2	-1.327639***	-1.331696***	-1.335568***
	(0.1093126)	(0.09854)	(0.0983877)
ilgtgamma	-0.8740387**	-0.890765***	-0.8955204***
	(0.3789595)	(0.3304859)	(0.3305397)
mu	0.9956765	1.21218	315.4458***
	(1.045597)	(5.705409)	(0.0606308)
eta	-0.003649		0.0000802
	(0.0414722)		(0.0000884)
sigma2	0.2651025	0.264029	0.2630087
	(0.028979)	(0.0260174)	(0.0258768)
gamma	0.2944146	0.290952	0.2899719
	(0.078723)	(0.0681789)	(0.0680542)
sigma_u2	0.07805	0.0224833	0.0762651
	(0.0266958)	(0.0768198)	(0.0223248)
sigma_v2	0.1870524	0.1872093	0.1867435
	(0.019077)	(0.019021)	(0.0189709)
Note:		*p<0.1; **p<0.05; ***p<0.01	

Source: *Compiled by Author from Stata output sheet*

Table 4.2.6 displays the various models utilized in the stochastic frontier analysis subsequent to the merger. The initial model pertains to the Time-Varying Decay Model (Truncated-Normal), while the second model pertains to the Time Invariant Inefficiency Model. Lastly, the third model pertains to the Time-Varying Decay Inefficiency Model.

In the context of a time-varying decay model, specifically the truncated-normal model, the coefficient of Mu is determined to be 0.9956765. This coefficient signifies that a one percent increase in the operating return on assets (OROA) and the five-year average turnover post-merger will lead to an increase in the growth rate. Nevertheless, the coefficient of Mu exhibited a negative value prior to the occurrence of the merger. Based on the calculated z value, it can be concluded that the post-operating return on assets and the post-five-year average turnover have a statistically significant influence on the operating margin, with significance levels of 1% and 10% respectively.

According to the Time Invariant Inefficiency Model, the Coefficient of Operating Return on Assets (OROA) experienced a significant increase from 0.8010874 before the merger to 0.9142983 after the merger. This indicates an approximate improvement of 11 percent in the operating performance subsequent to the merger. The coefficient of the five-year average turnover after the merger is positive, suggesting that the operating performance has improved compared to before the merger when the coefficient was negative. Additionally, the post-operating return on assets and the post-five-year average turnover has significant effects on the post-operating margin, with significant values at the 1% and 10% levels, respectively.

The merger has a positive impact on the operating margin, as evidenced by the positive influence of both the operating return on assets (OROA) and the five-year average turnover in the context of time-varying decay inefficiency. However, the only positive aspect in terms of operating return on assets (OROA) was observed prior to the merger. Hence, it can be asserted that both variables have exerted a positive influence on the operational performance of the company's post-merger. The significance levels of the coefficient values for OROA and the five-year average annual turnover in the post-merger context are 1% and 10% respectively. In the next segment, the impact of inventory turnover and return on assets on operating efficiency after merger using three different models of stochastic frontier analysis is discussed.

Table 4.2.7 displays the various models of Stochastic Frontier analysis subsequent to the merger. The initial model pertains to the Time-Varying Decay Model (Truncated-Normal), while the second model pertains to the Time Invariant Inefficiency Model. Lastly, the third model pertains to the Time-Varying Decay Inefficiency Model.

In the context of a time-varying decay model, specifically the truncated-normal model, the coefficient of Mu is estimated to be 0.0621751. This coefficient indicates that a one percent increase in both the return on assets (ROA) and inventory turnover following a merger will result in a decline of 6.21 percent in the growth rate. Nevertheless, the coefficient exhibited a positive value prior to the merger. Based on the calculated z value, it can be concluded that the influence of return on assets and inventory turnover

Table 4.2.7 -Impact of IT and ROA on Operating Efficiency After Merger

	Dependent variable		
	Operating Profit Margin		
	(1)	(2)	(3)
it	0.5090748***	0.5285834***	0.5090748***
	(0.0558719)	(0.0528863)	(0.0558714)
roa	0.1562663***	0.1545546***	0.1562663***
	(0.0266004)	(0.0268327)	(0.0266003)
constant	0.0230109	-0.0129856	0.0230118
	(0.2600295)	(0.2198516)	(0.2599977)
lnsigma2	0.1083923	0.3478557	0.1083894
	(0.4196521)	(0.9614658)	(0.4195589)
ilgtgamma	-1.479752	-0.5954745	-1.479765
	(2.272867)	(2.699881)	(2.272388)
mu	-0.0621751	-0.6258835	-0.0621627
	(1.690275)	(4.003949)	(1.689867)
eta	0.1335102		0.1335101
	(0.128131)		(0.1281303)
sigma2	1.114485	1.416028	1.114482
	(0.4676959)	(1.361462)	(0.4675907)
gamma	0.1854648	0.3553797	0.1854629
	(0.3433567)	(0.6185021)	(0.3432815)
sigma_u2	0.2066977	0.5032276	0.206695
	(0.4670728)	(1.357681)	(0.4669671)
sigma_v2	0.9077871	0.9128003	0.9077866
	(0.0979945)	(0.0986025)	(0.0979944)
Note:			*p<0.1; **p<0.05; ***p<0.01

Source: *Compiled by Author from Stata output sheet*

on operating margin is not statistically significant during the pre-merger period. However, following the merger, this relationship has become statistically significant at a 1% level of significance.

According to the Time Invariant Inefficiency Model, the coefficient of Return on Assets (ROA) after the merger is 0.1545546, compared to 0.00705 before the merger. This suggests that the operating performance has improved by approximately 15 percent after the merger, as indicated by the increased value of the ROA coefficient. Subsequent to the merger, the ROA and Inventory turnover have attained statistical significance at a 1% level. The previously negative inventory turnover has experienced a positive shift following the merger. This change has had a beneficial effect on the operational performance of the companies subsequent to the merger.

In time-varying decay inefficiency, the ROA and inventory turnover are positively influencing the operating margin after the merger which was influencing negatively before the merger. The coefficient value of ROA and inventory turnover are also significant at a 1% level after the merger which was insignificant before the merger. In the next table, the impact of sales on operating efficiency after the merger using three different models of stochastic frontier analysis.

Table 4.2.8 - Impact of Sales on Operating Efficiency After Merger

	Dependent variable		
	Operating Profit Margin		
	(1)	(2)	(3)
sales	0.657285***	0.6695934***	0.657285***
	(0.0488123)	(0.0471083)	(0.0488123)
constant	0.1258902	0.1256709	0.1258944
	(0.1010591)	(0.1023946)	(0.1010608)
lnsigma2	4.9138084	3.029328	4.900433
	(8.78181)	(7.462093)	(8.804767)
ilgtgamma	5.12129	3.203862	5.108564
	(8.835199)	(7.765217)	(8.85896)
mu	-390.0716	-47.9886	-385.1255
	(3452.628)	(380.8856)	(3418.145)
eta	0.0910236		0.0910217
	(0.1085107)		(0.1085102)
sigma2	136.0584	20.68332	134.348
	(1194.839)	(154.3409)	(1182.903)
gamma	0.9940671	0.9609793	0.9939916
	(0.0521074)	(0.2911805)	(0.0529087)
sigma_u2	135.2512	19.87625	133.5408
	(1194.84)	(154.3405)	(1182.903)
sigma_v^2	0.8072219	0.8070769	0.8072217
	(0.0741483)	(0.0742296)	(0.0741483)
Note:	*p<0.1; **p<0.05; ***p<0.01		

Source: *Compiled by Author from Stata output sheet*

Table 4.2.8 displays the various models used in Stochastic Frontier analysis after the merger. The initial model pertains to the Time-Varying Decay Model (Truncated-

Normal), while the second model pertains to the Time Invariant Inefficiency Model. Lastly, the third model pertains to the Time-Varying Decay Inefficiency Model.

The time-varying decay model, specifically the truncated-normal variant, indicates that the coefficient of Mu, denoted as 390.0716 after the merger was 0.5563 before the merger. Before the merger, the coefficient was positive which signifies that a one percent increase in turnover will result in a growth rate increase of 55.63 percent. However, it has become negative post-merger which means that a one percent increase in turnover will result in a decline in the growth rate of operating performance. Based on the calculated z value, it can be concluded that Sales exert a statistically significant influence on the operating margin at a significance level of 1% after the merger which was at 10% before the merger.

According to the Time Invariant Inefficiency Model, the Coefficient of Sales is determined to be 0.6695934 post-merger which was 0.1629605 pre-merger. This value suggests that the operating performance of all companies has become better due to the change in the percentage of coefficient of sales by approx. 50% after merger. The sales variable demonstrates a substantial impact on the operating margin, with statistical significance observed at a 1% level after the merger which was at a 5% level before the merger.

In the context of a time-varying decay inefficiency model, it is observed that the turnover has a positive influence on the operating margin post-merger and before the merger. The significance of the coefficient value of turnover is consistent with that observed in other models.

Further, in the next segment, the combined results of the impact of all the variables on the operating efficiency of the companies are reported under different models of stochastic frontier analysis.

Table 4.2.9 displays the various models used in the stochastic frontier analysis post-merger. The initial model pertains to the Time-Varying Decay Model (Truncated-Normal), while the second model pertains to the Time Invariant Inefficiency Model. Lastly, the third model pertains to the Time-Varying Decay Inefficiency Model. The time-varying decay model, particularly the truncated-normal variant, suggests that the coefficient of *mu*, represented as β, indicates that an increase in OROA and Sales will

Table 4.2.9 -Stochastic Frontier Results of Operating Efficiency After Merger

	Dependent variable		
	Operating Profit Margin		
	(1)	(2)	(3)
roa	0.0317301**	0.0341896**	0.0317322**
	(0.0146101)	(0.0150857)	(0.0145017)
oroa	0.9427254***	0.9377753***	0.9427228***
	(0.0366931)	(0.0374125)	(0.0366481)
sales	0.0342062	0.0264866	0.0342067
	(0.0503278)	(0.0496434)	(0.0503161)
fat	0.041961	0.0315763	0.0419532
	(0.0336833)	(0.0334757)	(0.0332611)
it	-0.0164117	-0.0193647	-0.0164143
	(0.0420087)	(0.0422075)	(0.0419751)
constant	0.21851***	0.223677***	0.2184618***
	(0.0689285)	(0.0541229)	(0.0601512)
lnsigma2	4.436206*	3.721752***	4.419817***
	(3.232594)	(0.007675)	(0.0076385)
/ilgtgamma	6.244077**	5.482485***	6.227621***
	(3.242136)	(0.1078816)	(0.1086098)
/mu	-344.4609	-238.1104	-339.8877
	(1114.057)		
/eta	-0.2763371**		-0.2763057**
	(0.1343286)		(0.1335839)
sigma2	84.45393	41.33674	83.08111
	(273.0052)	(0.3172608)	(0.6346118)
gamma	0.9980618	0.9958582	0.9980297
	(0.0062716)	(0.000445)	(0.0002136)
sigma_u2	84.29024	41.16553	82.91742
	(273.0054)	(0.3168223)	(0.6344458)
sigma_v2	0.1636851	0.1712068	0.1636908
	(0.0179765)	(0.0184161)	(0.0177285)
Note:			*p<0.1; **p<0.05; ***p<0.01

Source: *Compiled by Author from Stata output sheet*

lead to a decrease in the growth rate, as the coefficient of *mu* is negative. Based on the computed z value, it can be inferred that, with the exception of Sales, five-year average turnover, and inventory turnover, all other variables demonstrate a statistically significant impact on the operating margin at significance levels of 1% and 5%.

According to the Time Invariant Inefficiency Model, the Coefficient of ROA, OROA Sales, and five-year average turnover is determined to be 0.0341896, 0.9377753, 0.0264866, and 0.0315763 respectively. These values suggest that the operating performance of all companies after the merger has exhibited improvement. The ROA and OROA, demonstrate a substantial impact on the post-operating margin, with statistical significance observed at a 1% and 5% level. ROA, five-year average annual turnover, and inventory are negatively influencing the operating performance of the companies prior to the merger.

In the context of a model that accounts for time-varying decay inefficiency, empirical evidence suggests that the operating return on assets (ROA) exerts a positive impact on the operating margin in the period preceding the merger. Nevertheless, it is worth noting that all other variables exhibit a detrimental impact on the operational performance of the companies prior to the merger. However, after the merger, all the variables except inventory turnover have a positive influence on the operating performance of the companies. ROA and OROA exhibited a statistically significant impact at a significance level of 1% and 5% level after the merger.

In the above tables, the impact of all the variables on operating efficiency is discussed before and after the merger using three different models of stochastic frontier analysis. However, in the next segment, the impact of all the variables on operating efficiency is analyzed in the year of the merger using all three models of stochastic frontier analysis.

Table 4.2.10 displays the various models utilized in Stochastic Frontier analysis in the year of the merger. The initial model pertains to the Time-Varying Decay Model (Truncated-Normal), while the second model pertains to the Time Invariant Inefficiency Model. Lastly, the third model pertains to the Time-Varying Decay Inefficiency Model.

In the context of a time-varying decay model, specifically the truncated-normal model, the coefficient of Mu is determined to be 276.1189 which was 0.9956765 after the merger This coefficient signifies that a one percent increase in the operating return on assets (OROA), and the five-year average turnover during the year will lead to a decline in the growth rate. Nevertheless, the coefficient of Mu exhibited a positive value after the merger. Based on the calculated z value, it can be concluded that the post-operating return on assets and the post-five-year average turnover have a statistically significant influence on the operating margin, with significance levels of 1% and 10% respectively. However, during the merger, only OROA had a significant impact at the 1% level.

Based on the Time Invariant Inefficiency Model, the Coefficient of Operating Return on Assets (OROA) exhibits a value of 0.7315261 during the merger, which is observed

Table 4.2.10 -Impact of OROA and FAT on Operating Efficiency During Merger

	Dependent variable		
	Operating Profit Margin		
	(1)	(2)	(3)
oroa	0.7217486***	0.7315261***	0.7217619***
	(0.050064)	(0.0526043)	(0.0497912)
fat	-0.0038221	-0.0063934	-0.0038307
	(0.048021)	(0.0510478)	(0.0478734)
constant	0.1033331**	0.0066777	0.1032848***
	(0.039454)	(0.0380679)	(0.0353009)
lnsigma2	3.994682*	-1.67141	3.969867***
	(2.574814)		(0.0066504)
/ilgtgamma	5.908138**	-5.697941	5.883147***
	(2.588741)		(0.139603)
/mu	-276.1189	-0.9264593	-270.6612
	(710.8114)		
/eta	-33.56663		-30.78919
	(10500000)		(2610639)
sigma2	54.30857	0.1879819	52.9775
	(139.8345)		(0.3523209)
gamma	0.9972901	0.0033417	0.9972217
	(0.0069962)		(0.0003868)
sigma_u2	54.1614	0.0006282	52.83032
	(139.8349)		(0.3518126)
sigma_v2	0.1471696	0.1873537	0.1471855
	(0.0208036)		(0.0205199)
Note:		$^{*}p<0.1$; $^{**}p<0.05$; $^{***}p<0.01$	

Source: *Compiled by Author from Stata output sheet*

to be 0.8010874 prior to the merger and 0.9142983 subsequent to the merger. This suggests that the impact of return on assets (OROA) on the improvement of operating performance is higher both before and after a merger, compared to during the merger. The positive coefficient of the five-year average turnover subsequent to the merger indicates an enhancement in operating performance as compared to the pre-merger period, where the coefficient was negative. However, it should be noted that the coefficient exhibits a negative value during the year of the merger as well. Furthermore, it is observed that the post-operating return on assets (OROA) and the post-five-year average turnover have a considerable impact on the post-operating margin. Specifically, these variables exhibit significant values at the 1% and 10% levels, respectively. On the other hand, it is worth noting that only the operating return on assets (OROA) demonstrates a significant effect on the operating margin, with a significant value observed at the 1% level during the year of the merger.

The merger has a positive impact on the operating margin, as evidenced by the positive influence of the operating return on assets (OROA) in the context of time-varying decay inefficiency during the year of the merger. However, both operating return on assets and five-year average turnover have a positive aspect in terms of operating return on assets (OROA) observed after the merger. Hence, it can be asserted that both variables have exerted a positive influence on the operational performance of the company's post-merger but only OROA exerted a positive influence during the year of the merger. The significance level of the coefficient value for OROA is at a 1% level. Now, the impact of inventory turnover and return on assets on operating efficiency is examined in Table 4.2.11 during the merger.

Table 4.2.11 -Impact of IT and ROA on Operating Efficiency During Merger

	Dependent variable		
	Operating Profit Margin		
	(1)	(2)	(3)
it	0.2286602**	0.2344749**	0.2286609**
	(0.1125492)	(0.1093616)	(0.1125486)
roa	0.0430332*	0.043350**	0.0430335*
	(0.0232356)	(0.0224536)	(0.0232353)
constant	0.1399864	0.1399991*	0.1399893
	(0.1589074)	(0.0814437)	(0.1588892)
lnsigma2	4.418942	3.996292***	4.385617
	(12.28512)	(0.0071675)	(11.65757)
ilgtgamma	5.438524	5.002456***	5.405051
	(12.34395)	(0.1468953)	(11.71568)
mu	-340.0461	-274.5522	-328.8125
	(4199.566)		(3853.791)
eta	-0.4907447		-0.4907383
	(0.6921513)		(0.6920615)
sigma2	83.0084	54.3961	80.28771
	(1019.768)	(0.3898827)	(935.9596)
gamma	0.9956729	0.9933235	0.9955263
	(0.0531822)	(0.0009742)	(0.0521782)
sigma_u2	82.64921	54.03292	79.92853
	(1019.769)	(0.3866063)	(935.9612)
sigma_v2	0.3591846	0.3631778	0.3591847
	(0.0630186)	(0.0532673)	(0.0630151)
Note:			*p<0.1; **p<0.05; ***p<0.01

Source: *Compiled by Author from R output sheet*

Table 4.2.11 displays the various models of Stochastic Frontier analysis in the year of the merger. The initial model pertains to the Time-Varying Decay Model (Truncated-Normal), while the second model pertains to the Time Invariant Inefficiency Model. Lastly, the third model pertains to the Time-Varying Decay Inefficiency Model.

In the context of a time-varying decay model, specifically the truncated-normal model, the coefficient of Mu is estimated to be 340.0461. This coefficient indicates that a one percent increase in both the return on assets (ROA) and inventory turnover following a merger will result in a decline in the growth rate. Nevertheless, the coefficient exhibited a positive value prior to the merger. However, it was negative after the merger. Based on the calculated z value, it can be concluded that the influence of return on assets and inventory turnover on operating margin is not statistically significant during the pre-merger period. However, following the merger, this relationship has become statistically significant at a 1% level of significance, and during the year of the merger, the relationship has become statistically significant at a 5% and 10% level.

Based on the Time Invariant Inefficiency Model, the coefficient for Return on Assets (ROA) is observed to be 0.043350 during the year of the merger. This coefficient increases to 0.1545546 after the merger, while it stands at 0.00705 prior to the merger. This implies that operational efficiency has experienced a more significant growth rate subsequent to the merger, as evidenced by the heightened value of the ROA coefficient. Following the consolidation, the Return on Assets (ROA) and Inventory turnover have achieved statistical significance at a significance level of 1%. However, it is worth noting that in the year of the merger, both the return on assets (ROA) and inventory turnover exhibit statistical significance at a 5% level. The inventory turnover, which exhibited a negative trend in the past, has undergone a favorable transformation during and subsequent to the merger. The aforementioned alteration has had a significantly advantageous impact on the operational efficiency of the companies following the merger, as it is experiencing a higher rate of change.

In time-varying decay inefficiency, the ROA and inventory turnover positively influenced the operating margin after and during the merger which was influenced negatively before the merger. The coefficient value of ROA and inventory turnover are also significant at 1% level after the merger, 5% and 10% respectively during the merger which is insignificant before the merger.

In the next segment, the impact of Sales on operating efficiency is explored using three different models of stochastic frontier analysis during the merger.

Table 4.2.12 displays the various models used in Stochastic Frontier analysis during the year of the merger. The initial model pertains to the Time-Varying Decay Model (Truncated-Normal), while the second model pertains to the Time Invariant Inefficiency Model. Lastly, the third model pertains to the Time-Varying Decay Inefficiency Model.

Table 4.2.12 -Impact of Sales on Operating Efficiency During Merger

	Dependent variable		
	Operating Profit Margin		
	(1)	(2)	(3)
sales	0.3998576***	0.3835895***	0.3998583***
	(0.0889254)	(0.0897484)	(0.0888789)
constant	0.1126832	-0.0424587	0.1126636*
	(0.1596661)	(0.1247766)	(0.0838351)
lnsigma2	4.61142	-0.7774904**	4.59004***
	(6.368505)	(0.347648)	(0.0062883)
ilgtgamma	5.498954	-6.131744	5.477467***
	(6.404718)	(151.0785)	(0.1285181)
mu	-375.5967	-1.135194	-368.2067
	(2396.32)	(168.6608)	
eta	-1.624746		-1.625018
	(2.809931)		(2.078201)
sigma2	100.6269	0.4595579	98.49839
	(640.843)	(0.1597644)	(0.6193921)
gamma	0.9959256	0.0021681	0.9958375
	(0.0259889)	(0.3268396)	(0.0005327)
sigma_u2	100.2169	0.0009964	98.08839
	(640.8464)	(0.1505279)	(0.6175532)
sigma_v2	0.4099923	0.4585615	0.41
	(0.0639682)	(0.0536668)	(0.0526096)
Note:	*p<0.1; **p<0.05; ***p<0.01		

Source: *Compiled by Author from Stata output sheet*

The time-varying decay model, specifically the truncated-normal variant, indicates that the coefficient of *mu*, denoted as 375.5967 during the year of the merger which is 390.0716 after the merger and 0.5563 before the merger. Before the merger, the coefficient is positive which signifies that a one percent increase in turnover will result in a growth rate increase of 55.63 percent. However, it has become negative during and post-merger which means that a one percent increase in turnover will result in a decline in the growth rate of operating performance. Based on the calculated z value, it can be concluded that Sales exert a statistically significant influence on the operating margin at a significance level of 1% during and after the merger which was at 10% before the merger.

Based on the Time Invariant Inefficiency Model, the Coefficient of Sales is found to be 0.3835895 in the year of the merger, 0.6695934 after the merger, and 0.1629605 before the merger. This finding indicates that the operational efficiency of all companies has improved as a result of the merger, with a significant increase of approximately 50% in the coefficient of sales. During the fiscal year of the merger, there was an observed change of approximately 22 percent in comparison to the pre-merger period. However, following the merger, it has exerted a significant influence and is widely regarded as highly advantageous for enhancing operational performance. Thus, it can be inferred that the merger has been advantageous for the companies in enhancing their operational performance. The variable of sales exhibits a significant influence on the operating margin, as evidenced by statistical significance at a 1% level both during and after the merger. Prior to the merger, this significance was observed at a 5% level.

Within the framework of a time-varying decay inefficiency model, empirical evidence suggests that turnover exerts a favorable impact on the pre-merger, during-merger, and post-merger operating margins. The post-merger scenario has demonstrated the significant impact of mergers, thereby substantiating their benefits for companies by enhancing their operational performance. The coefficient value of turnover demonstrates a consistent significance, which aligns with findings observed in other models.

The stochastic frontier results of all the combined variables are discussed for pre- and post-merger under three different models. Now, in the next segment, the results are reported during the year of the merger.

Table 4.2.13 displays the various models used in Stochastic Frontier analysis during the year of the merger. The initial model pertains to the Time-Varying Decay Model (Truncated-Normal), while the second model pertains to the Time Invariant Inefficiency Model. Lastly, the third model pertains to the Time-Varying Decay Inefficiency Model.

The time-varying decay model, particularly the truncated-normal variant, suggests that the coefficient of Mu, represented as β, indicates that an increase in ROA, OROA, and Sales will lead to a decrease in the growth rate, as the coefficient of Mu is negative during the year and after the merger. Based on the computed z value, it can be inferred that with the exception of ROA, all other variables demonstrate a statistically significant impact on the operating margin at significance levels of 1%,5%, and 10%. According to the Time Invariant Inefficiency Model, the Coefficient of ROA, OROA, and Sales is determined to be 0.0079982,0.7212214, and 0.1070316 respectively. These values

Table 4.2.13 -Stochastic Frontier Results of Operating Efficiency During Merger

	Dependent variable		
	Operating Profit Margin		
	(1)	(2)	(3)
roa	0.0023522	0.0079982	0.0023545
	(0.0137507)	(0.0162686)	(0.013717)
oroa	0.7153701***	0.7212214***	0.7153906***
	(0.0518029)	(0.0606204)	(0.0515873)
sales	0.1836931**	0.1070316	0.1837553**
	(0.0836274)	(0.0932201)	(0.0819828)
fat	-0.0790494*	-0.0464837	-0.0790744*
	(0.0530314)	(0.0604683)	(0.0529582)
it	-0.1134706*	-0.0650156	-0.113482*
	(0.0727992)	(0.0855408)	(0.072408)
constant	0.0697485*	-0.0390751	0.06978*
	(0.049679)	(0.0559282)	(0.0473958)
lnsigma2	4.237075	-1.756678***	4.212781***
	(3.421507)	(0.1248993)	(0.0076861)
ilgtgamma	6.5659*	-2.138224***	6.541878***
	(3.432129)	(0.1398065)	(0.1637749)
mu	-311.8996	-5.030535	-304.7837
	(1068.558)		
eta	-32.06642		-42.60719
	(4083641)		(794000000)
sigma2	69.2051	0.1726174	67.54415
	(236.7857)	(0.0215598)	(0.5191533)
gamma	0.9985944	0.1054368	0.9985603
	(0.0048173)	(0.0131865)	(0.0002354)
sigma_u2	69.10783	0.0182002	67.4469
	(236.7859)	(0.0001394)	(0.5189609)
sigma_v2	0.0972732	0.1544172	0.0972435
	(0.0159947)	(0.021559)	(0.015906)
Note:		*p<0.1; **p<0.05; ***p<0.01	

Source: *Compiled by Author from Stata output sheet*

suggest that the operating performance of all companies during the year of the merger has exhibited improvement. The OROA, demonstrates a substantial impact on the operating margin, with statistical significance observed at a 1% level. Five-year average annual turnover and inventory are negatively influencing the operating performance of the companies during the year of the merger.

In the context of a model that accounts for time-varying decay inefficiency, empirical evidence suggests that the operating return on assets (ROA), ROA, and Sales exert a positive impact on the operating margin in the period during the year of the merger. Nevertheless, it is worth noting that all other variables exhibit a detrimental impact on the operational performance of the companies during the merger. However, after the merger, all the variables except inventory turnover have a positive influence on the operating performance of the companies which shows that the merger is beneficial for the companies as it has improved their operating performance. Except for ROA, all other variables exhibit a statistically significant impact at a significance level of 1%,5%, and 10% level during the year of the merger.

The impact of all variables on operating efficiency is explored in the above segments pre-, post-, and during the year of the merger. Now, the impact of all the variables on operating efficiency is analyzed under all the models considering the overall merger.

Table 4.2.14 displays the various models utilized in stochastic frontier analysis in the overall merger. The initial model pertains to the Time-Varying Decay Model (Truncated-Normal), while the second model pertains to the Time Invariant Inefficiency Model. Lastly, the third model pertains to the Time-Varying Decay Inefficiency Model.

In the context of a time-varying decay model, specifically the truncated-normal model, the coefficient of Mu is determined to be 0.2109052 in overall merger, 276.1189 in the year of merger, and 0.9956765 after merger This coefficient signifies that a one percent increase in the operating return on assets (OROA) and the five-year average turnover during the year will lead to a decline in the growth rate in the year of merger as well as in overall merger. Nevertheless, the coefficient of Mu exhibited a positive value after the merger. Based on the calculated z value, it can be concluded that the post-operating return on assets and the post-five-year average turnover have a statistically significant influence on the operating margin, with significance levels of 1% and 10% respectively.

Table 4.2.14 -Impact of OROA and FAT on Operating Efficiency considering Overall Merger

	Dependent variable		
	Operating Profit Margin		
	(1)	(2)	(3)
oroa	0.8726935***	0.8671949***	0.8352036***
	(0.0208862)	(0.0211174)	(0.0206103)
fat	0.0038258	-0.0073341	-0.0195233
	(0.0215598)	(0.0216835)	(0.0214541)
constant	0.099124***	0.0346768*	-0.0692715***
	(0.0262029)	(0.0193538)	(0.0239965)
lnsigma2	-1.487758***	-1.434361***	0.8264637
	(0.056765)	(0.0568629)	(2.079077)
ilgtgamma	-5.443679	-7.404432	2.409394
			(2.266799)
mu	-0.2109052	-0.4458611***	-3.415537
	(0.2405869)	(0.0127749)	(9.879528)
eta	0.4451116***		-0.5938538***
	(0.1150304)		(0.104095)
sigma2	0.2258784	0.2382675	2.285223
	(0.012822)	(0.0135486)	(4.751155)
gamma	0.0043049	0.0006082	0.9175409
			(0.1715051)
sigma_u2	0.0009724	0.0001449	2.096786
			(4.751167)
sigma_v2	0.2249061	0.2381225	0.1884375
			(0.0109103)
Note:			*p<0.1; **p<0.05; ***p<0.01

Source: *Compiled by Author from Stata output sheet*

However, in the overall merger, only OROA has a significant impact at the 1% level.

Based on the Time Invariant Inefficiency Model, the Coefficient of Operating Return on Assets (OROA) exhibits a value of 0.8671949 in the overall merger,0.7315261 during the merger, 0.8010874 prior to the merger, and 0.9142983 subsequent to the merger. This suggests that the impact of return on assets (OROA) on the improvement of operating performance is higher both after and overall merger, compared to during and prior to the merger. The positive coefficient of the five-year average turnover subsequent to the merger indicates an enhancement in operating performance as compared to the pre-merger period and overall merger, where the coefficient was negative. However, it should be noted that the coefficient exhibits a negative value during the year of the merger as well. Furthermore, it is observed that the post-operating return on assets (OROA) and the post-five-year average turnover have a considerable impact on the post-operating margin. Specifically, these variables exhibit significant values at the 1% and 10% levels, respectively. On the other hand, it is worth noting that only the operating return on assets (OROA) demonstrates a significant effect on the operating margin, with a significant value observed at the 1% level during the year and overall merger.

The merger has a positive impact on the operating margin, as evidenced by the positive influence of the operating return on assets (OROA) in the context of time-varying decay inefficiency during the year as well as the overall merger. However, both operating return on assets and five-year average turnover have a positive aspect in terms of operating return on assets (OROA) observed after the merger. Hence, it can be asserted that both variables have exerted a positive influence on the operational performance of the company's post-merger but only OROA exerted a positive influence during the year of merger and overall merger. The significance level of the coefficient value for OROA is at a 1% level.

In Table 4.2.15, the impact of inventory turnover and return on assets on operating efficiency is discussed under three different models of stochastic frontier analysis considering overall mergers.

Table 4.2.15 displays the various models of Stochastic Frontier analysis on the overall merger. The initial model pertains to the Time-Varying Decay Model (Truncated-Normal), while the second model pertains to the Time Invariant Inefficiency Model. Lastly, the third model pertains to the Time-Varying Decay Inefficiency Model.

In the context of a time-varying decay model, specifically the truncated-normal model, the coefficient of Mu is estimated to be 0.358711 in the overall merger which is very high during the year of the merger. This coefficient indicates that a one percent increase in both the return on assets (ROA) and inventory turnover following a merger will result in a decline in the growth rate of the overall merger. The percentage of decline would be very low as compared to during the merger. Nevertheless, the coefficient exhibited a positive value prior to the merger. However, it was negative after the merger. Based on the calculated z value, it can be concluded that the influence of return on assets and inventory turnover on operating margin is not statistically significant during the pre-

Table 4.2.15 - Impact of IT and ROA on Operating Efficiency considering Overall Merger

	Dependent variable		
	Operating Profit Margin		
	(1)	(2)	(3)
it	0.4071333***	0.4067461***	0.4048293***
	(0.0381436)	(0.038193)	(0.0381553)
roa	0.0714161***	0.0691192***	0.0698249***
	(0.0125003)	(0.0122677)	(0.0123494)
constant	-0.1127421**	-0.1386938***	-0.1185583**
	(0.0506624)	(0.0455586)	(0.0490347)
/lnsigma2	-0.3091999***	-0.2974427***	-0.3062114***
	(0.0602687)	(0.0595147)	(0.0618009)
/ilgtgamma	-8.995536*	-5.542477***	-11.43921
	(5.723873)	(0.0601774)	
/mu	-0.358711	-2.003593	-0.1045151***
	(0.8272614)		(0.0032537)
/eta	0.7109277		0.8253831***
	(0.5871191)		(0.1118586)
sigma2	0.734034	0.7427151	0.736231
	(0.0442393)	(0.0442025)	(0.0454998)
gamma	0.0001239	0.0039015	0.0000108
	(0.0007094)	(0.0002339)	
sigma_u2	0.000091	0.0028977	7.93E-06
	(0.0005207)	(0.0000208)	
sigma_v2	0.733943	0.7398174	0.736223
	(0.0442431)	(0.0442025)	
Note:		$^{*}p<0.1$; $^{**}p<0.05$; $^{***}p<0.01$	

Source: *Compiled by Author from Stata output sheet*

merger period. However, following the merger as well as in the overall merger, this relationship has become statistically significant at a 1% level of significance, and during the year of the merger, the relationship has become statistically significant at a 5% and 10% level.

Based on the Time Invariant Inefficiency Model, the coefficient for Return on Assets (ROA) is observed to be 0.0691192 in the overall merger, and 0.043350 during the year of the merger. This coefficient increases to 0.1545546 after the merger, while it stands at 0.00705 prior to the merger. This implies that operational efficiency has experienced a more significant growth rate subsequent to the merger, as evidenced by the heightened value of the ROA coefficient. Following the consolidation as well as in the overall merger, the Return on Assets (ROA) and Inventory turnover have achieved statistical significance at a significance level of 1%. However, it is worth noting that in the year of the merger, both the return on assets (ROA) and inventory turnover exhibit statistical significance at a 5% level. The inventory turnover, which exhibited a negative trend in the past, has undergone a favorable transformation during, subsequently as well as in the overall merger. The aforementioned alteration has had a significantly advantageous impact on the operational efficiency of the companies following the merger, as it is experiencing a higher rate of change.

In time-varying decay inefficiency, the ROA and inventory turnover positively influence the operating margin after, during, and in the overall merger which is influencing negatively before the merger. The coefficient value of ROA and inventory turnover are also significant at 1% level after and in the overall merger, 5% and 10% respectively during the merger which is insignificant before the merger.

Next, the impact of sales on operating efficiency considering the overall merger is discussed in Table 4.2.16.

Table 4.2.16 displays the various models used in Stochastic Frontier analysis in the overall merger. The initial model pertains to the Time-Varying Decay Model (Truncated-Normal), while the second model pertains to the Time Invariant Inefficiency Model. Lastly, the third model pertains to the Time-Varying Decay Inefficiency Model.

The time-varying decay model, specifically the truncated-normal variant, indicates that the coefficient of Mu, denoted as 0.87214 in overall merger,375.5967 during the year of merger which is 390.0716 after merger and 0.5563 before merger. Before the merger, the coefficient is positive which signifies that a one percent increase in turnover will result in a growth rate increase of 55.63 percent. However, it has become negative during, after, and in the overall merger which means that a one percent increase in turnover will result in a decline in the growth rate of operating performance. Based on the calculated z value, it can be concluded that Sales exert a statistically significant influence on the operating margin at a significance level of 1% during, after, and overall merger which was at 10% before the merger.

Based on the Time Invariant Inefficiency Model, the Coefficient of Sales is found to be 0.4464243 in the overall merger, 0.3835895 in the year of the merger, 0.6695934 after

Table 4.2.16 -Impact of Sales on Operating Efficiency considering Overall Merger

	Dependent variable		
	Operating Profit Margin		
	(1)	(2)	(3)
sales	0.4464243***	0.4674776***	0.5458106***
	(0.0330663)	(0.0332094)	(0.0349372)
constant	0.053928*	0.0214765	0.1794868***
	(0.0329754)		(0.0434673)
/lnsigma2	-0.321129***	-0.304265***	4.076825
	(0.0519221)	(0.0523424)	(9.082066)
/ilgtgamma	-7.201431	-9.575651	4.465364
			(9.186985)
/mu	-0.87214	-0.2662142***	-117.4584
	(1.076761)	(0.0333595)	(1089.34)
/eta	0.3853333**		-0.3122617***
	(0.1931752)		(0.0552707)
sigma2	0.7253296	0.7376654	58.958
	(0.0376607)	(0.0386111)	(535.4605)
gamma	0.000745	0.0000694	0.9886303
			(0.1032661)
sigma_u2	0.0005403	0.0000512	58.28766
			(535.4607)
sigma_v2	0.7247893	0.7376142	0.6703375
			(0.0365497)
Note:			*p<0.1; **p<0.05; ***p<0.01

Source: *Compiled by Author from Stata output sheet*

the merger, and 0.1629605 before the merger. This finding indicates that the operational efficiency of all companies has improved as a result of the merger, with a significant increase of approximately 50% in the coefficient of sales. During the fiscal year of the merger, there was an observed change of approximately 22 percent in comparison to the pre-merger period. However, following the merger, it has exerted a significant influence and is widely regarded as highly advantageous for enhancing operational performance. Thus, it can be inferred that the merger has been advantageous for the companies in enhancing their operational performance. The coefficient of the overall merger also indicates a growth in operating performance due to the merger. The variable of sales exhibits a significant influence on the operating margin, as evidenced by statistical significance at a 1% level both during, after, and overall merger. Prior to the merger, this significance was observed at a 5% level.

Within the framework of a time-varying decay inefficiency model, empirical evidence suggests that turnover exerts a favorable impact on the pre-merger, during-merger, post-merger, and overall merger operating margin. The post-merger scenario has demonstrated the significant impact of mergers, thereby substantiating their benefits for companies by enhancing their operational performance. The coefficient value of turnover demonstrates a consistent significance, which aligns with findings observed in other models. As in the above segments, the results of stochastic frontier analysis are investigated in all cases such as pre-, post-, and during merger under all the models. Similarly, in the next table, the results considering the overall merger are discussed.

Table 4.2.17 -Stochastic Frontier Results of Operating Efficiency considering Overall Merger

	Dependent variable		
	Operating Profit Margin		
	(1)	(2)	(3)
roa	0.0022843	0.0023211	-0.0018715
	(0.0076887)	(0.0077215)	(0.0081344)
oroa	0.8639503***	0.8536033***	0.8638058***
	(0.0250538)	(0.0246689)	(0.0244267)
sales	0.1123207***	0.1492094***	0.0698048**
	(0.0322887)	(0.0269361)	(0.0319167)
fat	-0.0208359	-0.0329473*	-0.0297612
	(0.0236491)	(0.0228725)	(0.0236799)
it	-0.0427846*	-0.0503805*	-0.06487**
	(0.0270594)	(0.0268502)	(0.0274584)
constant	0.1322383***	0.0000526	-0.0482587*
	(0.0389302)	(0.0300351)	(0.0289228)
/lnsigma2	-1.668849***	1.653954***	-0.1479984
	(0.0608698)	(0.1847692)	(1.684312)
/ilgtgamma	-49.40597	-5.042703	1.392432
		(27.04007)	(2.105755)
/mu	0.0669537	-1.29606	-1.343786
		(29.32669)	(4.211784)
/eta	0.1311349***		-0.6256659***
	(0.0382499)		(0.1942782)
sigma2	0.1884639	0.1912921	
	(0.0114717)	(0.0353449)	
gamma	3.49E-20	0.0064149	
		(0.1723455)	
sigma_u2	6.58E-23	0.0012271	
		(0.0331812)	
sigma_v2	0.1884639	0.190065	
		(0.0121421)	
Note:		*p<0.1; **p<0.05; ***p<0.01	

Source: *Compiled by Author from Stata output sheet*

Table 4.2.17 displays the various models used in Stochastic Frontier analysis in the overall merger. The initial model pertains to the Time-Varying Decay Model (Truncated-Normal), while the second model pertains to the Time Invariant Inefficiency Model. Lastly, the third model pertains to the Time-Varying Decay Inefficiency Model.

The time-varying decay model, particularly the truncated-normal variant, suggests that the coefficient of Mu, represented as β, indicates that an increase in ROA, OROA, and Sales will lead to a decrease in the growth rate, as the coefficient of *mu* is negative during the year, after an overall merger. Based on the computed z value, it can be inferred that with the exception of ROA, all other variables demonstrate a statistically significant impact on the operating margin at significance levels of 1%,5%, and 10% in the year of merger whereas in overall merger except ROA and five-year average turnover, all other variables have a significant impact on operating performance at 1% and 10%.

According to the Time Invariant Inefficiency Model, the Coefficient of ROA, OROA, and sales is determined to be 0.0023211, 0.8536033, and 0.1492094 respectively. These values suggest that the operating performance of all companies in the overall merger has exhibited improvement. Except for ROA, all other variables demonstrate a substantial impact on the operating margin, with statistical significance observed at a 1% and 10% level. Five-year average annual turnover and inventory are negatively influencing the operating performance of the companies in the overall merger.

In the context of a model that accounts for time-varying decay inefficiency, empirical evidence suggests that the operating return on assets (ROA), ROA, and Sales exert a positive impact on the operating margin in the period during the year of merger whereas in overall merger only OROA and Sales has a positive impact on operating performance. However, after the merger, all the variables except inventory turnover have a positive influence on the operating performance of the companies which shows that the merger is beneficial for the companies as it has improved their operating performance. Except for ROA and five-year average turnover, all other variables exhibit a statistically significant impact at a significance level of 1% and 5% level in the overall merger. In Table 4.21.18 the correlation of all the variables with each other is examined in case of merger.

Table 4.2.18 shows the correlation between the variables in the case of a merger. The operating margin, operating return on assets, sales, five-year average turnover, inventory turnover, and return on assets are positively correlated with each other. In the next table, the descriptive statistics of operating efficiency in the case of acquisition are studied.

Table 4.2.18 -Correlation Matrix of Operating Efficiency -Merger

	opm	oroa	sales	fat	it	roa
opm	1					
oroa	0.886	1				
sales	0.483	0.441	1			
fat	0.289	0.340	0.326	1		
it	0.391	0.424	0.606	0.329	1	
roa	0.265	0.293	0.107	0.074	0.081	1

Source: *Compiled by Author from Stata output sheet*

Table 4.2.19 -Comparison of Pre-and Post-Merger of Operating Efficiency

S.No.	Company Name	Pre-Mergers				Post-Mergers			
		2013	2014	2015	2016	2019	2020	2021	2022
1	Crystal Crop Protection Ltd	-0.6499	-0.1015	-1.1983	-0.1629	-0.9023	0.4190	2.0932	0.4190
2	Sterlite Power Transmission Ltd	0.5833	1.1928	0.5833	1.8024	0.1494	0.1659	-0.3902	1.2591
3	Olive Bar & Kitchen Pvt Ltd	0.1443	0.9667	0.7923	0.3457	-2.0692	-1.2475	-	-
4	Sembcorp Energy India Ltd	0.1814	0.3706	0.1814	0.5598	0.2993	3.0373	0.2993	-
5	Hero Future Energies Pvt Ltd	1.0334	1.0588	1.0334	1.0843	-0.3403	-0.1950	-0.9975	-0.1950
6	Reliance Industrial Investments & Holdings Ltd	0.5253	-0.4175	-1.6640	-0.3471	0.5990	0.9777	2.0509	0.9777
7	ECap Equities Ltd	0.6986	-0.4624	-0.4624	-0.3244	-0.3964	2.3779	-0.3964	-
8	Ashok Leyland Ltd	-2.1191	-0.6155	0.5446	0.6193	0.5171	-0.1278	-0.3670	1.4238
9	AMJ Land Holdings Ltd	2.0079	-0.4486	0.9194	-0.2001	-1.3407	-1.2621	0.1386	-0.2275
10	Anup Engineering Limited/The	-	-	-	0.3252	0.5020	-0.3602	-0.4670	3.0781
11	Arvind Ltd	1.2681	1.3615	0.8809	0.0035	-0.6938	-1.5117	-0.5724	1.1850
12	Astral Ltd	0.0192	-0.5050	-0.3872	-0.1777	0.1031	0.6950	0.2683	2.9805
13	Adani Total Gas Ltd	-0.2925	-0.4668	-0.1183	0.1261	2.8232	-0.4242	-	-
14	Bharti Airtel Ltd	-0.0429	0.3313	0.3191	0.2181	-0.5225	0.1665	0.7854	2.7104
15	Balaji Amines Ltd	-0.5725	-0.4838	-0.1693	0.1429	-0.2376	0.6553	0.5695	2.8997
16	Bank of Baroda	1.3856	0.9065	-1.9920	0.1628	-0.1911	-0.1345	0.7876	0.9920
17	Borosil Renewables Ltd	-0.3575	-0.3810	-0.2624	-0.3123	-0.4579	1.0222	1.0432	2.6192
18	Berger Paints India Ltd	-0.5485	-0.5006	-0.0104	0.1604	0.2392	0.4620	0.0771	3.0050
19	Birlasoft Ltd	0.2578	-0.5025	0.1270	-0.5009	-0.2377	0.3734	0.5670	2.9596
20	Chordia Food Products Ltd	1.1194	0.3675	-0.1958	0.5426	-1.7889	-1.3656	-1.7889	-
21	Chalet Hotels Ltd	0.1406	-0.1245	0.1038	0.4244	0.6910	-1.9335	-0.3050	-2.0955

S.No.	Company Name	Pre-Mergers				Post-Mergers			
		2013	2014	2015	2016	2019	2020	2021	2022
22	CL Educate Ltd	-	1.0684	0.5524	1.0684	-1.2417	-1.6838	0.9583	-0.6787
23	DiGiSPICE Technologies Ltd	1.1265	0.3591	-1.5925	1.4609	-1.2042	0.0152	0.3683	-0.2411
24	Dr Lal PathLabs Ltd	-0.1981	-0.2826	0.2009	0.2022	-0.1490	0.1710	0.0317	3.1169
25	Elpro International Ltd	-0.2535	0.2761	-0.1962	0.3087	-0.5183	0.2753	0.2649	2.4362
26	Foods & Inns Ltd	0.4681	2.0048	0.4910	-0.7765	-0.1986	-1.2399	0.2494	1.3751
27	Future Market Networks Ltd	0.6369	-0.1542	0.1193	-0.6698	0.4145	-1.9322	0.5258	-1.7297
28	Godrej Industries Ltd	0.4751	0.1320	-0.1587	1.0589	0.6345	-1.7253	0.6706	1.0838
29	Godrej Agrovet Ltd	0.2476	0.0976	0.4725	0.2235	0.0680	-0.2349	2.9608	-0.2349
30	GTL Infrastructure Ltd	-0.9716	0.1232	0.4344	1.9860	-0.8475	-0.6331	0.3814	-1.0523
31	Havells India Ltd	-0.4328	-0.6153	-0.3105	0.3639	-0.2659	0.6263	0.2232	2.9036
32	HealthCare Global Enterprises Ltd	-0.7547	0.9366	0.8868	0.8622	-0.6013	-2.2158	0.4583	-0.6096
33	Hexaware Technologies Ltd	1.3725	0.3958	0.1012	-0.1145	-0.3286	-0.5459	-0.6318	2.6009
34	Indiabulls Real Estate Ltd	-0.0966	-0.3278	-0.0765	-0.2206	1.5738	-0.8397	-1.3323	-0.8797
35	IDFC First Bank Ltd	1.0928	1.0458	1.0928	0.9988	-1.3497	0.0281	-0.1040	0.0620
36	IndusInd Bank Ltd	1.3388	1.4077	-0.3760	-0.5082	0.0568	-1.3386	-0.4356	1.7221
37	Indo Amines Ltd	-0.4092	-0.5486	0.1460	0.5514	-0.7264	0.8875	-0.6813	2.6063
38	Indus Towers Ltd	-0.6050	-0.3573	-0.3711	-0.1135	0.4649	0.2271	0.4692	2.9489
39	Infibeam Avenues Ltd	-1.9961	-1.0652	-0.3315	0.6575	0.6662	0.6425	0.2433	1.3652
40	Inox Leisure Ltd	0.2721	0.2361	0.2713	0.2375	0.3576	-2.0541	0.0822	-2.1621
41	JM Financial Ltd	-0.8612	-0.2325	0.0996	0.2279	0.1242	0.0095	0.0294	2.9707
42	JSW Steel Ltd	-0.3871	-0.1097	-0.8222	0.0669	-0.3908	0.4058	0.7873	2.8059
43	LTIMindtree Ltd	0.5551	-0.0104	-0.3880	-0.1364	-0.1429	0.3494	0.0279	3.0057
44	Morganite Crucible India Ltd	-0.3167	-0.8654	0.0809	1.3904	0.1444	1.0221	0.1444	-
45	Minda Corp Ltd	0.1606	-0.1474	-0.1675	-0.1680	0.6262	-0.6738	-0.3001	2.8930
46	Modern India Ltd	0.9336	0.4925	0.1444	0.5201	-1.2567	-2.2600	-1.2567	-
47	Mukand Ltd	0.1747	0.6649	0.6706	0.7825	-0.1155	-2.1744	0.1664	-1.7252
48	Narayana Hrudayalaya Ltd	-0.1001	-0.5588	0.0599	0.6305	0.3735	-1.5773	1.7039	1.7000
49	Nath Industries Ltd	0.2329	-0.2512	-0.1348	-0.7025	0.7658	1.0482	-0.1748	2.6434
50	NK Industries Ltd	-0.9080	-2.2683	0.4524	0.3530	0.5399	-0.3528	-0.0189	-1.3858
51	National Fittings Ltd	0.4366	0.6652	0.9815	1.3058	-1.1589	-1.1125	-1.2653	-0.6913
52	Optiemus Infracom Ltd	0.4449	0.4547	0.4507	0.3813	-0.6465	-1.8831	0.1268	-2.0988
53	Piramal Enterprises Ltd	-0.8320	-0.7092	-0.2513	0.3563	0.6664	1.0764	-2.0768	0.1981
54	Poonawalla Fincorp Ltd	-0.0552	-0.1087	0.1653	-1.2764	-0.9329	-0.9329	1.2355	1.5348
55	Reliance Industries Ltd	-1.2618	-0.9758	0.6866	0.4914	0.2905	0.1191	-0.0246	2.4342
56	RPSG Ventures Ltd	-	-	-	-	-0.8361	0.3031	0.5330	2.7235
57	Sastasundar Ventures Ltd	0.5565	-0.0519	-1.9212	-1.1938	0.7217	0.9518	0.8805	0.8232
58	S Chand & Co Ltd	0.6973	0.8525	1.0746	1.1343	-0.4833	-0.4768	-0.2116	-0.4768
59	Schaeffler India Ltd	-0.5515	-0.0938	0.4587	0.2135	-0.3317	-0.8003	0.4611	2.8352
60	Sundram Fasteners Ltd	-0.8792	-0.6089	-0.6231	0.5230	-0.0075	0.3394	0.1862	2.6817
61	Solara Active Pharma Sciences Ltd	-	-	-	0.1309	0.6300	1.5303	-2.2912	1.0354
62	Somany Ceramics Ltd	-0.7321	-0.5705	-0.0779	1.4840	-0.7501	0.2400	-0.0658	2.3791
63	Strides Pharma Science Ltd	0.4689	0.6669	0.0872	0.7823	0.5683	0.5035	-2.5561	-0.6732
64	Sundaram Finance Ltd	0.7959	0.7163	0.3440	-0.9410	-0.1161	0.1508	0.1227	2.4185
65	Thomas Cook India Ltd	0.5798	0.3199	0.3445	0.3230	-1.8184	-0.2571	-2.3326	-0.2571
66	Tech Mahindra Ltd	1.0232	0.3034	-0.1528	-0.5806	-0.4653	0.0338	0.0949	2.7998

S.No.	Company Name	Pre-Mergers				Post-Mergers			
		2013	2014	2015	2016	2019	2020	2021	2022
67	Investment Trust of India Ltd/The	-1.9963	-0.5773	-0.4242	0.8267	0.0921	0.6330	0.0202	1.5741
68	Timken India Ltd	-0.7437	-0.0381	-0.0573	-0.0955	0.6675	-0.0585	0.9127	2.7657
69	TV18 Broadcast Ltd	2.4259	-0.2150	-0.1480	-0.9179	-0.1582	0.1269	0.2405	1.1329
70	TV Today Network Ltd	-0.0224	-0.0768	0.2261	-0.0729	-0.2296	-0.2911	-0.0217	3.0945
71	Uniply Industries Ltd	-0.6938	0.1810	0.4098	0.4588	-1.9055	-0.3447	-1.9055	-
72	ATC Telecom Infrastructure Pvt Ltd	0.5314	-	0.5314	-0.5314	-	-	-	-
73	Wipro Ltd	0.3469	0.3057	0.0788	-0.2090	-0.1383	0.2788	-0.0768	3.0622

Source: *Compiled by Author*

Table 4.2.19 presents a comparative analysis of the operating margin of the firm before and after the merger. The operating margin of a corporation is a crucial metric for comprehending the financial standing of the organisation. The metric illustrates the company's net income following the deduction of expenditures, excluding interest and taxes. The operating margin is a crucial determinant of a company's growth for any organisation. The time period spanning from 2013 to 2016 is referred to as the pre-merger years, whereas the years from 2019 to 2022 are referred to as the post-merger years. The analysis of the provided table reveals that a majority of the business's operational margins have demonstrated improvement subsequent to the merger. Consequently, this has resulted in an increase in the company's profits, but not at a substantial rate. Nonetheless, this development has contributed to the overall growth of the firm. The merger has demonstrated its success by transforming the operating margin of firms from negative to positive. Hence, it may be posited that mergers have demonstrated advantageous outcomes for a significant proportion of organisations.

Table 4.2.20 -Descriptive Statistics of Operating Efficiency - Acquisition

Statistic	N	Mean	St. Dev.	Min	Max
PR_OPM	1524	0.098392	0.73137	-2.780273	3.160953
PR_OROA	1524	0.167498	0.893912	-3.170853	3.042495
PR_SALES	1524	-0.201013	0.560965	-1.828597	3.113171
PR_FAT	1524	0.225884	0.754866	-2.173624	3.131107
PR_IT	1524	0.123345	0.653582	-2.030061	3.115236
PR_ROA	1524	2.394004	8.553429	-14.211087	154.682886
PO_OPM	1524	0.114616	1.233637	-2.969229	3.162278
PO_OROA	1524	0.01469	1.189989	-3.162236	3.173694
PO_SALES	1524	0.628859	1.177573	-2.187062	3.165944
PO_FAT	1524	0.0474	1.205607	-3.162278	3.167063
PO_IT	1524	0.35054	1.21697	-2.179903	3.164768
PO_ROA	1524	2.144023	8.661626	-16.294183	156.765982

Source: *Compiled by Author from Stata output sheet*

Table 4.2.20 depicts the descriptive statistics of the dependent as well as independent variables used in this study in the case of pre- and post-acquisition. The mean of operating return on assets, five-year average turnover, inventory turnover, and return on assets is 0.167498, 0.225884, 0.123345, and 2.394004 respectively before acquisition which has become 0.01469, 0.0474, 0.35054, and 2.144023 after acquisition. The mean of only inventory turnover has increased post-acquisition, thereby indicating a positive impact of the inventory turnover on the operating performance of the company post-acquisition. However, the mean of sales was negative before the acquisition which has become positive after the acquisition. Thereby indicating a positive impact of sales on the operating performance of the companies after acquisition. The standard deviation defines the risk, in this case, the standard deviation of operating return on assets, sales, five-year average turnover, inventory turnover, and return on assets is high in the post-acquisition scenario thereby indicating that more risk is involved after acquisition. Further, in Table 4.2.20, the impact of operating return on assets and five-year average turnover is analyzed using stochastic frontier analysis in the case of pre-acquisition.

Table 4.2.21 presents the different models of Stochastic Frontier analysis before acquisition. The first model relates to the Time-varying decay model (truncated – normal), the second model relates to the Time invariant inefficiency model and the third model relates to the Time-varying decay inefficiency model. In the time-varying decay model (truncated -normal), the coefficient of *mu* i.e., 169.6808 implies that a one percent increase in operating OROA and a five-year average turnover of pre-acquisition will result in the decline of the growth rate. From the z value, it can be said that pre-operating return on assets and pre-five-year average turnover has a significant impact on operating margin at 1% and 5% levels respectively.

In the Time invariant inefficiency model, the coefficient of operating ROA is 0.6858719 which indicates that the operating performance has improved across all companies before acquisition. However, the five-year average turnover is influencing the operating performance negatively. Pre-operating ROA, pre-five-year average turnover significant values in influencing pre-operating margin at 1% level. In time-varying decay inefficiency, the operating ROA positively influences the operating margin before the acquisition. However, the five-year average turnover is negatively

Table 4.2.21 -Impact of OROA and FAT on Operating Efficiency Before Acquisition

	Dependent variable		
	Operating Profit Margin		
	(1)	(2)	(3)
oroa	0.6906096***	0.6858719***	0.6906096***
	(0.0198447)	(0.0201713)	(0.0198327)
fat	-0.0479146**	-0.053609***	-0.0479137**
	(0.0207365)	(0.0207697)	(0.0206143)
constant	0.1795821***	0.180972***	0.1765769***
	(0.02617)	(0.0527946)	(0.0192023)
lnsigma2	3.028849	-0.177314	3.016***
	(5.925988)	(3.745013)	(0.0031634)
ilgtgamma	4.531539	0.9804716	4.518549***
	(5.990032)	(5.137048)	(0.0453953)
mu	-169.6808	-3.033194	-167.5117
	(1018.195000)	(18.21209)	
eta	0.2471059***		0.2471221***
	(0.0589615)		(0.0366524)
sigma2	20.67343	0.8375165	20.4095
	(122.5105)	(3.13651)	(0.0645624)
gamma	0.9893505	0.7272018	0.9892128
	(0.0631113)	(1.019084)	(0.0004844)
sigma_u2	20.45327	0.6090435	20.18934
	(122.5105)	(3.134328)	(0.0638133)
sigma_v2	0.220161	0.228473	0.2201613
	(0.0101269)	(0.0107792)	(0.0099683)
Note:		*p<0.1; **p<0.05; ***p<0.01	

Source: *Compiled by Author from Stata output sheet*

influencing the operating margin. The coefficient value of OROA and five-year average annual turnover is significant in pre-acquisition at 1% and 5% levels.

In the next table, the impact of inventory turnover and return on assets on operating efficiency before acquisition is analyzed under the models of stochastic frontier analysis.

Table 4.2.22 displays the various models utilized in Stochastic Frontier analysis prior to acquisition. The initial model pertains to the Time-Varying Decay Model (Truncated-Normal), the second model pertains to the Time Invariant Inefficiency Model, and the third model pertains to the Time-Varying Decay Inefficiency Model.

In the time-varying decay model (truncated -normal), the coefficient of Mu i.e., 0.088367 implies that for a one percent increase in ROA and inventory turnover of pre-acquisition, the growth rate will rise by 8.83 percent. From the z value, it can be said that return on assets and inventory turnover have an insignificant impact on operating

Table 4.2.22 - Impact of IT and ROA on Operating Efficiency Before Acquisition

	Dependent variable		
	Operating Profit Margin		
	(1)	(2)	(3)
it	0.0404544	0.0189556	0.0404542
	(0.0340609)	(0.0341162)	(0.0340609)
roa	0.0019893	0.0023184	0.0019893
	(0.0032560)	(0.0030152)	(0.003256)
constant	0.5275875***	0.6010694***	0.5275912***
	(0.0732583)	(0.1181968)	(0.0732588)
lnsigma2	-0.6124693***	-0.5752009***	-0.6124746***
	(0.1019465)	(0.0900051)	(0.1019419)
ilgtgamma	-1.290261***	-1.31987***	-1.290286***
	(0.4587449)	(0.4230135)	(0.458733)
mu	0.088367	0.4071662*	0.0883831
	(0.2541306)	(0.2121454)	(0.2541179)
eta	0.1827079***		0.1827064***
	(0.049244)		(0.0492438)
sigma2	0.5420108	0.5625918	0.542008
	(0.0552561)	(0.0506361)	(0.0552533)
gamma	0.2158086	0.2108399	0.2158044
	(0.0776358)	(0.0703837)	(0.0776327)
sigma_u2	0.1169706	0.1186168	0.1169677
	(0.0528399)	(0.0489329)	(0.0528371)
sigma_v2	0.4250402	0.443975	0.4250402
	(0.0212982)	(0.0223136)	(0.0212982)
Note:		*p<0.1; **p<0.05; ***p<0.01	

Source: *Compiled by Author from Stata output sheet*

margin. According to the Time Invariant Inefficiency Model, the coefficient of inventory turnover is 0.0189556, while the return on assets is 0.0023184. These values suggest that the operating performance of all companies involved in the acquisition has exhibited improvement. Based on the analysis, it can be concluded that the return on assets (ROA) does not have a significant impact on the pre-operating margin.

In time-varying decay inefficiency, the ROA and inventory turnover positively influence the operating margin before the acquisition. The coefficient value of ROA and inventory turnover are also insignificant like in other models. In table 4.2.22, the impact of sales on operating efficiency before acquisition using three different models of stochastic frontier analysis.

Table 4.2.23 displays the various models used in Stochastic Frontier analysis prior to

Table 4.2.23 -Impact of Sales on Operating Efficiency Before Acquisition

	Dependent variable		
	Operating Profit Margin		
	(1)	(2)	(3)
sales	0.2837215***	0.2991654***	0.2837216***
	(0.0350157)	(0.034132)	(0.0350157)
constant	0.6931523***	0.9583491	0.6931536***
	(0.1616278)	(0.5391291)	(0.1616279)
lnsigma2	-0.6747937***	-0.6760518***	-0.6747941***
	(0.04993)	(0.0402991)	(0.0499332)
ilgtgamma	-1.690509***	-1.740169***	-1.690511***
	(0.2852513)	(0.2290384)	(0.2852497)
mu	0.4640823**	0.7981612*	0.4640842**
	(0.2167023)	(0.5481284)	(0.2167017)
eta	0.0546505*		0.0546503*
	(0.0380652)		(0.0380651)
sigma2	0.5092615	0.5086212	0.5092613
	(0.0254292)	(0.020497)	(0.0254291)
gamma	0.1557089	0.1492914	0.1557087
	(0.0375002)	(0.0290887)	(0.0374999)
sigma_u2	0.0792966	0.0759328	0.0792964
	(0.0217485)	(0.0162024)	(0.0217484)
sigma_v2	0.4299649	0.4326884	0.4299649
	(0.0179861)	(0.0181035)	(0.0179861)
Note:			*p<0.1; **p<0.05; ***p<0.01

Source: *Compiled by Author from Stata output sheet*

the occurrence of an acquisition. The initial model pertains to the Time-Varying Decay Model (Truncated-Normal), while the second model pertains to the Time Invariant Inefficiency Model. Lastly, the third model pertains to the Time-Varying Decay Inefficiency Model.

The time-varying decay model, specifically the truncated-normal variant, indicates that the coefficient of *mu*, denoted as 0.4640823, signifies that a one percent increase in turnover will result in a growth rate increase of 46.40 percent. Based on the calculated z value, it can be concluded that sales exert a statistically significant influence on the operating margin at a significance level of 1%.

According to the Time Invariant Inefficiency Model, the Coefficient of Sales is determined to be 0.2991654. This value suggests that the operating performance of all companies involved in the acquisition has exhibited improvement. The sales variable demonstrates a substantial impact on the pre-operating margin, with statistical significance observed at a 1% level. In the context of a time-varying decay inefficiency model, it is observed that the turnover has a positive influence on the operating margin prior to the acquisition. The significance of the coefficient value of turnover is consistent with that observed in other models at 1%.

In the next segment, the results of all the combined variables of operating efficiency before acquisition are reported under three different models of stochastic frontier analysis.

Table 4.2.24 -Stochastic Frontier Results of Operating Efficiency Before Acquisition

	Dependent variable		
	Operating Profit Margin		
	(1)	(2)	(3)
roa	-0.0149057	-0.0139719*	-0.0149055
	(0.0082025)	(0.0082958)	(0.0081997)
oroa	0.7615229***	0.7581025***	0.7615223***
	(0.0237425)	(0.0236259)	(0.0237397)
sales	-0.0281217	-0.0016721	-0.0281236
	(0.0345768)	(0.0340074)	(0.0345297)
fat	-0.0565243**	-0.0723487***	-0.0565251**
	(0.0233412)	(0.0231799)	(0.02329)
it	-0.0524664**	-0.0657279***	-0.0524664**
	(0.0251819)	(0.025181)	(0.0251782)
constant	0.2009946***	0.2009313***	0.2010095***
	(0.0304748)	(0.0248667)	(0.0250085)
lnsigma2	2.964074	3.765821*	2.946451***
	(3.535026)	(0.003626)	(0.0386887)
ilgtgamma	4.574947	5.332356*	4.557151***
	(3.572226)	(0.0514549)	(0.0521459)
mu	-164.3104	-245.2718	-161.4781
	(587.0926)		
eta	0.2761233***		0.276087***
	(0.0628548)		(0.0386887)
sigma2	19.37675	43.19916	19.03827
	(68.49733)	(0.1566591)	(0.0696463)
gamma	0.9897983	0.9951906	0.9896170
	(0.036071)	(0.0002463)	(0.0005358)
sigma_u2	19.17908	42.99139	18.84060
	(68.49741)	(0.1563486)	(0.0689067)
sigma_v2	0.1976758	0.2077632	0.1976738
	(0.0103995)	(0.01066)	(0.0102809)
Note:			*p<0.1; **p<0.05; ***p<0.01

Source: *Compiled by Author from Stata output sheet*

Table 4.2.24 displays the various models used in stochastic frontier analysis prior to the occurrence of an acquisition. The initial model pertains to the Time-Varying Decay Model (Truncated-Normal), while the second model pertains to the Time Invariant Inefficiency Model. Lastly, the third model pertains to the Time-Varying Decay Inefficiency Model.

The time-varying decay model, particularly the truncated-normal variant, suggests that the coefficient of *mu*, represented as β, indicates that an increase in ROA, five-year average turnover, inventory turnover, and sales will lead to a decrease in the growth rate, as the coefficient of *mu* is negative before acquisition. Based on the computed z value, it can be inferred that, with the exception of ROA and Sales, all other variables demonstrate a statistically significant impact on the operating margin at significance levels of 1% and 5%.

According to the Time Invariant Inefficiency Model, the Coefficient of operating ROA is determined to be 0.7581025. This value suggests that the operating performance of all companies before the acquisition has exhibited improvement. The OROA, ROA, FAT, and IT demonstrate a substantial impact on the pre-operating margin, with statistical significance observed at a 1% and 10% level. ROA, Sales, five-year average annual turnover, and inventory are negatively influencing the operating performance of the companies prior to the acquisition.

In the context of a model that accounts for time-varying decay inefficiency, empirical evidence suggests that the operating return on assets (ROA) exerts a positive impact on the operating margin in the period preceding the acquisition. Nevertheless, it is worth noting that all other variables exhibit a detrimental impact on the operational performance of the companies prior to the acquisition. With the exception of ROA and turnover, all other variables exhibit a statistically significant impact at a significance level of 1% and 5%.

Next, in Table 4.2.25, the impact of operating return on assets and five-year average turnover on operating efficiency after acquisition under the models of stochastic frontier analysis is explored, Table 4.2.25 displays the various models utilized in stochastic frontier analysis subsequent to the acquisition. The initial model pertains to the Time-Varying Decay Model (Truncated-Normal), while the second model pertains to the

Time Invariant Inefficiency Model. Lastly, the third model pertains to the Time-Varying Decay Inefficiency Model. In the context of a time-varying decay model, specifically the truncated-normal model, the coefficient of Mu is determined to be 575.1974 after acquisition which was 169.6808 before acquisition. This coefficient signifies that a one

Table 4.2.25 -Impact of OROA and FAT on Operating Efficiency After Acquisition

	Dependent variable		
	Operating Profit Margin		
	(1)	(2)	(3)
oroa	0.9149539***	0.903771***	0.9149508***
	(0.0170894)	(0.0168004)	(0.0170301)
fat	0.0634801***	0.0601197***	0.0634775***
	(0.016134)	(0.0160712)	(0.0160713)
constant	0.4395813***	0.4546642***	0.4395523***
	(0.0306502)	(0.053314)	(0.0248868)
lnsigma2	5.46082	1.505388	5.435092***
	(4.525301)	(3.983026)	(0.0031763)
ilgtgamma	6.822672*	2.79986	6.796903***
	(4.530307)	(4.209374)	(0.0462419)
mu	-575.1974	-10.62886	-560.6376
	(2610.234)	(49.25737)	
eta	-0.0876166***		-0.0875997***
	(0.0300963)		(0.0291297)
sigma2	235.2903	4.505902	229.314
	(1064.759)	(17.94712)	(0.7283665)
gamma	0.9989124	0.9426683	0.998884
	(0.0049219)	(0.2274948)	(0.0000515)
sigma_u2	235.0344	4.247571	229.0581
	(1064.759)	(17.94319)	(0.7283392)
sigma_v2	0.2559072	0.2583312	0.2559106
	(0.011986)	(0.0128051)	(0.0118011)
Note:			*p<0.1; **p<0.05; ***p<0.01

Source: *Compiled by Author from Stata output sheet*

percent increase in the operating return on assets (OROA) and the five-year average turnover post-merger will lead to a decline in the growth rate after acquisition. Based on the calculated z value, it can be concluded that the post-operating return on assets and the post-five-year average turnover have a statistically significant influence on the operating margin, with significance levels of 1%.

According to the Time Invariant Inefficiency Model, the Coefficient of Operating

Return on Assets (OROA) experienced a significant increase from 0.6858719 before the acquisition to 0.903771 after the acquisition. This indicates an approximate improvement of 2 percent in the operating performance subsequent to the acquisition. The coefficient of the five-year average turnover after the merger is positive, suggesting that the operating performance has improved compared to pre-acquisition when the coefficient was negative. Additionally, the post-operating return on assets and the post-five-year average turnover has significant effects on the post-operating margin, with significant values at the 1% level.

The acquisition has a positive impact on the operating margin, as evidenced by the positive influence of both the operating return on assets (OROA) and the five-year average turnover in the context of time-varying decay inefficiency. However, the only positive aspect in terms of operating return on assets (OROA) was observed prior to the acquisition. Hence, it can be asserted that both variables have exerted a positive influence on the operational performance of the company post-acquisition. The significance levels of the coefficient values for OROA and the five-year average annual turnover in the post-acquisition context is 1% level.

In this segment, the impact of operating return on assets and five-year average turnover on operating efficiency is explored. Further, in the next segment the impact of inventory turnover and return on assets on operating efficiency after acquisition is examined.

Table 4.2.26 displays the various models of stochastic frontier analysis subsequent to the acquisition. The initial model pertains to the Time-Varying Decay Model (Truncated-Normal), while the second model pertains to the Time Invariant Inefficiency Model. Lastly, the third model pertains to the Time-Varying Decay Inefficiency Model.

In the context of a time-varying decay model, specifically the truncated-normal model, the coefficient of Mu is estimated to be 0.8008007. This coefficient indicates that a one percent increase in both the return on assets (ROA) and inventory turnover following an acquisition will result in a decline of 80 percent in the growth rate. Nevertheless, the coefficient exhibited a positive value prior to the acquisition. Based on the calculated z value, it can be concluded that the influence of return on assets and inventory turnover on operating margin is not statistically significant during the pre-acquisition period.

However, following the acquisition, this relationship has become statistically significant at a 1% and 5% level of significance.

Table 4.2.26 - Impact of IT and ROA on Operating Efficiency After Acquisition

	Dependent variable		
	Operating Profit Margin		
	(1)	(2)	(3)
it	0.5551593***	0.5165574***	0.5551593***
	(0.0268164)	(0.0237176)	(0.0268164)
roa	0.0148774**	0.0172536***	0.0148774**
	(0.0071665)	(0.0061674)	(0.0071665)
constant	0.5766798***	0.697456***	0.5766793***
	(0.0856571)	(0.1114587)	(0.0856572)
lnsigma2	0.959776**	0.4103101**	0.9597796**
	(0.4601796)	(0.1959427)	(0.4601835)
ilgtgamma	0.8690288*	-0.0864632	0.869034*
	(0.6557066)	(0.4137133)	(0.655711)
mu	-0.8008007	0.356915	-0.8008129
	(1.506774)	(0.4702586)	(1.506793)
eta	-0.1128961***		-0.1128963***
	(0.0408663)		(0.0408663)
sigma2	2.611111	1.507285	2.611121
	(1.20158)	(0.2953416)	(1.201595)
gamma	0.7045436	0.4783976	0.7045447
	(0.1364931)	(0.1032353)	(0.1364938)
sigma_u2	1.839642	0.7210816	1.839651
	(1.201516)	(0.2945294)	(1.201531)
sigma_v2	0.7714697	0.7862034	0.7714697
	(0.0382366)	(0.0390937)	(0.0382366)
Note:		*p<0.1; **p<0.05; ***p<0.01	

Source: *Compiled by Author from Stata output sheet*

According to the Time Invariant Inefficiency Model, the coefficient of Return on Assets (ROA) after the acquisition is 0.0172536, compared to 0.0023184 before the acquisition. This suggests that the operating performance has improved by approximately 1.5 percent after the merger, as indicated by the increased value of the ROA coefficient. The change in return on assets (ROA) indicates that subsequent to the acquisition there is a positive impact on the post-operating margin. Nevertheless, subsequent to the acquisition, these values have attained statistical significance at a 1% level. The inventory turnover, which was previously 0.0189556, has experienced a shift to 0.5165574 following the acquisition indicating a positive percentage change of approx. 50%. This change has had a beneficial effect on the operational performance of the companies subsequent to the acquisition.

In time-varying decay inefficiency, the ROA and inventory turnover positively influence the operating margin after the acquisition. The coefficients are positive before acquisition as well. The coefficient value of inventory turnover and ROA are also significant at 1% and 5% levels after the acquisition which was insignificant before the acquisition.

In table 4.2.27, the impact of sales on operating efficiency after acquisition is examined under three different models of stochastic frontier analysis.

Table 4.2.27 - Impact of Sales on Operating Efficiency After Acquisition

	Dependent variable		
	Operating Profit Margin		
	(1)	(2)	(3)
sales	0.6559534***	0.6006861***	0.655958***
	(0.0227758)	(0.0210747)	(0.0228004)
constant	0.1904735***	0.3355839***	0.1904423***
	(0.0538336)	(0.0772709)	(0.0545961)
lnsigma2	2.61158	0.4063249*	2.614315
	(2.464196)	(0.2401505)	(2.585805)
ilgtgamma	2.818759	-0.1277604	2.821683
	(2.611033)	(0.5143528)	(2.739375)
mu	-17.8502	-0.2078588	-17.90738
	(50.51822)	(0.7123431)	(53.16275)
eta	-0.2346532***		-0.2346787***
	(0.0485804)		(0.0490279)
sigma2	13.62055	1.50129	13.65786
	(33.56372)	(0.360536)	(35.31656)
gamma	0.9436812	0.4681033	0.9438364
	(0.1387687)	(0.1280649)	(0.1452123)
sigma_u2	12.85346	0.7027589	12.89078
	(33.56331)	(0.3597173)	(35.31611)
sigma_v2	0.7670938	0.7985313	0.7670751
	(0.0312859)	(0.0327977)	(0.0312855)
Note:		*p<0.1; **p<0.05; ***p<0.01	

Source: *Compiled by Author from Stata output sheet*

Table 4.2.27 displays the various models used in Stochastic Frontier analysis after the acquisition. The initial model pertains to the Time-Varying Decay Model (Truncated-Normal), while the second model pertains to the Time Invariant Inefficiency Model. Lastly, the third model pertains to the Time-Varying Decay Inefficiency Model.

The time-varying decay model, specifically the truncated-normal variant, indicates that the coefficient of *mu*, denoted as 17.8502 after acquisition was 0.4640823 before acquisition. Before acquisition, the coefficient was positive which signifies that a one percent increase in turnover will result in a growth rate increase of 46.40 percent. However, it has become negative post-acquisition which means that a one percent increase in turnover will result in a decline in the growth rate of operating performance. Based on the calculated z value, it can be concluded that sales exert a statistically significant influence on the operating margin at a significance level of 1% after acquisition.

According to the Time Invariant Inefficiency model, the Coefficient of Sales is determined to be 0.6006861 post-acquisition which was 0.2991654 pre-acquisition. This value suggests that the operating performance of all companies has become better due to the change in the percentage of coefficient of sales by approx. 30% after acquisition. The sales variable demonstrates a substantial impact on the operating margin, with statistical significance observed at a 1% level after acquisition.

In the context of a time-varying decay inefficiency model, it is observed that the turnover has a positive influence on the operating margin post-acquisition and prior to the acquisition. The significance of the coefficient value of turnover is consistent with that observed in other models.

The results of the operating efficiency after acquisition under models of stochastic frontier analysis are presented in Table 4.2.28.

Table 4.2.28 displays the various models used in stochastic frontier analysis post-acquisition. The initial model pertains to the Time-Varying Decay Model (Truncated-Normal), while the second model pertains to the Time Invariant Inefficiency Model. Lastly, the third model pertains to the Time-Varying Decay Inefficiency Model.

The time-varying decay model, particularly the truncated-normal variant, suggests that the coefficient of Mu, represented as β, indicates that an increase in OROA, ROA, five-year average turnover, inventory turnover, and Sales will lead to an increase in the growth rate, as the coefficient of Mu is positive. Based on the computed z value, it can be inferred that OROA and Sales demonstrate a statistically significant impact on the operating margin at the significance level of 1%.

Table 4.2.28 -Stochastic Frontier Results of Operating Efficiency After Acquisition

	Dependent variable		
	Operating Profit Margin		
	(1)	(2)	(3)
roa	0.0050591	0.0057673	0.0050591
	(0.0117679)	(0.0117541)	(0.0117679)
oroa	0.8461069***	0.8446781***	0.8461068***
	(0.0221925)	(0.0221256)	(0.0221925)
sales	0.1486923***	0.1428267***	0.1486921***
	(0.0293112)	(0.0286028)	(0.0293112)
fat	-0.0144283	-0.013416	-0.0144283
	(0.0202428)	(0.0201861)	(0.0202428)
it	0.0047718	0.0012226	0.0047716
	(0.0252532)	(0.0249268)	(0.0252532)
constant	1.291978***	1.660759	1.292017***
	(0.3410618)	(4.240885)	(0.3411238)
lnsigma2	-1.056438***	-1.07144***	-1.056439***
	(0.062218)	(0.0583926)	(0.0622179)
ilgtgamma	-0.397832**	-0.4419606***	-0.3978341**
	(0.1639573)	(0.1565171)	(0.1639573)
mu	1.322746***	1.66379	1.322784***
	(0.3335685)	(4.241177)	(0.3336281)
eta	-0.0121814		-0.0121808
	(0.0147317)		(0.014732)
sigma2	0.347692	0.3425149	0.3476918
	(0.0216327)	(0.0200003)	(0.0216327)
gamma	0.4018333	0.3912739	0.4018328
	(0.0394093)	(0.037279)	(0.0394093)
sigma_u2	0.1397142	0.1340171	0.139714
	(0.0202861)	(0.0183714)	(0.0202861)
sigma_v2	0.2079778	0.2084978	0.2079778
	(0.0116005)	(0.0116234)	(0.0116005)
Note:	*p<0.1; **p<0.05; ***p<0.01		

Source: *Compiled by Author from Stata output sheet*

According to the Time Invariant Inefficiency Model, the Coefficient of ROA, OROA sales, and inventory turnover is determined to be 0.0057673, 0.8446781, 0.1428267, and 0.0012226 respectively. These values suggest that the operating performance of all companies after acquisition has exhibited improvement. The OROA and Sales demonstrate a substantial impact on the post-operating margin, with statistical significance observed at a 1% level. Except for OROA, all other variables are negatively influencing the operating performance of the companies prior to the acquisition.

In the context of a model that accounts for time-varying decay inefficiency, empirical evidence suggests that the operating return on assets (ROA) exerts a positive impact on the operating margin in the period preceding the acquisition. Nevertheless, it is worth noting that all other variables exhibit a detrimental impact on the operational performance of the companies prior to the acquisition. However, after the acquisition, all the variables except the five-year average turnover had a positive influence on the operating performance of the companies. OROA and Sales exhibit a statistically significant impact at a significance level of 1% level after acquisition.

In table 4.2.29, the impact of operating return on assets and five-year average turnover during acquisition under different models of stochastic frontier analysis is examined. Table 4.2.29 displays the various models utilized in stochastic frontier analysis in the year of the acquisition. The initial model pertains to the Time-Varying Decay Model (Truncated-Normal), while the second model pertains to the Time Invariant Inefficiency Model. Lastly, the third model pertains to the Time-Varying Decay Inefficiency Model.

Table 4.2.29 -Impact of OROA and FAT on Operating Efficiency During Acquisition

	Dependent variable		
	Operating Profit Margin		
	(1)	(2)	(3)
oroa	0.6953389***	0.6922742***	0.6953353***
	(0.0248897)	(0.0250246)	(0.0248488)
fat	-0.0249015	-0.0202516	-0.0248889
	(0.0275248)	(0.0277098)	(0.0273972)
constant	0.2206043***	0.2267823***	0.2207***
	(0.0287605)	(0.0195259)	(0.0207699)
lnsigma2	3.706425*	4.038027***	3.697646***
	(2.574171)	(0.0031621)	(0.0031517)
ilgtgamma	5.602967**	5.926752***	5.594262***
	(2.585712)	(0.0674075)	(0.067836)
mu	-238.9417	-279.8125	-236.8621
	(617.2939)		
eta	0.268915**		0.2683967***
	(0.1520537)		(0.1052603)
sigma2	40.70801	56.71436	40.35219
	(104.7894)	(0.1793354)	(0.1271768)
gamma	0.9963266	0.99734	0.9962946
	(0.0094634)	(0.0001788)	(0.0002504)
sigma_u2	40.55847	56.5635	40.20267
	(104.7895)	(0.1791207)	(0.1268103)
sigma_v2	0.1495354	0.1508622	0.1495195
	(0.0103916)	(0.0101546)	(0.0101301)
Note:			*p<0.1; **p<0.05; ***p<0.01

Source: *Compiled by Author from Stata output sheet*

In the context of a time-varying decay model, specifically the truncated-normal model, the coefficient of Mu is determined to be 238.9417 in the year of acquisition which is 575.1974 after acquisition. This coefficient signifies that a one percent increase in the operating return on assets (OROA) and the five-year average turnover during the year will lead to a decline in the growth rate. Based on the calculated z value, it can be concluded that the post-operating return on assets and the post-five-year average turnover have a statistically significant influence on the operating margin, with a significance level of 1%. However, during the acquisition only OROA had a significant impact at the 1% level.

Based on the Time Invariant Inefficiency Model, the Coefficient of Operating Return on Assets (OROA) exhibits a value of 0.6922742 during the acquisition, which is observed to be 0.6858719 before the acquisition and 0.903771 after the acquisition. This suggests that the impact of operating return on assets (OROA) on the improvement of operating performance is higher both before and after the acquisition compared to during the acquisition. The positive coefficient of the five-year average turnover subsequent to the acquisition indicates an enhancement in operating performance as compared to the pre-acquisition period, where the coefficient was negative. However, it should be noted that the coefficient exhibits a negative value during the year of acquisition as well. Furthermore, it is observed that the post-operating return on assets (OROA) and the post-five-year average turnover have a considerable impact on the post-operating margin. Specifically, these variables exhibit significant values at the 1% level. On the other hand, it is worth noting that only the operating return on assets (OROA) demonstrates a significant effect on the operating margin, with a significant value observed at the 1% level during the year of the acquisition.

The merger has a positive impact on the operating margin, as evidenced by the positive influence of the operating return on assets (OROA) in the context of time-varying decay inefficiency during the year of acquisition. However, both operating return on assets and five-year average turnover have a positive aspect in terms of operating return on assets (OROA) observed after the acquisition. Hence, it can be asserted that both variables have exerted a positive influence on the operational performance of the company's post-acquisition but only OROA exerted a positive influence during the year of acquisition. The significance level of the coefficient value for OROA is at a 1% level.

Further, in the next table, the impact of other variables such as return on assets and inventory turnover on operating efficiency is displayed under the models of stochastic frontier analysis.

Table 4.2.30 displays the various models of Stochastic Frontier analysis in the year of acquisition. The initial model pertains to the Time-Varying Decay Model (Truncated-Normal), while the second model pertains to the Time Invariant Inefficiency Model. Lastly, the third model pertains to the Time-Varying Decay Inefficiency Model.

In the context of a time-varying decay model, specifically the truncated-normal model, the coefficient of Mu is estimated to be 198.2539. This coefficient indicates that a one percent increase in both the return on assets (ROA) and inventory turnover following an acquisition will result in a decline in the growth rate. Nevertheless, the coefficient

Table 4.2.30 -Impact of IT and ROA on Operating Efficiency During Acquisition

	Dependent variable		
	Operating Profit Margin		
	(1)	(2)	(3)
it	0.2581636***	0.2560358***	0.2581695***
	(0.0434828)	(0.0434835)	(0.0434829)
roa	0.0041965	0.0047179	0.0041967
	(0.0036671)	(0.0051822)	(0.0036671)
constant	198.2493***	0.3555855***	376.6364***
	(0.0474685)	(0.0627932)	(0.0474675)
lnsigma2	-0.577936***	2.715644	-0.5779938***
	(0.062726)	(6.983929)	(0.0627226)
ilgtgamma	-1.425467***	3.423746	-1.425667***
	(0.3840492)	(7.208474)	(0.3840225)
mu	-198.2539	-48.47629	376.641
		(356.2182)	
eta	-0.0006352***		-0.0003343**
	(0.0002967)		(0.0001561)
sigma2	0.5610552	15.11435	0.5610228
	(0.0351927)	(105.5575)	(0.351888)
gamma	0.193806	0.9684385	0.1937748
	(0.0600059)	(0.2203299)	(0.0599943)
sigma_u2	0.1087359	14.63732	0.1087121
	(0.0356178)	(105.5559)	(0.0356071)
sigma_v2	0.4523193	0.4770319	0.4523107
	(0.0396179)	(0.0370504)	(0.0396172)
Note:			*p<0.1; **p<0.05; ***p<0.01

Source: *Compiled by Author from Stata output sheet*

exhibited a positive value prior to the acquisition. However, it was negative after the acquisition. Based on the calculated z value, it can be concluded that the influence of return on assets and inventory turnover on operating margin is not statistically significant during the pre-acquisition period. However, following the acquisition, this relationship has become statistically significant at a 1% and 5% level of significance. During the year of acquisition, only Inventory turnover is significant at a 1% level.

Based on the Time Invariant Inefficiency Model, the coefficient for Return on Assets (ROA) is observed to be 0.0047179 during the year of the acquisition. This coefficient increases to 0.0172536 after the acquisition, while it stands at 0.0023184 prior to the acquisition. This implies that operational efficiency has experienced a more significant growth rate subsequent to the merger, as evidenced by the heightened value of the ROA coefficient. Following the consolidation, the Return on Assets (ROA) and Inventory turnover have achieved statistical significance at a significance level of 1%. However, it is worth noting that in the year of the acquisition, only inventory turnover exhibited statistical significance at a 1% level. The inventory turnover, which was previously 0.0189556, has experienced a shift to 0.5165574 following the acquisition indicating a percentage change of approx. 50%. In the year of acquisition, the inventory turnover is 0.2560358 which signifies that the maximum change has occurred after the acquisition only. The aforementioned alteration has had a significantly advantageous impact on the operational efficiency of the companies following the acquisition, as it is experiencing a higher rate of change.

In time-varying decay inefficiency, the ROA and inventory turnover positively influence the operating margin after and during the acquisition. The coefficient value of ROA and inventory turnover are also significant at 1% and 5% level after the acquisition, only inventory turnover is significant during the acquisition. However, both variables were insignificant before acquisition.

In the next segment, the impact of sales on operating efficiency during acquisition is examined under the models of stochastic frontier analysis.

Table 4.2.31 displays the various models used in Stochastic Frontier analysis during the year of acquisition. The initial model pertains to the Time-Varying Decay Model (Truncated-Normal), while the second model pertains to the Time Invariant Inefficiency

Table 4.2.31 -Impact of Sales on Operating Efficiency During Acquisition

	Dependent variable		
	Operating Profit Margin		
	(1)	(2)	(3)
sales	0.3500072***	0.3395067***	0.3500107***
	(0.0381127)	(0.0380523)	(0.0381125)
constant	141.9936***	0.2650295***	271.2103***
	(0.0386594)	(0.0740867)	(0.0386584)
lnsigma2	-0.6586668***	0.7479212	-0.658722***
	(0.0516953)	(3.59866)	(0.0516926)
ilgtgamma	-1.865887***	1.280318	-1.866122***
	(0.4340295)	(4.58814)	(0.4339701)
mu	142.0493	-5.930403	271.266
		(30.72102)	
eta	-0.0008658***		-0.0004534***
	(0.0003463)		(0.0001813)
sigma2	0.5175408	2.112604	0.5175123
	(0.0267544)	(7.602543)	(0.0267516)
gamma	0.1340184	0.782504	0.1339911
	(0.0503724)	(0.7808625)	(0.0503568)
sigma_u2	0.06936	1.653121	0.069342
	(0.0267857)	(7.598457)	(0.0267747)
sigma_v2	0.4481809	0.4594829	0.4481702
	(0.0324806)	(0.0304719)	(0.0324799)
Note:			*p<0.1; **p<0.05; ***p<0.01

Source: *Compiled by Author from Stata output sheet*

Model. Lastly, the third model pertains to the Time-Varying Decay Inefficiency Model. The time-varying decay model, specifically the truncated-normal variant, indicates that the coefficient of Mu, denoted as 142.0493 during the year of acquisition which is 17.8502 after acquisition which was 0.4640823 before acquisition. Before acquisition, the coefficient was positive which signifies that a one percent increase in turnover will result in a growth rate increase of 46.40 percent. However, it has become negative post-acquisition which means that a one percent increase in turnover will result in a decline in the growth rate of operating performance. Based on the calculated z value, it can be concluded that sales exert a statistically significant influence on the operating margin at a significance level of 1% during and after acquisition.

Based on the Time Invariant Inefficiency Model, the Coefficient of Sales is found to be 0.3395067 in the year of acquisition, 0.6006861 post-acquisition, and 0.2991654 pre-acquisition. This finding indicates that the operational efficiency of the companies has improved after the acquisition, with a significant increase of approximately 30% in the coefficient of sales. During the fiscal year of the merger, there was an observed change of approximately 26 percent in comparison to the pre-acquisition period. However, following the acquisition, it has exerted a significant influence and is widely regarded as highly advantageous for enhancing operational performance. Thus, it can be inferred that the acquisition has been advantageous for the companies in enhancing their operational performance. The variable of sales exhibits a significant influence on the operating margin, as evidenced by statistical significance at a 1% level both during and after the acquisition.

Within the framework of a time-varying decay inefficiency model, empirical evidence suggests that turnover exerts a favorable impact on the pre-acquisition, during-acquisition, and post-acquisition operating margin. The post-merger scenario has demonstrated the significant impact of acquisition, thereby substantiating their benefits for companies by enhancing their operational performance. The coefficient value of turnover demonstrates a consistent significance, which aligns with findings observed in other models.

In table 4.2.32, the results of operating efficiency during acquisition under the models of stochastic frontier analysis are displayed.

Table 4.2.32 displays the various models used in stochastic frontier analysis during the year of acquisition. The initial model pertains to the Time-Varying Decay Model (Truncated-Normal), while the second model pertains to the Time Invariant Inefficiency Model. Lastly, the third model pertains to the Time-Varying Decay Inefficiency Model. The time-varying decay model, particularly the truncated-normal variant, suggests that the coefficient of *mu*, represented as β, indicates that an increase in ROA, OROA, and inventory turnover will lead to a decrease in the growth rate, as the coefficient of *mu* is negative during the year of acquisition. However, this coefficient is positive after acquisition thereby, a one percent increase in these variables will result rise in the growth rate post-acquisition. Based on the computed z value, it can be inferred that only OROA demonstrates a statistically significant impact on the operating margin at the significance level of 1% during the year of acquisition.

According to the Time Invariant Inefficiency Model, the Coefficient of ROA, OROA, Sales, and inventory turnover is determined to be 0.0034793,0.716772 0.0045292, and 0.0091602 respectively. These values suggest that the operating performance of all companies during the year of acquisition has exhibited improvement. The OROA, demonstrates a substantial impact on the operating margin, with statistical significance observed at a 1% level. Five-year average annual turnover is negatively influencing the operating performance of the companies during the year of acquisition.

Table 4.2.32 -Stochastic Frontier Results of Operating Efficiency During Acquisition

	Dependent variable		
	Operating Profit Margin		
	(1)	(2)	(3)
roa	0.0023516	0.0034793	0.0023516
	(0.0098748)	(0.0097937)	(0.0098739)
oroa	0.7210818***	0.7167772***	0.721082***
	(0.0306283)	(0.0302093)	(0.0305698)
sales	-0.0102527	0.0045292	-0.0102548
	(0.0536285)	(0.0504656)	(0.052892)
fat	-0.0375369	-0.0371702	-0.0375373
	(0.0347558)	(0.0348208)	(0.0346947)
it	0.0106426	0.0091602	0.010643
	(0.0351259)	(0.0352081)	(0.0351108)
constant	0.2084661***	0.2061407***	0.2084624***
	(0.0395484)	(0.0294151)	(0.0336804)
lnsigma2	3.796871	3.951833***	3.787707***
	(3.543049)	(0.0036529)	(0.0036385)
ilgtgamma	5.700059*	5.852065***	5.690862***
	(3.556935)	(0.0776274)	(0.0788701)
mu	-250.038	-267.8686	-247.8166
	(889.4469)		
eta	0.1495228		0.1495518
	(0.1910507)		(0.1448391)
sigma2	44.56153	52.03068	44.15504
	(157.8837)	(0.1900626)	(0.1606592)
gamma	0.9966654	0.9971343	0.9966347
	(0.0118214)	(0.0002218)	(0.0002645)
sigma_u2	44.41293	51.88157	44.00644
	(157.8838)	(0.1897955)	(0.1602795)
sigma_v2	0.1485954	0.1491055	0.1485957
	(0.0120376)	(0.0115578)	(0.0117051)
Note:			*p<0.1; **p<0.05; ***p<0.01

Source: *Compiled by Author from Stata output sheet*

In the context of a model that accounts for time-varying decay inefficiency, empirical evidence suggests that the operating return on assets (OROA), ROA, and inventory exert a positive impact on the operating margin in the period during the year of acquisition. Nevertheless, it is worth noting that all other variables exhibit a detrimental impact on the operational performance of the companies during the acquisition. However, after the merger, all the variables except the five-year average turnover have a positive influence on the operating performance of the companies which shows that acquisition is beneficial for the companies as it has improved their operating performance. Only OROA exhibits a statistically significant impact at a significance level of 1% during the year of acquisition. In the above tables, the impact of all the variables on operating efficiency is analysed under various models of stochastic frontier analysis in pre-, post-and during the acquisition. Further, in the next segment the impact of these variables is examined considering overall acquisition.

Table 4.2.33 displays the various models utilized in Stochastic Frontier analysis in the overall acquisition. The initial model pertains to the Time-Varying Decay Model (Truncated-Normal), while the second model pertains to the Time Invariant Inefficiency Model. Lastly, the third model pertains to the Time-Varying Decay Inefficiency Model. In the context of a time-varying decay model, specifically the truncated-normal model, the coefficient of Mu is determined to be 1.428802 in overall acquisition, 238.9417 in the year of acquisition, and 575.1974 after acquisition. This coefficient signifies that a one percent increase in the operating return on assets (ROA) and the five-year average turnover during the year will lead to a decline in the growth rate in the year of acquisition as well as in overall acquisition. Based on the calculated z value, it can be concluded that the post-operating return on assets and the post-five-year average turnover have a statistically significant influence on the operating margin, with a significance level of 1%. However, in the overall merger, both OROA and five-year average turnover have a significant impact at the 1% level.

Based on the Time Invariant Inefficiency Model, the Coefficient of Operating Return on Assets (OROA) exhibits a value of 0.8049481 in the overall acquisition,0.6922742 during the acquisition, which is observed to be 0.6858719 before the acquisition, and 0.903771 after the acquisition. This suggests that the impact of return on assets (ROA) on the improvement of operating performance is higher both after and overall acquisition, compared to during and prior to the acquisition. The positive coefficient of the five-year average turnover subsequent to the acquisition indicates an enhancement in operating performance as compared to the pre-acquisition period, where the coefficient was negative. However, it should be noted that the coefficient exhibits a

Table 4.2.33 -Impact of OROA and FAT on Operating Efficiency considering Overall Acquisition

	Dependent variable		
	Operating Profit Margin		
	(1)	(2)	(3)
oroa	0.8109941***	0.8049481***	0.8115162***
	(0.011674)	(0.0116798)	(0.0116825)
fat	0.0293603***	0.0250097**	0.0274323**
	(0.0118136)	(0.0118617)	(0.0117929)
constant	0.0650312***	0.0212372*	0.0825026***
	(0.0124584)	(0.0134978)	(0.0124008)
/lnsigma2	-1.189422***	-1.160361***	3.752583***
	(0.030595)	(0.0263621)	(0.0031324)
/ilgtgamma	-5.341824*	-6.981377	4.952944***
	(3.077014)		(0.0273764)
/mu	-1.428802	-0.6371556***	-243.4128
	(4.229146)	(0.011895)	
/eta	0.5885286***		-0.3064067***
	(0.0915575)		(0.0464624)
sigma2	0.3043971	0.3133732	42.63105
	(0.009313)	(0.0082612)	(0.1335357)
gamma	0.0047643	0.0009282	0.9929869
	(0.01459)		(0.0001906)
sigma_u2	0.0014502	0.0002909	42.33207
	(0.0044622)		(0.1333156)
sigma_v2	0.3029469	0.3130823	0.298974
	(0.0081766)		(0.0081273)
Note:			*p<0.1; **p<0.05; ***p<0.01

Source: *Compiled by Author from Stata output sheet*

negative value during the year of acquisition as well. Furthermore, it is observed that the post-operating return on assets (OROA) and the post-five-year average turnover have a considerable impact on the post-operating margin. Specifically, these variables exhibit significant values at the 1% level. On the other hand, it is worth noting that only the operating return on assets (OROA) demonstrates a significant effect on the operating margin, with a significant value observed at the 1% level during the year of acquisition. But in overall acquisition both OROA and five-year average turnover at 1% and 5% overall acquisition respectively.

The acquisition has a positive impact on the operating margin, as evidenced by the positive influence of the operating return on assets (ROA) in the context of time-varying decay inefficiency during the year. However, both operating return on assets and five-year average turnover have a positive aspect in terms of operating return on assets (ROA) observed after the acquisition as well as in overall acquisition. Hence, it can be asserted that both variables have exerted a positive influence on the operational performance of the company's post-merger and overall acquisition but only ROA exerted a positive influence during the year of acquisition. The significance level of the coefficient value for OROA and five-year average turnover is at 1% and 5% level respectively.

In table 4.2.34 the impact of inventory turnover and return on assets on operating efficiency is presented considering overall acquisition.

Table 4.2.34 -Impact of IT and ROA on Operating Efficiency considering Overall Acquisition

	Dependent variable		
	Operating Profit Margin		
	(1)	(2)	(3)
it	0.3710408***	0.368436***	0.4265749***
	(0.0167857)	(0.0184744)	(0.0184154)
roa	0.0073799***	0.0064355***	0.0044642***
	(0.0017742)	(0.0017962)	(0.0018152)
constant	0.1510805***	0.014026	0.1517276***
	(0.0215194)	(0.0183875)	(0.0215376)
lnsigma2	-0.4245414***	-0.2079091***	5.942017***
	(0.0252927)	(0.0274092)	(0.0032744)
ilgtgamma	-7.805556***	-5.532101***	6.25695***
	(1.906048)	(0.0277166)	(0.0289942)
mu	-0.6123785***	-2.100352	-731.0268
	(0.1566639)		
eta	0.7411615***		-0.4269286***
	(0.2104786)		(0.0430991)
sigma2	0.6540697	0.8122809	380.7019
	(0.0165432)	(0.022264)	(1.246569)
gamma	0.0004073	0.0039421	0.9980866
	(0.000776)	(0.0001088)	(0.0000554)
sigma_u2	0.0002664	0.0032021	379.9734
	(0.0005077)	(0.0000106)	(1.246478)
sigma_v2	0.6538033	0.8090788	0.7284412
	(0.016535)	(0.022264)	(0.0209752)
Note:		*p<0.1; **p<0.05; ***p<0.01	

Source: *Compiled by Author from Stata output sheet*

Table 4.2.34 displays the various models of stochastic frontier analysis in the year of acquisition. The initial model pertains to the Time-Varying Decay Model (Truncated-Normal), while the second model pertains to the Time Invariant Inefficiency Model. Lastly, the third model pertains to the Time-Varying Decay Inefficiency Model. In the context of a time-varying decay model, specifically the truncated-normal model, the coefficient of Mu is estimated to be 198.2539. This coefficient indicates that a one percent increase in both the return on assets (ROA) and inventory turnover following an acquisition will result in a decline in the growth rate. Nevertheless, the coefficient exhibited a positive value prior to the acquisition. However, it was negative after the acquisition as well as in the overall acquisition. Based on the calculated z value, it can be concluded that the influence of return on assets and inventory turnover on operating margin is not statistically significant during the pre-acquisition period. However, following the acquisition, this relationship has become statistically significant at a 1% and 5% level of significance. During the year of acquisition, only Inventory turnover is significant at a 1% level. However, in overall acquisition, the coefficient of ROA and Inventory turnover is statistically significant at the 1% level.

Based on the Time Invariant Inefficiency Model, the coefficient for Return on Assets (ROA) is observed to be 0.0047179 during the year of the acquisition. This coefficient increases to 0.0172536 after the acquisition, while it stands at 0.0023184 prior to the acquisition. In overall acquisition, the coefficient of ROA is 0.0064355. This implies that operational efficiency has experienced a more significant growth rate subsequent to the merger, as evidenced by the heightened value of the ROA coefficient. Following the consolidation as well as in overall acquisition, the Return on Assets (ROA) and Inventory turnover have achieved statistical significance at a significance level of 1%. However, it is worth noting that in the year of the acquisition, only inventory turnover exhibited statistical significance at a 1% level. The inventory turnover, which was previously 0.0189556, has experienced a shift to 0.5165574 following the acquisition indicating a percentage change of approx. 50%. In the year of acquisition, the inventory turnover is 0.2560358 which signifies that the maximum change has occurred after the acquisition only. The aforementioned alteration has had a significantly advantageous impact on the operational efficiency of the companies following the acquisition, as it is experiencing a higher rate of change.

In time-varying decay inefficiency, the ROA and inventory turnover positively influence the operating margin before, after, and during as well as in overall acquisition.

The coefficient value of ROA and inventory turnover are also significant at 1% and 5% level after the acquisition, only inventory turnover is significant during the acquisition. However, both variables were insignificant before acquisition. Both ROA and inventory turnover are statistically significant at a 1% level in overall acquisition.

The impact of sales on operating efficiency is also important to evaluate. Therefore, in the next table, the impact of sales on operating efficiency considering overall acquisition is examined.

Table 4.2.35 -Impact of Sales on Operating Efficiency considering Overall Acquisition

	Dependent variable		
	Operating Profit Margin		
	(1)	(2)	(3)
sales	0.4320169***	0.443625***	0.5448451***
	(0.0154859)	(0.0147334)	(0.0147236)
constant	-0.0390305***	0.0069567	0.1662887***
	(0.015389)		(0.0166899)
/lnsigma2	-0.1821964***	-0.2778363***	6.405321***
	(0.0240678)	(0.022912)	(0.0027414)
/ilgtgamma	-7.254415	-8.63767	6.841055***
			(0.0240492)
/mu	-0.910454**	-0.4314499***	-917.2337
	(0.3838189)	(0.0152736)	
/eta	0.3891906***		-0.4451229***
	(0.0712845)		(0.0291615)
sigma2	0.8334376	0.7574208	605.0562
	(0.020059)	(0.017354)	(1.658699)
gamma	0.0007065	0.0001773	0.9989322
			(0.0000257)
sigma_u2	0.0005889	0.0001343	604.4101
			(1.65867)
sigma_v2	0.8328488	0.7572865	0.646099
			(0.0154318)
Note:			*p<0.1; **p<0.05; ***p<0.01

Source: *Compiled by Author from Stata output sheet*

Table 4.2.35 displays the various models used in stochastic frontier analysis during the year of acquisition. The initial model pertains to the Time-Varying Decay Model (Truncated-Normal), while the second model pertains to the Time Invariant Inefficiency

Model. Lastly, the third model pertains to the Time-Varying Decay Inefficiency Model. The time-varying decay model, specifically the truncated-normal variant, indicates that the coefficient of *mu*, denoted as 142.0493 during the year of acquisition which is 17.8502 after acquisition which was 0.4640823 before acquisition. Before acquisition, the coefficient was positive which signifies that a one percent increase in turnover will result in a growth rate increase of 46.40 percent. However, it has become negative post-acquisition and in overall acquisition which means that a one percent increase in turnover will result in a decline in the growth rate of operating performance. Based on the calculated z value, it can be concluded that sales exert a statistically significant influence on the operating margin at a significance level of 1% during, after, and overall acquisition.

Based on the Time Invariant Inefficiency Model, the Coefficient of Sales is found to be 0.3395067 in the year of acquisition, 0.6006861 post-acquisition, 0.2991654 pre-acquisition, and 0.443625 in overall acquisition. This finding indicates that the operational efficiency of the companies has improved after the acquisition, with a significant increase of approximately 30 percent in the coefficient of sales. During the fiscal year of the merger, there was an observed change of approximately 26 percent in comparison to the pre-acquisition period. It has increased 14 percent in comparison to overall acquisition. However, following the acquisition, it has exerted a significant influence and is widely regarded as highly advantageous for enhancing operational performance. Thus, it can be inferred that the acquisition has been advantageous for the companies in enhancing their operational performance. The variable of sales exhibits a significant influence on the operating margin, as evidenced by statistical significance at a 1% level during, and after as well as in overall acquisition.

Within the framework of a time-varying decay inefficiency model, empirical evidence suggests that turnover exerts a favorable impact on the pre-, during, post, and overall acquisition operating margin. The post-merger scenario has demonstrated the significant impact of acquisition, thereby substantiating their benefits for companies by enhancing their operational performance. The coefficient value of turnover demonstrates a consistent significance, which aligns with findings observed in other models.

The results of operating efficiency considering overall acquisition is explored in the next tables under the different models of stochastic frontier analysis.

Table 4.2.36 displays the various models used in stochastic frontier analysis in overall acquisition. The initial model pertains to the Time-Varying Decay Model (Truncated-Normal), while the second model pertains to the Time Invariant Inefficiency Model. Lastly, the third model pertains to the Time-Varying Decay Inefficiency Model.

Table 4.2.36 -Stochastic Frontier Results of Operating Efficiency considering Overall Acquisition

	Dependent variable		
	Operating Profit Margin		
	(1)	(2)	(3)
roa	0.0024993	0.00299	0.0007985
	(0.007055)	(0.0050414)	(0.0142729)
oroa	0.778099***	0.7744317***	0.7704458***
	(0.0199926)	(0.0142256)	(0.0142729)
sales	0.1325923***	0.1506905***	0.1974449***
	(0.0232178)	(0.0157205)	(0.015872)
fat	-0.0315547*	-0.0391032***	-0.0519322***
	(0.0195766)	(0.0138255)	(0.0137199)
it	0.0087624	0.0056011	0.0088521
	(0.0216007)	(0.0153803)	(0.0153293)
constant	0.0201356	-0.0016962	0.0692368***
	(0.0221167)	(0.0143977)	(0.0160758)
/lnsigma2	-0.6060316***	-1.27347***	4.469686***
	(0.0425862)	(0.0312181)	(0.0036356)
/ilgtgamma	-7.25218	-6.163193	5.81902***
			(0.0315606)
/mu	-0.7374091	-0.8976279***	-348.1753
	(0.8804653)	(0.0141182)	
/eta	0.519755***		-0.381204***
	(0.1591026)		(0.0440035)
sigma2	0.5455114	0.2798587	87.32933
	(0.0232312)	(0.0087367)	(0.317498)
gamma	0.0007081	0.0021011	0.9970383
			(0.0000932)
sigma_u2	0.0003863	0.000588	87.07069
			(0.3174165)
sigma_v2	0.5451251	0.2792707	0.2586446
			(0.0081058)
Note:		*p<0.1; **p<0.05; ***p<0.01	

Source: *Compiled by Author from Stata output sheet*

The time-varying decay model, particularly the truncated-normal variant, suggests that the coefficient of *mu*, represented as β, indicates that an increase in ROA, OROA, and inventory turnover will lead to a decrease in the growth rate, as the coefficient of Mu is negative during the year of acquisition as well as in overall acquisition. In the case of overall acquisition an increase in sales will also lead to an adverse effect on growth rate. However, this coefficient is positive after acquisition thereby, a one percent increase in these variables will result rise in the growth rate post-acquisition. Based on the computed z value, it can be inferred that only OROA demonstrates a statistically significant impact on the operating margin at a significance level of 1% during the year of acquisition. OROA and Sales are statistically significant at a 1% level in overall acquisition and five-year average turnover at a 10% level.

According to the Time Invariant Inefficiency Model, the Coefficient of ROA, OROA, sales, and inventory turnover is determined to be 0.00299, 0.7744317, 0.1506905, and 0.0056011 respectively. These values suggest that the operating performance of all companies in overall acquisition has exhibited improvement. The OROA, sales, and five-year average turnover demonstrate a substantial impact on the operating margin, with statistical significance observed at a 1% level. Five-year average annual turnover is negatively influencing the operating performance of the companies in overall acquisition.

In the context of a model that accounts for time-varying decay inefficiency, empirical evidence suggests that the operating return on assets (OROA), ROA, and inventory exert a positive impact on the operating margin in the period during the year of acquisition. Nevertheless, it is worth noting that all other variables exhibit a detrimental impact on the operational performance of the companies during the acquisition. However, after the merger, all the variables except the five-year average turnover have a positive influence on the operating performance of the companies which shows that acquisition is beneficial for the companies as it has improved their operating performance. In overall acquisition except for five-year average turnover, all other variables are positively influencing the operating performance of the companies. Only OROA exhibits a statistically significant impact at a significance level of 1% during the year of acquisition. Except for ROA and inventory turnover, all other variables are statistically significant at a 1% level. Further, the correlation of all the other variables with each other in case of acquisition is presented in correlation matrix table 4.2.36.

Table 4.2.37 -Correlation Matrix of Operating Efficiency - Acquisition

	opm	oroa	sales	fat	it	roa
opm	1					
oroa	0.827	1				
sales	0.462	0.419	1			
fat	0.339	0.404	0.414	1		
it	0.372	0.375	0.605	0.386	1	
roa	0.255	0.308	0.079	0.098	0.075	1

Source: *Compiled by Author from Stata output sheet*

Table 4.2.37 shows the correlation between the variables in the case of acquisition. The operating margin, operating return on assets, sales, five-year average turnover, inventory turnover, and return on assets are positively correlated with each other. Further, Table 4.2.37 shows the null hypotheses of operating efficiency which reflects which variable significantly impacts the operating efficiency of the company in different cases.

Table 4.2.38 -Comparison of Pre-and Post-Acquisitions of Operating Efficiency

S.No.	Company Name	Pre-Acquisition				Post-Acquisition			
		2013	2014	2015	2016	2019	2020	2021	2022
1	Fortis Hospitals Ltd	0.0896	0.4931	0.9978	0.7993	0.8675	-0.5541	-0.7975	-0.5541
2	Virtusa Consulting Services Pvt Ltd	0.8164	0.7715	0.5670	-0.7978	-0.9342	0.0154	2.4395	0.0154
3	TVS Automobile Solutions Pvt Ltd	-	-	-	-	-0.9026	0.9026	-2.5258	0.9026
4	Haldia Energy Ltd	0.1153	-0.2849	0.5155	0.0238	-0.3538	-0.0375	3.0574	-0.0375
5	Tata Power Renewable Energy Ltd	0.4410	0.1588	-0.0255	-0.2943	-0.0769	-0.2211	3.0399	-0.2211
6	Karvy Data Management Services Ltd	-	0.0113	-0.0113	3.1610	-	-	-	-
7	Casagrand Builder Pvt Ltd	1.1000	0.5659	1.6341	0.0284	-1.0957	-1.1127	-	-
8	Valuefirst Digital Media Pvt Ltd	0.2550	0.3724	0.2550	0.4898	0.5004	-1.9192	-1.1037	-1.9192
9	JM Financial Asset Reconstruction Co Ltd	-	0.0981	-0.4612	0.0981	0.2698	0.4146	2.8447	0.4146
10	IDFC Alternatives Ltd	-0.0267	-0.1132	-0.3352	-1.0467	0.5469	1.1030	2.3879	1.1030
11	Tata Realty & Infrastructure Ltd	1.0658	1.1063	-0.3442	-0.5817	0.0351	0.6012	1.2000	0.6012
12	Srei Equipment Finance Ltd	-0.0196	0.0686	-0.0490	3.1551	-	-	-	-
13	ReNew Power Pvt Ltd	0.0579	0.0579	-0.3126	-0.1124	0.1373	3.1436	0.1373	-
14	Wearit Global Ltd	0.2229	0.8036	0.2229	1.3844	-1.6072	-	-	-
15	Shriji Polymers India Ltd	-0.1143	-0.7986	0.2083	0.4602	0.1086	0.2617	2.9962	0.2617
16	Lalitpur Power Generation Co Ltd	1.4499	-1.5393	-1.1301	-1.3569	0.4996	0.2740	0.6364	0.7778
17	Assets Care & Reconstruction Enterprise Ltd	-	-	-	-	0.4355	-0.4355	3.0261	-0.4355
18	HomeShop18	0.3525	0.2013	-1.1411	-0.0588	0.0790	0.2843	2.8839	0.2843
19	GMR Airports Ltd	0.4733	-0.6100	0.3956	1.2712	1.8712	-1.2423	-	-
20	Athanas Enterprise Pvt Ltd	0.4159	1.5805	-0.7487	-0.8317	-	-	-	-
21	SVP Builders India Ltd	-0.3834	-0.6281	-0.1388	-0.2627	-0.8297	-0.5267	-0.2320	-0.5267
22	Jain Farm Fresh Foods Ltd	0.2850	0.6850	0.2850	1.0850	-0.8475	-1.3339	-1.7028	-1.3339
23	Bharti Enterprises Ltd	-1.4864	-	-1.4864	1.4864	-	-	-	-
24	Salzer Magnet Wires Ltd	1.1132	0.3158	0.1676	-0.2354	-1.3611	-	-	-
25	Choicest Enterprises Ltd	-	0.7943	0.7332	0.7943	-0.2980	-1.0026	-2.2154	-1.0026
26	MRC Logistics India Pvt Ltd	0.7283	1.1133	0.4569	0.4262	-0.5663	-0.1431	1.9049	-0.1431
27	World Resorts Ltd	0.1980	-1.6769	-0.1735	1.1129	0.5396	-	-	-
28	Escorts Heart Institute and Research Centre Ltd	-0.8899	-1.9262	0.1463	0.1531	0.0652	1.2712	1.1925	1.2712
29	Alivira Animal Health Ltd	-	-1.2627	-0.5455	-1.2627	0.6644	2.1251	0.6644	-
30	Biocon Biologics Ltd/India	-	-	-	1.3922	0.1817	-1.0766	-0.4972	2.2401

S.No.	Company Name	Pre-Acquisition				Post-Acquisition			
		2013	2014	2015	2016	2019	2020	2021	2022
31	OmniActive Health Technologies Ltd	1.2527	-0.4099	1.1046	-0.1866	-1.7607	-	-	-
32	Nowrosjee Wadia & Sons Ltd	-	0.3518	0.5857	0.3518	-1.4493	-1.2486	0.4365	-1.2486
33	Edel Land Ltd	-	-	-	-	1.4997	-1.4997	-0.0619	-1.4997
34	Telesonic Networks Ltd	-0.4149	-0.4192	-0.4149	-0.4234	1.6475	1.7958	1.6475	-
35	Amtek Auto Ltd	0.4845	0.5378	0.4312	0.4312	0.2613	-1.6788	-1.7541	-1.6788
36	Takasago Thermal Engineering Co Ltd	-0.7192	-0.7797	-0.4777	0.1344	0.6064	-0.0322	0.1297	2.7047
37	Flipkart India Pvt Ltd	-	1.2662	0.4328	1.2662	-0.3289	0.5700	-1.8653	0.5700
38	20 Microns Ltd	-0.9267	-1.0456	0.1110	0.3789	0.1283	-0.0883	0.2849	2.6046
39	Smartchem Technologies Ltd	1.1131	-0.8558	-1.6735	1.0711	0.3451	-	-	-
40	Lotte Confectionery Co Ltd	-	-	-	-0.4816	-0.0421	0.3562	0.1675	2.9674
41	Jasper Industries Pvt Ltd	-0.2202	-1.1050	-0.4387	2.3326	-1.2765	-0.1745	0.1108	-0.1745
42	CavinKare Pvt Ltd	1.4212	-0.6980	0.7043	-0.0884	1.3508	0.6110	-	-
43	Reliance Jio Infocomm Ltd	-0.0047	0.0435	-0.0528	-2.4364	0.8153	0.8156	0.8153	-
44	ProConnect Supply Chain Solutions Ltd	0.5132	0.7437	0.5377	0.3442	-2.1928	1.0058	-0.3147	1.0058
45	Ebixcash Ltd	-1.0246	0.1671	-0.2619	-0.0426	0.8508	2.7142	0.8508	-
46	TATA Advanced Systems Ltd	-0.1540	1.8897	-0.3687	-1.3443	0.0515	-1.0982	-	-
47	Tata Sons Pvt Ltd	1.9514	-2.2321	0.1448	0.1068	0.0292	-	-	-
48	Indian Farmers Fertilizer Cooperative Ltd	0.6346	1.5218	-0.3356	0.2036	0.0726	0.5806	-0.6034	1.2242
49	Inditrade Business Consultants Ltd	0.2710	1.6258	0.1771	-0.1328	-0.8217	-1.1546	0.0710	2.1632
50	Jaquar & Co Pvt Ltd	0.2684	0.7382	0.2684	1.2081	-0.8517	-0.4513	2.5037	-0.4513
51	Minda SAI Ltd	-0.0490	-	-0.0490	0.0490	-	-	-	-
52	Tata Capital Ltd	-0.1808	-0.2218	-0.2228	-0.3171	0.2977	0.3477	0.2459	3.0642
53	SFO Technologies Pvt Ltd	-1.8446	-0.7031	-1.8446	0.4384	0.2703	0.5120	0.9024	0.5120
54	Sistema Smart Technologies Ltd	0.8827	0.8523	0.9130	0.3800	0.6532	-0.7206	-1.1370	-0.7206
55	Adani Harbour Services Ltd/The	0.8221	0.3903	0.3914	0.7853	-1.8265	0.1108	0.4921	0.2073
56	EbixCash World Money Ltd	0.4470	0.1367	0.4470	-0.1737	2.2888	-1.1789	-	-
57	Indian Seamless Enterprises Ltd	-0.3002	0.5455	-0.3002	1.3912	-1.4307	-1.1072	-1.4307	-
58	Avana Logistek Ltd	0.0671	1.1230	-1.1392	-0.0503	-1.2872	0.5695	0.9969	0.5695
59	Royal Highland Distilleries Ltd	0.8417	0.9835	-1.2602	-0.5651	-	-	-	-
60	Poly Hose India Rubber Pvt Ltd	-0.5853	-1.3569	0.1864	0.5762	0.2985	-0.2724	2.4638	-0.2724
61	Minda Rinder Pvt Ltd	0.1719	0.1445	0.1719	0.1170	-0.2890	-	-	-
62	Olive Commercial Co Ltd	-0.3417	-0.5987	-0.2314	0.1224	0.0474	0.2141	0.3211	3.0174
63	BCL Secure Premises Pvt Ltd	-1.0948	-2.4926	0.3030	0.4199	0.4634	0.4560	0.5679	0.4560
64	JSW Cement Ltd	0.0134	-0.2411	0.0134	-0.4956	3.0766	0.3299	-	-
65	Aditya Birla Capital Ltd	-	-	-0.0123	-0.1447	0.2587	-0.0879	0.1185	3.1123
66	Carysil Ltd	-0.1429	0.2928	-0.0109	-0.3418	-0.1402	0.5089	0.5317	2.9553
67	Adani Power Ltd	0.0286	0.0843	0.7330	-0.2000	-0.6523	0.3843	0.7055	2.7241
68	Adani Green Energy Ltd	-	-0.6970	-0.5998	-0.6970	0.2477	0.7488	0.6061	2.5332
69	Adani Transmission Ltd	1.0457	0.6088	1.4827	0.5808	-0.7718	-0.9464	-1.0612	0.7069
70	Redribbon Modulex Buildings Ltd	-0.1430	-0.2316	-0.4351	-0.0987	0.2599	0.0398	0.5646	3.0434
71	Adani Enterprises Ltd	0.2627	2.5931	-0.3150	-0.3167	-0.4734	-0.1807	-0.4787	1.0022
72	Advanced Enzyme Technologies Ltd	-0.0207	-0.1911	0.4581	0.2899	0.1072	0.1630	-0.6646	3.0140
73	Allcargo Logistics Ltd	-0.0771	0.4681	0.3439	0.2632	-0.5406	-0.3588	0.7485	2.8273
74	Veecon Media & Television Ltd	0.7790	0.0487	0.3849	1.1100	-0.8005	-0.6506	-1.6846	-0.3195
75	Asian Hotels East Ltd	0.3319	0.2950	0.4500	0.3912	0.1566	-1.5475	-0.7645	-2.4031
76	Asahi India Glass Ltd	-1.0157	-0.3483	0.1819	0.2339	-0.2184	-0.0391	0.9155	2.7541
77	AJR Infra and Tolling Ltd	0.7377	0.4101	0.6802	0.6137	-1.1692	-1.5083	-1.5628	-1.5083
78	Amarjothi Spinning Mills Ltd	2.0914	0.7879	-0.5291	0.2394	-0.3975	-0.9442	-0.7322	1.4487
79	Alankit Ltd	-0.4266	2.2542	0.1072	0.5608	-0.5508	-0.5049	-1.4883	-0.3949
80	Altran Technologies SASU	-0.5783	-0.1911	-0.0224	0.3443	0.3468	3.0455	0.3468	-
81	Amber Enterprises India Ltd	0.9242	0.4201	1.4284	-0.1241	0.0441	-1.0408	-1.1964	1.9860
82	Nettle Infrastructure Investments Ltd	0.4196	0.1756	0.4942	0.3887	0.0007	-0.9969	-0.1344	2.8505
83	Asian Paints Ltd	-0.3823	-0.3709	0.0623	0.2741	0.1338	0.5058	-0.4264	3.0108
84	Apollo Tyres Ltd	0.7921	1.0136	1.1192	0.5142	-1.2555	-0.0550	-0.9863	1.7058
85	Aurobindo Pharma Ltd	0.8397	-0.0547	0.3964	0.3669	-0.2963	-0.2369	-0.9757	2.7358
86	Arco Leasing Ltd	0.6474	0.5673	-0.0702	0.3440	0.3304	-0.9606	-0.8787	-2.4689
87	Anant Raj Ltd	0.4319	2.2403	0.3201	0.6916	-0.7892	-1.2677	-0.7627	-0.0974
88	Ajmera Realty & Infra India Ltd	-0.1119	0.1244	0.0941	0.7594	0.3212	0.1764	-2.5426	-1.0901
89	Adani Power Mundra Ltd	-0.8026	0.3264	0.4762	3.0008	-	-	-	-
90	Aarvee Denims & Exports Ltd	0.5069	0.3533	0.4379	0.3342	-0.1848	-1.4420	-0.9768	-2.3027
91	Arvind Fashions Ltd	-	-	0.7948	0.8579	-0.2878	-1.5924	0.1644	-1.8740

S.No.	Company Name	Pre-Acquisition				Post-Acquisition			
		2013	2014	2015	2016	2019	2020	2021	2022
92	IndusInd Media & Communications Ltd	-0.0051	0.0520	0.1618	0.2706	-1.6360	-0.0774	0.7145	2.4844
93	Ashapura Minechem Ltd	1.0504	0.9902	0.7736	-0.1464	-2.3363	0.3604	0.1158	0.6347
94	Vipani Hotels & Resorts Ltd	0.0101	0.3864	0.3833	-0.1282	0.2162	-0.0578	0.1274	2.7418
95	Asya Infosoft Ltd	1.3608	1.4158	1.1526	-0.8887	-0.7671	-0.7518	-0.5644	-0.7518
96	AXISCADES Technologies Ltd	0.0944	0.9107	1.0804	-0.1210	0.3178	0.2532	0.2816	1.7370
97	Sembcorp Energy India Ltd	0.9140	0.9355	0.8649	-0.4509	-1.0605	-0.1715	0.6215	1.8343
98	Bazel International Ltd	-	-	-	-1.1744	-0.8777	0.2377	1.8145	1.0918
99	BCL Industries Ltd	-0.7826	-0.1729	-0.5201	-0.1767	0.0168	0.0948	0.6625	2.6974
100	Birla Corp Ltd	-0.8115	-0.7478	-0.2686	-0.1169	0.9239	0.9268	0.1077	2.5732
101	Bharat Forge Ltd	-0.5617	0.6906	0.6626	0.2715	-1.1355	-1.8955	0.0803	1.0604
102	Bhagyanagar India Ltd	-0.4301	0.1122	-0.7999	1.6967	-0.4574	-0.6406	-0.7369	1.5791
103	Bio Green Papers Ltd	0.5959	0.5836	0.5834	-0.3678	0.4215	0.4215	0.2613	0.4215
104	Bajaj Electricals Ltd	-1.1017	-1.1137	0.6106	0.5337	-0.5089	0.5339	-0.0074	2.2777
105	Bal Pharma Ltd	0.9170	0.3463	-0.1243	-0.3328	-1.8996	0.4836	0.2234	2.0939
106	Balasore Alloys Ltd	0.6488	0.3750	0.0880	0.8512	-1.7881	-1.5180	-1.7881	-
107	Heritage Nutrivet Ltd	-0.0482	0.0750	0.3534	0.2221	-0.1044	0.1535	-0.3485	3.0876
108	Bodal Chemicals Ltd	1.0786	0.6533	0.3425	0.7206	-1.1302	-1.9122	-1.0138	0.0340
109	Balrampur Chini Mills Ltd	-0.9773	-1.4961	-0.0230	1.5359	0.1634	0.2005	0.1417	1.8874
110	Bharat Road Network Ltd	0.2037	0.1261	-2.7803	0.3532	0.5870	0.2352	0.3672	0.3941
111	BSE Ltd	1.5118	1.8951	1.1285	-0.2961	-0.6049	-0.9581	-0.5118	0.1159
112	Infutec Healthcare Ltd	0.2314	0.3943	0.2314	0.5571	2.3253	-1.2455	-	-
113	Blueblood Ventures Ltd	-	-	-1.3506	-	-1.3760	1.3506	-	-
114	Babcock Borsig Ltd	-0.1027	0.2384	-0.6440	-0.1133	0.0738	-0.2937	0.4859	3.0024
115	Indigrid 2 Ltd	-0.0802	-0.1278	-0.0888	0.2200	-0.0041	-0.1164	0.1103	3.1430
116	Byke Hospitality Ltd/The	0.3136	0.3152	0.4757	0.5091	-0.1622	-1.5496	-0.9415	-1.9523
117	Future Speciality Retail Ltd	-0.0770	-0.0174	-0.2873	0.3817	-	-	-	-
118	Calcom Vision Ltd	-1.0018	-1.4619	-1.0076	0.4038	0.3476	0.4238	0.1694	1.4284
119	Cartrade Tech Ltd	-	-	-	0.6194	0.6932	0.7084	-2.0209	-1.6584
120	Chembond Chemicals Ltd	0.9085	1.0667	-0.1565	-0.3969	-1.6074	-0.1586	-0.7796	1.7326
121	Coffee Day Enterprises Ltd	0.2866	0.3322	0.5485	0.6020	-0.6895	-1.5344	-0.5154	-2.2506
122	Ceat Ltd	0.9055	0.8709	1.4686	-0.1735	-0.5170	0.1488	-1.7900	1.2006
123	Centrum Capital Ltd	0.5230	0.5362	0.5562	0.5562	-2.5668	-0.0344	0.1281	-0.7879
124	Choice International Ltd	0.0811	1.4289	-1.1354	0.0619	-0.2577	-0.9330	0.9444	1.8937
125	California Software Co Ltd	-1.0601	-1.0601	-1.0601	-1.0601	0.6603	0.5075	1.0527	0.8573
126	Zuari Finserv Ltd	0.3644	0.0183	-0.6244	-1.3039	0.7049	-0.1538	1.0744	2.3173
127	Chemfab Alkalis Ltd	-	-	0.9812	1.1631	0.1265	-2.0582	-0.3943	0.1049
128	Cholamandalam Financial Holdings Ltd	-0.7426	-0.7010	-0.7351	-0.8800	0.5706	0.6139	0.6049	2.3001
129	Cian Agro Industries & Infrastructure Ltd	-0.2915	-1.3851	0.8021	0.2551	0.3279	-	-	-
130	Spice Money Ltd	-0.1523	-0.1308	-0.2100	-0.1726	0.3032	0.2770	3.1299	0.2770
131	Colorchips New Media Ltd	0.1854	0.2085	0.2292	0.3863	0.0402	-1.8099	-0.1743	-2.3397
132	Confidence Petroleum India Ltd	-0.0547	-1.1532	-0.6644	-0.6162	0.2298	0.4622	0.5526	2.4478
133	Century Plyboards India Ltd	-0.6177	0.1746	0.5014	0.3189	-0.6347	0.0644	0.5411	2.8765
134	Capital Trust Ltd/India	0.0584	0.7158	0.9601	0.8646	-0.2768	-1.4259	-1.0301	-1.9176
135	Cravatex Ltd	0.9335	1.2717	0.4462	-0.7495	0.1341	-1.2532	-0.5699	-1.8151
136	Crest Ventures Ltd	-0.4139	-0.6214	0.3192	-0.0494	0.6930	-0.5147	-1.6065	-1.5366
137	Coromandel International Ltd	-0.0109	-0.1535	-0.8894	-0.2533	0.4127	0.6519	0.1402	2.8863
138	CRISIL Ltd	0.7085	0.5513	0.2413	0.0494	-0.1068	-0.8692	-0.4872	2.8137
139	Cyient Ltd	0.9431	0.1655	-0.1512	-0.1792	-0.7553	-0.5063	0.5802	2.7603
140	Dalmia Bharat Ltd	0.4626	0.6143	0.4626	0.7660	-1.0051	0.6540	-0.1600	2.5997
141	Datamatics Global Services Ltd	0.3594	-0.1133	-0.5028	-0.4639	-0.2549	0.1020	0.9953	2.8208
142	Dilip Buildcon Ltd	1.1042	0.9662	0.3793	0.2993	-0.2234	-0.3236	-2.5122	0.3073
143	Deep Industries Ltd	-	-	-	-	-	-1.5852	1.5852	1.2145
144	DEN Networks Ltd	1.2875	-0.4164	-2.3425	-0.3324	0.1432	0.4000	0.7375	0.7724
145	Deepak Fertilisers & Petrochemicals Corp Ltd	0.4132	-0.4071	-0.3254	-0.0155	-0.4153	0.6472	0.9128	2.7388
146	Digicontent Ltd	-	-	-	0.0103	-1.3247	-0.9665	2.2809	0.8245
147	Avenue Supermarts Ltd	-0.3070	-0.4245	-0.0309	0.2893	0.2224	-0.6175	-0.0936	2.9123
148	Donear Industries Ltd	-0.0153	-0.0248	0.3739	-0.1709	0.4140	-2.5527	0.2745	0.8242
149	Dr Reddy's Laboratories Ltd	0.9831	0.6526	0.8901	-0.7234	-0.7954	-0.0113	-0.0208	2.3095
150	Synegra EMS Ltd	0.9643	1.0322	0.5540	0.5797	-0.2865	-1.1395	-2.1764	0.3827
151	ABM Knowledgeware Ltd	0.3721	0.4454	0.1663	0.0074	0.1548	-1.4022	2.0368	-1.4022
152	Den Broadband Ltd	0.4321	0.3958	0.5418	0.6419	-2.0507	-1.0265	-0.4146	-1.2579

S.No.	Company Name	Pre-Acquisition				Post-Acquisition			
		2013	2014	2015	2016	2019	2020	2021	2022
153	Eiko Lifesciences Ltd	-	1.5445	0.9130	1.5445	-1.2669	0.0073	-1.2410	0.0073
154	Emami Realty Ltd	2.8099	-0.3583	-0.3589	-0.3283	-0.3589	-0.3589	-0.3589	-0.3588
155	Eurofins Scientific SE	-0.2569	-0.2323	-0.1276	-0.0044	-0.4018	0.4598	0.9777	2.8756
156	Eris Lifesciences Ltd	-0.8034	-0.7322	-0.2652	0.3308	0.1094	0.3020	0.2380	2.8075
157	ESAB India Ltd	-0.0050	-0.2989	-0.2831	-0.4936	0.6046	0.1816	0.5508	2.9227
158	Max Estates Gurgaon Ltd	-1.3449	-0.4002	-0.1374	-1.8269	0.1427	0.3935	1.2297	0.2326
159	Nihilent Ltd	-0.3320	0.6002	-0.6828	-0.2237	-0.0170	0.4012	0.6265	2.8562
160	Fermenta Biotech Ltd	-0.2469	-0.9549	-0.6315	-1.2180	0.2893	0.2064	-0.4715	1.0480
161	Flomic Global Logistics Ltd	-0.5388	0.6702	-1.7477	1.0775	-	-	-	-
162	Fortis Healthcare Ltd	-0.8875	-0.7203	-0.4065	0.0970	0.7001	0.1335	1.6619	2.1272
163	Future Retail Ltd	-	0.3892	0.4170	0.3892	0.4683	-1.7729	-1.4826	-1.7729
164	Atul Finserve Ltd	-	-	-	-	0.7558	0.4798	-1.2356	-2.4140
165	Future Supply Chain Solutions Ltd	-	-	0.4619	0.5564	0.7593	-1.7719	-0.1002	-2.0546
166	Gallantt Ispat Ltd/Old	1.9038	1.7908	-0.6473	-0.5436	-0.8131	-0.3681	-0.6634	-0.0063
167	Garnet International Ltd	0.5977	0.6543	0.5608	1.1011	-1.6206	-0.0284	0.3119	-0.0751
168	GBL Industries Ltd	-	-	-	-	-	3.1623	-	-
169	Godrej Consumer Products Ltd	-0.5755	-0.4128	0.0089	0.1507	0.2476	0.2743	-0.0369	3.0324
170	Goodricke Group Ltd	1.8638	1.0526	-0.5710	0.7618	-0.9637	-0.3554	-1.3898	-0.2615
171	Genesis IBRC India Ltd	-0.1599	0.6766	0.6766	0.6766	-0.5279	-0.5279	-0.5279	-2.6725
172	Gillanders Arbuthnot & Co Ltd	-0.1660	-0.1705	-0.5172	0.0878	0.1762	0.4654	2.5177	0.4654
173	Gloster Ltd	-	-	-	0.1310	-0.2094	0.5925	-0.5141	3.0481
174	JK Investors Bombay Ltd	0.3145	0.0249	0.1116	0.1595	-0.3800	-0.2287	0.6103	2.9888
175	Grandeur Products Ltd	-0.9857	0.3958	-2.3671	1.0747	0.5626	-0.0064	-	-
176	Grasim Industries Ltd	-0.5252	-0.6391	-0.3157	-0.0001	0.3085	0.5095	0.2173	2.9278
177	Greenpanel Industries Ltd	-	-	-	-0.7329	-0.4651	0.1719	1.0261	2.5322
178	Greatship India Ltd	0.9300	0.7870	0.7797	0.3211	-0.5304	-1.6045	-1.3444	-1.6045
179	Gajanan Securities Services Ltd	-1.1895	0.1635	-2.5426	0.3773	0.3959	0.4218	0.4107	0.4509
180	GTPL Hathway Ltd	-0.7336	-1.5941	0.1269	-1.1921	0.1517	0.3364	0.5896	1.3350
181	Gujarat State Petronet Ltd	1.1692	1.1058	1.0836	1.0896	-0.8763	-0.6990	-1.1223	-0.0150
182	Happiest Minds Technologies Ltd	-	-	-1.5197	-0.1927	-0.2877	0.3948	0.2782	1.6559
183	Harish Textile Engineers Ltd	-	-	-	-0.4873	-0.7450	1.2323	2.2641	1.2323
184	Hester Biosciences Ltd	-0.0012	-0.1615	0.3620	0.2558	-0.5808	0.4015	-0.9860	2.7978
185	HCL Technologies Ltd	-0.0392	0.6173	-0.0377	-0.0029	-0.1159	0.0135	-0.2261	3.0784
186	Hindustan Foods Ltd	-0.8880	-2.4651	0.3850	0.5598	0.5092	0.4619	0.4236	0.7482
187	Hindware Home Innovation Ltd	-	-	-	-	-0.8460	0.4116	0.4344	2.7277
188	HFCL Ltd	-0.4483	-0.3293	0.1702	-0.2839	0.5235	0.3267	0.5894	2.9254
189	Hindustan Media Ventures Ltd	0.4060	0.4182	1.0668	0.5846	-1.3567	-1.2700	-1.6238	-1.2700
190	Himatsingka Seide Ltd	-1.1429	-0.9562	0.0460	0.7270	0.1810	-1.1896	-0.0004	1.5177
191	Hi-Tech Gears Ltd/The	-1.5622	0.4162	0.8913	0.1892	-0.1784	0.1385	-1.4172	1.6038
192	HT Media Ltd	0.6593	0.4569	0.5598	0.4314	-0.1489	-1.6500	-0.5580	-2.1550
193	Huhtamaki India Ltd	0.1490	0.0973	0.3393	0.4574	-1.9007	0.9720	-1.9007	-
194	FIITJEE Ltd	0.7995	0.7552	-0.0608	-0.3279	-0.2177	0.1310	0.5900	2.5331
195	IFB Industries Ltd	-0.1579	0.5672	-0.4663	0.7350	-0.7157	0.6666	-2.1710	-0.2245
196	Sintex Prefab & Infra Ltd	-1.1177	-1.1177	0.8995	0.4453	2.3879	0.4453	-	-
197	360 ONE WAM Ltd	0.8154	0.2132	1.4175	-0.9926	2.4027	-0.3617	-	-
198	IL&FS Investment Managers Ltd	1.1444	1.1760	0.9380	0.0203	-2.1314	-0.5771	-0.4245	-0.6143
199	Imagicaaworld Entertainment Ltd	0.3289	0.3662	0.3917	0.3976	-1.9203	0.1211	-2.2476	0.1211
200	India Motor Parts and Accessories Ltd	-0.3107	-0.4518	-0.6024	0.0204	0.2516	0.6007	0.1470	2.9416
201	Inditrade Capital Ltd	-1.6776	0.7849	-0.7689	0.2987	0.8503	0.2432	-1.3278	-1.0062
202	India Grid Trust	-	-	0.2012	-0.0750	0.4326	-0.1900	-0.0927	3.0980
203	India Finsec Ltd	0.2851	-0.7926	1.3627	-0.6284	1.0038	0.3113	2.1972	0.3113
204	Infosys Ltd	-0.0297	0.1667	0.1264	0.1177	-0.3219	0.0950	-0.0992	3.1267
205	Info Edge India Ltd	-0.1989	-1.3347	-0.7800	-0.1595	0.5799	0.2489	0.5845	2.4098
206	Scott Edil Pharmacia Ltd	0.7210	0.6043	0.7210	0.4876	0.1511	-1.1276	-1.1489	-2.0826
207	Infronics Systems Ltd	0.6055	-2.1296	0.4680	0.8051	0.2282	0.8375	0.3777	0.8375
208	Indian Oil Corp Ltd	-0.5811	-0.9934	0.1322	0.6682	-0.9916	0.7831	0.2175	2.3474
209	Ipca Laboratories Ltd	0.7153	-0.2622	-0.8660	-0.4867	0.0889	0.9501	0.3995	2.6064
210	ICICI Prudential Life Insurance Co Ltd	0.9547	0.0728	1.9249	-0.0756	0.2279	-1.3324	-1.2879	-0.7211
211	IRB Infrastructure Developers Ltd	-0.2093	0.1992	-0.1240	0.0678	-0.0020	0.0335	0.0385	3.1417
212	IRB InvIT Fund	-	-	0.3010	0.0909	-0.4262	-0.2083	0.4527	3.0956
213	Raymond Apparel Ltd	-0.2201	-0.0350	-0.0581	-0.4626	0.0563	0.5964	0.1445	3.0360

S.No.	Company Name	Pre-Acquisition				Post-Acquisition			
		2013	2014	2015	2016	2019	2020	2021	2022
214	Bharti Hexacom Ltd	-0.9102	-0.0933	0.1903	0.2705	-0.0920	0.3190	0.4015	2.9216
215	Jaykay Enterprises Ltd	0.1456	0.0063	-0.0721	-0.3548	-0.4123	1.9858	-0.4323	1.9858
216	Jiya Eco-Products Ltd	-0.1834	-0.1012	0.0725	-0.0905	-1.0975	2.3919	-1.0975	-
217	Jindal Worldwide Ltd	-0.0142	-0.0456	1.1936	0.4233	-1.0196	-0.6515	0.2504	2.3774
218	Josts Engineering Co Ltd	0.5221	-0.4343	-1.2343	-0.5325	0.8017	0.7988	2.4154	0.7988
219	Jaiprakash Associates Ltd	1.3934	1.3266	0.9087	-0.4846	-0.4691	-0.2138	-1.2770	-1.1463
220	Jindal Saw Ltd	-0.9689	0.3283	-0.6088	-0.2349	0.7757	-0.0013	-0.1396	2.6847
221	JSW Energy Ltd	0.1843	0.4015	0.6165	0.2247	-0.5471	-0.1929	0.3280	2.8612
222	Jayshree Chemicals Ltd	0.9579	0.9069	0.6658	-0.8789	-0.9239	-1.4545	0.8396	-1.5927
223	Kalyan Jewellers India Ltd	-0.9746	-0.4629	-0.9746	0.0487	0.4125	-0.0073	0.4998	2.5235
224	KDDL Ltd	-1.6146	-1.8391	0.3856	0.2512	0.3877	0.3036	0.7206	1.0696
225	Khemani Distributors & Marketing Ltd	0.0947	0.1037	0.1037	0.1037	-2.3375	1.0614	0.5196	1.5033
226	Karma Energy Ltd	1.1643	0.2487	-0.2797	0.8178	0.3972	-1.8480	-0.2332	-1.8108
227	Kajaria Ceramics Ltd	-0.0751	0.1108	0.2071	0.2511	-0.5130	0.2307	-0.0015	3.0722
228	Anup Engineering Ltd/The	0.1522	-0.1539	-0.2698	-0.0112	0.0479	-0.2343	0.0914	3.1167
229	Kirloskar Oil Engines Ltd	0.5400	-0.3564	-0.0836	-0.1870	-0.3355	0.6255	0.1915	2.9002
230	KPIT Technologies Ltd	-	-	-	0.2710	-0.5323	-0.4661	0.7274	2.9611
231	Kalpataru Power Transmission Ltd	-0.9256	-0.6052	-0.3780	1.2583	-0.2778	-0.2704	-1.2470	1.2245
232	Kridhan Infra Ltd	0.5765	0.5310	0.5039	0.6089	-0.9127	-0.4237	-1.6886	-1.9651
233	Kesoram Industries Ltd	0.2189	-0.4561	-1.2242	-0.5600	0.3184	0.9011	1.0529	2.1136
234	Kemistar Corp Ltd	-0.1018	-0.8336	-0.4708	-0.4012	1.1988	2.4262	1.1988	-
235	Kothari Products Ltd	1.6495	0.1878	0.2995	0.5731	-1.1758	-1.4803	-0.5263	-1.4287
236	Kothari Petrochemicals	-0.7684	-0.2781	-0.3757	-0.0724	2.7954	0.6517	-	-
237	Life Insurance Corp of India	-	-	-	-0.1780	-1.8299	1.2200	0.7878	1.5770
238	Dishnet Wireless Ltd	0.9475	-0.3854	-0.1627	0.0390	1.3498	-1.0650	-1.4290	-1.7251
239	Larsen & Toubro Ltd	0.1275	-0.1350	-0.3323	-0.4295	-0.1750	0.7507	0.4257	2.9567
240	Lloyds Metals & Energy Ltd	-0.7239	-0.3729	-0.3427	-0.0075	1.9002	1.7092	-	-
241	Mahesh Developers Ltd	-	-	-	-	-	-	-	-
242	Maithan Alloys Ltd	-0.8531	-0.5416	-0.4173	0.2360	-0.2416	0.1172	1.3531	2.5228
243	Asianet Communications Ltd	0.4748	0.4905	0.4894	0.4854	-2.3388	0.3989	-0.9792	-1.0496
244	CE Info Systems Ltd	-	-	-	-0.6419	-0.5772	0.2637	0.9554	2.5818
245	Matrimony.com Ltd	-0.8250	-0.7371	-1.3370	0.8264	-0.3285	0.1468	0.4923	1.8429
246	McNally Bharat Engineering Co Ltd	1.1917	0.9315	0.8134	-0.3047	-1.9395	0.5794	-0.5952	-0.9109
247	Kosmo One Business Park Ltd	-0.2122	-0.2778	-0.1466	-0.5201	-0.0703	0.0752	1.3162	2.7205
248	Megri Soft Ltd	0.3806	-0.0991	0.3806	-0.5789	-0.4471	0.6055	0.8730	2.7499
249	Midas Infra Trade Ltd	0.4766	0.3507	-2.7267	-0.0844	0.5001	0.3305	0.3418	0.3305
250	Mahindra Lifespace Developers Ltd	0.5854	0.9792	0.4576	0.1502	-0.2810	-1.5799	-0.6411	-2.2150
251	Mahindra & Mahindra Ltd	-0.4633	-0.7684	-0.7788	-0.8199	0.7418	0.8613	0.6050	2.3711
252	MM Forgings Ltd	0.4830	0.4213	-0.5576	-0.9148	0.5681	-	-	-
253	Mega Nirman and Industries Ltd	-1.3517	-1.3112	-1.3921	1.2526	0.7025	0.6129	-	-
254	Marathon Nextgen Realty Ltd	2.1772	-0.9048	1.0706	-0.6403	-0.7848	-0.6689	-0.8138	0.0040
255	Moschip Technologies Ltd	-1.0073	-0.0223	-2.2608	0.7523	0.2906	0.7173	0.8853	0.8448
256	Marico Ltd	-0.1727	-0.4884	-0.1093	0.2716	0.3068	0.2583	-0.0591	3.0697
257	Majestic Research Services and Solutions Ltd	0.2530	0.2565	0.2614	0.2648	0.2519	-1.8124	-1.8089	-1.8124
258	Mirza International Ltd	0.8228	0.3637	1.1115	0.6860	-0.8587	-1.9211	-0.4057	0.9371
259	HCL Comnet Ltd	-	0.3907	0.1167	0.3907	0.0023	0.5053	0.5423	2.7415
260	Belrise Industries Ltd	-	-	-	-	-1.6798	0.8801	0.7998	1.3546
261	Adani Ports & Special Economic Zone Ltd	-0.2950	-0.4964	-0.3515	-0.1603	0.2375	0.3740	0.3348	3.0081
262	Mawana Sugars Ltd	-1.6675	-1.3556	0.4462	1.4725	-0.3508	0.2425	0.4220	0.9873
263	Mayur Leather Products Ltd	1.2550	0.9740	0.8201	0.0184	-2.0035	-0.4051	0.3315	-1.0171
264	Nazara Technologies Ltd	1.8361	0.7683	1.8361	-0.2995	0.2565	0.3643	0.2565	-
265	NBCC India Ltd	0.6360	0.9646	0.4689	0.9867	-1.5561	-1.3732	-0.8814	-0.0713
266	Satchmo Holdings Ltd	0.7729	0.7970	0.6211	0.5577	-0.3972	-0.9182	0.5524	-1.0048
267	Nettlinx Ltd	-2.3049	-0.8077	0.1887	0.8298	-0.0036	0.0958	0.4791	0.8565
268	Nila Spaces Ltd	-	-	0.4060	0.5468	0.4395	0.4889	-2.0220	-1.8602
269	Nila Infrastructures Ltd	1.9203	0.6926	0.0138	-0.1448	-0.6326	-1.2111	-1.5745	0.1002
270	Natco Pharma Ltd	-0.4908	-0.4930	-0.3492	0.7337	0.0477	-0.0980	-1.9761	0.5643
271	Orient Beverages Ltd	0.7831	0.1886	0.2052	0.2156	0.1341	-1.7615	-0.4883	-2.2678
272	Orient Bell Ltd	0.3888	0.0301	0.1419	0.8463	-1.5939	-0.8998	0.7620	2.0732
273	Oracle Financial Services Software Ltd	-0.3231	-0.0480	-0.1915	-0.2001	0.1560	0.3779	0.2981	3.0799
274	Onesource Ideas Venture Ltd	0.4583	0.4617	0.4583	0.4652	-2.7144	0.4293	0.4293	0.3868

S.No.	Company Name	Pre-Acquisition				Post-Acquisition			
		2013	2014	2015	2016	2019	2020	2021	2022
275	Om Infra Ltd	-0.1724	-0.1590	1.9022	-0.1097	-1.5897	-0.0598	-0.5041	1.3747
276	Oil & Natural Gas Corp Ltd	1.5260	0.7881	1.3108	-0.3660	-1.2500	-0.9999	-0.3908	1.1561
277	Oriental Rail Infrastructure Ltd	-1.3781	-1.0938	0.0960	0.4100	0.6098	0.1806	0.5664	2.3132
278	Padmanabh Industries Ltd	0.2271	0.1132	0.3410	0.3284	0.3284	-1.7677	-1.8048	-1.7677
279	Parsvnath Developers Ltd	1.2182	1.4973	0.4009	0.4504	-0.1148	-0.8145	-0.7198	-1.3269
280	Paul Merchants Ltd	-0.4367	-0.5313	-0.3421	0.1079	0.6976	0.2631	2.9085	0.2631
281	One 97 Communications Ltd	-0.9084	-1.8447	0.0278	0.6004	1.2165	-	-	-
282	Shree Pushkar Chemicals & Fertilisers Ltd	-0.0627	-0.4562	0.1757	1.0538	-0.1078	-1.1048	-0.2478	2.5895
283	Pervasive Commodities Ltd	-1.1371	-2.2309	-0.3345	0.6782	0.5929	0.6087	0.6146	0.6042
284	Peninsula Land Ltd	1.7441	0.2818	-0.6682	-0.3127	-0.9312	0.3456	1.0388	0.7547
285	Prestige Estates Projects Ltd	0.7984	0.8365	-0.5425	-0.7384	0.1154	-0.2177	-0.6019	2.6473
286	Phoenix Mills Ltd/The	0.4031	-0.0139	-0.1196	0.0002	0.3455	-0.9895	-0.0027	2.8978
287	Pidilite Industries Ltd	-0.6303	-0.6791	0.3253	0.3900	0.2018	0.3611	-0.2454	2.8930
288	Pacheli Industrial Finance Ltd	0.2788	0.2788	0.2674	0.3153	0.2377	0.4154	-2.2441	-1.9143
289	Pil Italica Lifestyle Ltd	-0.6823	-0.6650	-0.4177	0.0498	1.2944	1.4677	-0.6396	1.6186
290	Panacea Biotec Ltd	-1.5005	0.5170	0.8054	0.8974	0.4151	0.5737	-0.2907	0.0278
291	Prakash Pipes Ltd	-	-	-	-	-0.4186	0.1758	0.2428	3.0271
292	Praxis Home Retail Ltd	-	-	0.6503	0.5765	0.3734	-1.6139	0.0876	-2.2171
293	Precision Camshafts Ltd	0.2635	1.3472	1.3260	0.6099	-0.7446	-1.5100	-0.8720	-1.1958
294	Pricol Ltd	-0.0308	-1.2833	0.1671	0.0610	-0.5151	0.7455	0.8358	1.9800
295	Prime Urban Development India Ltd	-0.1616	0.2527	1.8606	1.0242	-0.9314	-0.4866	-1.2515	-1.3086
296	Power Grid Corp of India Ltd	0.0833	-0.0437	0.0878	0.0664	-0.0245	-0.0772	-0.0141	3.1569
297	Ravinder Heights Ltd	-	-	-	-	-	-0.7171	0.7171	-2.9692
298	AGI Greenpac Ltd	-0.0803	0.6002	0.7335	0.8457	-0.7669	-0.8674	-1.9580	-1.0991
299	Reliance Capital Ltd	0.4287	0.4509	0.4872	0.3789	-0.0453	-0.1077	-1.8729	-2.2752
300	Reliance Communications Ltd	0.6109	0.8350	0.7095	0.4607	-0.9206	-0.9568	-1.0428	-2.1842
301	Rane Holdings Ltd	0.9732	0.6434	0.7880	0.5416	-1.2123	-1.6530	-0.9520	-1.1103
302	Rain Industries Ltd	-0.3049	-0.6797	0.0145	0.2571	-0.7194	-0.2226	0.2188	2.5354
303	Rajapalayam Mills Ltd	1.3689	0.1023	0.3436	1.1268	-1.3068	-1.7397	0.7781	0.3959
304	Royal Orchid Hotels Ltd	0.2629	0.1879	0.2164	0.1313	0.3078	-2.1557	0.1292	-2.0115
305	Raymond Ltd	0.6384	0.3208	0.3016	0.0131	-0.1239	-2.5212	0.7088	-1.2011
306	Saksoft Ltd	-0.6455	-0.4708	0.1919	-0.2098	0.2903	0.2875	0.2943	2.9618
307	Samvardhana Motherson International Ltd/IN	0.2306	0.3980	0.3403	0.5692	-1.7364	-1.7819	-1.7364	-
308	Sat Industries Ltd	0.0737	-2.7464	0.2451	0.3126	0.3397	0.4198	0.5009	0.6543
309	Aegis Logistics Ltd	0.7636	0.7909	0.2356	-0.8614	0.2953	0.2773	0.7407	1.9320
310	Sembcorp Industries Ltd	0.2375	0.2609	-0.7007	0.0764	0.6847	0.1709	0.2037	2.7539
311	SEAMEC Ltd	-0.0386	0.9801	-0.0898	-2.5290	0.9286	0.0981	0.3812	0.4657
312	Steel Exchange India Ltd	0.6321	0.7046	0.3681	-0.2861	0.0678	0.7815	0.3535	1.9953
313	Setubandhan Infrastructure Ltd	0.6567	0.3147	0.4701	0.4066	-0.8380	-1.8387	0.0533	-2.0250
314	Aksh Optifibre Ltd	-	-	0.6156	0.5809	0.0411	-1.2029	2.2872	-1.2029
315	Sagar Cements Ltd	-1.0947	-0.2414	0.2292	-0.1715	-0.0367	1.3732	0.2003	2.5099
316	Smartlink Holdings Ltd	-0.3276	-0.7742	2.4712	-0.8434	-1.0170	0.0169	0.3793	-0.0537
317	SH Kelkar & Co Ltd	0.8668	-0.3950	0.2204	0.7032	-0.6417	0.2776	-0.7668	2.6112
318	Ashok Leyland Ltd	0.3352	-0.3412	-0.5573	-0.5384	0.0600	-0.1173	-0.2669	2.7826
319	Sical Logistics Ltd	0.4072	0.2879	0.4825	0.6160	-0.4332	-0.8010	-1.4446	-2.3150
320	Shristi Infrastructure Development Corp Ltd	0.7967	0.7750	0.7649	1.0422	-0.3356	-1.3449	-1.3559	-1.5217
321	Singer India Ltd	0.1684	1.5980	0.0546	0.4414	0.0119	-0.7350	1.1593	-2.0017
322	Alkem Laboratories Ltd	-0.1732	-0.2425	-0.2724	-0.0943	0.2535	0.4506	0.5457	3.0070
323	Sobha Ltd	0.1319	-0.0481	0.0315	-0.5759	0.3951	0.4336	0.5736	2.8920
324	Span Divergent Ltd	1.0875	0.9693	0.9693	-1.4139	-0.8689	-0.3483	0.8250	-0.6194
325	Srei Infrastructure Finance Ltd	0.2738	0.2710	0.2683	0.2720	0.2726	-2.0484	0.1366	-2.1765
326	SRF Ltd	-0.7702	-0.3644	0.1051	0.0266	0.0862	0.6356	0.7194	2.8280
327	SRS Ltd	1.1538	1.1504	-0.8248	-0.8248	-0.6546	-	-	-
328	TVS Srichakra Ltd	-0.4703	0.1174	1.8791	1.2432	-0.8293	-0.4680	-1.5089	0.6847
329	Saraswati Commercial India Ltd	0.2092	0.2244	0.2274	0.3738	-2.7188	0.4891	0.4999	0.7924
330	Sonata Software Ltd	-1.1921	0.3283	0.3154	0.6212	0.0268	-0.3411	-0.5476	2.5748
331	S&S Power Switchgear Ltd	0.6671	0.0553	1.1601	0.3756	-1.2914	0.3871	-1.6281	-1.4609
332	Stride Gaming plc	1.1655	0.8061	1.1655	0.4467	-1.9287	-0.6009	-	-
333	Systematix Corporate Services	-0.6800	-0.6800	-0.6800	-0.6800	-0.0290	1.3690	1.9140	1.3690
334	Sunil Hitech Engineers Ltd	0.6841	0.3580	0.7561	-0.2224	-1.5758	-	-	-
335	Sun Pharmaceutical Industries Ltd	1.9496	0.1634	0.2336	0.6030	-0.8170	-0.4041	-0.2203	1.7441

S.No.	Company Name	Pre-Acquisition				Post-Acquisition			
		2013	2014	2015	2016	2019	2020	2021	2022
336	Seven Hill Industries Ltd	-	-	-0.6461	-0.6461	-0.6461	-0.6461	2.5845	-0.1057
337	Swan Energy Ltd	0.4606	-0.0509	0.0710	-0.0016	1.6070	0.7642	-2.0408	0.6314
338	Surya Roshni Ltd	0.4093	0.4225	0.4260	0.4550	-0.4547	-0.2195	-0.6846	2.8704
339	Talwalkars Better Value Fitness Ltd	0.2201	0.3183	0.4250	0.2418	2.2263	-1.3611	-	-
340	Tata Steel Ltd	-0.3236	-0.5647	-0.7898	-0.0691	-0.4169	0.3348	1.2058	2.5826
341	TeamLease Services Ltd	-0.9512	-0.3230	-0.5675	-0.3909	0.0355	0.0871	0.4749	2.5513
342	Tube Investments of India Ltd	-	-0.3470	-0.5231	-0.3470	0.5437	-0.1355	0.6383	2.7628
343	Thermax Ltd	0.7141	-0.0239	0.5586	1.0877	-0.7720	-1.2281	-0.8982	2.0261
344	Ramco Cements Ltd/The	-1.1806	-0.4692	0.5722	0.7934	-0.1549	0.7262	-0.2311	2.5167
345	Trejhara Solutions Ltd	-		-	-0.1785	-0.5913	0.2475	0.5223	2.9447
346	Trent Ltd	-0.9999	-0.0129	-0.2295	0.1302	1.2330	-2.1699	0.4643	-0.4930
347	Torrent Pharmaceuticals Ltd	0.1765	-0.3997	1.7356	-0.3310	-0.2511	0.1417	-0.0885	2.3773
348	Tata Chemicals Ltd	-0.8442	-0.4499	-0.2777	1.0610	0.2233	-1.1562	0.0850	2.0442
349	TVS Motor Co Ltd	0.8362	0.1246	0.9729	0.8074	-0.7561	-1.1888	-1.2072	-1.8216
350	Universal Autofoundry Ltd	0.2309	0.1726	0.2891	0.5365	-1.7162	-0.2654	-1.4619	-0.5082
351	Uniply Decor Ltd	0.4233	0.3729	0.4537	0.1274	-1.6439	-1.8381	-	-
352	UFO Moviez India Ltd	0.3260	0.3411	0.3551	0.3213	0.2595	-1.6702	-0.5635	-2.3978
353	Ugro Capital Ltd	0.9128	-2.4224	0.4613	-0.8921	0.1723	0.2883	0.2891	0.3551
354	Umiya Tubes Ltd	-0.1507	0.1243	-0.4256	0.3013	-	-	-	-
355	UNO Minda Ltd	-1.3444	-0.9902	0.1097	0.4719	-0.1532	-0.0669	0.1003	2.1565
356	UPL Ltd	0.0939	0.2044	-0.4409	-0.1132	-0.2750	0.2200	0.3193	3.0543
357	Varroc Engineering Ltd	0.2501	0.5370	0.2426	0.9507	-2.0795	-0.2655	-1.7197	-0.2655
358	Varun Beverages Ltd	-1.1240	-0.7237	-0.2265	0.3349	0.6233	-0.0071	0.4827	2.6295
359	Vibrant Global Capital Ltd	-0.1170	-0.0239	-0.1431	-0.0980	-1.0070	0.8267	1.2930	2.4302
360	Vikas Lifecare Ltd	-	-	-	-	-	1.6346	-1.6346	1.3747
361	Visco Trade Associates Ltd	-0.1451	-0.0897	-0.1451	-0.0342	-0.9229	1.9498	-0.1278	2.0593
362	Hemisphere Properties India Ltd	-1.7639	-0.0400	-0.2972	0.3083	0.4304	0.7069	0.7938	2.0702
363	Vidhi Specialty Food Ingredients Ltd	-0.5489	-0.7044	-0.3934	-0.3602	0.4109	-0.3698	2.5831	-0.3698
364	Vardhman Textiles Ltd	0.9986	-0.6229	0.0761	0.1898	-0.6389	-0.8844	1.1547	2.3321
365	Vinayak Vanijya Ltd	-1.0584	-1.7538	-0.3630	-0.3630	1.2249	0.6414	1.2548	0.9202
366	Waaree Renewable Technologies Ltd	0.7183	0.7183	0.7183	0.7183	-0.6354	-1.8301	-0.4908	-1.4991
367	Natco Economicals Ltd	0.0476	-0.1044	-0.4391	0.4057	-0.5569	2.8882	-0.5569	-
368	White Organic Agro Ltd	1.8045	1.5877	0.4436	-0.7522	-0.8552	-0.8642	-0.4605	-0.5813
369	Williamson Magor & Co Ltd	-2.5502	0.0630	0.6780	0.5365	0.8311	0.6849	-	-
370	Windsor Machines Ltd	1.2843	-0.8651	0.1741	0.4869	-1.6095	0.5214	0.3277	1.5926
371	WPIL Ltd	0.4526	0.0925	-1.0808	-0.9475	-0.1234	0.3170	0.5893	2.3943
372	Yaari Digital Integrated Services Ltd	0.6641	0.6252	0.6717	0.4407	-1.9620	-0.2444	-0.9463	-1.6184
373	Spencer's Retail Ltd	0.7006	0.6749	0.6680	0.6493	-2.2592	-1.0669	0.0020	-0.8061
374	Vineet Laboratories Ltd	0.3584	0.3514	0.3654	0.2464	0.4920	-1.8289	0.2084	-2.2992
375	Zee Entertainment Enterprises Ltd	0.4346	0.1027	-0.0223	0.2467	-1.0659	-0.6290	-0.9121	2.2724
376	Zee Media Corp Ltd	-0.8674	-1.2066	-0.4186	0.2922	0.1931	0.7326	0.5966	2.4418
377	Zensar Technologies Ltd	0.5649	0.3894	0.3383	-0.0551	-0.8167	0.4294	-0.4093	2.8414
378	Zee Learn Ltd	-1.0129	-0.0085	0.4048	0.8472	0.2889	-1.5521	-0.9951	-1.2076
379	Zomato Ltd	-	-	-	-1.8358	-0.1158	1.1636	0.7881	0.1557
380	Zuari Agro Chemicals Ltd	-1.0326	-0.9359	-0.2494	0.6756	0.4554	1.0816	-0.5728	2.2358
381	Zydus Lifesciences Ltd	-0.6296	-0.0537	0.7510	-0.1736	-0.4288	0.2331	-0.1780	2.9059

Source: *Compiled by Author*

The operating margin of the business before and after the acquisition is compared in Table 4.2.38. The assessment of a corporation's financial position is significantly enhanced by the consideration of its operating margin, which serves as a vital statistic. The ratio provides a representation of the company's net income after subtracting expenses, minus interest and taxes. The operating margin is a vital factor in assessing a company's growth potential across various organisations. The interval including the years 2013 to 2016 is commonly denoted as the pre-acquisition era, whereas the years

2019 to 2022 are commonly designated as the post-acquisition era. The examination of the presented table indicates that the operating margin of the firms has experienced a rise subsequent to the acquisition. This suggests that the acquisition has been advantageous to the companies, as it has enhanced their profitability. In the instance of Hemisphere Properties India Ltd., it is observed that the company's operating margin has experienced growth subsequent to the acquisition. Furthermore, during the post-acquisition period, the company's earnings have nearly doubled within a span of four years. Although there were a limited number of firms, such as Pricol Ltd, whose operating margin saw a decline following an acquisition, it subsequently increased after one year, resulting in an overall enhancement of the company's profitability.

Table 4.2.39 -Comparison of Pre- and Post-Merger and Acquisition

Variable	Merger		Acquisition	
	Pre	**Post**	**Pre**	**Post**
Objective 2: Operating Efficiency				
Under Time-varying decay model				
Return on Assets	-0.0355***	0.03173**	-0.01491	0.00506
Operating Return on Assets	0.7676***	0.9427***	0.76152***	0.84611***
Sales	0.0055	0.03421	-0.02812	0.14869***
Five-Year Average Turnover	-0.1129***	0.04196	-0.05652**	-0.01443
Inventory Turnover	-0.0854**	-0.01641	-0.05247**	0.00477
Under Time invariant inefficiency model				
Return on Assets	-0.0334***	0.0342**	-0.01397*	0.00577
Operating Return on Assets	0.7706***	0.9378***	0.75810***	0.84468***
Sales	0.0272	0.0265	-0.00167	0.14283***

Variable	Merger		Acquisition	
	Pre	Post	Pre	Post
Five-Year Average Turnover	-0.1248***	0.03158	-0.07235***	-0.013416
Inventory Turnover	-0.0828**	-0.01936	-0.06573***	0.00122
Under Time-varying decay inefficiency model				
Return on Assets	-0.03574***	0.03173**	-0.01491	0.00506
Operating Return on Assets	0.76623***	0.9427***	0.7615***	0.84611***
Sales	-0.0032	0.0342	-0.0281	0.14869***
Five-Year Average Turnover	-0.0977***	0.04195	-0.0565**	-0.01443
Inventory Turnover	-0.07552**	-0.0164	-0.05246**	0.00477

Note: *p<0.1, **p<0.05, ***p<0.01

Table 4.2.39 presents the effects of return on assets, operating return on assets, sales, five-year average turnover, and inventory turnover on the operating performance of corporations both before to and following a merger or acquisition. The analysis reveals that, according to the time varying decay model, the return on assets, five-year average turnover, and inventory turnover exhibited negative values before to the merger and acquisition. However, these metrics have subsequently shown positive values, indicating a favourable influence of the merger and acquisition on the operating effectiveness of the businesses. In a similar vein, it can be observed that in the context of the time invariant inefficiency model, the coefficients have exhibited a shift towards positivity or a decrease in negativity subsequent to the occurrence of a merger and acquisition. According to the time-varying decay inefficiency model, the coefficients have exhibited a positive trend, indicating an improvement in the operational efficiency of organisations following merger and acquisition activities.

Table 4.2.40 -Regression Analysis of Operating Efficiency

Null Hypotheses	Description	Accept/Reject
$Ho_{2.1}$	There is no impact of OROA and FAT on OPM before the merger	Rejected
$Ho_{2.2}$	There is no impact of Sales on OPM before the merger	Fail to Reject
$Ho_{2.3}$	There is no impact of IT and ROA on OPM before the merger	Rejected
$Ho_{2.4}$	There is no impact of OROA and FAT on OPM after the merger	Rejected
$Ho_{2.5}$	There is no impact of Sales on OPM after the merger	Fail to Reject
$Ho_{2.6}$	There is no impact of IT and ROA on OPM after the merger	Rejected
$Ho_{2.7}$	There is no impact of OROA and FAT on OPM during the merger	Rejected
$Ho_{2.8}$	There is no impact of Sales on OPM during the merger	Fail to Reject
$Ho_{2.9}$	There is no impact of IT and ROA on OPM during the merger	Fail to Reject
$Ho_{2.10}$	There is no impact of OROA and FAT on OPM on the overall merger	Rejected
$Ho_{2.11}$	There is no impact of Sales on OPM on the overall merger	Rejected
$Ho_{2.12}$	There is no impact of IT and ROA on OPM on the overall merger	Fail to Reject
$Ho_{2.13}$	There is no impact of OROA and FAT on OPM before acquisition	Rejected
$Ho_{2.14}$	There is no impact of Sales on OPM before acquisition	Fail to Reject

Null Hypotheses	Description	Accept/Reject
$Ho_{2.15}$	There is no impact of IT and ROA on OPM before acquisition	Rejected
$Ho_{2.16}$	There is no impact of OROA and FAT on OPM after acquisition	Rejected
$Ho_{2.17}$	There is no impact of Sales on OPM after acquisition	Rejected
$Ho_{2.18}$	There is no impact of IT and ROA on OPM after acquisition	Fail to Reject
$Ho_{2.19}$	There is no impact of OROA and FAT on OPM during acquisition	Rejected
$Ho_{2.20}$	There is no impact of Sales on OPM during acquisition	Fail to Reject
$Ho_{2.21}$	There is no impact of IT and ROA on OPM during acquisition	Fail to Reject
$Ho_{2.22}$	There is no impact of OROA and FAT on OPM on overall acquisition	Rejected
$Ho_{2.23}$	There is no impact of Sales on OPM on overall acquisition	Rejected
$Ho_{2.24}$	There is no impact of IT and ROA on OPM on overall acquisition	Fail to Reject

It may be concluded from the above Hypotheses that after the merger the inventory turnover and return on assets also have a significant impact on the operating efficiency of the companies. Similarly, before the merger, these variables have a significant impact on the operating efficiency of the companies. Besides this, Sales are insignificant before and after the merger. Similarly in the case of acquisition, the inventory turnover and return on assets have a significant impact on the operating efficiency of the companies in pre-acquisition which has become insignificant post-acquisition. However, Sales has a significant impact post-acquisition as compared to pre-acquisition.

4.4 Regression results of the objective three

Table 4.3.1 -Descriptive Statistics of Financial Performance - Merger

Statistic	N	Mean	St. Dev.	Min	Max
PR_NI	292	-0.233967	0.832195	-2.021393	2.801108
PR_EBITDA	292	-0.309824	0.874327	-2.215868	2.471736
PR_EBIT	292	-0.214425	0.857242	-2.127256	2.484069
PR_ROA	292	0.120202	0.925316	-2.653465	2.791997
PR_ROC	292	0.17345	0.887028	-2.767618	2.788882
PR_ROCE	292	0.046203	1.001289	-2.31421	2.755984
PR_FL	292	0.111745	1.038039	-2.209638	2.799004
PR_DFL	292	0.068101	1.027626	-2.841993	2.815709
PR_DOL	292	0.068584	0.928543	-2.39009	2.839449
PR_CFNI	292	-0.250716	0.844246	-2.023143	2.838838
PO_NI	292	0.184964	1.045492	-2.6092	2.824574
PO_EBITDA	292	0.289856	0.972437	-2.368395	2.501152
PO_EBIT	292	0.165345	1.01791	-2.677693	2.658487
PO_ROA	292	-0.142424	0.991219	-2.680413	2.463593
PO_ROC	292	-0.20226	0.986008	-2.637613	2.478916
PO_ROCE	292	-0.015515	0.892793	-2.203372	2.456072
PO_FL	292	-0.119342	0.897633	-1.937827	2.150218
PO_DFL	292	-0.047345	0.875022	-2.843964	2.760237
PO_DOL	292	-0.039464	0.95391	-2.63002	2.611263
PO_CFNI	292	0.236858	1.032679	-2.628288	2.508658

Source: *Compiled by Author from R output sheet*

Table 4.3.1 depicts the descriptive statistics of the dependent as well as independent variables used in this study in the case of pre-merger and post-merger. The mean of EBITDA, EBIT, and CFNI is negative 0.233967, 0.309824, and 0.250716 respectively before the merger which has become positive 0.289856,0.165345, and 0.236858 after the merger. The mean of only these variables has increased post-merger, thereby indicating a positive impact on the financial performance post-merger. However, the mean of other variables was positive before the merger which became negative after the merger. Thereby indicating a negative impact on the financial performance of the companies after the merger. The standard deviation defines the risk, in this case, the standard deviation of ROCE, FL, and DFL is reduced after the merger, other than these all-other variables involving high risk after the merger. In the next table, the impact of earnings on the financial performance of the company before the merger is discussed.

Table 4.3.2 displays both random effect and fixed effect regression results. The values under (1) and (3) represent random effect variable coefficients, while (2) and (4) represent fixed effect variable coefficients. The coefficient of EBITDA is 0.579 under

Table 4.3.2 -Impact of Earnings on Financial Performance Before Merger

	Dependent variable:			
	ni			
	(1)	(2)	(3)	(4)
ebitda	0.579***	0.540***		
	(0.047)	(0.059)		
ebit			0.676***	0.541***
			(0.041)	(0.056)
Constant	−0.058		−0.092**	
	(0.052)		(0.038)	
Observations	280	280	280	280
R^2	0.358	0.286	0.489	0.308
Adjusted R^2	0.356	0.047	0.488	0.076
F Statistic (df = 1; 209)	155.082***	83.792***	266.512***	92.934***
Note:				*p<0.1; **p<0.05; ***p<0.01

Source: *Compiled by Author from R output sheet*

random effect and 0.540 under fixed effect before the merger. This indicates that the change in EBITDA under random effect will impact the financial performance at a greater rate. Similarly, EBIT also impacts at a higher rate under random effect as compared to fixed effect in pre-merger as the coefficient of EBIT is 0.676 under random effect and 0.541 under fixed effect. The coefficient values of EBIT and EBITDA have a significant impact at the 1% level. Table 4.3.3 shows the impact of returns on the financial performance of the company before the merger.

Table 4.3.3 displays both random effect and fixed effect regression results. The values under (1) and (3) represent random effect variable coefficients, while (2) and (4) represent fixed effect variable coefficients. The coefficient of ROA was 0.512 under random effect and 0.515 under fixed effect before the merger. This indicates that the change in ROA under fixed effect will impact the financial performance at a greater rate. However, ROC impacts at the same rate under random as well as fixed effect in pre-merger as the coefficient of ROC is 0.494 under random effect as well as fixed effect. The coefficient values of ROA and ROC have a significant impact at the 1%

Table 4.3.3 -Impact of Returns on Financial Performance Before Merger

	Dependent variable:			
	ni			
	(1)	(2)	(3)	(4)
roa	0.512***	0.515***		
	(0.038)	(0.040)		
roc			0.494***	0.494***
			(0.040)	(0.043)
Constant	−0.302***		−0.324***	
	(0.062)		(0.064)	
Observations	288	288	284	284
R^2	0.393	0.432	0.350	0.385
Adjusted R^2	0.391	0.241	0.347	0.179
F Statistic	185.361***	163.321*** (df = 1; 215)	151.542***	132.909*** (df = 1; 212)
Note:				*p<0.1; **p<0.05; ***p<0.01

Source: *Compiled by Author from R output sheet*

Table 4.3.4 -Impact of Returns and Liquidity on Financial Performance Before Merger

	Dependent variable:			
	ni			
	(1)	(2)	(3)	(4)
roce	0.207***	0.219***		
	(0.047)	(0.050)		
fl			−0.127***	−0.115**
			(0.046)	(0.053)
Constant	−0.240***		−0.224***	
	(0.078)		(0.070)	
Observations	236	236	284	284
R^2	0.078	0.098	0.027	0.022
Adjusted R^2	0.074	−0.204	0.023	−0.306
F Statistic	19.729***	19.219*** (df = 1; 176)	7.745***	4.771** (df = 1; 212)
Note:				*p<0.1; **p<0.05; ***p<0.01

Source: *Compiled by Author from R output sheet*

level. Further, in the next table, the impact of return on capital employed and financial leverage on the financial performance of the companies before the merger is analyzed.

Table 4.3.4 displays both random effect and fixed effect regression results before the merger. The values under (1) and (3) represent random effect variable coefficients, while (2) and (4) represent fixed effect variable coefficients. The coefficient of ROCE is 0.207 under random effect and 0.219 under fixed effect before the merger. This indicates that the change in ROCE under fixed effect will impact the financial performance at a greater rate. However, Financial leverage (FL) impacts at a higher rate under random effect in pre-merger as the coefficient of FL is 0.127 under random effect as well as 0.115 fixed effects. Financial leverage affects the financial performance of the companies negatively under both the random effect and fixed effect models. The coefficient values of ROCE and FL have a significant impact at the 1% level. In this table only financial leverage is examined, however, in the next table, the impact of the degree of financial leverage and degree of operating leverage on financial performance before the merger is examined.

Table 4.3.5 -Impact of Leverages on Financial Performance Before Merger

	Dependent variable:			
	ni			
	(1)	(2)	(3)	(4)
dfl	−0.113**	−0.135***		
	(0.048)	(0.052)		
dol			0.064	0.054
			(0.051)	(0.055)
Constant	−0.237***		−0.235***	
	(0.075)		(0.077)	
Observations	244	244	248	248
R^2	0.023	0.036	0.006	0.005
Adjusted R^2	0.018	−0.287	0.002	−0.328
F Statistic	5.573**	6.837*** (df = 1; 182)	1.531	0.973 (df = 1; 185)
Note:				*p<0.1; **p<0.05; ***p<0.01

Source: *Compiled by Author from R output sheet*

Table 4.3.5 displays both random effect and fixed effect regression results before the merger. The values under (1) and (3) represent random effect variable coefficients, while (2) and (4) represent fixed effect variable coefficients. The coefficient of Degree of Financial leverage (DFL) is 0.113 under random effect and 0.135 under fixed effect before merger. This indicates that the change in DFL under fixed effect will impact the financial performance at a greater rate negatively. However, the degree of operating leverage (DOL) impacts at a higher rate under random effect in pre-merger as the coefficient of DOL is 0.064 under random effect as well as 0.054 under fixed effect. The degree of Operating leverage affects the financial performance of the companies positively under both the random effect and fixed effect models. The coefficient values of DFL have a significant impact at 5% and 1% level under random and fixed models respectively. The DOL has an insignificant impact under both models. The earnings, returns, and leverage ratios are already discussed in the above tables. In the next table, the impact of cash flow on financial performance before the merger is examined.

Table 4.3.6 -Impact of Cash Flow on Financial Performance Before Merger

	Dependent variable:	
	ni	
	(1)	(2)
cfni	0.988***	1.055***
	(0.008)	(0.010)
Constant	0.014*	
	(0.008)	
Observations	292	292
R^2	0.979	0.980
Adjusted R^2	0.979	0.973
F Statistic	13,672.390***	10,422.100*** (df = 1; 218)
Note:		*p<0.1; **p<0.05; ***p<0.01

Source: *Compiled by Author from R output sheet*

Table 4.3.6 displays both random effect and fixed effect regression results before the merger. The values under (1) represent random effect variable coefficients, while (2) represent fixed effect variable coefficients. The coefficient of cash flow from net income (CFNI) was 0.988 under random effect and 1.055 under fixed effect before the merger. This indicates that the change in CFNI under fixed effect will impact the financial performance at a greater rate. The coefficient values of CFNI have a significant impact at a 1% level under both models. Further, the regression results of financial performance before the merger are reported in the next table on the basis of the Hausman test.

Table 4.3.7 -Regression Results of Financial Performance Before Merger

	Dependent variable:			
	ni			
	(1)	(2)	(3)	(4)
ebitda	0.579***			
	(0.047)			
ebit		0.541***		
		(0.056)		
roa			0.512***	
			(0.038)	
roc				0.494***
				(0.040)
Constant	−0.058		−0.302***	−0.324***
	(0.052)		(0.062)	(0.064)
Observations	280	280	288	284
R^2	0.358	0.308	0.393	0.350
Adjusted R^2	0.356	0.076	0.391	0.347
F Statistic	155.082***	92.934*** (df = 1; 209)	185.361***	151.542***
Note:				*p<0.1; **p<0.05; ***p<0.01

Source: *Compiled by Author from R output sheet*

Table 4.3.7 -Regression Results of Financial Performance Before Merger (Contd)

	Dependent variable:				
	ni				
	(5)	(6)	(7)	(8)	(9)
roce	0.207***				
	(0.047)				
fl		−0.127***			
		(0.046)			
dfl			−0.113**		
			(0.048)		
dol				0.064	
				(0.051)	
cfni					1.055***
					(0.010)
Constant	−0.240***	−0.224***	−0.237***	−0.235***	
	(0.078)	(0.070)	(0.075)	(0.077)	
Observations	236	284	244	248	292
R^2	0.078	0.027	0.023	0.006	0.980
Adjusted R^2	0.074	0.023	0.018	0.002	0.973
F Statistic	19.729***	7.745***	5.573**	1.531	10,422.100*** (df = 1; 218)
Note:					*p<0.1; **p<0.05; ***p<0.01

Source: *Compiled by Author from R output sheet*

Table 4.3.7 displays the regression results of all the variables impacting the financial performance of the companies. In these tables, either a random or fixed effect model is taken on the basis of the result obtained after applying the Hausman test. Specifically, if the p-value is less than 0.05, fixed effects are employed, whereas if the p-value is greater than 0.05, random effects are used. The coefficients of EBIT and CFNI are the only variables that are less than 0.05, hence, the coefficient under the fixed effect model is taken. However, the coefficients of all other variables except EBIT and CFNI under the random effect model are taken. Except for DFL and DOL, all the coefficient values are statistically significant at a 1% level. The coefficient of DFL is statistically significant at 5% but the coefficient of DOL has an insignificant value. In the above tables, the impact of earnings, returns, and leverages on financial performance before the merger are discussed. Further, in the next table the impact of earnings on financial performance after the merger is analyzed.

Table 4.3.8 -Impact of Earnings on Financial Performance After Merger

	Dependent variable:			
	ni			
	(1)	(2)	(3)	(4)
ebitda	0.627***	0.624***		
	(0.053)	(0.072)		
ebit			0.771***	0.729***
			(0.041)	(0.049)
Constant	0.001		0.055	
	(0.053)		(0.042)	
Observations	280	280	280	280
R^2	0.339	0.265	0.561	0.516
Adjusted R^2	0.336	0.019	0.559	0.354
F Statistic (df = 1; 209)	142.373***	75.441***	354.797***	223.190***
Note:				*p<0.1; **p<0.05; ***p<0.01

Source: *Compiled by Author from R output sheet*

Table 4.3.8 presents the regression outcomes for both random effect and fixed effect models. The coefficients corresponding to values (1) and (3) pertain to random effect variables, whereas the coefficients corresponding to values (2) and (4) pertain to fixed effect variables. After the merger, the coefficient of EBITDA is observed to be 0.627 under the random effect model and 0.624 under the fixed effect model. The values observed were 0.579 under the random effect model and 0.540 under the fixed effect model prior to the merger. This finding suggests that there is a statistically significant change in EBITDA, with an approximate increase of 5 percent under random effects and 1 percent under fixed effects. This implies that the post-merger EBITDA has had a greater impact on the financial performance. Likewise, it can be observed that Earnings Before Interest and Taxes (EBIT) exhibit a more pronounced effect following a merger in both models, suggesting an enhanced financial performance of the companies subsequent to the merger. The coefficient of EBIT is 0.676 under the random effects model and 0.541 under the fixed effects model prior to the merger. Following the merger, the coefficient of EBIT is 0.771 under the random effects model and 0.729 under the fixed effects model. The coefficient values associated with EBIT and EBITDA exhibit a statistically significant impact at a significance level of 1%. In table 4.3.9 the impact of returns on financial performance after the merger is examined.

Table 4.3.9 -Impact of Returns on Financial Performance After Merger

	Dependent variable:			
	ni			
	(1)	(2)	(3)	(4)
roa	0.769***	0.834***		
	(0.045)	(0.051)		
roc			0.773***	0.840***
			(0.046)	(0.052)
Constant	0.299***		0.341***	
	(0.059)		(0.060)	
Observations	288	288	284	284
R^2	0.503	0.558	0.497	0.552
Adjusted R^2	0.501	0.410	0.495	0.403
F Statistic	289.073***	271.828*** (df = 1; 215)	278.418***	261.645*** (df = 1; 212)
Note:				*p<0.1; **p<0.05; ***p<0.01

Source: *Compiled by Author from R output sheet*

The regression results for both random effect and fixed effect models are presented in Table 4.3.9. The coefficients corresponding to values (1) and (3) pertain to random effect variables, whereas the coefficients corresponding to values (2) and (4) pertain to fixed effect variables. The coefficient of Return on Assets (ROA) is found to be 0.512 under the random effects model and 0.515 under the fixed effects model prior to the merger. Following the merger, the coefficient of ROA is estimated to be 0.769 under the random effects model and 0.834 under the fixed effects model. This suggests that the alteration in Return on Assets (ROA) will have a more pronounced effect on the financial performance in both models after the merger. The financial performance of the companies has demonstrated improvement subsequent to the merger. The coefficient of the ROC is 0.494 in both the random effect and fixed effect models prior to the merger. However, after the merger, the coefficient has increased to 0.773 and 0.840 in the random effect and fixed effect models, respectively. This indicates a stronger influence of the ROC post-merger. The coefficient values of Return on Assets (ROA) and Return on Capital (ROC) exhibit a statistically significant impact at a significance level of 1% both before and after the merger. Further, in the next table, the impact of return on capital employed and financial leverage on financial performance after merger is analyzed.

Table 4.3.10 - Impact of Returns and Liquidity on Financial Performance After Merger

	Dependent variable:			
	ni			
	(1)	(2)	(3)	(4)
roce	0.451***	0.538***		
	(0.074)	(0.092)		
fl			−0.194***	−0.242**
			(0.072)	(0.107)
Constant	0.183**		0.162**	
	(0.076)		(0.070)	
Observations	236	236	284	284
R^2	0.136	0.164	0.025	0.024
Adjusted R^2	0.132	−0.116	0.021	−0.303
F Statistic	36.823***	34.546*** (df = 1; 176)	7.152***	5.138** (df = 1; 212)
Note:				*p<0.1; **p<0.05; ***p<0.01

Source: *Compiled by Author from R output sheet*

Table 4.3.10 presents the regression outcomes, encompassing both random effect and fixed effect models, subsequent to the merger. The coefficients corresponding to values (1) and (3) represent the random effect variables, whereas the coefficients corresponding to values (2) and (4) represent the fixed effect variables. The coefficient values for the Return on Capital Employed (ROCE) variable are 0.451 and 0.538 when estimated using the random effects and fixed effects models, respectively. Prior to the merger, the coefficient of Return on Capital Employed (ROCE) was observed to be 0.207 under the random effects model and 0.219 under the fixed effects model. This suggests that the rise in the proportion of Return on Capital Employed (ROCE) subsequent to the merger has enhanced the financial performance of the companies. However, it should be noted that financial leverage exhibits a negative trend both prior to and subsequent to the merger. In the event of a pre-merger scenario, the coefficient of FL was observed to be 0.127 under the random effect and 0.115 under the fixed effect model. Subsequently, this coefficient increased to 0.194 and 0.242 under the random and fixed models, respectively. The financial performance of companies is being adversely impacted by financial leverage, as observed in both the random effect and fixed effect models before and after the merger. However, subsequent to the merger, there has been an increase in this percentage, consequently leading to a detrimental impact of financial leverage on the financial performance of the companies. The coefficient values of Return on Capital Employed (ROCE) exhibit a statistically significant impact at a significance level of 1% in both the pre-merger and post-merger periods. Nevertheless, the variable FL demonstrates a substantial influence at a significance level of 1% in both pre-merger models. However, in the post-merger scenario, FL exhibits a significant impact at a significance level of 1% in the random effect model and at a significance level of 5% in the fixed effect model. In this table, only financial leverage is discussed. However, in Table 4.3.11 the impact of the degree of operating leverage and degree of financial leverage on operating performance after merger is examined.

The regression results following the merger are presented in Table 4.3.11, encompassing both random effect and fixed effect models. The coefficients corresponding to values (1) and (3) represent random effect variables, whereas the coefficients corresponding to values (2) and (4) represent fixed effect variables. The coefficient for the Degree of Financial Leverage (DFL) is 0.113 under the random effects model and 0.135 under the fixed effects model prior to the merger. However, following the merger, the value decreased to 0.047 under the random effect model and 0.106 under the fixed effect model. This suggests that the decrease in the negative

Table 4.3.11 -Impact of Leverages on Financial Performance After Merger

	Dependent variable:			
	ni			
	(1)	(2)	(3)	(4)
dfl	−0.047	−0.106		
	(0.078)	(0.097)		
dol			0.113	0.054
			(0.069)	(0.081)
Constant	0.189**		0.195***	
	(0.076)		(0.074)	
Observations	244	244	248	248
R^2	0.002	0.007	0.011	0.002
Adjusted R^2	−0.003	−0.326	0.007	−0.332
F Statistic	0.364	1.195 (df = 1; 182)	2.630	0.452 (df = 1; 185)
Note:			*p<0.1; **p<0.05; ***p<0.01	

Source: *Compiled by Author from R output sheet*

coefficient of DFL has mitigated the adverse impact of this variable on the financial performance of the companies following the merger. During the pre-merger period, the coefficient of DOL was observed to be 0.064 under the random effects model and 0.054 under the fixed effects model. Subsequently, there was an increase in the coefficient to 0.113 under the random effects model. However, under the fixed effect model, the coefficient remains the same as in the pre-merger case. The rise in the proportion of degree of operating leverage (DOL) due to random effects has resulted in enhanced financial performance among companies. In general, DOL and DFL have yielded enhancements in the financial performance of the companies subsequent to the merger.

The coefficient values of DFL exhibit a statistically significant impact at the 5% and 1% significance levels in the random and fixed models, respectively. The DOL had a negligible influence in both models before the merger. Following the merger, it can be observed that both DFL and DOL have minimal or negligible effects in both of the models. In the next table, the impact of cashflow on financial performance after the merger is analyzed.

Table 4.3.12 presents the regression outcomes for both random effect and fixed effect models subsequent to the merger. The values denoted by (1) correspond to coefficients of random effect variables, whereas the values denoted by (2) correspond to coefficients of fixed effect variables. The coefficient of cash flow from net income (CFNI) is

Table 4.3.12 - Impact of Cash Flow on Financial Performance After Merger

	Dependent variable:	
	ni	
	(1)	(2)
cfni	0.870***	0.898***
	(0.030)	(0.045)
Constant	−0.021	
	(0.032)	
Observations	292	292
R^2	0.738	0.642
Adjusted R^2	0.737	0.522
F Statistic	815.266***	390.898*** (df = 1; 218)
Note:		*p<0.1; **p<0.05; ***p<0.01

Source: *Compiled by Author from R output sheet*

observed to be 0.870 under the random effect model and 0.898 under the fixed effect model following the merger. Prior to the merger, these coefficients were recorded as 0.988 under the random effect model and 1.055 under the fixed effect model. This suggests that the CFNI has decreased following the merger in both models, indicating a decline in financial performance after the merger. The coefficient values of CFNI exhibit a statistically significant impact at a 1% level in both the pre-merger and post-merger models. The regression results of financial performance before the merger are already discussed in table 4.3.7 and now, in table 4.3.13 the regression results of financial performance after the merger are reported on the basis of the Hausman test.

Table 4.3.13 displays the regression results of all the variables impacting the financial performance of the companies after the merger. In these tables, either a random or fixed effect model is taken on the basis of the result obtained after applying the Hausman test. Specifically, if the p-value is less than 0.05, fixed effects are employed, whereas if the p-value is greater than 0.05, random effects are used. The coefficients of ROA and ROC are the only variables that are less than 0.05, thereby coefficients of these variables under fixed effect are taken and coefficients of all other variables except these two are under random effect after the merger. However, the coefficient of EBIT and CFNI are the only variables which are less than 0.05, hence, the coefficient under the fixed effect model is taken and the coefficient of all other variables except EBIT and CFNI under the random effect model are taken before the merger. Except for DFL and DOL, all the coefficient values are statistically significant at a 1% level. The coefficient of DFL is statistically significant at 5% but the coefficient of DOL has an insignificant value

Table 4.3.13 -Regression Results of Financial Performance After Merger

	Dependent variable:			
	ni			
	(1)	(2)	(3)	(4)
ebitda	0.627***			
	(0.053)			
ebit		0.771***		
		(0.041)		
roa			0.834***	
			(0.051)	
roc				0.840***
				(0.052)
Constant	0.001	0.055		
	(0.053)	(0.042)		
Observations	280	280	288	284
R^2	0.339	0.561	0.558	0.552
Adjusted R^2	0.336	0.559	0.410	0.403
F Statistic	142.373***	354.797***	271.828*** (df = 1; 215)	261.645*** (df = 1; 212)
Note:				*p<0.1; **p<0.05; ***p<0.01

Source: *Compiled by Author from R output sheet*

Table 4.3.13 - Regression Results of Financial Performance After Merger (Contd)

	Dependent variable:				
	ni				
	(5)	(6)	(7)	(8)	(9)
roce	0.451***				
	(0.074)				
fl		−0.194***			
		(0.072)			
dfl			−0.047		
			(0.078)		
dol				0.113	
				(0.069)	
cfni					0.870***
					(0.030)
Constant	0.183**	0.162**	0.189**	0.195***	−0.021
	(0.076)	(0.070)	(0.076)	(0.074)	(0.032)
Observations	236	284	244	248	292
R^2	0.136	0.025	0.002	0.011	0.738
Adjusted R^2	0.132	0.021	−0.003	0.007	0.737
F Statistic	36.823***	7.152***	0.364	2.630	815.266***
Note:					*p<0.1; **p<0.05; ***p<0.01

Source: *Compiled by Author from R output sheet*

before the merger. Except for DOL and DFL, all the variables are statistically significant at a 1% level after the merger. In the next segment, the impact of earnings on financial performance during the merger is evaluated.

The regression results for both random effect and fixed effect models are displayed in Table 4.3.14. The coefficients associated with values (1) and (3) are related to random

Table 4.3.14 -Impact of Earnings on Financial Performance During Merger

	Dependent variable:			
	ni			
	(1)	(2)	(3)	(4)
ebitda	0.528***	0.443***		
	(0.073)	(0.103)		
ebit			0.550***	0.428***
			(0.067)	(0.104)
Constant	0.088		0.055	
	(0.069)		(0.064)	
Observations	140	140	140	140
R^2	0.274	0.210	0.326	0.199
Adjusted R^2	0.269	−0.591	0.321	−0.614
F Statistic (df = 1; 69)	52.138***	18.367***	66.796***	17.097***
Note:		*p<0.1; **p<0.05; ***p<0.01		

Source: *Compiled by Author from R output sheet*

effect variables, while the coefficients associated with values (2) and (4) are related to fixed effect variables. Following the merger, it has been observed that the coefficient of EBITDA is 0.627 under the random effect model and 0.624 under the fixed effect model. Prior to the merger, the observed values were 0.579 under the random effect model and 0.540 under the fixed effect model. In the year of the merger, the coefficient of EBITDA is 0.528 and 0.443 under the random and fixed effect models, respectively. The aforementioned discovery implies that there is a statistically noteworthy alteration in EBITDA following a merger, exhibiting an approximate rise of 5 percent under random effects and 1 percent under fixed effects compared to the pre-merger period. However, there is a marginal 1% variation observed in both models after the merger, compared to the year of the merger. This suggests that the financial performance has been more significantly influenced by the post-merger EBITDA. Similarly, it is evident that the impact of Earnings Before Interest and Taxes (EBIT) is more prominent after a merger in both models, indicating an improved financial performance of the companies during and after the merger.

The coefficient of EBIT is 0.676 under the random effects model and 0.541 under the fixed effects model prior to the merger. Following the merger, the coefficient of EBIT is 0.771 under the random effects model and 0.729 under the fixed effects model. During the year of the merger, the coefficient of EBIT is 0.550 and 0.428 under the random effect and fixed model respectively. The coefficient values associated with EBIT and EBITDA exhibit a statistically significant impact at a significance level of 1% in pre-, post, and during the merger. Further, the impact of returns on financial performance is analyzed during the merger in the next table.

Table 4.3.15 -Impact of Returns on Financial Performance During Merger

	Dependent variable:			
	ni			
	(1)	(2)	(3)	(4)
roa	0.789***	0.761***		
	(0.051)	(0.071)		
roc			0.642***	0.602***
			(0.058)	(0.082)
Constant	0.067		0.070	
	(0.049)		(0.059)	
Observations	144	144	142	142
R^2	0.630	0.615	0.467	0.435
Adjusted R^2	0.628	0.225	0.463	−0.138
F Statistic	242.262***	113.510*** (df = 1; 71)	122.770***	53.951*** (df = 1; 70)
Note:				*p<0.1; **p<0.05; ***p<0.01

Source: *Compiled by Author from R output sheet*

The regression results for both random effect and fixed effect models are presented in Table 4.3.15. The coefficients corresponding to values (1) and (3) pertain to random effect variables, whereas the coefficients corresponding to values (2) and (4) pertain to fixed effect variables. The coefficient of Return on Assets (ROA) is found to be 0.512 under the random effects model and 0.515 under the fixed effects model prior to the merger. Following the merger, the coefficient of ROA is estimated to be 0.769 under the random effects model and 0.834 under the fixed effects model. However, during the merger, these values are 0.789 under the random effect and 0.761 under the fixed effect model. This suggests that the alteration in Return on Assets (ROA) will have a more pronounced effect on the financial performance in both models after the merger as compared to pre-merger. However, as compared to during the year of the merger there is a more profound effect under the fixed effect model post-merger. The financial performance of the companies has demonstrated improvement subsequent to the merger.

The coefficient of the ROC is 0.494 in both the random effect and fixed effect models prior to the merger. During the year of the merger, the values are 0.642 and 0.602 under the random effect and fixed effect model respectively. However, after the merger, the coefficient has increased to 0.773 and 0.840 in the random effect and fixed effect models, respectively. This indicates a stronger influence of the ROC post-merger as compared to both pre-and during the merger. The coefficient values of Return on Assets (ROA) and Return on Capital (ROC) exhibit a statistically significant impact at a significance level of 1% both before, during, and after the merger. In the next table, the impact of return on capital employed and financial leverage on financial performance is examined.

Table 4.3.16 presents the regression outcomes, encompassing both random effect and fixed effect models, in the year of the merger. The coefficients corresponding to values (1) and (3) represent the random effect variables, whereas the coefficients corresponding to values (2) and (4) represent the fixed effect variables. The coefficient values for the Return on Capital Employed (ROCE) variable are 0.451 and 0.538 when estimated using the random effects and fixed effects models, respectively. Prior to the merger, the coefficient of Return on Capital Employed (ROCE) was observed to be 0.207 under the random effects model and 0.219 under the fixed effects model. During the year, the coefficient of ROCE is 0.487 and 0.330 under random and fixed effect models respectively. This suggests that the rise in the proportion of Return on Capital Employed (ROCE) subsequent to the merger has enhanced the financial performance of the companies as compared to pre-merger. If we compare the post-merger from the year of merger then the coefficient of ROCE under random effect in the year of merger is higher.

Table 4.3.16 -Impact of Returns and Liquidity on Financial Performance During Merger

	Dependent variable:			
	ni			
	(1)	(2)	(3)	(4)
roce	0.487***	0.330**		
	(0.073)	(0.134)		
fl			−0.171*	−0.363***
			(0.090)	(0.135)
Constant	0.137*		0.110	
	(0.072)		(0.085)	
Observations	118	118	142	142
R^2	0.277	0.094	0.025	0.094
Adjusted R^2	0.270	−0.828	0.018	−0.825
F Statistic	44.350***	6.019** (df = 1; 58)	3.639*	7.272*** (df = 1; 70)
Note:			*p<0.1; **p<0.05; ***p<0.01	

Source: *Compiled by Author from R output sheet*

However, it should be noted that financial leverage exhibits a negative trend both prior to and subsequent to the merger. In the event of a pre-merger scenario, the coefficient of FL was observed to be 0.127 under the random effect and 0.115 under the fixed effect model. During the year, it is 0.171 and 0.363 under random and fixed effect models respectively. Subsequent to the merger, this coefficient is 0.194 and 0.242 under the random and fixed models, respectively. The financial performance of companies is being adversely impacted by financial leverage, as observed in both the random effect and fixed effect models before, during, and after the merger. However, subsequent to the merger, there has been an increase in this percentage, consequently leading to a detrimental impact of financial leverage on the financial performance of the companies under the random effect model. The coefficient values of Return on Capital Employed (ROCE) exhibit a statistically significant impact at a significance level of 1% in the pre-, during, and post-merger periods. Nevertheless, the variable FL demonstrates a substantial influence at a significance level of 1% in both pre-merger models. However, in the post-merger scenario, FL exhibits a significant impact at a significance level of 1% in the random effect model and at a significance level of 5% in the fixed effect model. However, during the year of the merger FL has a significant impact at a 10% level under the random effect model and 1% under the fixed effect model. Further, the impact of the degree of financial leverage and operating leverage during the merger is analyzed in table 4.3.17.

The regression results following the merger are presented in Table 4.3.17, encompassing both random effect and fixed effect models. The coefficients corresponding to values (1) and (3) represent random effect variables, whereas the coefficients corresponding to values (2) and (4) represent fixed effect variables. The

Table 4.3.17 -Impact of Leverages on Financial Performance During Merger

	Dependent variable:			
	ni			
	(1)	(2)	(3)	(4)
dfl	−0.140*	−0.012		
	(0.083)	(0.111)		
dol			0.141*	0.067
			(0.080)	(0.103)
Constant	0.102		0.111	
	(0.087)		(0.089)	
Observations	122	122	124	124
R^2	0.023	0.0002	0.025	0.007
Adjusted R^2	0.015	−1.016	0.017	−1.002
F Statistic	2.861*	0.011 (df = 1; 60)	3.126*	0.424 (df = 1; 61)
Note:			*p<0.1; **p<0.05; ***p<0.01	

Source: *Compiled by Author from R output sheet*

coefficient for the Degree of Financial Leverage (DFL) is 0.113 under the random effects model and 0.135 under the fixed effects model prior to the merger. During the merger, these values are 0.140 and 0.012 under random and fixed effect models respectively. However, following the merger, the value has changed to 0.047 under the random effect model and 0.106 under the fixed effect model. This suggests that the decrease in the negative coefficient of DFL has mitigated the adverse impact of this variable on the financial performance of the companies following the merger in the case of the random effect model. However, the value under fixed effect has increased from the year of the merger.

During the pre-merger period, the coefficient of DOL was observed to be 0.064 under the random effects model and 0.054 under the fixed effects model. During the year, this has increased to 0.141 and 0.067 under the random effect and fixed effect model respectively. Subsequently, the coefficient is 0.113 under the random effects model. However, under the fixed effect model, the coefficient remains the same as in the pre-merger case. The rise in the proportion of degree of operating leverage (DOL) due to random effects has resulted in enhanced financial performance among companies as compared to pre-merger. However, the coefficient is highest under both models during the merger. In general, DOL and DFL have yielded enhancements in the financial performance of the companies subsequent to the merger.

The coefficient values of DFL exhibit a statistically significant impact at the 5% and 1% significance levels in the random and fixed models, respectively. The DOL had a negligible influence in both models before the merger. Following the merger, it can be observed that both DFL and DOL have minimal or negligible effects under both models. During the merger, the DFL and DOL have a significant impact at a 10% level under the random effect model and an insignificant impact under the fixed effect model. In the next table, the impact of cash flow on financial performance during the merger is examined.

Table 4.3.18 -Impact of Cash Flow on Financial Performance During Merger

	Dependent variable:	
	ni	
	(1)	(2)
cfni	0.989***	1.005***
	(0.024)	(0.031)
Constant	0.071**	
	(0.028)	
Observations	146	146
R^2	0.919	0.938
Adjusted R^2	0.919	0.875
F Statistic	1,638.131***	1,084.235*** (df = 1; 72)
Note:		*p<0.1; **p<0.05; ***p<0.01

Source: *Compiled by Author from R output sheet*

Table 4.3.18 presents the regression outcomes for both random effect and fixed effect models in the year of the merger. The values denoted by (1) correspond to coefficients of random effect variables, whereas the values denoted by (2) correspond to coefficients of fixed effect variables. The coefficient of cash flow from net income (CFNI) is observed to be 0.870 under the random effect model and 0.898 under the fixed effect model following the merger. Prior to the merger, these coefficients were recorded as 0.988 under the random effect model and 1.055 under the fixed effect model. During the year of the merger, these values are 0.989 and 1.005 under random effect and fixed effect respectively. This suggests that the CFNI has decreased following the merger in both models, indicating a decline in financial performance after the merger. The coefficient values of CFNI exhibit a statistically significant impact at a 1% level in the pre-, during, and post-merger under both models. The regression results of financial performance during the merger are reported in table 4.3.19.

Table 4.3.19 -Regression Results of Financial Performance During Merger

	Dependent variable:			
	ni			
	(1)	(2)	(3)	(4)
ebitda	0.528***			
	(0.073)			
ebit		0.550***		
		(0.067)		
roa			0.789***	
			(0.051)	
roc				0.642***
				(0.058)
Constant	0.088	0.055	0.067	0.070
	(0.069)	(0.064)	(0.049)	(0.059)
Observations	140	140	144	142
R^2	0.274	0.326	0.630	0.467
Adjusted R^2	0.269	0.321	0.628	0.463
F Statistic	52.138***	66.796***	242.262***	122.770***
Note:	*p<0.1; **p<0.05; ***p<0.01			

Source: *Compiled by Author from R output sheet*

Table 4.3.19 displays the regression results of all the variables impacting the financial performance of the companies in the year of the merger. In these tables, either a random or fixed effect model is taken on the basis of the result obtained after applying the Hausman test. Specifically, if the p-value is less than 0.05, fixed effects are employed, whereas if the p-value is greater than 0.05, random effects are used. The coefficient of all the variables is more than 0.05, thereby coefficients of these variables under random effect are taken. However, the coefficient of EBIT and CFNI are the only variables that are less than 0.05, hence, the coefficient under the fixed effect model is taken and the coefficient of all other variables except EBIT and CFNI under the random effect model that are less than 0.05, thereby coefficients of these variables under fixed effect are

Table 4.3.19 -Regression Results of Financial Performance During Merger (Contd)

	Dependent variable:				
	ni				
	(5)	(6)	(7)	(8)	(9)
roce	0.487***				
	(0.073)				
fl		−0.171*			
		(0.090)			
dfl			−0.140*		
			(0.083)		
dol				0.141*	
				(0.080)	
cfni					0.989***
					(0.024)
Constant	0.137*	0.110	0.102	0.111	0.071**
	(0.072)	(0.085)	(0.087)	(0.089)	(0.028)
Observations	118	142	122	124	146
R^2	0.277	0.025	0.023	0.025	0.919
Adjusted R^2	0.270	0.018	0.015	0.017	0.919
F Statistic	44.350***	3.639*	2.861*	3.126*	1,638.131***
Note:			*p<0.1; **p<0.05; ***p<0.01		

Source: *Compiled by Author from R output sheet*

taken and coefficients of all other variables except these two are under random effect after the merger.

Except for DFL and DOL, all the coefficient values were statistically significant at a 1% level before the merger. The coefficient of DFL is statistically significant at 5% but the coefficient of DOL has an insignificant value before the merger. However, during the year of the merger EBITDA, EBIT, ROA, ROC, ROCE, and CFNI had a significant impact at the 1% level and FL, DFL, and DOL at the 10% level. Except for DOL and DFL, all the variables are statistically significant at a 1% level after the merger. The impact of earnings, returns and leverages is discussed in case of pre-, post- and during the merger. Now, the impact of earnings on financial performance considering overall merger is analyzed in table 4.3.20.

The regression results for both random effect and fixed effect models are displayed in Table 4.3.20. The coefficients associated with values (1) and (3) are related to random

Table 4.3.20 -Impact of Earnings on Financial Performance considering Overall Merger

	Dependent variable:			
	ni			
	(1)	(2)	(3)	(4)
ebitda	0.611***	0.611***		
	(0.030)	(0.032)		
ebit			0.717***	0.717***
			(0.026)	(0.028)
Constant	−0.000		−0.000	
	(0.028)		(0.025)	
Observations	700	700	700	700
R^2	0.373	0.373	0.515	0.515
Adjusted R^2	0.372	0.303	0.514	0.461
F Statistic (df = 1; 629)	415.520***	374.445***	740.036***	666.880***
Note:				*p<0.1; **p<0.05; ***p<0.01

Source: *Compiled by Author from R output sheet*

effect variables, while the coefficients associated with values (2) and (4) are related to fixed effect variables. Following the merger, it has been observed that the coefficient of EBITDA is 0.627 under the random effect model and 0.624 under the fixed effect model. Prior to the merger, the observed values were 0.579 under the random effect model and 0.540 under the fixed effect model. In the year of the merger, the coefficient of EBITDA is 0.528 and 0.443 under the random and fixed effect models, respectively. In the overall merger, the value is 0.611 under both models.

The aforementioned discovery implies that there is a statistically noteworthy alteration in EBITDA following a merger, exhibiting an approximate rise of 5 percent under random effects and 1 percent under fixed effects compared to the pre-merger period. However, there is a marginal variation observed in both models after the merger, compared to the year of the merger and overall merger. This suggests that the financial performance has been more significantly influenced by the post-merger EBITDA.

Similarly, it is evident that the impact of Earnings Before Interest and Taxes (EBIT) is more prominent after a merger in both models, indicating an improved financial performance of the companies during and after the merger. The coefficient of EBIT is 0.676 under the random effects model and 0.541 under the fixed effects model prior to the merger. Following the merger, the coefficient of EBIT is 0.771 under the random effects model and 0.729 under the fixed effects model. During the year of the merger, the coefficient of EBIT is 0.550 and 0.428 under the random effect and fixed model respectively. In the case of an overall merger, the coefficient of EBIT is 0.717 under both models. The coefficient values associated with EBIT and EBITDA exhibit a statistically significant impact at a significance level of 1% in pre-, post, during, and overall merger. In table 4.3.21, the impact of returns on financial performance considering the overall merger is examined.

Table 4.3.21 - Impact of Returns on Financial Performance considering Overall Merger

	Dependent variable:			
	ni			
	(1)	(2)	(3)	(4)
roa	0.618***	0.618***		
	(0.029)	(0.031)		
roc			0.574***	0.574***
			(0.031)	(0.032)
Constant	−0.000		−0.000	
	(0.028)		(0.029)	
Observations	720	720	710	710
R^2	0.382	0.382	0.330	0.330
Adjusted R^2	0.381	0.313	0.329	0.255
F Statistic	443.687***	399.813*** (df = 1; 647)	348.740***	314.260*** (df = 1; 638)
Note:				*p<0.1; **p<0.05; ***p<0.01

Source: *Compiled by Author from R output sheet*

The regression results for both random effect and fixed effect models are presented in Table 4.3.21. The coefficients corresponding to values (1) and (3) pertain to random effect variables, whereas the coefficients corresponding to values (2) and (4) pertain to fixed effect variables. The coefficient of Return on Assets (ROA) is found to be 0.512 under the random effects model and 0.515 under the fixed effects model prior to the merger. Following the merger, the coefficient of ROA is estimated to be 0.769 under the random effects model and 0.834 under the fixed effects model. However, during the merger, these values were 0.789 under the random effect and 0.761 under the fixed effect model. In the case of the overall merger, the coefficient of ROA is 0.618 under both models. This suggests that the alteration in Return on Assets (ROA) will have a more pronounced effect on the financial performance in both models after the merger as compared to pre-merger as well as overall merger. However, as compared to during the year of the merger there is a more profound effect under the fixed effect model post-merger. The financial performance of the companies has demonstrated improvement subsequent to the merger.

The coefficient of the ROC is 0.494 in both the random effect and fixed effect models prior to the merger. During the year of the merger, the values are 0.642 and 0.602 under the random effect and fixed effect model respectively. However, after the merger, the coefficient has increased to 0.773 and 0.840 in the random effect and fixed effect models, respectively. In the case of an overall merger, the coefficient of ROC is 0.574 under both models. This indicates a stronger influence of the ROC post-merger as compared to both pre-, during, and overall merger. The coefficient values of Return on Assets (ROA) and Return on Capital (ROC) exhibit a statistically significant impact at a significance level of 1% both before, during, after, and overall merger. Further, in table 4.3.22 the impact of return on capital employed and financial leverage on financial performance considering the overall merger.

Table 4.3.22 presents the regression outcomes, encompassing both random effect and fixed effect models in the overall merger. The coefficients corresponding to values (1) and (3) represent the random effect variables, whereas the coefficients corresponding to values (2) and (4) represent the fixed effect variables. The coefficient values for the Return on Capital Employed (ROCE) variable are 0.451 and 0.538 when estimated using the random effects and fixed effects models, respectively after the merger. Prior

Table 4.3.22 - Impact of Returns and Liquidity on Financial Performance considering Overall Merger

	Dependent variable:			
	ni			
	(1)	(2)	(3)	(4)
roce	0.324***	0.335***		
	(0.039)	(0.042)		
fl			−0.174***	−0.174***
			(0.037)	(0.039)
Constant	−0.0003		−0.000	
	(0.037)		(0.035)	
Observations	590	590	710	710
R^2	0.105	0.108	0.030	0.030
Adjusted R^2	0.103	0.009	0.029	−0.078
F Statistic	68.853***	64.377*** (df = 1; 530)	22.090***	19.906*** (df = 1; 638)
Note:				*p<0.1; **p<0.05; ***p<0.01

Source: *Compiled by Author from R output sheet*

to the merger, the coefficient of Return on Capital Employed (ROCE) was observed to be 0.207 under the random effects model and 0.219 under the fixed effects model. During the year, the coefficient of ROCE is 0.487 and 0.330 under random and fixed effect models respectively. In the case of an overall merger, the values are 0.324 and 0.335 under the random and fixed effect model respectively. This suggests that the rise in the proportion of Return on Capital Employed (ROCE) subsequent to the merger has enhanced the financial performance of the companies as compared to pre-merger and overall mergers. If we compare the post-merger from the year of merger then the coefficient of ROCE under random effect in the year of merger is higher.

However, it should be noted that financial leverage exhibits a negative trend both prior to and subsequent to the merger. In the event of a pre-merger scenario, the coefficient of FL was observed to be 0.127 under the random effect and 0.115 under the fixed effect model. During the year, it is 0.171 and 0.363 under random and fixed effect models respectively. Subsequent to the merger, this coefficient is 0.194 and 0.242 under the random and fixed models, respectively. In the case of the overall merger, the coefficient is 0.174 under both models. The financial performance of companies is adversely impacted by financial leverage, as observed in both the random effect and fixed effect models before, during, after, and in the overall merger. However, subsequent to the merger, there has been an increase in this percentage, consequently leading to a detrimental impact of financial leverage on the financial performance of the companies under the random effect model. The coefficient values of Return on Capital Employed (ROCE) exhibit a statistically significant impact at a significance level of 1% in the pre-, during, and post-merger periods. Nevertheless, the variable FL demonstrates a substantial influence at a significance level of 1% in both pre-merger models. However, in the post-merger scenario, FL exhibits a significant impact at a significance level of 1% in the random effect model and at a significance level of 5% in the fixed effect model. However, during the year of the merger FL had a significant impact at a 10% level under the random effect model and 1% under the fixed effect model. Both the variables have a significant impact at 1% under both the models in the overall merger. Further, in the next table, the impact of leverages on financial performance considering the overall merger is explored.

Table 4.3.23 - Impact of Leverages on Financial Performance considering Overall Merger

	Dependent variable:			
	ni			
	(1)	(2)	(3)	(4)
dfl	−0.096**	−0.096**		
	(0.040)	(0.043)		
dol			0.100**	0.104**
			(0.040)	(0.043)
Constant	−0.000		0.003	
	(0.038)		(0.038)	
Observations	610	610	620	620
R^2	0.009	0.009	0.010	0.010
Adjusted R^2	0.008	−0.101	0.008	−0.100
F Statistic	5.666**	5.107** (df = 1; 548)	6.285**	5.850** (df = 1; 557)
Note:				*p<0.1; **p<0.05; ***p<0.01

Source: *Compiled by Author from R output sheet*

The regression results of overall merger are presented in Table 4.3.23, encompassing both random effect and fixed effect models. The coefficients corresponding to values (1) and (3) represent random effect variables, whereas the coefficients corresponding to values (2) and (4) represent fixed effect variables. The coefficient for the Degree of Financial Leverage (DFL) is 0.113 under the random effects model and 0.135 under the fixed effects model prior to the merger. During the merger, these values are 0.140 and 0.012 under random and fixed effect models respectively. However, following the merger, the value has changed to 0.047 under the random effect model and 0.106 under the fixed effect model. In the case of an overall merger, the coefficient of DFL is 0.096 under both models. This suggests that the decrease in the negative coefficient of DFL has mitigated the adverse impact of this variable on the financial performance of the companies following the merger in the case of the random effect model. However, the value under fixed effect has increased from the year of the merger.

During the pre-merger period, the coefficient of DOL was observed to be 0.064 under the random effects model and 0.054 under the fixed effects model. During the year, this has increased to 0.141 and 0.067 under the random effect and fixed effect model respectively. Subsequently, the coefficient is 0.113 under the random effects model. However, under the fixed effect model, the coefficient remains the same as in the pre-merger case. In the case of the overall merger, the coefficient of DOL is 0.100 and 0.104 under the random and fixed effect model respectively. The rise in the proportion of degree of operating leverage (DOL) due to random effects has resulted in enhanced financial performance among companies as compared to pre-merger. However, the coefficient is highest under both models during the merger. In general, DOL and DFL have yielded enhancements in the financial performance of the companies subsequent to the merger.

The coefficient values of DFL exhibit a statistically significant impact at the 5% and 1% significance levels in the random and fixed models, respectively. The DOL had a negligible influence in both models before the merger. Following the merger, it can be observed that both DFL and DOL have minimal or negligible effects under both models. During the merger, the DFL and DOL had a significant impact at a 10% level under the random effect model and an insignificant impact under the fixed effect model. Both the variables have a significant impact under both the models at the 5% level. In the next table, the impact of cash flow on financial performance considering overall merger is analyzed.

Table 4.3.24 - Impact of Cash Flow on Financial Performance considering Overall Merger

	Dependent variable:	
	ni	
	(1)	(2)
cfni	0.920***	0.920***
	(0.015)	(0.015)
Constant	0.000	
	(0.014)	
Observations	730	730
R^2	0.847	0.847
Adjusted R^2	0.846	0.830
F Statistic	4,017.299***	3,619.984*** (df = 1; 656)
Note:		*p<0.1; **p<0.05; ***p<0.01

Source: *Compiled by Author from R output sheet*

Table 4.3.24 presents the regression outcomes for both random effect and fixed effect models in the overall merger. The values denoted by (1) correspond to coefficients of random effect variables, whereas the values denoted by (2) correspond to coefficients of fixed effect variables. The coefficient of cash flow from net income (CFNI) is observed to be 0.870 under the random effect model and 0.898 under the fixed effect model following the merger. Prior to the merger, these coefficients were recorded as 0.988 under the random effect model and 1.055 under the fixed effect model. During the year of the merger, these values were 0.989 and 1.005 under random effect and fixed effect respectively. In the case of an overall merger, the coefficient is 0.920 under both models. This suggests that the CFNI has decreased following the merger in both models, indicating a decline in financial performance after the merger. The coefficient values of CFNI exhibit a statistically significant impact at a 1% level in the pre, during, post, and overall merger under both models. In the next table, the regression results of financial performance considering the overall merger are reported on the basis of the Hausman test.

Table 4.3.25 displays the regression results of all the variables impacting the financial performance of the companies in the overall merger. In these tables, either a random or fixed effect model is taken on the basis of the result obtained after applying the Hausman test. Specifically, if the p-value is less than 0.05, fixed effects are employed,

Table 4.3.25 -Regression Results of Financial Performance considering Overall Merger

	Dependent variable:			
	ni			
	(1)	(2)	(3)	(4)
ebitda	0.611***			
	(0.030)			
ebit		0.717***		
		(0.026)		
roa			0.618***	
			(0.029)	
roc				0.574***
				(0.031)
Constant	−0.000	−0.000	−0.000	−0.000
	(0.028)	(0.025)	(0.028)	(0.029)
Observations	700	700	720	710
R^2	0.373	0.515	0.382	0.330
Adjusted R^2	0.372	0.514	0.381	0.329
F Statistic	415.520***	740.036***	443.687***	348.740***
Note:		*p<0.1; **p<0.05; ***p<0.01		

Source: *Compiled by Author from R output sheet*

Table 4.3.25 -Regression Results of Financial Performance considering Overall Merger (Contd)

	Dependent variable:				
	ni				
	(5)	(6)	(7)	(8)	(9)
roce	0.324***				
	(0.039)				
fl		−0.174***			
		(0.037)			
dfl			−0.096**		
			(0.040)		
dol				0.100**	
				(0.040)	
cfni					0.920***
					(0.015)
Constant	−0.0003	−0.000	−0.000	0.003	0.000
	(0.037)	(0.035)	(0.038)	(0.038)	(0.014)
Observations	590	710	610	620	730
R^2	0.105	0.030	0.009	0.010	0.847
Adjusted R^2	0.103	0.029	0.008	0.008	0.846
F Statistic	68.853***	22.090***	5.666**	6.285**	4,017.299***
Note:			*p<0.1; **p<0.05; ***p<0.01		

Source: *Compiled by Author from R output sheet*

whereas if the p-value is greater than 0.05, random effects are used. The coefficient of all the variables is more than 0.05, thereby coefficients of these variables under random effect are taken in the year of merger. However, the coefficient of EBIT and CFNI are the only variables which are less than 0.05, hence, the coefficient under the fixed effect model is taken and the coefficient of all other variables except EBIT and CFNI under the random effect model are taken before the merger. The coefficients of ROA and ROC are the only variables which are less than 0.05, thereby coefficients of these variables under fixed effect are taken and coefficients of all other variables except these two are under random effect after the merger. In the case of overall except ROCE and DOL, all other variables have a p-value less than 0.05, hence its fixed effect coefficients are taken.

Except for DFL and DOL, all the coefficient values were statistically significant at a 1% level before the merger. The coefficient of DFL is statistically significant at 5% but the coefficient of DOL has an insignificant value before the merger. However, during the year of the merger EBITDA, EBIT, ROA, ROC, ROCE, and CFNI had a significant impact at the 1% level and FL, DFL, and DOL at the 10% level. Except for DOL and DFL, all the variables are statistically significant at a 1% level after the merger as well as in the overall merger. DOL and DFL are significant at a 5% level in the overall merger. In the next table, the correlation of all the variables impacting the financial performance is presented in the case of a merger.

Table 4.3.26 -Correlation Matrix of Financial Performance - Merger

	ni	ebitda	ebit	roa	roc	roce	fl	dfl	dol	cfni
ni	1									
ebitda	0.622	1								
ebit	0.709	0.883	1							
roa	0.610	0.279	0.339	1						
roc	0.569	0.269	0.326	0.945	1					
roce	0.320	0.150	0.165	0.561	0.580	1				
fl	-0.164	-0.044	-0.070	-0.167	-0.043	0.016	1			
dfl	-0.097	-0.095	-0.086	-0.168	-0.092	-0.098	0.199	1		
dol	0.073	0.166	0.187	0.141	0.168	0.125	0.014	0.001	1	
cfni	0.922	0.684	0.663	0.645	0.602	0.341	-0.168	-0.104	0.077	1

Source: *Compiled by Author from R output sheet*

The correlation between the variables in the case of a merger is displayed in Table 4.3.26. Positive coefficients exist between EBITDA and net income, EBIT, ROA, ROC, ROCE, DOL, and CFNI. The negative correlation between FL and EBITDA as well as DFL and EBITDA indicates that these variables are inversely correlated. FL is negatively correlated to the coefficient of all the variables except ROCE, DFL, and DOL. Similarly, DFL is also negatively correlated to the coefficient of all the variables FL and DOL. In table 4.3.28 the descriptive statistics of financial performance in case of an acquisition are presented.

Table 4.3.27 displays the pre-merger and post-merger net income of the firms. The net income of a firm refers to the total revenue or money earned by the company after

Table 4.3.27 -Comparison of Pre-and Post-Merger of Net Income

S.No.	Company Name	Pre-Mergers				Post-Mergers			
		2013	2014	2015	2016	2019	2020	2021	2022
1	Crystal Crop Protection Ltd	-0.7384	-0.7585	-0.7182	-0.4465	-1.0195	2.3235	0.0820	0.0820
2	Sterlite Power Transmission Ltd	-0.3446	-0.7151	-0.3446	-1.0856	1.6036	1.4552	0.5683	0.1325
3	Olive Bar & Kitchen Pvt Ltd	0.6496	0.9612	0.9647	0.6759	-	-	-	-
4	Sembcorp Energy India Ltd	-0.8851	-0.8482	-0.8851	-0.8113	2.3706	0.2167	0.2167	0.2167
5	Hero Future Energies Pvt Ltd	0.7404	0.7410	0.7412	0.7537	-1.5780	-1.6375	0.0000	0.0000
6	Reliance Industrial Investments & Holdings Ltd	-0.4911	-0.5671	-0.7999	-0.5444	0.5655	2.6214	-	-
7	ECap Equities Ltd	0.2342	0.9235	0.9612	1.4498	-0.6313	0.0000	0.0000	0.0000
8	Ashok Leyland Ltd	-0.9375	-0.5963	0.0311	1.0700	-0.3642	-0.9388	-1.1602	-0.0000
9	AMJ Land Holdings Ltd	1.0126	2.2669	-0.3179	-0.3822	0.1791	-0.8466	-0.0044	-
10	Anup Engineering Limited/The	0.2451	0.2451	0.2451	-1.0173	-0.8698	0.7514	2.1162	0.2451
11	Arvind Ltd	0.9472	0.8390	0.6115	0.6152	-1.2363	-2.1847	-0.0314	-0.0000
12	Astral Ltd	-0.9768	-0.9990	-0.8150	-0.4939	0.2641	1.4133	1.9963	-
13	Adani Total Gas Ltd	-1.2874	-1.5349	-1.0399	0.8022	0.1430	0.1430	0.1430	0.1430
14	Bharti Airtel Ltd	0.4484	0.6485	0.7227	0.5337	-2.4529	-1.0336	0.5715	-
15	Balaji Amines Ltd	-0.9142	-0.9068	-0.6803	-0.4402	-0.2224	1.0721	2.3358	-0.0000
16	Bank of Baroda	0.9336	0.6267	-1.9045	0.0356	-0.2145	-0.0397	1.7367	-
17	Borosil Renewables Ltd	-0.6407	-0.4267	-0.3181	1.2328	-1.4594	0.4209	2.0274	0.0000
18	Berger Paints India Ltd	-1.3399	-1.2589	-0.7028	-0.1530	0.8217	1.1495	1.7479	-
19	Birlasoft Ltd	-0.5038	-0.6754	-0.0452	-0.6537	-0.8568	0.5278	2.5771	-0.0000
20	Chordia Food Products Ltd	1.6138	0.2248	-0.3964	0.3316	-2.4221	-	-	-
21	Chalet Hotels Ltd	-0.6350	-0.8219	-0.6741	1.8767	1.5810	-0.9568	-0.3450	0.0000
22	CL Educate Ltd	-0.1386	0.6710	0.4378	0.6710	-2.5168	-0.6376	0.5835	-0.1386
23	DiGiSPICE Technologies Ltd	1.0040	-0.2150	-1.6793	-0.4883	-1.2147	1.0089	1.0492	-
24	Dr Lal PathLabs Ltd	-1.3045	-1.1265	-0.6773	-0.4067	0.4551	1.2485	1.8913	-
25	Elpro International Ltd	-0.4214	-0.4153	-0.4197	-0.3905	-0.3658	-0.3482	2.8163	-
26	Foods & Inns Ltd	-0.3804	-0.1612	-0.5256	-0.5857	-0.2040	-0.4225	-0.0757	-
27	Future Market Networks Ltd	-1.2144	-1.2468	2.2043	-0.2754	0.8002	-0.3508	-0.3007	-
28	Godrej Industries Ltd	-0.4872	0.0048	-1.5578	-0.9392	0.9832	-0.4338	1.6292	-
29	Godrej Agrovet Ltd	-1.4899	-0.4108	-0.6791	-1.0270	0.4731	2.0499	-	-
30	GTL Infrastructure Ltd	1.0632	1.1292	1.0703	0.9705	-1.3079	-0.2368	-0.6053	-
31	Havells India Ltd	-1.0798	-1.2748	1.6535	-0.9255	-0.1545	0.8346	1.3217	-
32	HealthCare Global Enterprises Ltd	-0.0853	0.4198	0.3880	0.7161	-1.0728	-2.2772	1.1541	-
33	Hexaware Technologies Ltd	-0.9733	-1.4059	-0.8700	-0.6796	0.9502	0.8046	1.7386	0.0000
34	Indiabulls Real Estate Ltd	-0.3178	-0.2834	-0.2153	-0.0722	-0.4641	-0.6293	-0.8294	-0.0000
35	IDFC First Bank Ltd	0.3298	0.1402	0.5194	0.9651	-2.1541	0.5326	0.2492	-0.0366
36	IndusInd Bank Ltd	-1.5326	-1.1727	-0.7130	-0.1704	1.3131	-0.1126	1.6367	-
37	Indo Amines Ltd	-1.1179	-1.1695	-0.7794	-0.0580	-0.4020	2.1125	0.6362	0.0000
38	Indus Towers Ltd	-1.0923	-0.7411	-0.5524	-0.1826	0.2258	0.5813	2.5013	-

S.No.	Company Name	Pre-Mergers				Post-Mergers			
		2013	2014	2015	2016	2019	2020	2021	2022
39	Infibeam Avenues Ltd	-1.5979	-1.2872	-0.9050	-0.2235	1.0298	0.3302	0.6085	-0.0000
40	Inox Leisure Ltd	0.3511	0.2402	0.6174	0.3096	0.2071	-2.1084	-1.4635	-0.0000
41	JM Financial Ltd	-1.8354	-1.0686	-0.6253	-0.1833	0.2907	0.5769	1.7370	-
42	JSW Steel Ltd	-0.9027	-0.6137	-1.0354	-0.3850	-0.2996	0.3546	2.5045	-0.0000
43	LTIMindtree Ltd	-0.7814	-1.0984	-0.9647	-0.6970	0.3974	1.2261	1.9446	0.0000
44	Morganite Crucible India Ltd	-0.4523	-0.6846	-0.3188	0.0737	2.5723	-	-	-
45	Minda Corp Ltd	-0.0216	0.0728	0.2373	0.1894	-2.6092	-0.2676	1.0218	-
46	Modern India Ltd	1.3000	0.3583	0.7920	0.3263	-2.5235	-	-	-
47	Mukand Ltd	-0.4097	-0.0913	-0.1534	-0.1662	-0.9270	-0.8068	0.4623	0.0000
48	Narayana Hrudayalaya Ltd	-0.4195	-0.8902	-0.5417	0.0791	0.4273	-0.8663	2.5929	-
49	Nath Industries Ltd	-0.6940	-0.6937	-0.7441	-0.8505	1.6263	1.1851	1.3941	-
50	NK Industries Ltd	-0.7228	-2.0214	0.5757	0.5110	0.3284	0.8408	0.9349	0.0803
51	National Fittings Ltd	-0.4095	0.2929	0.9141	1.8196	-1.0743	-0.9737	-1.0718	0.0000
52	Optiemus Infracom Ltd	0.8363	0.4150	0.1266	0.0035	-1.8157	1.7482	-0.1487	-
53	Piramal Enterprises Ltd	-1.3527	0.8076	-0.4463	-0.2222	-1.0140	-0.1706	0.2102	-
54	Poonawalla Fincorp Ltd	0.1794	0.2908	0.4094	-0.3280	-0.3025	-2.5660	1.0418	0.0000
55	Reliance Industries Ltd	-1.2250	-1.1326	-0.6009	-0.5875	0.2259	1.0670	2.0632	-0.0000
56	RPSG Ventures Ltd	-0.1709	-0.1709	-0.1709	1.3510	-1.3190	-1.6299	0.9144	-0.1709
57	Sastasundar Ventures Ltd	-0.2806	-0.3172	-0.4115	-0.3768	-0.4210	-0.2977	2.8246	0.0000
58	S Chand & Co Ltd	0.2942	0.6135	0.8494	1.5886	-0.2319	0.0416	-	-
59	Schaeffler India Ltd	-1.2135	-1.0100	-0.7178	-0.7337	0.3971	-0.1052	2.1105	-
60	Sundram Fasteners Ltd	-1.3739	-1.2936	-1.3334	0.2871	0.1904	0.4532	1.2006	-
61	Solara Active Pharma Sciences Ltd	0.0328	0.0328	0.0328	-0.3351	0.4805	2.0587	-2.0728	0.0328
62	Somany Ceramics Ltd	-1.1171	-0.4357	0.2764	1.6838	-1.6566	-0.0220	1.2097	-0.0000
63	Strides Pharma Science Ltd	2.2602	0.6925	-0.5830	-0.0647	-0.6827	-0.2881	-1.5273	0.0000
64	Sundaram Finance Ltd	-0.9866	-1.0073	-0.9781	-0.5760	-0.1427	1.3548	1.3879	-
65	Thomas Cook India Ltd	-0.3389	-0.4134	-0.3489	2.8011	-0.5071	-0.4938	-0.0000	-0.0000
66	Tech Mahindra Ltd	-0.7770	-1.2203	-0.8167	-1.0156	0.3328	0.7694	2.0272	-0.0000
67	Investment Trust of India Ltd/The	-0.7549	-0.6449	-0.4762	0.4377	-0.9445	-0.0967	-0.6410	0.0000
68	Timken India Ltd	-1.1324	-0.7108	-0.5803	-0.5171	1.2298	0.0223	2.1802	0.0000
69	TV18 Broadcast Ltd	-0.5245	-0.8387	-0.0421	-0.9741	0.2131	1.3464	2.0320	-
70	TV Today Network Ltd	-1.3744	-0.8426	-1.3194	-0.2711	0.7312	0.5191	1.8686	-0.0000
71	Uniply Industries Ltd	-0.6031	-0.4251	-0.2435	0.2636	-1.9626	-0.0000	-0.0000	-0.0000
72	ATC Telecom Infrastructure Pvt Ltd	1.5855	-0.1762	1.5855	-1.9378	-0.1762	-0.1762	-0.1762	-0.1762
73	Wipro Ltd	-1.1124	-0.4739	-0.2839	-0.5957	0.3235	1.1236	2.1861	-0.0000

Source: *Compiled by Author*

deducting all costs and taxes. This data illustrates the financial performance of the organisation. The table provided above outlines the time span from 2013 to 2016 as the pre-merger period, whereas the years 2019 to 2022 are designated as the post-merger period. The net income of the firms has shown improvement in the subsequent year, shown by Astral Ltd.'s transition to positive net income after the merger. Nevertheless, several corporations, such as Ashok Leyland Ltd., have seen a shift in their net income towards negative figures subsequent to a merger. Therefore, it may be inferred that the merger has had varying effects on the financial performance of different companies, with some seeing improvements and others experiencing declines.

Table 4.3.28 depicts the descriptive statistics of the dependent as well as independent variables used in this study in the case of pre-acquisition and post-acquisition. The mean of EBITDA, EBIT, and DFL is negative 0.288625, 0.194172, and 0.005015

Table 4.3.28 -Descriptive Statistics of Financial Performance – Acquisition

Statistic	N	Mean	St. Dev.	Min	Max
PR_NI	1540	-0.135119	0.872673	-2.684895	2.801681
PR_EBITDA	1540	-0.288625	0.87964	-2.751074	2.84605
PR_EBIT	1540	-0.194172	0.88379	-2.468259	2.77746
PR_ROA	1540	0.122815	0.924039	-2.761458	2.836015
PR_ROC	1540	0.140209	0.923916	-2.835009	2.82668
PR_ROCE	1540	0.051398	0.956122	-2.49317	2.845819
PR_FL	1540	0.018484	1.006115	-2.409294	2.842805
PR_DFL	1540	-0.005015	1.006978	-2.84605	2.84605
PR_DOL	1540	0.085989	0.92662	-2.84605	2.845915
PR_CFNI	1540	-0.150317	0.870845	-2.590138	2.818806
PO_NI	1540	0.080245	1.004009	-2.797541	2.810242
PO_EBITDA	1540	0.249192	0.971892	-2.427486	2.578156
PO_EBIT	1540	0.128186	0.980825	-2.703278	2.778493
PO_ROA	1540	-0.138359	0.958189	-2.711292	2.619669
PO_ROC	1540	-0.173834	0.948785	-2.724847	2.516265
PO_ROCE	1540	-0.09253	0.932227	-2.553747	2.707247
PO_FL	1540	0.015265	0.924143	-2.488895	2.830734
PO_DFL	1540	0.023	0.91161	-2.84605	2.816261
PO_DOL	1540	-0.082146	0.962974	-2.84605	2.663735
PO_CFNI	1540	0.106685	1.017807	-2.704202	2.693021

respectively before the acquisition which has become positive 0.249192,0.128186, and 0.023 after acquisition. The mean of only these variables has increased post-acquisition, thereby indicating a positive impact on the financial performance post-acquisition. However, the mean of other variables was positive before the merger which became negative after the merger except for EBITDA, EBIT, FL, and DFL. Thereby indicating a negative impact on the financial performance of the companies after the acquisition. The standard deviation defines the risk, in this case, the standard deviation of ROCE, FL, and DFL is reduced after the acquisition, other than these all-other variables involving high risk after the acquisition. In the above few tables, the impact of earnings, returns, and leverages on financial performance is evaluated in the case of a merger. Now the same will be analysed in the case of acquisition.

Table 4.3.29 displays both random effect and fixed effect regression results before acquisition. The values under (1) and (3) represent random effect variable coefficients, while (2) and (4) represent fixed effect variable coefficients. The coefficient of EBITDA is 0.590 under random effect and fixed effect before acquisition. As EBITDA is the same under both models, therefore the impact of this variable on the financial performance is the same before acquisition. However, EBIT impacts at a higher rate

Table 4.3.29 -Impact of Earnings on Financial Performance Before Acquisition

	Dependent variable:			
	ni			
	(1)	(2)	(3)	(4)
ebitda	0.590***	0.590***		
	(0.022)	(0.027)		
ebit			0.615***	0.581***
			(0.020)	(0.025)
Constant	0.039*		−0.019	
	(0.023)		(0.021)	
Observations	1,488	1,488	1,496	1,496
R^2	0.335	0.295	0.379	0.322
Adjusted R^2	0.335	0.060	0.379	0.096
F Statistic	749.869***	466.204*** (df = 1; 1115)	913.697***	532.727*** (df = 1; 1121)
Note:				*p<0.1; **p<0.05; ***p<0.01

Source: *Compiled by Author from R output sheet*

under random effect as compared to fixed effect in pre-acquisition as the coefficient of EBIT is 0.615 under random effect and 0.581 under fixed effect. The coefficient values of EBIT and EBITDA have a significant impact at the 1% level. Further, in table 4.3.30, the impact of returns on the financial performance before acquisition is examined.

Table 4.3.30 - Impact of Returns on Financial Performance Before Acquisition

	Dependent variable:			
	ni			
	(1)	(2)	(3)	(4)
roa	0.645***	0.671***		
	(0.018)	(0.020)		
roc			0.549***	0.567***
			(0.020)	(0.023)
Constant	−0.216***		−0.216***	
	(0.023)		(0.025)	
Observations	1,512	1,512	1,480	1,480
R^2	0.465	0.498	0.339	0.363
Adjusted R^2	0.464	0.330	0.339	0.150
F Statistic	1,310.888***	1,123.164*** (df = 1; 1133)	758.298***	631.108*** (df = 1; 1109)
Note:				*p<0.1; **p<0.05; ***p<0.01

Source: *Compiled by Author from R output sheet*

Table 4.3.30 displays both random effect and fixed effect regression results before acquisition. The values under (1) and (3) represent random effect variable coefficients, while (2) and (4) represent fixed effect variable coefficients. The coefficient of ROA is 0.645 under random effect and 0.671 under fixed effect before acquisition. This indicates that the change in ROA under fixed effect impacts the financial performance at a greater rate. Similarly, ROC also impacts at a higher rate under the fixed effect model as the coefficient of ROC is 0.549 under random effect and 0.567 under fixed effect. The coefficient values of ROA and ROC have a significant impact at the 1% level. In the next table, the impact of return on capital employed and financial leverage on financial performance is discussed before acquisition.

Table 4.3.31 displays both random effect and fixed effect regression results before acquisition. The values under (1) and (3) represent random effect variable coefficients, while (2) and (4) represent fixed effect variable coefficients. The coefficient of ROCE

Table 4.3.31 - Impact of Returns and Liquidity on Financial Performance Before Acquisition

	Dependent variable:			
	ni			
	(1)	(2)	(3)	(4)
roce	0.345***	0.366***		
	(0.025)	(0.030)		
fl			−0.173***	−0.164***
			(0.023)	(0.029)
Constant	−0.217***		−0.128***	
	(0.031)		(0.028)	
Observations	1,148	1,148	1,496	1,496
R^2	0.140	0.150	0.036	0.027
Adjusted R^2	0.139	−0.134	0.036	−0.297
F Statistic	186.927***	151.173*** (df = 1; 860)	56.583***	31.679*** (df = 1; 1121)
Note:				*p<0.1; **p<0.05; ***p<0.01

Source: *Compiled by Author from R output sheet*

is 0.345 under random effect and 0.366 under fixed effect before acquisition. This indicates that the change in ROCE under fixed effect will impact the financial performance at a greater rate. However, Financial leverage (FL) impacts at a higher rate under random effect in pre-acquisition as the coefficient of FL is 0.173 under random effect as well as 0.164 fixed effect. Financial leverage affects the financial performance of the companies negatively under both the random effect and fixed effect models. The coefficient values of ROCE and FL have a significant impact at the 1% level. Further, in table 4.3.32 the impact of leverage ratios on financial performance before acquisition is analyzed.

Table 4.3.32 displays both random effect and fixed effect regression results before acquisition. The values under (1) and (3) represent random effect variable coefficients, while (2) and (4) represent fixed effect variable coefficients. The coefficient of Degree of Financial leverage (DFL) is 0.121 under random effect and 0.124 under fixed effect before acquisition. This indicates that the change in DFL under fixed effect will impact the financial performance at a greater rate negatively. Similarly, the degree of operating leverage (DOL) also impacts at a higher rate under fixed effect in pre-acquisition as the coefficient of DOL is 0.137 under random effect as well as 0.157 under fixed effect. The degree of operating leverage affects the financial performance of the companies

Table 4.3.32 - Impact of Leverages on Financial Performance Before Acquisition

	Dependent variable:			
	ni			
	(1)	(2)	(3)	(4)
dfl	−0.121***	−0.124***		
	(0.024)	(0.027)		
dol			0.137***	0.157***
			(0.026)	(0.030)
Constant	−0.169***		−0.168***	
	(0.032)		(0.033)	
Observations	1,220	1,220	1,228	1,228
R^2	0.020	0.022	0.021	0.029
Adjusted R^2	0.019	−0.304	0.021	−0.295
F Statistic	25.014***	20.723*** (df = 1; 914)	26.771***	27.462*** (df = 1; 920)
Note:				*p<0.1; **p<0.05; ***p<0.01

Source: *Compiled by Author from R output sheet*

positively under both random effect and fixed effect models. The coefficient values of DFL and DOL have a significant impact at a 1% level under random and fixed models.

Further, in table 4.3.33 the impact of cash flow on financial performance before acquisition is examined.

Table 4.3.33 - Impact of Cash Flow on Financial Performance Before Acquisition

	Dependent variable:	
	ni	
	(1)	(2)
cfni	0.984***	1.033***
	(0.007)	(0.008)
Constant	0.015**	
	(0.007)	
Observations	1,528	1,528
R^2	0.935	0.934
Adjusted R^2	0.935	0.912
F Statistic	21,896.040***	16,229.510*** (df = 1; 1145)
Note:		*p<0.1; **p<0.05; ***p<0.01

Source: *Compiled by Author from R output sheet*

Table 4.3.33 displays both random effect and fixed effect regression results before acquisition. The values under (1) represent random effect variable coefficients, while (2) represent fixed effect variable coefficients. The coefficient of cash flow from net income (CFNI) is 0.984 under random effect and 1.033 under fixed effect before acquisition. This indicates that the change in CFNI under fixed effect will impact the financial performance at a greater rate. The coefficient values of CFNI have a significant impact at a 1% level under both models. Further, in table 4.3.34 the regression results of financial performance before acquisition are reported on the basis of the Hausman test.

Table 4.3.34 displays the regression results of all the variables impacting the financial performance of the companies. In these tables, either a random or fixed effect model is taken on the basis of the result obtained after applying the Hausman test. Specifically, if the p-value is less than 0.05, fixed effects are employed, whereas if the p-value is greater than 0.05, random effects are used. The coefficients of EBIT, ROA, and CFNI are the only variables that are less than 0.05, hence, the coefficient under the fixed effect model is taken. However, the coefficients of all other variables except EBIT, ROA, and CFNI under the random effect model are taken. Coefficient values of all the variables are statistically significant at a 1% level. Further, in table 4.3.35 the impact of earnings

Table 4.3.34 -Regression Results of Financial Performance Before Acquisition

	Dependent variable:			
	ni			
	(1)	(2)	(3)	(4)
ebitda	0.590***			
	(0.022)			
ebit		0.581***		
		(0.025)		
roa			0.671***	
			(0.020)	
roe				0.549***
				(0.020)
Constant	0.039*			−0.216***
	(0.023)			(0.025)
Observations	1,488	1,496	1,512	1,480
R^2	0.335	0.322	0.498	0.339
Adjusted R^2	0.335	0.096	0.330	0.339
F Statistic	749.869***	532.727*** (df = 1; 1121)	1,123.164*** (df = 1; 1133)	758.298***
Note:				*p<0.1; **p<0.05; ***p<0.01

Source: *Compiled by Author from R output sheet*

Table 4.3.34 -Regression Results of Financial Performance Before Acquisition (Contd)

	Dependent variable:				
	ni				
	(5)	(6)	(7)	(8)	(9)
roce	0.345***				
	(0.025)				
fl		−0.173***			
		(0.023)			
dfl			−0.121***		
			(0.024)		
dol				0.137***	
				(0.026)	
cfni					1.033***
					(0.008)
Constant	−0.217***	−0.128***	−0.169***	−0.168***	
	(0.031)	(0.028)	(0.032)	(0.033)	
Observations	1,148	1,496	1,220	1,228	1,528
R^2	0.140	0.036	0.020	0.021	0.934
Adjusted R^2	0.139	0.036	0.019	0.021	0.912
F Statistic	186.927***	56.583***	25.014***	26.771***	16,229.510*** (df = 1; 1145)
Note:					*p<0.1; **p<0.05; ***p<0.01

Source: *Compiled by Author from R output sheet*

on financial performance after acquisition is explored.

Table 4.3.35 -Impact of Earnings on Financial Performance After Acquisition

	Dependent variable:			
	ni			
	(1)	(2)	(3)	(4)
ebitda	0.605***	0.643***		
	(0.022)	(0.030)		
ebit			0.747***	0.748***
			(0.018)	(0.022)
Constant	−0.075***		−0.017	
	(0.022)		(0.018)	
Observations	1,488	1,488	1,496	1,496
R^2	0.344	0.293	0.536	0.511
Adjusted R^2	0.344	0.057	0.535	0.347
F Statistic	780.847***	461.254*** (df = 1; 1115)	1,722.608***	1,169.931*** (df = 1; 1121)
Note:				*p<0.1; **p<0.05; ***p<0.01

Source: *Compiled by Author from R output sheet*

Table 4.3.35 presents the regression outcomes for both random effect and fixed effect models. The coefficients corresponding to values (1) and (3) pertain to random effect variables, whereas the coefficients corresponding to values (2) and (4) pertain to fixed effect variables. After the acquisition, the coefficient of EBITDA is observed to be 0.605 under the random effect model and 0.643 under the fixed effect model. The values observed were 0.590 under the random effect model and the fixed effect model prior to the acquisition. This finding suggests that there is a minute change in EBITDA, with under-random effects and fixed effects post-acquisition. Still, the post-acquisition EBITDA has had a greater impact on the financial performance. Likewise, it can be observed that Earnings Before Interest and Taxes (EBIT) exhibit a more pronounced effect following an acquisition in both models, suggesting an enhanced financial performance of the companies subsequent to the acquisition. The coefficient of EBIT is 0.615 under the random effects model and 0.581 under the fixed effects model prior to the acquisition. Following the acquisition, the coefficient of EBIT is 0.747 under the random effects model and 0.748 under the fixed effects model. The coefficient values associated with EBIT and EBITDA exhibit a statistically significant impact at a significance level of 1% in pre and post-acquisition. In the next table, the impact of returns on financial performance after acquisition is analyzed.

Table 4.3.36 - Impact of Returns on Financial Performance After Acquisition

	Dependent variable:			
	ni			
	(1)	(2)	(3)	(4)
roa	0.766***	0.854***		
	(0.019)	(0.023)		
roc			0.704***	0.788***
			(0.021)	(0.026)
Constant	0.189***		0.210***	
	(0.021)		(0.023)	
Observations	1.512	1,512	1,480	1.480
R^2	0.508	0.543	0.425	0.462
Adjusted R^2	0.508	0.391	0.424	0.282
F Statistic	1.561.166***	1,346.263*** (df = 1: 1133)	1,090.729***	951.526*** (df = 1; 1109)
Note:				*p<0.1; **p<0.05; ***p<0.01

Source: *Compiled by Author from R output sheet*

The regression results for both random effect and fixed effect models are presented in Table 4.3.36. The coefficients corresponding to values (1) and (3) pertain to random effect variables, whereas the coefficients corresponding to values (2) and (4) pertain to fixed effect variables. The coefficient of Return on Assets (ROA) is found to be 0.645 under the random effects model and 0.671 under the fixed effects model prior to the acquisition. Following the acquisition, the coefficient of ROA is estimated to be 0.766 under the random effects model and 0.854 under the fixed effects model. This suggests that the change in Return on Assets (ROA) will have a more pronounced effect on the financial performance of both models after the acquisition. The financial performance of the companies has demonstrated improvement subsequent to the acquisition. The coefficient of the ROC is 0.549 under the random effect and 0.567 under fixed effect models prior to the acquisition. However, after the acquisition, the coefficient increased to 0.704 and 0.788 in the random effect and fixed effect models, respectively. This indicates a stronger influence of the ROC post-acquisition. The coefficient values of Return on Assets (ROA) and Return on Capital (ROC) exhibit a statistically significant impact at a significance level of 1% both before and after the acquisition. The impact of return on capital employed and financial leverage on the financial performance of the companies after the acquisition is examined in table 4.3.37.

Table 4.3.37 presents the regression outcomes, encompassing both random effect and

Table 4.3.37 - Impact of Returns and Liquidity on Financial Performance After Acquisition

	Dependent variable:			
	ni			
	(1)	(2)	(3)	(4)
roce	0.466***	0.577***		
	(0.030)	(0.037)		
fl			−0.174***	−0.115***
			(0.028)	(0.043)
Constant	0.156***		0.085***	
	(0.031)		(0.027)	
Observations	1,148	1,148	1,496	1,496
R^2	0.177	0.225	0.025	0.006
Adjusted R^2	0.176	−0.034	0.024	−0.325
F Statistic	246.338***	249.155*** (df = 1; 860)	37.875***	7.163*** (df = 1; 1121)
Note:				*p<0.1; **p<0.05; ***p<0.01

Source: *Compiled by Author from R output sheet*

fixed effect models, subsequent to the acquisition. The coefficients corresponding to values (1) and (3) represent the random effect variables, whereas the coefficients corresponding to values (2) and (4) represent the fixed effect variables. The coefficient values for the Return on Capital Employed (ROCE) variable are 0.466 and 0.577 when estimated using the random effects and fixed effects models, respectively. Prior to the acquisition, the coefficient of Return on Capital Employed (ROCE) was observed to be 0.345 under the random effects model and 0.366 under the fixed effects model. This suggests that the rise in the proportion of Return on Capital Employed (ROCE) subsequent to the acquisition has enhanced the financial performance of the companies.

However, it should be noted that financial leverage exhibits a negative trend both prior to and subsequent to the acquisition. In the event of a pre-acquisition scenario, the coefficient of FL was observed to be 0.173 under the random effect and 0.164 under the fixed effect model. Subsequently, this coefficient increased to 0.194 and 0.242 under the random and fixed models, respectively. The financial performance of companies is being adversely impacted by financial leverage, as observed in both the random effect and fixed effect models before and after the acquisition. However, subsequent to the acquisition, there has been an increase in this percentage, consequently leading to an adverse impact of financial leverage on the financial performance of the companies under both models. The coefficient values of Return on Capital Employed (ROCE) exhibit a statistically significant impact at a significance level of 1% in both the pre and post-acquisition periods. Further, the impact of leverage ratios on financial performance after acquisition is analyzed in Table 4.3.38.

Table 4.3.38 -Impact of Leverages on Financial Performance After Acquisition

	Dependent variable:			
	ni			
	(1)	(2)	(3)	(4)
dfl	−0.184***	−0.214***		
	(0.032)	(0.040)		
dol			0.216***	0.281***
			(0.029)	(0.036)
Constant	0.103***		0.113***	
	(0.031)		(0.031)	
Observations	1,220	1,220	1,228	1,228
R^2	0.027	0.030	0.042	0.062
Adjusted R^2	0.026	−0.293	0.041	−0.252
F Statistic	34.144***	28.659*** (df = 1; 914)	53.821***	60.324*** (df = 1; 920)
Note:				*p<0.1; **p<0.05; ***p<0.01

Source: *Compiled by Author from R output sheet*

The regression results following the merger are presented in Table 4.3.38, encompassing both random effect and fixed effect models. The coefficients corresponding to values (1) and (3) represent random effect variables, whereas the coefficients corresponding to values (2) and (4) represent fixed effect variables. The coefficient for the Degree of Financial Leverage (DFL) is 0.121 under the random effects model and 0.124 under the fixed effects model prior to the acquisition. However, following the acquisition, the value has increased to 0.184 under the random effect model and 0.214 under the fixed effect model. This suggests that the increase in the negative coefficient of DFL has enhanced the adverse impact of this variable on the financial performance of the companies following the acquisition. During the pre-acquisition period, the coefficient of DOL was observed to be 0.137 under the random effects model and 0.157 under the fixed effects model. Subsequently, there was an increase in the coefficient to 0.216 under the random effect model and 0.281 under the fixed effect model. The rise in the proportion of degree of operating leverage (DOL) under both models has resulted in enhanced financial performance among companies.

In general, DOL has yielded enhancements in the financial performance of the companies subsequent to the acquisition.

The coefficient values of DFL and DOL exhibit a statistically significant impact at a 1% significance level in both the models pre and post-acquisition. In the next table, the impact of cash flow on financial performance after acquisition is examined.

Table 4.3.39 -Impact of Cash Flow on Financial Performance After Acquisition

	Dependent variable:	
	ni	
	(1)	(2)
cfni	0.856***	0.879***
	(0.013)	(0.018)
Constant	−0.010	
	(0.013)	
Observations	1,528	1,528
R^2	0.750	0.670
Adjusted R^2	0.750	0.560
F Statistic	4,588.607***	2,322.876*** (df = 1; 1145)
Note:		*p<0.1; **p<0.05; ***p<0.01

Source: *Compiled by Author from R output sheet*

Table 4.3.39 presents the regression outcomes for both random effect and fixed effect models subsequent to the acquisition. The values denoted by (1) correspond to coefficients of random effect variables, whereas the values denoted by (2) correspond to coefficients of fixed effect variables. The coefficient of cash flow from net income (CFNI) is observed to be 0.856 under the random effect model and 0.879 under the fixed effect model following the acquisition. Prior to the acquisition, these coefficients were recorded as 0.984 under the random effect model and 1.033 under the fixed effect model. This suggests that the CFNI has decreased following the acquisition in both models, indicating a decline in financial performance after the acquisition. The coefficient values of CFNI exhibit a statistically significant impact at a 1% level in both the pre-and post-acquisition models. The regression results of financial performance after acquisition are reported in Table 4.3.40 on the basis of the Hausman test.

Table 4.3.40 displays the regression results of all the variables impacting the financial

Table 4.3.40 -Regression Results of Financial Performance After Acquisition

	Dependent variable:			
	ni			
	(1)	(2)	(3)	(4)
ebitda	0.605***			
	(0.022)			
ebit		0.747***		
		(0.018)		
roa			0.854***	
			(0.023)	
roe				0.788***
				(0.026)
Constant	−0.075***	−0.017		
	(0.022)	(0.018)		
Observations	1,488	1,496	1,512	1,480
R^2	0.344	0.536	0.543	0.462
Adjusted R^2	0.344	0.535	0.391	0.282
F Statistic	780.847***	1,722.608***	1,346.263*** (df = 1; 1133)	951.526*** (df = 1; 1109)
Note:				*p<0.1; **p<0.05; ***p<0.01

Source: *Compiled by Author from R output sheet*

Table 4.3.40 -Regression Results of Financial Performance After Acquisition (Contd)

	Dependent variable:				
	ni				
	(5)	(6)	(7)	(8)	(9)
roce	0.577***				
	(0.037)				
fl		−0.174***			
		(0.028)			
dfl			−0.184***		
			(0.032)		
dol				0.281***	
				(0.036)	
cfni					0.856***
					(0.013)
Constant		0.085***	0.103***		−0.010
		(0.027)	(0.031)		(0.013)
Observations	1,148	1,496	1,220	1,228	1,528
R^2	0.225	0.025	0.027	0.062	0.750
Adjusted R^2	−0.034	0.024	0.026	−0.252	0.750
F Statistic	249.155*** (df = 1; 860)	37.875***	34.144***	60.324*** (df = 1; 920)	4,588.607***
Note:					*p<0.1; **p<0.05; ***p<0.01

Source: *Compiled by Author from R output sheet*

performance of the companies after acquisition. In these tables, either a random or fixed effect model is taken on the basis of the result obtained after applying the Hausman test.

Specifically, if the p-value is less than 0.05, fixed effects are employed, whereas if the p-value is greater than 0.05, random effects are used. The coefficients of ROA, ROC, ROCE, and DOL are the only variables that are less than 0.05, thereby coefficients of these variables under fixed effect are taken and coefficients of all other variables except these four are under random effect after acquisition. However, the coefficient of EBIT, ROA, and CFNI are the only variables that are less than 0.05, hence, the coefficient under the fixed effect model is taken and the coefficient of all other variables except EBIT and CFNI under the random effect model are taken before acquisition. All the variables are statistically significant at 1% level pre- and post-acquisition. In the above few tables, the impact of earnings, returns, and leverages is analyzed in pre- and post-acquisition. Further, in the next table, the impact of earnings on financial performance during acquisition is examined.

Table 4.3.41 -Impact of Earnings on Financial Performance During Acquisition

	Dependent variable:			
	ni			
	(1)	(2)	(3)	(4)
ebitda	0.657***	0.696***		
	(0.032)	(0.046)		
ebit			0.690***	0.655***
			(0.027)	(0.038)
Constant	0.069**		0.019	
	(0.030)		(0.026)	
Observations	744	744	748	748
R^2	0.366	0.381	0.474	0.437
Adjusted R^2	0.365	−0.240	0.473	−0.127
F Statistic	427.900***	228.424*** (df = 1; 371)	672.034***	289.566*** (df = 1; 373)
Note:				*p<0.1; **p<0.05; ***p<0.01

Source: *Compiled by Author from R output sheet*

Table 4.3.41 presents the regression outcomes for both random effect and fixed effect models. The coefficients corresponding to values (1) and (3) pertain to random effect variables, whereas the coefficients corresponding to values (2) and (4) pertain to fixed effect variables. After the acquisition, the coefficient of EBITDA is observed to be 0.605 under the random effect model and 0.643 under the fixed effect model. The values observed were 0.590 under the random effect model and the fixed effect model prior to the acquisition. During the year the coefficient of EBITDA is 0.657 and 0.696 under random and fixed effect models respectively. This finding suggests that there is a minute change in EBITDA, with under-random effects and fixed effects post-acquisition. Still, the post-acquisition EBITDA has had a greater impact on the financial performance if compared to pre-merger. However, the coefficient has decreased minutely under both the models as compared to the year of acquisition.

Likewise, it can be observed that Earnings Before Interest and Taxes (EBIT) exhibit a more pronounced effect following an acquisition in both models, suggesting an enhanced financial performance of the companies subsequent to the acquisition. The coefficient of EBIT is 0.615 under the random effects model and 0.581 under the fixed effects model prior to the acquisition. During the year the coefficient of EBIT is 0.690 and 0.655 in the year of acquisition. Following the acquisition, the coefficient of EBIT is 0.747 under the random effects model and 0.748 under the fixed effects model. The coefficient values associated with EBIT and EBITDA exhibit a statistically significant impact at a significance level of 1% in pre-, during, and post-acquisition. In the next table, the impact of returns on financial performance during acquisition is explored.

The regression results for both random effect and fixed effect models are presented in Table 4.3.42. The coefficients corresponding to values (1) and (3) pertain to random effect variables, whereas the coefficients corresponding to values (2) and (4) pertain to fixed effect variables. The coefficient of Return on Assets (ROA) is found to be 0.645 under the random effects model and 0.671 under the fixed effects model prior to the acquisition. During the year of acquisition, the coefficient of ROA is 0.783 and 0.814 under the random and fixed effect model, respectively. Following the acquisition, the coefficient of ROA is estimated to be 0.766 under the random effects model and 0.854 under the fixed effects model. This suggests that the change in Return on Assets (ROA) will have a more pronounced effect on the financial performance of both models after the acquisition. The financial performance of the companies has demonstrated improvement subsequent to the acquisition. However, under the random effect model, the coefficient of ROA is higher than during the year of acquisition. Since it's a very marginal change it won't affect the profitability of the companies post-acquisition.

Table 4.3.42 -Impact of Returns on Financial Performance During Acquisition

	Dependent variable:			
	ni			
	(1)	(2)	(3)	(4)
roa	0.783***	0.814***		
	(0.023)	(0.033)		
roc			0.709***	0.733***
			(0.026)	(0.037)
Constant	0.083***		0.075***	
	(0.024)		(0.027)	
Observations	756	756	740	740
R^2	0.600	0.617	0.495	0.519
Adjusted R^2	0.599	0.233	0.495	0.036
F Statistic	1,130.508***	606.778*** (df = 1; 377)	724.068***	397.859*** (df = 1; 369)
Note:				*p<0.1; **p<0.05; ***p<0.01

Source: *Compiled by Author from R output sheet*

The coefficient of the ROC is 0.549 under the random effect and 0.567 under fixed effect models prior to the acquisition. During the acquisition, it increased to 0.709 and 0.733 under the random effect and fixed effect model respectively. However, after the acquisition, the coefficient decreased to 0.704 in the random effect and increased to 0.788 in the fixed effect model. This indicates a stronger influence of the ROC post-acquisition under both models as compared to pre-acquisition. However, if compared to the year of acquisition ROA exhibits a greater influence under the fixed effect model. The coefficient values of Return on Assets (ROA) and Return on Capital (ROC) exhibit a statistically significant impact at a significance level of 1% before, during, and after the acquisition. Further, in table 4.3.43 the impact of return on capital employed and financial leverage on financial performance during acquisition is examined.

Table 4.3.43 presents the regression outcomes, encompassing both random effect and fixed effect models, in the year of acquisition. The coefficients corresponding to values (1) and (3) represent the random effect variables, whereas the coefficients corresponding to values (2) and (4) represent the fixed effect variables. The coefficient values for the Return on Capital Employed (ROCE) variable are 0.466 and 0.577 when estimated using the random effects and fixed effects models, respectively post-acquisition. Prior to the acquisition, the coefficient of Return on Capital Employed

Table 4.3.43 -Impact of Returns and Liquidity on Financial Performance During Acquisition

	Dependent variable:			
	ni			
	(1)	(2)	(3)	(4)
roce	0.454***	0.474***		
	(0.036)	(0.051)		
fl			−0.095**	−0.074
			(0.040)	(0.065)
Constant	0.143***		0.090**	
	(0.037)		(0.037)	
Observations	574	574	748	748
R^2	0.219	0.231	0.007	0.003
Adjusted R^2	0.217	−0.541	0.006	−0.996
F Statistic	160.181***	85.735*** (df = 1; 286)	5.533**	1.270 (df = 1; 373)
Note:				*p<0.1; **p<0.05; ***p<0.01

Source: *Compiled by Author from R output sheet*

(ROCE) was observed to be 0.345 under the random effects model and 0.366 under the fixed effects model. During the year of acquisition, the coefficient of ROCE is 0.454 and 0.474 under the random effect and fixed effect model. This suggests that the rise in the proportion of Return on Capital Employed (ROCE) subsequent to the acquisition has enhanced the financial performance of the companies.

However, it should be noted that financial leverage exhibits a negative trend both prior to and subsequent to the acquisition. In the event of a pre-acquisition scenario, the coefficient of FL was observed to be 0.173 under the random effect and 0.164 under the fixed effect model. During the year of acquisition, the coefficient of FL is 0.095 and 0.074 under random effect and fixed effect respectively. Subsequently, this coefficient increased to 0.194 and 0.242 under the random and fixed models, respectively. The financial performance of companies is being adversely impacted by financial leverage, as observed in both the random effect and fixed effect models before and after the acquisition. However, subsequent to the acquisition, there has been an increase in this percentage, consequently leading to an adverse impact of financial leverage on the financial performance of the companies under both models. The coefficient values of Return on Capital Employed (ROCE) exhibit a statistically significant impact at a significance level of 1% in both the pre-, during, and post-acquisition periods. The coefficient value of FL is also significant at 5% under random effect in the year of acquisition. The impact of the degree of operating leverage and financial leverage on financial performance during acquisition is explored in Table 4.3.44.

Table 4.3.44 - Impact of Leverages on Financial Performance During Acquisition

	Dependent variable:			
	ni			
	(1)	(2)	(3)	(4)
dfl	−0.198***	−0.150**		
	(0.042)	(0.060)		
dol			0.195***	0.203***
			(0.039)	(0.056)
Constant	0.132***		0.123***	
	(0.040)		(0.040)	
Observations	610	610	614	614
R^2	0.036	0.020	0.039	0.041
Adjusted R^2	0.034	−0.963	0.038	−0.920
F Statistic	22.586***	6.194** (df = 1; 304)	25.073***	13.240*** (df = 1; 306)
Note:				*p<0.1; **p<0.05; ***p<0.01

Source: *Compiled by Author from R output sheet*

The regression results following the merger are presented in Table 4.3.44, encompassing both random effect and fixed effect models. The coefficients corresponding to values (1) and (3) represent random effect variables, whereas the coefficients corresponding to values (2) and (4) represent fixed effect variables. The coefficient for the Degree of Financial Leverage (DFL) is 0.121 under the random effects model and 0.124 under the fixed effects model prior to the acquisition. During the acquisition, the coefficient of DFL is 0.198 and 0.150 under random and fixed effect models respectively. However, following the acquisition, the value is 0.184 under the random effect model and 0.214 under the fixed effect model. This suggests that the increase in the negative coefficient of DFL has enhanced the adverse impact of this variable on the financial performance of the companies following the acquisition as compared to pre-acquisition. However, in the case of the random effect model, the coefficient of DFL is highest during the year of acquisition.

During the pre-acquisition period, the coefficient of DOL was observed to be 0.137 under the random effects model and 0.157 under the fixed effects model. In the year of acquisition, the coefficient is 0.195 and 0.203 under the random effect and fixed effect model. Subsequently, there was an increase in the coefficient to 0.216 under the random effect model and 0.281 under the fixed effect model. The rise in the proportion of degree of operating leverage (DOL) under both models has resulted in enhanced financial performance among companies. In general, DOL has yielded enhancements in the financial performance of the companies subsequent to the acquisition.

The coefficient values of DOL and DFL exhibit a statistically significant impact at a 1% significance level in both the models pre-, during, and post-acquisition. Further, the impact of cash flow on financial performance during acquisition is analyzed in table 4.3.45.

Table 4.3.45 - Impact of Cash Flow on Financial Performance During Acquisition

	Dependent variable:	
	ni	
	(1)	(2)
cfni	0.999***	1.028***
	(0.010)	(0.015)
Constant	0.015	
	(0.010)	
Observations	764	764
R^2	0.924	0.924
Adjusted R^2	0.924	0.847
F Statistic	9,241.088***	4,601.267*** (df = 1; 381)
Note:		*p<0.1; **p<0.05; ***p<0.01

Source: *Compiled by Author from R output sheet*

Table 4.3.45 presents the regression outcomes for both random effect and fixed effect models in the year of acquisition. The values denoted by (1) correspond to coefficients of random effect variables, whereas the values denoted by (2) correspond to coefficients of fixed effect variables. The coefficient of cash flow from net income (CFNI) is observed to be 0.856 under the random effect model and 0.879 under the fixed effect model following the acquisition. During the acquisition, the coefficient of CFNI is 0.999 under random effect and 1.028 under the fixed effect model. Prior to the acquisition, these coefficients were recorded as 0.984 under the random effect model and 1.033 under the fixed effect model. This suggests that the CFNI has decreased following the acquisition in both models, indicating a decline in financial performance after the acquisition. However, the financial performance has improved if we compare the coefficient of CFNI after acquisition to the year of acquisition under the fixed effect model. The coefficient values of CFNI exhibit a statistically significant impact at a 1% level in the pre-, during, and post-acquisition under both models. Further, the regression results of financial performance during acquisition are presented in table 4.3.46.

Table 4.3.46 -Regression Results of Financial Performance During Acquisition

	Dependent variable:			
	ni			
	(1)	(2)	(3)	(4)
ebitda	0.657***			
	(0.032)			
ebit		0.690***		
		(0.027)		
roa			0.783***	
			(0.023)	
roc				0.709***
				(0.026)
Constant	0.069**	0.019	0.083***	0.075***
	(0.030)	(0.026)	(0.024)	(0.027)
Observations	744	748	756	740
R^2	0.366	0.474	0.600	0.495
Adjusted R^2	0.365	0.473	0.599	0.495
F Statistic	427.900***	672.034***	1,130.508***	724.068***
Note:		*p<0.1; **p<0.05; ***p<0.01		

Source: *Compiled by Author from R output sheet*

Table 4.3.46 displays the regression results of all the variables impacting the financial performance of the companies in the year of acquisition. In these tables, either a random or fixed effect model is taken on the basis of the result obtained after applying the Hausman test. Specifically, if the p-value is less than 0.05, fixed effects are employed, whereas if the p-value is greater than 0.05, random effects are used. The coefficients of ROA, ROC, ROCE, and DOL are the only variables that are less than 0.05, thereby coefficients of these variables under fixed effect are taken and coefficients of all other variables except these four are under random effect after acquisition. However, the

Table 4.3.46 -Regression Results of Financial Performance During Acquisition (Contd)

	Dependent variable:				
	ni				
	(5)	(6)	(7)	(8)	(9)
roce	0.454***				
	(0.036)				
fl		−0.095**			
		(0.040)			
dfl			−0.198***		
			(0.042)		
dol				0.195***	
				(0.039)	
cfni					1.028***
					(0.015)
Constant	0.143***	0.090**	0.132***	0.123***	
	(0.037)	(0.037)	(0.040)	(0.040)	
Observations	574	748	610	614	764
R^2	0.219	0.007	0.036	0.039	0.924
Adjusted R^2	0.217	0.006	0.034	0.038	0.847
F Statistic	160.181***	5.533**	22.586***	25.073***	4,601.267*** (df = 1; 381)
Note:					*p<0.1; **p<0.05; ***p<0.01

Source: *Compiled by Author from R output sheet*

coefficient of EBIT, ROA, and CFNI are the only variables that are less than 0.05, hence, the coefficient under the fixed effect model is taken and the coefficient of all other variables except EBIT and CFNI under the random effect model are taken before acquisition. In the case of during the year of acquisition except CFNI all other variables have p value greater than 0.05 thereby coefficient of the random effect model is taken. All the variables are statistically significant at 1% level pre- and post-acquisition. Except FL all the variables are statistically significant at 1% level. FL is statistically significant at the 5% level. In the above tables, the impact of earnings, returns and leverages on financial performance is discussed before, after and during acquisition. Now, in the next segment the impact of all these variables on financial performance is examined in overall acquisition.

Table 4.3.47 presents the regression outcomes for both random effect and fixed effect

Table 4.3.47 -Impact of Earnings on Financial Performance considering Overall Acquisition

	Dependent variable:			
	ni			
	(1)	(2)	(3)	(4)
ebitda	0.595***	0.597***		
	(0.013)	(0.014)		
ebit			0.692***	0.692***
			(0.012)	(0.012)
Constant	0.002		−0.002	
	(0.013)		(0.011)	
Observations	3,720	3,720	3,740	3,740
R^2	0.354	0.355	0.480	0.480
Adjusted R^2	0.354	0.283	0.479	0.423
F Statistic	2,037.120***	1,841.489*** (df = 1; 3347)	3,443.964***	3,111.464*** (df = 1; 3365)
Note:				*p<0.1; **p<0.05; ***p<0.01

Source: *Compiled by Author from R output sheet*

models. The coefficients corresponding to values (1) and (3) pertain to random effect variables, whereas the coefficients corresponding to values (2) and (4) pertain to fixed effect variables. After the acquisition, the coefficient of EBITDA is observed to be 0.605 under the random effect model and 0.643 under the fixed effect model. The values observed were 0.590 under the random effect model and the fixed effect model prior to the acquisition. During the year the coefficient of EBITDA is 0.657 and 0.696 under random and fixed effect models respectively. In the case of overall acquisition, the coefficient is 0.595 under random effect and 0.597 under fixed effect model. This finding suggests that there is a minute change in EBITDA, with under-random effects and fixed effects post-acquisition as well as in overall acquisition. Still, the post-acquisition EBITDA has had a greater impact on the financial performance if compared to pre-merger. However, the coefficient has decreased minutely post-acquisition under both models as compared to the year of acquisition.

Likewise, it can be observed that Earnings Before Interest and Taxes (EBIT) exhibit a more pronounced effect following an acquisition in both models, suggesting an enhanced financial performance of the companies subsequent to the acquisition. The coefficient of EBIT is 0.615 under the random effects model and 0.581 under the fixed effects model prior to the acquisition. During the year the coefficient of EBIT is 0.690 and 0.655 in the year of acquisition. Following the acquisition, the coefficient of EBIT is 0.747 under the random effects model and 0.748 under the fixed effects model. In the case of overall acquisition the coefficient of EBIT is 0.692 under both the models The coefficient values associated with EBIT and EBITDA exhibit a statistically significant impact at a significance level of 1% in pre-, during, post, and overall acquisition.

Further, in table 4.3.48 the impact of returns on financial performance considering overall acquisition is evaluated.

Table 4.3.48 -Impact of Returns on Financial Performance considering Overall Acquisition

	Dependent variable:			
	ni			
	(1)	(2)	(3)	(4)
roa	0.679***	0.694***		
	(0.012)	(0.013)		
roc			0.600***	0.610***
			(0.013)	(0.014)
Constant	−0.000		0.003	
	(0.011)		(0.012)	
Observations	3,780	3,780	3,700	3,700
R^2	0.461	0.471	0.360	0.366
Adjusted R^2	0.461	0.413	0.360	0.295
F Statistic	3,236.658***	3,032.855*** (df = 1; 3401)	2,078.551***	1,919.687*** (df = 1; 3329)
Note:				*p<0.1; **p<0.05; ***p<0.01

Source: *Compiled by Author from R output sheet*

The regression results for both random effect and fixed effect models are presented in Table 4.3.48. The coefficients corresponding to values (1) and (3) pertain to random effect variables, whereas the coefficients corresponding to values (2) and (4) pertain to fixed effect variables. The coefficient of Return on Assets (ROA) is found to be 0.645 under the random effects model and 0.671 under the fixed effects model prior to the acquisition. During the year of acquisition, the coefficient of ROA is 0.783 and 0.814 under the random and fixed effect model, respectively. Following the acquisition, the coefficient of ROA is estimated to be 0.766 under the random effects model and 0.854

under the fixed effects model. In the case of overall acquisition, the coefficient of ROA is 0.679 and 0.694 under the random effect and fixed effect model respectively. This suggests that the change in Return on Assets (ROA) will have a more pronounced effect on the financial performance of both models after the acquisition. The financial performance of the companies has demonstrated improvement subsequent to the acquisition. However, under the random effect model, the coefficient of ROA is higher than during the year of acquisition. Since it's a very marginal change it won't affect the profitability of the companies post-acquisition.

The coefficient of the ROC is 0.549 under the random effect and 0.567 under fixed effect models prior to the acquisition. During the acquisition, it increased to 0.709 and 0.733 under the random effect and fixed effect models respectively. However, after the acquisition, the coefficient decreased to 0.704 in the random effect and increased to 0.788 in the fixed effect model. In the case of an overall merger, the coefficient of ROC is 0.600 and 0.610 under the random effect and fixed effect model. This indicates a stronger influence of the ROC post-acquisition under both the models as compared to pre-acquisition as well as overall acquisition. However, if compared to the year of acquisition ROA exhibits a greater influence under the fixed effect model. The coefficient values of Return on Assets (ROA) and Return on Capital (ROC) exhibit a statistically significant impact at a significance level of 1% before, during, after, and overall acquisition. The impact of return on capital employed and financial leverage on financial performance considering overall acquisition is analyzed in table 4.3.49.

Table 4.3.49 presents the regression outcomes, encompassing both random effect and fixed effect models, in overall acquisition. The coefficients corresponding to values (1) and (3) represent the random effect variables, whereas the coefficients corresponding to values (2) and (4) represent the fixed effect variables. The coefficient values for the return on capital employed (ROCE) variable are 0.466 and 0.577 when estimated using the random effects and fixed effects models, respectively post-acquisition. Prior to the acquisition, the coefficient of return on capital employed (ROCE) was observed to be 0.345 under the random effects model and 0.366 under the fixed effects model. During the year of acquisition, the coefficient of ROCE is 0.454 and 0.474 under the random effect and fixed effect model. In overall acquisition, the coefficient is 0.388 under the random effect and 0.403 under the fixed effect model. This suggests that the rise in the proportion of return on capital employed (ROCE) subsequent to the acquisition has enhanced the financial performance of the companies.

Table 4.3.49 -Impact of Returns and Liquidity on Financial Performance considering Overall Acquisition

	Dependent variable:			
	ni			
	(1)	(2)	(3)	(4)
roce	0.388***	0.403***		
	(0.017)	(0.018)		
fl			−0.166***	−0.170***
			(0.016)	(0.017)
Constant	0.001		−0.0004	
	(0.016)		(0.015)	
Observations	2,870	2,870	3,740	3,740
R^2	0.150	0.156	0.027	0.028
Adjusted R^2	0.150	0.062	0.027	−0.080
F Statistic	506.890***	477.890*** (df = 1; 2582)	105.328***	97.223*** (df = 1; 3365)
Note:				*p<0.1; **p<0.05; ***p<0.01

Source: *Compiled by Author from R output sheet*

However, it should be noted that financial leverage exhibits a negative trend both prior to and subsequent to the acquisition. In the event of a pre-acquisition scenario, the coefficient of FL was observed to be 0.173 under the random effect and 0.164 under the fixed effect model. During the year of acquisition, the coefficient of FL is 0.095 and 0.074 under random effect and fixed effect respectively. Subsequently, this coefficient increased to 0.194 and 0.242 under the random and fixed models, respectively. In the case of overall acquisition, the coefficient is 0.166 and 0.170 under random and fixed effect models respectively. The financial performance of companies is adversely impacted by financial leverage, as observed in both the random effect and fixed effect models before, during, after, and overall acquisition. However, subsequent to the acquisition, there has been an increase in this percentage, consequently leading to an adverse impact of financial leverage on the financial performance of the companies under both models. The coefficient values of Return on Capital Employed (ROCE) exhibit a statistically significant impact at a significance level of 1% in both the pre-, during, post, and overall acquisition periods. The coefficient value of FL is also significant at 5% under random effect in the year of acquisition. However, the coefficient of FL is statistically significant at a 1% level in overall acquisition under both models. Further, in the next table, the impact of the degree of financial leverage and operating leverage considering overall acquisition is explored.

Table 4.3.50 -Impact of Leverages on Financial Performance considering Overall Acquisition

	Dependent variable:			
	ni			
	(1)	(2)	(3)	(4)
dfl	−0.156***	−0.159***		
	(0.018)	(0.019)		
dol			0.160***	0.167***
			(0.018)	(0.019)
Constant	−0.000		−0.000	
	(0.017)		(0.017)	
Observations	3,050	3,050	3,070	3,070
R^2	0.024	0.025	0.026	0.027
Adjusted R^2	0.024	−0.083	0.025	−0.081
F Statistic	76.330***	70.131*** (df = 1; 2744)	80.400***	75.935*** (df = 1; 2762)
Note:				*p<0.1; **p<0.05; ***p<0.01

Source: *Compiled by Author from R output sheet*

The regression results following the merger are presented in Table 4.3.50, encompassing both random effect and fixed effect models. The coefficients corresponding to values (1) and (3) represent random effect variables, whereas the coefficients corresponding to values (2) and (4) represent fixed effect variables. The coefficient for the Degree of Financial Leverage (DFL) is 0.121 under the random effects model and 0.124 under the fixed effects model prior to the acquisition. During the acquisition, the coefficient of DFL is 0.198 and 0.150 under random and fixed effect models respectively. However, following the acquisition, the value is 0.184 under the random effect model and 0.214 under the fixed effect model. In the case of overall acquisition, the value is 0.156 and 0.159 under the random and fixed effect model respectively. This suggests that the increase in the negative coefficient of DFL has enhanced the adverse impact of this variable on the financial performance of the companies following the acquisition as compared to pre-acquisition and overall acquisition. However, in the case of the random effect model, the coefficient of DFL is highest during the year of acquisition.

During the pre-acquisition period, the coefficient of DOL was observed to be 0.137 under the random effects model and 0.157 under the fixed effects model. In the year of acquisition, the coefficient is 0.195 and 0.203 under the random effect and fixed effect model. Subsequently, there was an increase in the coefficient to 0.216 under the random effect model and 0.281 under the fixed effect model. In the case of overall acquisition, the coefficient of DOL is 0.160 and 0.167 under the random and fixed effect model respectively. The rise in the proportion of degree of operating leverage (DOL) under both models has resulted in enhanced financial performance among companies. In general, DOL has yielded enhancements in the financial performance of the companies subsequent to the acquisition.

The coefficient values of DOL and DFL exhibit a statistically significant impact at a 1% significance level in both the models pre-, during, post, and overall acquisition. The impact of cash flow on financial performance considering overall acquisition is examined in table 4.3.51.

Table 4.3.51 -Impact of Cash Flow on Financial Performance considering Overall Acquisition

	Dependent variable:	
	ni	
	(1)	(2)
cfni	0.920***	0.920***
	(0.006)	(0.007)
Constant	0.000	
	(0.006)	
Observations	3,820	3,820
R^2	0.847	0.847
Adjusted R^2	0.847	0.830
F Statistic	21,151.580***	19,040.850*** (df = 1; 3437)
Note:		*p<0.1; **p<0.05; ***p<0.01

Source: *Compiled by Author from R output sheet*

Table 4.3.51 presents the regression outcomes for both random effect and fixed effect models in overall acquisition. The values denoted by (1) correspond to coefficients of random effect variables, whereas the values denoted by (2) correspond to coefficients of fixed effect variables. The coefficient of cash flow from net income (CFNI) is observed to be 0.856 under the random effect model and 0.879 under the fixed effect model following the acquisition. During the acquisition, the coefficient of CFNI is 0.999 under the random effect and 1.028 under the fixed effect model. Prior to the acquisition, these coefficients were recorded as 0.984 under the random effect model and 1.033 under the fixed effect model. In the case of overall acquisition, the coefficient is 0.920 under both models. This suggests that the CFNI has decreased following the acquisition in both models, indicating a decline in financial performance after the acquisition as compared to before and overall acquisition. However, the financial performance has improved if we compare the coefficient of CFNI after acquisition to the year of acquisition under the fixed effect model. The coefficient values of CFNI exhibit a statistically significant impact at a 1% level in the pre-, during, post, and overall acquisition under both models. The regression results of financial performance considering overall acquisition are reported in Table 4.3.52 on the basis of the Hausman test.

Table 4.3.52 displays the regression results of all the variables impacting the financial performance of the companies in overall acquisition. In these tables, either a random or fixed effect model is taken on the basis of the result obtained after applying the Hausman test. Specifically, if the p-value is less than 0.05, fixed effects are employed, whereas if the p-value is greater than 0.05, random effects are used. The coefficients of ROA, ROC, ROCE, and DOL are the only variables that are less than 0.05, thereby coefficients of these variables under fixed effect are taken and coefficients of all other variables except these four are under random effect after acquisition. However, the coefficient of EBIT, ROA, and CFNI are the only variables that are less than 0.05, hence, the coefficient under the fixed effect model is taken and the coefficient of all other variables except EBIT and CFNI under the random effect model are taken before acquisition. In the case of during the year of acquisition except CFNI all other variables have p value greater than 0.05 thereby coefficient of the random effect model is taken. In the case of overall acquisition except for ROA, ROC, and ROCE, all other variables have p value greater than 0.05, hence coefficients under the random effect model are taken of them. All the variables are statistically significant at 1% level pre-, post-, and overall acquisition. Except FL all the variables are statistically significant at 1% level.

Table 4.3.52 -Regression Results of Financial Performance considering Overall Acquisition

	Dependent variable:			
	ni			
	(1)	(2)	(3)	(4)
ebitda	0.595***			
	(0.013)			
ebit		0.692***		
		(0.012)		
roa			0.694***	
			(0.013)	
roc				0.610***
				(0.014)
Constant	0.002	−0.002		
	(0.013)	(0.011)		
Observations	3,720	3,740	3,780	3,700
R^2	0.354	0.480	0.471	0.366
Adjusted R^2	0.354	0.479	0.413	0.295
F Statistic	2,037.120***	3,443.964***	3,032.855*** (df = 1; 3401)	1,919.687*** (df = 1; 3329)
Note:				*p<0.1; **p<0.05; ***p<0.01

Source: *Compiled by Author from R output sheet*

Table 4.3.52 -Regression Results of Financial Performance considering Overall Acquisition (Contd)

	Dependent variable:				
	ni				
	(5)	(6)	(7)	(8)	(9)
roce	0.403***				
	(0.018)				
fl		−0.166***			
		(0.016)			
dfl			−0.156***		
			(0.018)		
dol				0.160***	
				(0.018)	
cfni					0.920***
					(0.006)
Constant		−0.0004	−0.000	−0.000	0.000
		(0.015)	(0.017)	(0.017)	(0.006)
Observations	2,870	3,740	3,050	3,070	3,820
R^2	0.156	0.027	0.024	0.026	0.847
Adjusted R^2	0.062	0.027	0.024	0.025	0.847
F Statistic	477.890*** (df = 1; 2582)	105.328***	76.330***	80.400***	21,151.580***
Note:					*p<0.1; **p<0.05; ***p<0.01

Source: *Compiled by Author from R output sheet*

FL is statistically significant at the 5% level. The correlation of all the variables in relation to financial performance with each other is presented in Table 4.3.53 in case of an acquisition.

Table 4.3.53 -Correlation Matrix of Financial Performance – Acquisition

	ni	ebitda	ebit	roa	roc	roce	fl	dfl	dol	cfni
ni	1									
ebitda	0.626	1								
ebit	0.723	0.883	1							
roa	0.688	0.373	0.433	1						
roc	0.607	0.356	0.415	0.879	1					
roce	0.397	0.218	0.268	0.537	0.623	1				
fl	-0.173	-0.064	-0.071	-0.253	-0.117	0.009	1			
dfl	-0.155	-0.079	-0.105	-0.226	-0.163	-0.123	0.189	1		
dol	0.149	0.137	0.156	0.230	0.222	0.201	0.036	-0.069	1	
cfni	0.923	0.669	0.665	0.716	0.628	0.412	-0.198	-0.163	0.157	1

Source: *Compiled by Author from R output sheet*

The correlation between the variables in the case of an acquisition is displayed in Table 4.3.53. The relationship between net income and EBITDA, EBIT, ROA, and ROCE are positively correlated. However, the relationship of fl is negatively correlated with all the variables except ROCE, DFL, and DOL. Similarly, CFNI is negatively correlated to FL and DFL. In the next table, the null hypotheses are formed to analyze whether the variable has an impact on financial performance or not.

Table 4.3.54 -Comparison of Pre-and Post-Acquisition of Net Income

S.No.	Company Name	Pre-Acquisition				Post-Acquisition			
		2013	2014	2015	2016	2019	2020	2021	2022
1	Fortis Hospitals Ltd	1.0596	0.9411	0.8306	0.5914	-1.7910	0.1830	0.0000	0.0000
2	Television Eighteen India Ltd	-1.1339	-1.1339	-1.1339	-1.1339	-1.1339	-	-	-
3	Virtusa Consulting Services Pvt Ltd	-0.3561	-0.2663	-0.1872	-1.5634	2.2211	0.8808	-	-
4	TVS Automobile Solutions Pvt Ltd	-0.1762	-0.1762	-0.1762	-0.1762	1.5855	-1.9378	-0.1762	-0.1762
5	Haldia Energy Ltd	-1.7439	-1.8333	0.0601	0.5135	0.6685	0.9826	-	-
6	Tata Power Renewable Energy Ltd	-0.6102	-0.5819	-0.4512	0.3489	-1.3804	-0.3608	-	-
7	Karvy Data Management Services Ltd	-	2.1213	-2.1213	-	-	-	-	-
8	Casagrand Builder Pvt Ltd	-1.0961	-1.1027	-1.0894	-0.3574	0.1218	0.1218	0.1218	0.1218
9	Valuefirst Digital Media Pvt Ltd	0.1475	0.2750	0.1475	0.4025	1.0381	-2.7026	-0.0528	-0.0528
10	JM Financial Asset Reconstruction Co Ltd	0.1138	-0.1379	-0.7726	-0.1379	-0.4352	0.0693	0.1138	0.1138
11	IDFC Alternatives Ltd	-0.0517	0.1130	-0.0429	-1.3026	-0.6980	0.5330	-0.0000	-0.0000
12	Tata Realty & Infrastructure Ltd	0.8714	1.0406	1.4370	0.4929	-1.2980	-0.7053	0.0000	0.0000
13	Srei Equipment Finance Ltd	-1.6540	-0.7377	2.3917	-0.0000	-0.0000	-0.0000	-0.0000	-0.0000
14	ReNew Power Pvt Ltd	0.2306	0.2713	0.7113	0.4251	-2.7443	-	-	-
15	Wearit Global Ltd	0.8143	0.8825	0.8143	0.9507	-0.2121	-0.2121	-0.2121	-0.2121
16	Shriji Polymers India Ltd	-1.2804	-1.2821	-0.8006	0.1743	1.0817	1.9208	0.0000	0.0000
17	Lalitpur Power Generation Co Ltd	0.9964	-0.0366	1.4919	-0.9733	0.2467	-1.3055	0.5188	0.9794
18	Assets Care & Reconstruction Enterprise Ltd	-0.1762	-0.1762	-0.1762	-0.1762	1.5855	-1.9378	-0.1762	-0.1762

S.No.	Company Name	Pre-Acquisition				Post-Acquisition			
		2013	2014	2015	2016	2019	2020	2021	2022
19	HomeShop18	-0.4102	-0.3203	-0.6112	-0.5320	-0.3685	-0.6803	-	-
20	GMR Airports Ltd	-1.1854	-1.9542	0.1456	0.9212	-	-	-	-
21	Athanas Enterprise Pvt Ltd	-0.0854	1.8911	-2.2788	0.4730	0.0000	0.0000	0.0000	0.0000
22	SVP Builders India Ltd	0.9890	0.4911	1.4868	0.7221	-0.9133	0.0935	-0.1099	-0.1099
23	Jain Farm Fresh Foods Ltd	0.3295	0.8929	0.3295	1.4563	-1.3964	-1.6103	-0.1528	-0.1528
24	Salzer Magnet Wires Ltd	0.8153	-1.3642	-1.0892	-0.5857	-0.0000	-0.0000	-0.0000	-0.0000
25	Nettle Infrastructure Investments Ltd	0.1934	-1.4795	-0.0678	-1.4795	1.5148	0.1934	0.1934	0.1934
26	Choicest Enterprises Ltd	-0.2086	0.6966	0.9724	0.6966	-2.1726	-0.8218	-0.2086	-0.2086
27	MRC Logistics India Pvt Ltd	-0.7003	-0.6750	-0.8135	-0.8815	1.2072	1.8575	-	-
28	World Resorts Ltd	-1.0522	-1.9284	0.1180	1.6088	-0.0000	-0.0000	-0.0000	-0.0000
29	Escorts Heart Institute and Research Centre Ltd	-0.0208	-0.0391	-0.0024	0.0281	-1.2173	2.4810	0.0023	0.0023
30	Alivira Animal Health Ltd	-1.3154	-0.8259	-1.3154	-0.3363	1.0273	0.2677	0.2677	0.2677
31	Biocon Biologics Ltd/India	-0.2153	-0.2153	-0.2153	1.4391	-0.8726	-1.8996	0.4719	-0.2153
32	OmniActive Health Technologies Ltd	1.2470	-0.5867	1.5568	-0.0552	-	-	-	-
33	Nowrosjee Wadia & Sons Ltd	-0.0920	0.9318	-0.1959	0.9318	-0.9672	-0.9837	-0.0920	-0.0920
34	Edel Land Ltd	0.0890	0.0890	0.0890	-1.2275	2.2580	-0.7634	0.0890	0.0890
35	Telesonic Networks Ltd	-0.4931	-0.5379	-0.4931	-0.5827	2.7072	0.1289	0.1289	0.1289
36	Amtek Auto Ltd	0.6382	0.9447	0.3317	0.3317	0.5377	0.2996	-0.0709	-0.0709
37	Takasago Thermal Engineering Co Ltd	-1.6713	-1.2978	-0.8394	-0.2043	1.2350	0.2531	0.7004	-
38	Flipkart India Pvt Ltd	-0.2840	1.5278	0.7439	1.5278	-0.9749	-0.3679	-0.2840	-0.2840
39	20 Microns Ltd	-1.5865	-1.6032	-0.4584	-0.0467	0.6557	0.5585	1.5441	-0.0000
40	Smartchem Technologies Ltd	-0.1676	-0.8545	-1.1757	-0.3918	-	-	-	-
41	Lotte Confectionery Co Ltd	0.2630	0.2630	0.2630	-1.7125	0.9291	1.1981	0.6374	0.2630
42	Jasper Industries Pvt Ltd	-0.1321	-0.6027	0.1344	-1.9811	-0.5957	0.4281	-	-
43	CavinKare Pvt Ltd	2.0776	-0.7555	-1.0678	0.3623	0.0000	0.0000	0.0000	0.0000
44	Reliance Jio Infocomm Ltd	-0.5896	-0.5924	-0.5926	-0.5943	2.7221	-0.0000	-0.0000	-0.0000
45	ProConnect Supply Chain Solutions Ltd	0.3380	0.4891	0.5306	0.7797	-2.2250	0.8127	-	-
46	Ebixcash Ltd	-1.0806	0.0488	-0.8653	-0.6281	2.1558	-	-	-
47	TATA Advanced Systems Ltd	-0.4230	0.5733	0.5139	0.9846	-	-	-	-
48	Tata Sons Pvt Ltd	-1.7257	-0.1372	2.0890	0.7851	-	-	-	-
49	Indian Farmers Fertilizer Cooperative Ltd	-1.3437	-0.6721	-0.5521	-0.5947	0.0601	1.5940	1.8599	-0.0000
50	Inditrade Business Consultants Ltd	-1.8066	-0.3659	-0.6313	-0.2705	0.0955	-0.4514	1.8357	-
51	Jaquar & Co Pvt Ltd	-1.4096	-0.6744	-1.4096	0.0609	1.1312	1.7640	0.2605	0.2605
52	Minda SAI Ltd	-1.5855	0.1762	-1.5855	1.9378	0.1762	0.1762	0.1762	0.1762
53	Tata Capital Ltd	-1.0191	-0.8140	-0.5905	-0.4680	-0.8356	1.0290	2.2026	0.0000
54	SFO Technologies Pvt Ltd	1.6383	0.3275	1.6383	-0.9834	-0.9530	0.3892	-0.2457	-0.2457
55	Sistema Smart Technologies Ltd	0.1721	0.6351	-0.2909	-2.5505	0.2307	0.0123	-0.0191	-0.0191
56	Adani Harbour Services Ltd/The	0.3380	0.1633	-0.0651	1.4762	-1.7744	-1.1549	0.3452	0.0000
57	EbixCash World Money Ltd	0.6186	-0.6381	0.6186	-1.8947	0.0024	0.0024	0.0024	0.0024
58	Indian Seamless Enterprises Ltd	0.7570	0.9475	0.7570	1.1380	-1.7506	-0.2131	-0.2131	-0.2131
59	Avana Logistek Ltd	0.3359	0.3993	0.3046	0.3686	-2.7975	0.5231	-0.0000	-0.0000
60	Royal Highland Distilleries Ltd	-0.4997	0.2876	-1.9730	2.1852	0.0000	0.0000	0.0000	0.0000
61	Poly Hose India Rubber Pvt Ltd	-1.1770	-1.8817	-0.4723	0.0804	0.5297	0.8894	0.1308	0.1308
62	Minda Rinder Pvt Ltd	-1.6981	-0.1850	-1.6981	1.3280	0.2354	0.2354	0.2354	0.2354
63	Olive Commercial Co Ltd	-1.2613	-1.6297	-0.4292	-0.0882	0.2133	0.5460	1.9937	0.0000
64	BCL Secure Premises Pvt Ltd	-1.2055	-1.6977	-0.7133	-0.2785	1.6380	0.7397	0.1339	0.1339
65	JSW Cement Ltd	-0.3010	-0.9103	-0.3010	-1.5195	0.1514	0.1514	0.1514	0.1514
66	Aditya Birla Capital Ltd	0.2205	0.2205	-1.0326	-0.7316	-0.2652	0.4347	2.3962	0.2205
67	Carysil Ltd	-0.7372	-0.6815	-0.5613	-0.7627	0.0545	0.9949	2.4091	-0.0000
68	Adani Power Ltd	0.1298	-0.0564	0.4281	-1.9562	-0.5737	0.6831	1.9742	-
69	Adani Green Energy Ltd	0.0591	-0.1437	-0.3293	-0.1437	-0.0479	0.9054	2.0457	0.0591
70	Adani Transmission Ltd	-1.0858	-1.5195	-0.6522	-0.5400	0.1314	1.3293	1.2843	0.1206
71	Redribbon Modulex Buildings Ltd	-0.8724	-0.8107	2.5006	-0.7087	0.1882	-0.1433	0.6388	-
72	Adani Enterprises Ltd	2.0629	1.5304	-0.3000	-0.3449	-0.0511	-0.4720	-0.7572	-
73	Advanced Enzyme Technologies Ltd	-1.9501	-1.1147	-0.4498	-0.0300	0.9792	1.4241	0.7196	-
74	Allcargo Logistics Ltd	-0.6107	-0.2131	-0.2132	-0.2485	-0.2873	-0.5072	2.7980	-
75	Veecon Media & Television Ltd	0.7915	0.2608	0.3008	0.9263	-0.8954	-0.2011	-1.7851	-
76	Asian Hotels East Ltd	0.4288	-0.7023	0.5119	0.7412	0.4260	-1.5725	-1.6923	-
77	Asahi India Glass Ltd	-1.8019	-0.9301	-0.4890	0.1256	0.1665	-0.0363	2.0421	-
78	AJR Infra and Tolling Ltd	0.5304	0.7834	0.3712	0.0721	-0.1033	-2.6364	0.0000	0.0000
79	Amarjothi Spinning Mills Ltd	1.4478	-0.3060	-1.4786	-0.1620	-1.0419	0.4815	1.6962	-0.0000

S.No.	Company Name	Pre-Acquisition				Post-Acquisition			
		2013	2014	2015	2016	2019	2020	2021	2022
80	Alankit Ltd	-1.2329	-1.2039	-0.7351	0.6048	0.7001	0.2967	-0.9225	-
81	Altran Technologies SASU	-1.5891	-0.8948	-0.1379	0.7819	1.6819	0.0000	0.0000	0.0000
82	Amber Enterprises India Ltd	-0.9258	-0.8737	-0.9779	-1.0217	2.0200	0.3054	0.9214	0.1029
83	Nettle Infrastructure Investments Ltd	1.0858	0.5148	1.3322	0.5794	0.1145	-2.1020	-0.3863	-0.0000
84	Asian Paints Ltd	-1.4453	-1.1716	-0.6577	-0.3268	0.8618	1.5357	1.3669	-
85	Apollo Tyres Ltd	0.8356	0.7309	1.2852	1.1938	-1.1805	-1.6617	-0.5619	-
86	Aurobindo Pharma Ltd	-1.2154	-0.8522	-0.4472	-0.1979	0.2919	2.5360	0.1144	0.0000
87	Arco Leasing Ltd	0.9918	0.8551	0.5232	0.6273	-0.4620	-0.5673	-0.8937	-0.0000
88	Anant Raj Ltd	0.9303	2.0811	0.0799	0.2917	-1.0259	-1.4702	-0.2717	0.0000
89	Ajmera Realty & Infra India Ltd	-0.0798	0.0517	0.2840	0.5999	0.1492	0.1141	-2.6958	-0.0000
90	Adani Power Mundra Ltd	-2.2907	0.3940	1.8967	-0.0000	-0.0000	-0.0000	-0.0000	-0.0000
91	Aarvee Denims & Exports Ltd	0.6857	0.5682	0.8365	0.6299	-1.0837	-1.9570	-1.0639	-
92	Arvind Fashions Ltd	-0.2517	-0.2517	1.0041	1.0093	-1.0182	-1.8902	-0.3687	-0.2517
93	IndusInd Media & Communications Ltd	-0.3198	-0.0146	-0.0156	0.0620	-2.1876	0.2527	1.8737	-
94	Ashapura Minechem Ltd	0.6580	-0.4750	0.5941	-0.3804	1.8059	0.1916	0.1864	-0.0000
95	Vipani Hotels & Resorts Ltd	-1.0943	-0.4130	0.1017	-0.3249	1.0434	0.7068	1.4147	-
96	Asya Infosoft Ltd	-1.0027	-0.8946	-0.0190	-0.4011	-0.4317	-0.6874	-0.0000	-0.0000
97	AXISCADES Technologies Ltd	0.3328	0.5313	1.0616	0.2251	1.1295	-1.8444	0.6945	-
98	Sembcorp Energy India Ltd	0.0609	0.3625	0.6016	-0.5640	-1.1207	0.2956	2.1312	-
99	Bazel International Ltd	-0.0752	0.2728	0.3289	0.2728	1.4534	-0.8531	0.6084	-0.0752
100	BCL Industries Ltd	-0.8599	-0.8202	-0.8388	-0.6952	-0.0511	0.7240	2.3282	-0.0000
101	Birla Corp Ltd	-0.9741	-0.7027	-0.7476	-0.4385	1.2684	2.0150	0.6316	-0.0000
102	Bharat Forge Ltd	-0.4040	0.3595	0.1164	0.1920	-0.8340	-2.2112	1.2827	0.0000
103	Bhagyanagar India Ltd	-0.5591	-0.8181	-0.7231	0.0076	-1.1155	-0.4802	1.4997	-
104	Bio Green Papers Ltd	0.8551	0.8385	0.8353	-0.3922	0.3637	-2.0270	0.0000	0.0000
105	Bajaj Electricals Ltd	-1.2301	-1.3519	0.3641	0.2847	-1.2861	1.5303	0.6561	-
106	Bal Pharma Ltd	0.6461	0.3523	-0.2845	0.0494	-2.6969	0.5823	0.7503	-
107	Balasore Alloys Ltd	0.6941	0.3660	0.1592	1.4338	-2.3446	-	-	-
108	Heritage Nutrivet Ltd	-1.1321	-1.1303	-0.6578	-0.7442	1.2120	1.2083	0.8737	-
109	Bodal Chemicals Ltd	-1.7526	-0.0532	-0.2131	1.0810	-0.1806	-1.4267	0.3848	-
110	Balrampur Chini Mills Ltd	-1.3097	-1.5854	-0.9288	1.1174	0.8116	0.6473	0.5844	-0.0000
111	Bharat Road Network Ltd	0.1691	0.4793	0.3171	0.1551	0.5737	-0.3140	-2.6812	-0.0000
112	BSE Ltd	-0.4378	-0.4975	-0.3780	-0.5108	-0.1211	-0.5734	-0.4405	0.2021
113	Infutec Healthcare Ltd	1.4920	0.2099	1.4920	-1.0722	-0.2127	-0.2127	-0.2127	-0.2127
114	Blueblood Ventures Ltd	-0.1009	1.2836	-0.4766	1.2836	-0.1009	-0.1009	-0.1009	-0.1009
115	Babcock Borsig Ltd	-0.4479	-0.1669	-0.7617	-0.5377	0.1493	-0.5335	2.7382	-
116	Indigrid 2 Ltd	-1.0700	-0.9582	-0.5724	-0.5864	0.3958	0.8406	2.3012	-
117	Byke Hospitality Ltd/The	0.2169	0.4479	0.7773	1.1165	-0.4384	-1.6872	-1.3851	-
118	Future Speciality Retail Ltd	-2.3296	1.8566	0.3211	0.1519	-0.0000	-0.0000	-0.0000	-0.0000
119	Calcom Vision Ltd	-0.8591	-1.1730	-0.7438	-0.1564	-0.3936	-0.1246	-0.0390	-
120	Cartrade Tech Ltd	-0.0613	-0.0613	-0.0613	0.2200	0.3201	1.6573	-2.4425	-0.0613
121	Chembond Chemicals Ltd	-0.4996	-0.3951	2.8017	-0.2378	-0.6328	-0.2149	-0.3602	-
122	Coffee Day Enterprises Ltd	-0.3346	-0.3450	-0.2812	-0.1431	2.6937	-1.1176	-0.4019	0.0000
123	Ceat Ltd	-0.1736	0.2247	1.3781	0.6654	-0.5466	1.3267	-2.0399	0.0000
124	Centrum Capital Ltd	0.0573	0.1961	0.4645	0.4645	1.3836	0.0586	-0.7400	-2.4314
125	Choice International Ltd	-0.6633	-0.5547	-0.6088	-0.4746	-0.0610	0.2272	2.7101	-0.0000
126	California Software Co Ltd	-2.6849	0.1792	-0.0254	0.5587	0.2220	0.1662	1.1195	-
127	Zuari Finserv Ltd	-0.4104	-0.4309	-0.5473	-0.5196	-0.1011	-0.1376	2.7974	-0.0000
128	Chemfab Alkalis Ltd	-0.1085	-0.1085	0.6440	0.2243	0.6412	-2.5915	0.9590	-0.1085
129	Cholamandalam Financial Holdings Ltd	-1.0841	-0.6881	1.4644	-1.5874	-0.2451	0.7139	1.4089	-0.0000
130	Cian Agro Industries & Infrastructure Ltd	0.4587	0.4715	0.4458	1.4049	-0.0510	-0.0510	-0.0510	-0.0510
131	Spice Money Ltd	-1.3123	-1.1045	-0.5940	-0.1412	-0.2523	0.5574	-	-
132	Colorchips New Media Ltd	0.3002	0.3097	0.3028	0.5308	-0.0140	-2.7850	0.5910	0.0000
133	Confidence Petroleum India Ltd	-0.8043	-1.5365	-0.8366	-0.7219	0.6583	0.5611	1.6897	-
134	Century Plyboards India Ltd	-1.7763	-0.3481	-0.0264	0.3200	-0.3221	0.3363	2.2940	-
135	Capital Trust Ltd/India	-0.2300	0.2463	0.8919	1.9645	-0.0808	-1.7800	-0.9713	-
136	Cravatex Ltd	1.0505	0.8463	0.0009	-0.4864	0.2641	-1.8594	-0.9801	-
137	Crest Ventures Ltd	-0.9337	-0.4656	0.1054	0.1399	0.4174	-1.2092	-0.8588	0.0000
138	Coromandel International Ltd	-0.9968	-0.8876	-0.9946	-0.7062	0.7126	1.3498	1.8306	-
139	CRISIL Ltd	-0.5808	-1.0979	-0.8039	-0.6425	0.2301	0.4197	2.3731	-
140	Cyient Ltd	-1.5001	-0.3318	-0.6930	-0.4578	-0.4752	-0.1899	1.9336	0.0000

S.No.	Company Name	Pre-Acquisition				Post-Acquisition			
		2013	2014	2015	2016	2019	2020	2021	2022
141	Dalmia Bharat Ltd	-0.7307	-0.5255	-0.7307	-0.3203	-0.6405	1.8701	1.7986	0.1570
142	Datamatics Global Services Ltd	-0.7642	-0.9295	-0.8807	0.4848	-0.3106	0.1717	2.5150	0.0000
143	Dilip Buildcon Ltd	-0.1539	-0.4642	-0.0144	0.3903	0.5414	0.1021	-2.4785	-0.0000
144	Deep Industries Ltd	0.1762	0.1762	0.1762	0.1762	0.1762	-1.5855	1.9378	0.1762
145	DEN Networks Ltd	0.5305	-0.3776	-1.8086	-0.6979	0.6876	1.3247	1.2151	0.0000
146	Deepak Fertilisers & Petrochemicals Corp Ltd	0.1090	-0.7997	-0.5454	-0.3450	-0.6982	0.9509	2.4151	-0.0000
147	Digicontent Ltd	0.0030	0.0030	0.0030	0.3070	-0.9692	-1.6040	2.2781	0.0030
148	Avenue Supermarts Ltd	-1.2875	-1.1780	-0.9417	-0.5964	1.1942	0.7552	1.6111	-
149	Donear Industries Ltd	-0.7109	-0.1818	-0.4596	-0.0040	0.3745	-2.0301	1.8026	-
150	Dr Reddy's Laboratories Ltd	0.6933	0.8463	0.3471	-1.4907	0.2284	0.1480	1.1665	0.0000
151	Synegra EMS Ltd	-1.6018	-1.3129	-0.2357	0.7295	0.9233	0.6304	-1.0007	-
152	ABM Knowledgeware Ltd	-1.0110	0.5657	1.3677	-1.0647	1.8672	-0.9164	-	-
153	Den Broadband Ltd	0.0188	0.1480	0.2500	0.4821	-2.6787	0.0725	-0.0186	0.0000
154	Eiko Lifesciences Ltd	-0.1392	0.5504	0.5631	0.5504	-2.5779	0.9928	-0.1392	-0.1392
155	Emami Realty Ltd	0.4163	0.6627	-0.1989	0.6798	-2.6804	0.0542	0.8072	-
156	Eurofins Scientific SE	-0.8424	-0.8119	-0.7757	-0.3938	-0.3004	1.2160	2.2875	-
157	Eris Lifesciences Ltd	-1.5382	-1.3731	-0.9760	0.0378	0.4830	1.0081	1.4647	-
158	ESAB India Ltd	0.5858	-1.4065	-0.8046	-0.8723	1.1668	0.6121	1.7573	-
159	Max Estates Gurgaon Ltd	0.2475	0.1403	2.2608	-0.4521	-1.2359	-1.4138	0.2211	-
160	Nihilent Ltd	-0.7653	-0.2999	-1.5780	-0.7270	0.8686	1.0568	1.7401	-
161	Fermenta Biotech Ltd	-0.5738	-0.7687	-0.8107	-1.0811	0.7834	0.4150	-0.3749	-
162	Flomic Global Logistics Ltd	-0.8697	-0.8660	-0.8623	2.5981	-0.0000	-0.0000	-0.0000	-0.0000
163	Fortis Healthcare Ltd	0.3889	-0.2370	0.1441	1.0920	0.2370	-0.1572	1.4057	-0.0000
164	Future Retail Ltd	-0.1256	0.5843	0.4208	0.5843	0.2779	-2.6658	-0.1256	-0.1256
165	Atul Finserve Ltd	-0.2369	-0.2369	-0.2369	-0.2369	1.0866	0.5311	-2.3285	-0.2369
166	Future Supply Chain Solutions Ltd	-0.1744	-0.1744	0.6632	0.7317	0.5033	-0.2855	-2.5531	-0.1744
167	Gallantt Ispat Ltd/Old	1.6148	2.0153	-0.7895	-0.7466	-0.7248	-0.4025	-0.1336	-0.0000
168	Garnet International Ltd	0.3074	0.3476	0.3267	0.7884	-0.2705	0.0983	0.2013	-
169	GBL Industries Ltd	-0.4636	-0.5963	-0.3310	0.3585	-1.8165	0.0515	0.0515	0.0515
170	Godrej Consumer Products Ltd	-1.3383	-1.0393	-1.2006	-0.2340	0.1565	0.6114	0.7383	0.0000
171	Goodricke Group Ltd	0.6647	-0.1790	1.9513	0.6477	-0.6281	-0.3847	-1.4664	-
172	Genesis IBRC India Ltd	-1.0488	-1.5886	2.2001	0.5473	0.0409	-0.0158	-0.0178	-0.0000
173	Gillanders Arbuthnot & Co Ltd	0.1236	-2.4335	0.5014	0.1406	-0.2476	1.5110	-0.0000	-0.0000
174	Gloster Ltd	0.0804	0.0804	0.0804	0.2201	-1.9470	-0.0346	2.0832	0.0804
175	JK Investors Bombay Ltd	-0.8159	-0.7435	-0.6292	-0.4675	0.3005	0.6067	2.4544	-
176	Grandeur Products Ltd	-0.1739	0.4803	-0.8282	1.9210	0.0193	0.0193	0.0193	0.0193
177	Grasim Industries Ltd	-0.7223	-0.9084	-0.4970	-0.0999	0.6069	0.5462	2.3892	-
178	Greenpanel Industries Ltd	0.1820	0.1820	0.1820	-0.6131	-1.0725	-0.0861	2.4996	0.1820
179	Greatship India Ltd	1.1049	1.2835	1.3065	0.0660	-0.6716	-0.8947	-	-
180	Gajanan Securities Services Ltd	-0.7482	-0.8753	-0.6211	-0.5010	-0.8969	1.6028	1.5259	0.0831
181	GTPL Hathway Ltd	-0.7543	-0.8746	-0.6340	-0.7192	-0.5494	0.2328	1.6993	1.8529
182	Gujarat State Petronet Ltd	-1.0336	-0.8999	-0.9399	-0.8004	1.4442	1.2968	1.2836	0.0000
183	Happiest Minds Technologies Ltd	0.2637	0.2637	-1.1824	-0.9271	0.1285	1.3917	1.6525	0.2637
184	Harish Textile Engineers Ltd	-0.0551	-0.0551	-0.0551	-0.4092	2.1091	-1.8652	-0.0551	-0.0551
185	Hester Biosciences Ltd	-1.5722	-1.1766	-0.6716	-0.2987	0.4859	0.8133	1.2804	0.0000
186	HCL Technologies Ltd	-1.7853	-0.9762	-0.6387	-0.2318	0.6748	1.1939	1.5443	-0.0000
187	Hemisphere Properties India Ltd	-0.1762	-0.1762	-0.1762	-0.1762	-0.1762	1.5855	-1.9378	-0.1762
188	Hindustan Foods Ltd	-1.0058	-0.7092	-0.7752	-0.7813	0.4991	1.4544	1.9155	0.0000
189	Hindware Home Innovation Ltd	0.2385	0.2385	0.2385	0.2385	-1.1061	-0.4975	2.3191	0.2385
190	HFCL Ltd	2.2154	0.7307	-0.9148	-1.2431	-0.2184	-0.1029	0.6252	-
191	Hindustan Media Ventures Ltd	-0.3561	0.2699	1.0694	1.2971	-1.2379	-1.8469	-	-
192	Himatsingka Seide Ltd	-0.5348	-0.1440	0.2192	0.9115	-1.1448	-1.9559	0.4087	-
193	Hi-Tech Gears Ltd/The	-1.2938	-0.0205	0.1999	0.1177	-0.8341	0.8115	-1.5865	0.0000
194	HT Media Ltd	0.7936	0.6156	0.5749	0.5542	-1.9365	-0.9940	-0.4248	-
195	Huhtamaki India Ltd	-0.3174	-0.0919	0.1323	0.3106	-2.0294	-	-	-
196	FIITJEE Ltd	-0.1779	0.0294	-0.3260	-0.3245	-0.4315	1.0846	2.2410	-
197	IFB Industries Ltd	-0.4842	0.2876	-0.2165	0.3847	-0.3248	0.6821	-2.3983	-0.0000
198	Sintex Prefab & Infra Ltd	-1.6202	-1.6202	0.1332	0.8214	0.0000	0.0000	0.0000	0.0000
199	360 ONE WAM Ltd	-0.6034	-1.7417	0.5348	-0.9303	0.0670	0.0670	0.0670	0.0670
200	IL&FS Investment Managers Ltd	1.5016	1.5181	1.0008	-0.5244	-1.1347	-0.4714	-0.4736	0.0000
201	Imagicaaworld Entertainment Ltd	1.0984	1.1326	0.9899	0.6121	-0.5032	-0.2593	-	-

S.No.	Company Name	Pre-Acquisition				Post-Acquisition			
		2013	2014	2015	2016	2019	2020	2021	2022
202	India Motor Parts and Accessories Ltd	-0.8648	-0.7380	-1.1098	-0.6320	0.8751	1.1665	1.8505	-
203	Inditrade Capital Ltd	-2.4000	0.5957	0.6717	-0.3051	0.4111	-0.2272	-0.3868	-0.0000
204	India Grid Trust	0.2212	0.2212	-0.7482	-1.0216	2.1133	0.4468	0.5893	0.2212
205	India Finsec Ltd	-0.8120	-1.4125	-0.2114	-0.6167	1.0018	2.2012	0.0902	0.0902
206	Infosys Ltd	-1.4909	-0.9838	-0.6332	-0.3732	0.3029	1.1347	1.9670	-0.0000
207	Info Edge India Ltd	-0.4083	-0.4250	-0.3967	-0.4371	-0.4914	-0.0715	2.8089	-
208	Scott Edil Pharmacia Ltd	0.6795	0.8636	0.6795	1.0477	-0.6517	-1.6837	-1.5902	-0.1929
209	Infronics Systems Ltd	0.3771	-2.5564	0.5756	0.4947	0.5958	0.6773	-	-
210	Indian Oil Corp Ltd	-0.8571	-1.1130	-0.2758	0.6458	-1.7965	0.8564	1.2642	-
211	Ipca Laboratories Ltd	-0.0096	-0.6978	-1.1921	-0.8810	0.3824	2.0199	1.2346	-0.0000
212	ICICI Prudential Life Insurance Co Ltd	0.6485	0.8819	0.9184	1.0039	-0.8120	-1.1394	-1.7212	-
213	IRB Infrastructure Developers Ltd	-0.5575	-0.2043	0.1874	0.5232	0.5459	-1.9992	-0.9695	-0.0000
214	IRB InvIT Fund	-0.0364	-0.0364	0.3886	-0.0976	-1.2871	-1.0587	2.3593	-0.0364
215	Raymond Apparel Ltd	-1.2509	0.6407	-1.0304	-1.1821	0.1569	0.7772	1.6629	0.0000
216	Bharti Hexacom Ltd	0.9306	-1.6449	0.0581	-0.3952	-1.2040	1.3645	0.9679	-
217	Jaykay Enterprises Ltd	-0.4157	-0.3845	-0.3612	-0.3802	2.7933	-0.4564	-	-
218	Jiya Eco-Products Ltd	-0.8659	-0.5609	-0.4417	-0.0968	-1.2760	-	-	-
219	Jindal Worldwide Ltd	-0.8647	-0.8168	-0.2893	0.7225	-0.7463	-0.1377	2.3992	-
220	Josts Engineering Co Ltd	0.8263	-0.2550	-1.5081	-1.6476	-0.2540	1.3462	-	-
221	Jaiprakash Associates Ltd	0.5138	0.1577	-0.3179	-2.5694	1.2651	0.5776	0.2582	-
222	Jindal Saw Ltd	-1.1583	-0.9160	-1.0036	-0.4787	1.0248	0.2204	0.5372	-0.0000
223	JSW Energy Ltd	-0.4180	0.8355	1.0418	-0.6830	0.3095	-0.3322	1.6346	-
224	Jayshree Chemicals Ltd	-1.1433	-1.9755	1.8468	0.3476	0.2198	0.2784	0.2702	-
225	Kalyan Jewellers India Ltd	-0.5155	-0.2971	-0.5155	-0.0788	0.8627	-1.2231	1.9972	0.1016
226	KDDL Ltd	-1.4466	-2.1269	0.3417	0.2603	0.1918	0.3508	1.0176	-
227	Khemani Distributors & Marketing Ltd	-0.5186	0.8494	-0.5283	0.3518	-2.2177	1.5386	0.5635	0.0000
228	Karma Energy Ltd	1.0289	-0.2758	0.1690	1.1205	0.6491	-2.3937	0.0054	-0.0000
229	Kajaria Ceramics Ltd	-1.7463	-0.9901	-0.1699	0.1466	0.1833	0.9592	1.9736	-
230	Anup Engineering Ltd/The	-1.2703	-1.0850	-0.9530	-0.4798	0.6867	1.1327	1.8031	-
231	Kirloskar Oil Engines Ltd	0.1326	-1.4480	-0.4507	-0.0715	0.4339	0.8716	-0.0433	-
232	KPIT Technologies Ltd	0.2490	0.2490	0.2490	-1.3685	0.1220	0.0990	2.1433	0.2490
233	Kalpataru Power Transmission Ltd	-1.0300	-1.0396	-1.0541	-0.6982	0.3508	1.8042	1.1292	-0.0000
234	Kridhan Infra Ltd	0.6032	0.5355	0.4806	0.9634	0.2015	0.2184	-2.1957	-
235	Kesoram Industries Ltd	-1.1782	-0.5680	1.4968	-0.0574	0.1663	1.5091	0.6179	-
236	Kemistar Corp Ltd	-1.5110	-1.2218	-0.6976	-0.1455	1.7098	-0.0000	-0.0000	-0.0000
237	Kothari Products Ltd	0.2444	0.4797	0.5613	0.5084	-0.3517	-2.2629	-0.7728	-0.0000
238	Kothari Petrochemicals	-1.0585	-0.5130	-0.8365	-0.8318	-0.0000	-0.0000	-0.0000	-0.0000
239	Life Insurance Corp of India	0.1583	0.1583	0.1583	-0.1947	-1.9490	1.4888	1.2882	0.1583
240	Dishnet Wireless Ltd	0.0957	-0.4679	-0.2502	0.0365	2.0954	-1.1477	-1.5024	0.0000
241	Larsen & Toubro Ltd	-1.0220	-1.0796	-1.3030	-0.5435	0.9298	1.7841	0.5603	0.0000
242	Lloyds Metals & Energy Ltd	-1.4197	-0.5539	-0.0597	0.3075	-0.0000	-0.0000	-0.0000	-0.0000
243	Mahesh Developers Ltd	-0.2802	0.0737	1.4808	-2.3564	-0.0000	-0.0000	-0.0000	-0.0000
244	Maithan Alloys Ltd	-1.0077	-0.8243	-0.7076	-0.2588	-0.0704	-0.0311	2.5822	0.0000
245	Asianet Communications Ltd	1.1531	1.9388	0.3827	-0.0197	-0.4418	-0.2666	-0.3070	-0.0000
246	CE Info Systems Ltd	0.2147	0.2147	0.2147	-0.7192	-1.2778	0.6953	2.1605	0.2147
247	Matrimony.com Ltd	-0.7345	-0.5866	-2.2992	0.5029	0.1841	0.4509	0.7552	-0.0000
248	McNally Bharat Engineering Co Ltd	0.7682	0.7729	-0.3241	0.8455	-0.5325	0.8967	0.6128	-0.0000
249	Kosmo One Business Park Ltd	-0.6248	-0.6804	-0.5693	-0.6804	-0.0486	0.0660	2.7042	0.0694
250	Megri Soft Ltd	1.7237	0.4535	1.7237	-0.8167	-0.8275	-0.4418	0.0086	-0.2722
251	Midas Infra Trade Ltd	-0.2806	0.3266	-0.2106	-0.4098	0.1791	-2.2324	0.0000	0.0000
252	Mahindra Lifespace Developers Ltd	0.2074	1.5308	0.1471	0.2202	-2.1431	-1.1705	0.6379	-
253	Mahindra & Mahindra Ltd	0.3073	-0.3967	-0.3916	-0.1386	-1.7822	-1.0065	1.1866	-
254	MM Forgings Ltd	-0.2308	1.0787	-1.5712	-1.2278	-0.0000	-0.0000	-0.0000	-0.0000
255	Mega Nirman and Industries Ltd	-0.9350	-0.9033	-0.9667	-0.8054	0.1039	0.1039	0.1039	0.1039
256	Marathon Nextgen Realty Ltd	1.0010	-0.3378	1.2892	1.6750	-0.9686	-1.3599	-0.3330	-
257	Moschip Technologies Ltd	0.2021	0.5467	0.0592	0.9352	-2.2169	0.2454	1.2876	-0.0000
258	Marico Ltd	-1.5686	-1.2180	-0.6686	-0.3218	0.5635	1.1646	1.3756	0.0000
259	Majestic Research Services and Solutions Ltd	-0.1169	-0.0766	0.0655	0.3530	-0.0256	-2.4878	-	-
260	Mirza International Ltd	-0.5953	-0.3108	0.6726	0.4407	-0.4386	-1.9095	1.8539	-0.0000
261	HCL Comnet Ltd	0.0451	-0.2888	-0.0719	-0.2888	-1.5125	1.3443	1.7977	0.0451
262	Belrise Industries Ltd	0.2039	0.2039	0.2039	0.2039	-1.6615	1.7223	0.5510	0.2039

S.No.	Company Name	Pre-Acquisition				Post-Acquisition			
		2013	2014	2015	2016	2019	2020	2021	2022
263	Adani Ports & Special Economic Zone Ltd	-1.0050	-1.0926	-0.9774	-0.6681	0.8883	1.4231	1.5935	-
264	Mawana Sugars Ltd	-1.1447	-0.8872	-0.1439	2.5255	-0.6379	0.2839	0.0058	-
265	Mayur Leather Products Ltd	1.5547	1.1438	0.9830	-0.9823	-0.7727	-0.0999	0.4131	-
266	Nazara Technologies Ltd	-0.8819	-0.0114	-0.8819	0.8592	2.1373	0.1117	0.1117	0.1117
267	NBCC India Ltd	-0.1503	0.0907	0.2182	0.9753	-2.2245	-0.5629	-0.5338	-0.0000
268	Satchmo Holdings Ltd	0.8878	0.8739	0.5136	0.1829	-2.5875	-0.1217	0.5493	-
269	Nettlinx Ltd	-1.0971	-1.0688	0.2859	0.9004	0.3367	-1.4644	1.1204	-0.0000
270	Nila Spaces Ltd	-0.1377	-0.1377	0.2955	0.8058	0.7444	-2.2964	-0.7479	-0.1377
271	Nila Infrastructures Ltd	0.0012	0.0167	0.2871	0.4001	0.6144	-1.6499	-1.8257	-
272	Natco Pharma Ltd	-1.2174	-1.0699	-0.9659	0.5558	0.4393	0.3472	-0.9062	-
273	Orient Beverages Ltd	0.4259	0.0617	0.5555	0.0917	0.1375	-2.7550	0.2738	-
274	Orient Bell Ltd	-0.9347	-0.7138	-0.5803	-0.0063	-0.5260	-0.4809	1.4891	-
275	Oracle Financial Services Software Ltd	-0.1225	-0.7619	-1.3110	-0.7884	0.2715	1.4187	1.9049	-0.0000
276	Onesource Ideas Venture Ltd	0.1298	0.3435	0.3472	0.3516	0.1151	0.3731	0.3670	-0.0000
277	Om Infra Ltd	0.9817	0.5289	0.6216	-1.0488	-0.8242	-1.4805	0.3388	0.0000
278	Oil & Natural Gas Corp Ltd	0.3466	-0.4720	-1.0187	0.1375	-1.2262	-0.6753	2.2512	-
279	Oriental Rail Infrastructure Ltd	-1.3867	-1.0153	-0.9891	-0.3719	1.9564	0.7072	0.7306	-
280	Padmanabh Industries Ltd	0.6820	0.6620	0.6764	0.7740	-2.2874	0.0481	-0.0000	-0.0000
281	Palco Metals Ltd	1.1475	0.1962	2.0987	-1.5669	-0.5047	-0.4705	-0.3989	-0.1275
282	Parsvnath Developers Ltd	1.5639	0.8403	1.1809	0.5997	-0.6523	-1.0272	-1.4061	-
283	Parvati Sweetners & Power Ltd	-0.2417	-0.2417	1.6922	0.2417	-1.2087	-0.2417	-0.2417	-0.2417
284	Paul Merchants Ltd	-0.5461	-0.4827	-0.6096	2.7652	-0.2628	-0.1498	0.0607	0.0607
285	One 97 Communications Ltd	-1.0191	-2.0538	0.0155	1.7822	0.1132	0.1132	0.1132	0.1132
286	Shree Pushkar Chemicals & Fertilisers Ltd	-1.6431	-0.9836	-0.6926	-0.0602	0.3784	-0.1943	1.9619	-0.0000
287	Pervasive Commodities Ltd	-0.8661	-1.7998	-1.3971	1.0474	0.6205	0.6661	0.2812	-
288	Peninsula Land Ltd	1.1479	0.9125	0.7350	-0.0609	-1.1686	0.8084	0.4388	-
289	Prestige Estates Projects Ltd	-0.5532	-0.5296	-0.1676	-0.6177	-0.4373	2.6678	0.5375	-
290	Phoenix Mills Ltd/The	-0.4960	-1.2508	-0.8766	-0.1759	1.1773	-1.0707	0.3874	-
291	Pidilite Industries Ltd	-1.7438	-1.4925	-0.3302	-0.1013	0.9255	0.9847	1.2905	-
292	Pacheli Industrial Finance Ltd	0.1969	-2.3536	0.5915	0.6046	0.3874	0.8602	-1.1487	-
293	Pil Italica Lifestyle Ltd	1.9993	-0.6879	-1.0148	0.8125	-0.9314	-0.3235	-0.5727	-
294	Panacea Biotec Ltd	-0.4208	-0.4056	-0.1679	-0.2923	-0.6422	-0.5166	2.7858	-
295	Prakash Pipes Ltd	0.2588	0.2588	0.2588	0.2588	-1.4671	0.2614	1.9820	0.2588
296	Praxis Home Retail Ltd	-0.1734	-0.1734	0.8654	0.5220	-1.3022	-1.9211	1.3120	-0.1734
297	Precision Camshafts Ltd	-0.4767	0.3766	1.2416	1.3600	-0.1818	-1.7743	0.3576	-
298	Pricol Ltd	0.8638	-0.1744	0.3537	0.4661	-1.0633	0.9235	1.1156	-
299	Prime Urban Development India Ltd	-0.0368	0.2909	1.8204	1.2348	-0.7434	-0.1605	-0.2606	-
300	Power Grid Corp of India Ltd	-1.2068	-1.0722	-0.8259	-0.4231	0.5512	0.8149	2.1075	-
301	Ravinder Heights Ltd	0.1762	0.1762	0.1762	0.1762	0.1762	-1.5855	1.9378	0.1762
302	AGI Greenpac Ltd	-0.9844	-0.5896	-0.2955	0.2365	0.4204	0.5214	-1.8766	-
303	Reliance Capital Ltd	0.7955	0.8616	0.8876	0.8837	0.2895	-1.8134	-1.5088	-
304	Reliance Communications Ltd	0.7606	0.7365	0.7311	0.5832	-2.4044	0.2655	0.2055	-
305	Rane Holdings Ltd	-0.2446	0.2313	0.1379	1.3117	-1.0434	-1.8714	-0.5786	-0.0000
306	Rain Industries Ltd	-0.2941	-1.8561	-0.6170	-0.7879	-0.2579	0.6223	0.7383	-0.0000
307	Rajapalayam Mills Ltd	-1.1775	-1.4581	-1.2091	1.1110	0.0860	0.2619	1.5236	-
308	Royal Orchid Hotels Ltd	-1.7539	-0.0329	0.0985	-0.0121	0.4165	-1.4971	1.6680	0.0000
309	Raymond Ltd	0.1301	0.1646	-0.0219	-0.4165	0.7191	-2.5635	1.1466	-
310	Saksoft Ltd	-0.9760	-0.8639	-0.7519	-0.8391	0.5184	0.9631	2.0959	0.0000
311	Samvardhana Motherson International Ltd/IN	-0.8308	-0.6069	-0.2569	0.3225	-1.1982	0.0000	0.0000	0.0000
312	Sat Industries Ltd	-0.6371	-1.7651	-0.6552	0.9397	-0.3342	0.0961	1.9673	-0.0000
313	Aegis Logistics Ltd	0.0819	0.3224	-0.0843	-1.1061	0.5588	0.7837	1.8895	0.0000
314	Sembcorp Industries Ltd	1.0053	0.9669	0.4664	0.1609	-0.1326	-2.6010	-0.0691	-0.0000
315	SEAMEC Ltd	-0.5235	0.9642	-0.4341	-2.2836	1.0989	0.6831	0.4990	0.0000
316	Steel Exchange India Ltd	0.3190	0.2471	0.0413	-1.5659	0.5971	1.3363	1.1068	-
317	Setubandhan Infrastructure Ltd	0.8339	0.2913	0.5691	0.7564	-2.2137	-1.3191	-0.0152	-0.0000
318	Aksh Optifibre Ltd	-0.0933	-0.0933	-0.0603	0.8065	0.3366	-2.3226	-0.0933	-0.0933
319	Sagar Cements Ltd	-0.9753	2.2987	-0.2656	-0.7552	-0.4440	1.1799	-0.0128	-
320	Smartlink Holdings Ltd	-0.3069	1.3977	0.4083	-1.1722	-1.6502	1.0798	1.0815	-
321	SH Kelkar & Co Ltd	-0.4160	-0.6730	-0.5949	0.3436	-1.6993	1.5221	1.6365	-
322	Ashok Leyland Ltd	-0.8882	-1.3697	-1.1429	-1.0231	0.7984	0.7788	1.1036	0.0000
323	Sical Logistics Ltd	0.4476	0.4662	0.4719	0.5288	0.1300	-2.7382	-0.2879	-

S.No.	Company Name	Pre-Acquisition				Post-Acquisition			
		2013	2014	2015	2016	2019	2020	2021	2022
324	Shristi Infrastructure Development Corp Ltd	0.6590	0.6567	0.6511	0.6456	-0.4926	-0.6499	-2.4670	-
325	Singer India Ltd	2.5122	-0.7628	-0.9879	-0.2699	0.1338	-0.3123	0.6672	-0.4893
326	Alkem Laboratories Ltd	-0.7027	-0.6473	-0.8097	-0.6096	0.6894	1.3351	1.7908	-
327	Sobha Ltd	0.5354	0.5758	-0.5788	-0.4769	1.1707	-1.8188	-1.0747	0.0000
328	Span Divergent Ltd	-0.2845	2.6851	0.3453	-0.1280	-0.3811	-0.2379	-0.5143	-0.0000
329	Srei Infrastructure Finance Ltd	0.4385	0.4351	0.4113	0.4816	0.4180	-2.6398	-0.6663	-
330	SRF Ltd	-1.1176	-0.8439	-0.5960	-0.4301	0.5531	0.9019	2.2496	-
331	SRS Ltd	0.8588	0.8543	0.3205	-2.6542	-0.0000	-0.0000	-0.0000	-0.0000
332	TVS Srichakra Ltd	-1.0576	-0.0398	2.0054	1.0947	-0.4486	-0.6477	-1.3676	-
333	Saraswati Commercial India Ltd	-0.6482	-0.3173	0.0310	-0.3930	-1.1234	0.4000	2.5465	0.0000
334	Sonata Software Ltd	-1.5364	-0.8729	-0.5776	-0.6047	0.8264	0.4352	2.0068	0.0000
335	S&S Power Switchgear Ltd	0.6818	0.4567	1.2090	0.2856	-1.8440	0.0833	-1.6636	-
336	Stride Gaming plc	0.8253	0.7739	0.8253	0.7225	-0.1999	-0.1999	-0.1999	-0.1999
337	Systematix Corporate Services	-0.2594	-0.5999	0.1962	0.5963	-0.2365	2.4193	-	-
338	Sunil Hitech Engineers Ltd	-0.2848	1.1648	1.1714	0.4036	-0.0000	-0.0000	-0.0000	-0.0000
339	Sun Pharmaceutical Industries Ltd	-0.4569	0.5659	0.5705	2.3401	-0.0007	-0.6308	-0.3609	-
340	Seven Hill Industries Ltd	0.2043	0.2054	0.1794	0.2013	-1.0556	-0.5079	2.2217	0.0000
341	Swan Energy Ltd	0.2339	0.3303	0.2406	0.2629	0.0821	-0.8215	-2.2037	0.0000
342	Surya Roshni Ltd	-1.0935	-1.0783	-0.9115	-0.4044	-0.0639	1.1033	2.0789	-0.0000
343	Talwalkars Better Value Fitness Ltd	0.5561	1.1723	1.7534	-1.4227	0.0000	0.0000	0.0000	0.0000
344	Tata Steel Ltd	-0.3069	-0.8914	-0.6160	-0.9159	-0.4653	-0.0042	2.5344	0.0000
345	TeamLease Services Ltd	-1.2526	-0.7547	-0.9852	0.2770	-0.5933	1.0447	-0.4603	0.0000
346	Tube Investments of India Ltd	0.1695	-0.6502	-0.7055	-0.6502	0.1077	-0.0622	2.6346	0.1695
347	Thermax Ltd	-0.0932	-0.9368	0.7518	-0.6284	-0.8743	-1.0111	1.4514	-0.0000
348	Ramco Cements Ltd/The	-1.9003	-1.3206	-0.0028	0.5149	0.2567	1.0476	1.4786	0.0000
349	Trejhara Solutions Ltd	-0.0752	-0.0752	-0.0752	1.1815	-2.3407	0.3966	0.4617	-0.0752
350	Trent Ltd	-0.9141	0.8647	-0.0300	0.3298	0.7860	-2.4492	0.5821	-0.0000
351	Torrent Pharmaceuticals Ltd	-0.6952	-0.4558	2.2461	0.0465	0.2973	0.9221	-0.3836	-0.0000
352	Tata Chemicals Ltd	-1.1841	-0.4204	-0.3388	-0.2344	2.5853	-0.5799	-0.1104	-0.0000
353	TVS Motor Co Ltd	-1.9621	-1.1563	-0.5836	-0.1176	0.5259	0.3536	1.2764	-
354	Universal Autofoundry Ltd	0.0601	0.1088	0.0114	0.3608	-1.6175	0.0666	-1.5684	-0.0067
355	Uniply Decor Ltd	0.5234	0.7537	0.0552	-0.5234	-0.0000	-0.0000	-0.0000	-0.0000
356	UFO Moviez India Ltd	0.2406	0.4505	0.6723	0.6276	0.2985	-2.0684	-1.6030	0.0000
357	Ugro Capital Ltd	-0.5581	-0.7882	-0.6440	-0.7547	1.1560	2.1589	0.6150	-0.0000
358	Umiya Tubes Ltd	-0.9038	-0.8778	-0.8158	2.5975	-	-	-	-
359	UNO Minda Ltd	-1.6270	-1.0707	-0.6758	-0.1813	-0.2727	0.1981	1.5630	-0.0000
360	UPL Ltd	-1.0449	-0.8165	-1.0564	-0.1311	-0.0735	1.2138	2.1015	-
361	Varroc Engineering Ltd	0.1222	0.7781	0.6451	0.9402	-1.2281	-2.1858	-	-
362	Varun Beverages Ltd	-1.1887	-1.1040	-0.5215	-0.8305	1.0349	0.4228	2.0192	-0.0000
363	Vibrant Global Capital Ltd	-0.2068	-0.1221	-0.2568	-0.1977	-1.4359	1.4213	1.9684	0.0000
364	Vikas Lifecare Ltd	0.1762	0.1762	0.1762	0.1762	0.1762	-1.5855	1.9378	0.1762
365	Visco Trade Associates Ltd	0.3396	0.3581	0.3396	0.3765	-2.6540	0.9002	0.4277	-0.0872
366	Hemisphere Properties India Ltd	2.7712	0.0218	-0.5353	-0.5743	-0.3393	-0.2942	-0.2078	-0.0000
367	Vidhi Specialty Food Ingredients Ltd	-0.9586	-1.0370	-0.8801	-0.8114	0.6599	2.2073	0.1065	0.1065
368	Vardhman Textiles Ltd	-0.0334	-0.9889	-0.3450	0.7567	-0.4564	-0.9464	2.4550	-0.0000
369	Vinayak Vanijya Ltd	-0.4215	-0.7742	1.2080	-1.1696	1.1071	-1.6097	0.7925	-0.0000
370	Waaree Renewable Technologies Ltd	-0.3881	-0.3946	-0.3929	-0.4126	-0.4368	-0.0384	2.8102	-0.0000
371	Natco Economicals Ltd	2.4502	-0.5273	-0.6615	-1.0912	-0.9035	-	-	-
372	White Organic Agro Ltd	-0.7315	-0.7308	-0.6899	-0.4046	-0.7141	-0.7110	1.5553	-
373	Williamson Magor & Co Ltd	0.1146	0.2034	0.8730	-2.5245	-	-	-	-
374	Windsor Machines Ltd	1.5910	-0.8974	-0.1926	0.6733	-1.5799	0.7944	-0.3258	-0.0000
375	WPIL Ltd	-0.5146	-0.8030	-1.2327	-1.0829	0.1246	0.8122	1.1354	0.0000
376	Yaari Digital Integrated Services Ltd	0.8201	0.5959	0.5009	0.2503	-2.1936	-0.4034	-1.1293	-
377	Spencer's Retail Ltd	0.3307	0.3947	0.4830	0.6174	-2.6628	-0.5155	0.2399	-
378	Vineet Laboratories Ltd	0.4615	0.5434	0.3795	-2.3389	0.6030	0.4036	0.8097	-0.0513
379	Zee Entertainment Enterprises Ltd	-0.5021	-0.3284	-0.6421	2.2002	-1.2453	-0.6891	-0.3547	-0.0000
380	Zee Media Corp Ltd	0.6094	-0.0755	0.3394	0.2060	-2.4196	1.2027	-0.8176	-0.0000
381	Zensar Technologies Ltd	-0.8786	-0.3734	0.0924	-0.9281	-0.3953	0.2879	2.4578	-
382	Zee Learn Ltd	-0.9521	-0.5142	-0.3222	0.3599	0.7365	-1.2057	-0.9812	-
383	Zomato Ltd	-0.0104	-0.0104	-0.0104	0.8392	-2.3518	1.1861	0.2850	-0.0104
384	Zuari Agro Chemicals Ltd	0.3212	0.5200	0.0561	0.4045	-2.5095	-0.1002	0.9736	-

S.No.	Company Name	Pre-Acquisition				Post-Acquisition			
		2013	2014	2015	2016	2019	2020	2021	2022
385	Zydus Lifesciences Ltd	-1.0500	-0.7092	0.0669	-0.3740	-0.6814	0.2642	2.5900	-

Source: *Compiled by Author*

The net income of the businesses before and after the acquisition is presented in Table 4.3.54. The net income of a corporation is defined as the aggregate revenue generated by the organisation, less all expenses and taxes. The provided data serves to depict the financial performance of the company. The aforementioned table delineates a time period ranging from 2013 to 2016, denoted as the pre-acquisition period, while the years 2019 to 2022 are marked as the post-acquisition period. The succeeding year has shown an improvement in the net income of enterprises, as evidenced by Sonata Software Ltd, which experienced growth in its net income following its acquisition. Nevertheless, several firms, such as Varroc Engineering Ltd, have seen a decrease in their net income subsequent to an acquisition. Therefore, it may be inferred that acquisitions are advantageous for the majority of firms, as evidenced by the subsequent enhancement of their net income.

Table 4.3.55 -Comparison of Pre- and Post-Merger and Acquisition

Variable	Merger		Acquisition	
	Pre	**Post**	**Pre**	**Post**
Objective 3: Financial Performance				
Earnings Before Interest, Taxes, Depreciation and Amortisation	0.579***	0.627***	0.590***	0.605***
Earnings Before Interest and Taxes	0.541***	0.771***	0.581***	0.747***
Return on Assets	0.512***	0.834***	0.671***	0.854***
Return on Capital	0.494***	0.840***	0.549***	0.788***
Return on Capital Employed	0.207***	0.451***	0.345***	0.577***
Financial Leverage	-0.127***	-0.194***	-0.173***	-0.174***
Degree of Financial Leverage	-0.113**	-0.047	-0.121***	-0.184***

Variable	Merger		Acquisition	
	Pre	Post	Pre	Post
Degree of Operating Leverage	0.064	0.113	0.137***	0.281
Cash Flow from Net Income	1.055***	0.870***	1.033***	0.856

Note: *p<0.1, **p<0.05, ***p<0.01

Table 4.3.55 presents the effects of various financial indicators, including earnings before interest, taxes, depreciation and amortisation (EBITDA), earnings before interest and taxes (EBIT), return on assets (ROA), return on capital (ROC), return on capital employed (ROCE), financial leverage, degree of financial leverage, degree of operating leverage, and cash flow from net income, on the financial performance of companies both prior to and following a merger or acquisition. The financial performance of the firms has shown improvement following the merger and acquisition, as evidenced by considerable increases in profits before interest, taxes, depreciation and amortisation (EBITDA), earnings before interest and taxes (EBIT), return on assets and capital, and the degree of operating leverage. Nevertheless, there has been a detrimental increase in financial leverage, and the cash flow derived from net income has seen a decline subsequent to the merger and acquisition. In summary, it can be inferred that the merger and acquisition of enterprises have resulted in an overall enhancement of their financial performance.

Table 4.3.56 -Regression Analysis of Financial Performance

Null Hypotheses	Description	Accept/Reject
$Ho_{3.1}$	There is no impact of EBITDA and EBIT on financial performance before the merger	Rejected
$Ho_{3.2}$	There is no impact of ROA and ROC on financial performance before the merger	Rejected
$Ho_{3.3}$	There is no impact of ROCE and FL on financial performance before the merger	Rejected

Null Hypotheses	Description	Accept/Reject
$Ho_{3.4}$	There is no impact of DFL and DOL on financial performance before the merger	Rejected
$Ho_{3.5}$	There is no impact of CFNI on financial performance before the merger	Rejected
$Ho_{3.6}$	There is no impact of EBITDA and EBIT on financial performance after the merger	Rejected
$Ho_{3.7}$	There is no impact of ROA and ROC on financial performance after the merger	Rejected
$Ho_{3.8}$	There is no impact of ROCE and FL on financial performance after the merger	Rejected
$Ho_{3.9}$	There is no impact of DFL and DOL on financial performance after the merger	Fail to reject
$Ho_{3.10}$	There is no impact of CFNI on financial performance after the merger	Rejected
$Ho_{3.11}$	There is no impact of EBITDA and EBIT on financial performance during the merger	Rejected
$Ho_{3.12}$	There is no impact of ROA and ROC on financial performance during the merger	Rejected
$Ho_{3.13}$	There is no impact of ROCE and FL on financial performance during the merger	Rejected
$Ho_{3.14}$	There is no impact of DFL and DOL on financial performance during the merger	Rejected
$Ho_{3.15}$	There is no impact of CFNI on financial performance during the merger	Rejected
$Ho_{3.16}$	There is no impact of EBITDA and EBIT on financial performance considering the overall merger	Rejected
$Ho_{3.17}$	There is no impact of ROA and ROC on financial performance considering the overall merger	Rejected
$Ho_{3.18}$	There is no impact of ROCE and FL on financial performance considering the overall merger	Rejected

Null Hypotheses	Description	Accept/Reject
$Ho_{3.19}$	There is no impact of DFL and DOL on financial performance considering the overall merger	Rejected
$Ho_{3.20}$	There is no impact of CFNI on financial performance considering the overall merger	Rejected
$Ho_{3.21}$	There is no impact of EBITDA and EBIT on financial performance before the acquisition	Rejected
$Ho_{3.22}$	There is no impact of ROA and ROC on financial performance before the acquisition	Rejected
$Ho_{3.23}$	There is no impact of ROCE and FL on financial performance before the acquisition	Rejected
$Ho_{3.24}$	There is no impact of DFL and DOL on financial performance before the acquisition	Rejected
$Ho_{3.25}$	There is no impact of CFNI on financial performance before the acquisition	Rejected
$Ho_{3.26}$	There is no impact of EBITDA and EBIT on financial performance after the acquisition	Rejected
$Ho_{3.27}$	There is no impact of ROA and ROC on financial performance after the acquisition	Rejected
$Ho_{3.28}$	There is no impact of ROCE and FL on financial performance after the acquisition	Rejected
$Ho_{3.29}$	There is no impact of DFL and DOL on financial performance after the acquisition	Rejected
$Ho_{3.30}$	There is no impact of CFNI on financial performance after the acquisition	Rejected
$Ho_{3.31}$	There is no impact of EBITDA and EBIT on financial performance during the acquisition	Rejected
$Ho_{3.32}$	There is no impact of ROA and ROC on financial performance during the acquisition	Rejected
$Ho_{3.33}$	There is no impact of ROCE and FL on financial performance during the acquisition	Rejected

Null Hypotheses	Description	Accept/Reject
$Ho_{3.34}$	There is no impact of DFL and DOL on financial performance during the acquisition	Rejected
$Ho_{3.35}$	There is no impact of CFNI on financial performance during the acquisition	Rejected
$Ho_{3.36}$	There is no impact of EBITDA and EBIT on financial performance considering overall acquisition	Rejected
$Ho_{3.37}$	There is no impact of ROA and ROC on financial performance considering overall acquisition	Rejected
$Ho_{3.38}$	There is no impact of ROCE and FL on financial performance considering overall acquisition	Rejected
$Ho_{3.39}$	There is no impact of DFL and DOL on financial performance considering overall acquisition	Rejected
$Ho_{3.40}$	There is no impact of CFNI on financial performance considering overall acquisition	Rejected

Source: *Compiled by Author from R output sheet*

Based on the analysis conducted, it can be inferred that the levels of financial leverage and operating leverage do not exert a substantial influence on operational efficiency after the merger. With the exception of this factor, all remaining variables exert a substantial influence on the operational efficiency of organizations following the merger. However, subsequent to the merger, these factors have demonstrated an enhancement in the financial performance of the firms, thus suggesting that the merger has been advantageous for the companies. In the case of an acquisition, all the variables have a significant impact on the financial performance of the companies before and after the acquisition. During the year of acquisition as well as in case of overall acquisition also all the variables has a significant impact on the financial performance of the companies. Hence, the acquisition and merger both has a significant positive impact on the financial performance of the company.

4.5 Regression results of the objective four

The purpose of this section is to list the many ways in which volatility presents itself in the sample companies as a result of M&A announcements. The goal is to figure out what might be the underlying causes of the sample companies' vulnerability to volatility and the risk that comes with it. The findings of the paired t-test to assess the mean variance pre and post-announcement of M &As are presented.

Table 4.4.1 -Descriptive Statistics of Value of the Firm - Merger

Statistic	N	Mean	St. Dev.	Min	Max
PR_MA_30D	252	1.791262	0.604803	0.161727	3.025278
PR_MA_20D	252	1.817435	0.626542	0.085398	3.103734
PR_MA_5D	252	1.860322	0.645685	-0.059683	3.11087
PR_RSI_30D	252	1.704325	0.133248	1.140904	1.938099
PR_LP	252	1.884129	0.649269	-0.102373	3.136882
PR_TA	252	1.010502	7.562736	-31.753437	96.103579
PO_MA_30D	252	2.23974	0.615467	-0.152859	3.569653
PO_MA_20D	252	2.238221	0.641965	-0.218245	3.668217
PO_MA_5D	252	2.241304	0.690844	-0.408935	3.811806
PO_RSI_30D	252	1.708213	0.092696	1.230094	1.891207
PO_LP	252	2.209592	0.721692	-0.60206	3.789256
PO_TA	252	-0.209835	12.641997	-185.973458	29.311674

Source: *Compiled by Author from R output sheet*

In the pre-merger and post-merger cases, Table 4.4.1 depicts the descriptive statistics of the dependent and independent variables used in this study. Before the merger, the moving average of 30 days, the moving average of 20 days, the moving average of 5 days, and the relative strength index of 30 days had respective means of 0.1791262, 1.817435, 1.860322, and 1.704325, which increased to 2.23974, 2.238221, 2.241304, and 1.708254 after the merger. Post-merger, the mean of only these variables has increased, indicating a positive impact on the stock price. Before the merger, the mean total assets were positive, but after the merger, they turned negative. Consequently, indicating a negative impact on the stock prices of the merged companies. The standard deviation defines risk; in this case, only the standard deviation of the 30-day relative strength index is reduced after the merger, whereas the standard deviation of all other variables is elevated after the merger. Further, in the next table the impact of the moving average of 30 and 20 days on the share price before the merger is analyzed.

Both random effect and fixed effect regression results are displayed in Table 4.4.2. The

Table 4.4.2 -Impact of Moving Averages on Value of the Firm Before Merger

	Dependent variable:			
	lp			
	(1)	(2)	(3)	(4)
ma_30d	1.046***	1.057***		
	(0.025)	(0.073)		
ma_20d			1.022***	0.990***
			(0.017)	(0.054)
Constant	−0.007		0.013	
	(0.047)		(0.032)	
Observations	197	197	198	198
R^2	0.904	0.592	0.950	0.699
Adjusted R^2	0.903	0.452	0.950	0.596
F Statistic	1,809.675***	211.436*** (df = 1; 146)	3,695.003***	341.093*** (df = 1; 147)
Note:				*p<0.1; **p<0.05; ***p<0.01

Source: *Compiled by Author from R output sheet*

values under (1) and (3) represent coefficients for random effect variables, while (2) and (4) represent coefficients for fixed effect variables. Before the merger, the coefficient of the 30-day moving average is 1.046 under random effect and 1.057 under fixed effect. This indicates that the change in the 30-day moving average under fixed effect will have a greater impact on the stock price of the company. However, the moving average of 20 days impacts at a higher rate under random effect as compared to fixed effect in pre-merger as the coefficient of moving average of 20 days is 1.022 under random effect and 0.990 under fixed effect. The coefficient values of the 30-day and 20-day moving averages have a significant effect at the 1% level. In this table, the impact of the moving average of 30 days and 20 days is discussed on the stock price before the merger. In the next table, the impact of the moving average of 5 days and the relative strength index of 30 days on stock price before the merger is examined.

Table 4.4.3 displays the findings of both random effect and fixed effect regression. The coefficients for random effect variables are represented by (1) and (3), whereas the coefficients for fixed effect variables are represented by (2) and (4). Prior to the merger, the 5-day moving average coefficient is 0.999 under random effect and 0.932 under fixed effect. This shows that a change in the 5-day moving average under the random effect will have a higher impact on the company's stock price. Similarly, the random

Table 4.4.3 -Impact of Moving Average and Relative Strength Index on Value of the Firm Before Merger

	Dependent variable:			
	lp			
	(1)	(2)	(3)	(4)
ma_5d	0.999***	0.932***		
	(0.008)	(0.021)		
rsi_30d			2.663***	2.610***
			(0.153)	(0.158)
Constant	0.015		−2.666***	
	(0.015)		(0.270)	
Observations	202	202	197	197
R^2	0.989	0.932	0.615	0.651
Adjusted R^2	0.989	0.908	0.613	0.531
F Statistic	17,290.180***	2,029.294*** (df = 1; 149)	302.605***	271.828*** (df = 1; 146)
Note:				*p<0.1; **p<0.05; ***p<0.01

Source: *Compiled by Author from R output sheet*

effect has a bigger impact on the relative strength index of 30 days, as the coefficient of the relative strength index of 30 days is 2.663 under random effect and 2.610 under fixed effect. At the 1% level, the coefficient values of the 5-day moving average and the relative strength index of 30 days have a substantial effect. Further, in the next table, the impact of total assets on the value of the firm is examined.

Table 4.4.4 -Impact of Total Assets on Value of the Firm Before Merger

	Dependent variable:	
	lp	
	(1)	(2)
ta	−0.001	−0.001
	(0.002)	(0.002)
Constant	1.908***	
	(0.084)	
Observations	206	206
R^2	0.082	0.001
Adjusted R^2	0.077	−0.365
F Statistic	0.262	0.147 (df = 1; 150)
Note:	*p<0.1; **p<0.05; ***p<0.01	

Source: *Compiled by Author from R output sheet*

The results of both random effect and fixed effect regression are shown in Table 4.4.4.

(1) represents the coefficients for random effect variables, while (2) represents the coefficients for fixed effect variables. Prior to the merger, the coefficient of total assets is 0.001 for both the random and fixed effects. According to both models, overall assets have a negative impact on the company's stock price prior to the merger. The coefficient values of total assets have no significant influence. In the next table, the regression results of all the variables are reported on the basis of the Hausman test.

Table 4.4.5 -Regression Results of Value of the Firm Before Merger

	Dependent variable:				
	lp				
	(1)	(2)	(3)	(4)	(5)
ma_30d	1.046***				
	(0.025)				
ma_20d		1.022***			
		(0.017)			
ma_5d			0.932***		
			(0.021)		
rsi_30d				2.663***	
				(0.153)	
ta					−0.001
					(0.002)
Constant	−0.007	0.013		−2.666***	1.908***
	(0.047)	(0.032)		(0.270)	(0.084)
Observations	197	198	202	197	206
R^2	0.904	0.950	0.932	0.615	0.082
Adjusted R^2	0.903	0.950	0.908	0.613	0.077
F Statistic	1,809.675***	3,695.003***	2,029.294*** (df = 1; 149)	302.605***	0.262
Note:					*p<0.1; **p<0.05; ***p<0.01

Source: *Compiled by Author from R output sheet*

On the basis of the results of the Hausman test, Table 4.4.5 displays the regression results that include either random or fixed effects. Specifically, fixed effects are employed if the p-value is less than 0.05, whereas random effects are employed if the p-value is greater than 0.05. In this table, the p-value of the moving average of 5 days coefficient is less than 0.05, so its value is fixed. However, the p-value of all other variables is greater than 0.05, so their random values are taken. Except for total assets, all other variables are statistically significant at 1%, before the merger. In the above tables, the impact of moving averages, relative strength index, and total assets on stock price is examined in pre-merger. Now, in the next table impact of moving averages on stock price after the merger is analyzed.

Table 4.4.6 presents the outcomes of both random effect and fixed effect regression analyses. The coefficients for random effect variables are represented by values (1) and

Table 4.4.6 -Impact of Moving Averages on Value of the Firm After Merger

	Dependent variable:			
	lp			
	(1)	(2)	(3)	(4)
ma_30d	1.112***	0.662***		
	(0.028)	(0.139)		
ma_20d			1.085***	0.893***
			(0.022)	(0.091)
Constant	−0.292***		−0.225***	
	(0.065)		(0.050)	
Observations	240	240	245	245
R^2	0.870	0.114	0.912	0.348
Adjusted R^2	0.869	−0.203	0.911	0.121
F Statistic	1,591.598***	22.697*** (df = 1; 176)	2,503.007***	96.601*** (df = 1; 181)
Note:				*p<0.1; **p<0.05; ***p<0.01

Source: *Compiled by Author from R output sheet*

(3), whereas values (2) and (4) correspond to the coefficients for fixed effect variables. Prior to the consolidation, the coefficient of the 30-day moving average was found to be 1.046 under the random effect model and 1.057 under the fixed effect model. Following the merger, it is observed that the coefficient of the 30-day moving average is 1.112 under random effect, while the coefficient of the 30-day moving average (ma_30d) under fixed effect is 0.662. This suggests that the rise in the 30-day moving average following a merger, when considering random effects, will exert a more significant influence on the post-merger stock price of the company. Under the fixed effect model, it is observed that the moving average of the stock price over a 30-day period is higher prior to the merger. This suggests a declining impact on the stock price following the merger.

The moving average coefficient for a 20-day period is 1.022 under the random effect model and 0.990 under the fixed effect model prior to the merger. Following the merger, the coefficient has increased to 1.085 under the random effect model and decreased to 0.893 under the fixed effect model. This finding indicates that the application of a random effect model demonstrates a significant impact of a 20-day moving average on the stock prices of companies following a merger, with a heightened level of influence.The coefficient values associated with the 30-day and 20-day moving averages exhibit a statistically significant impact at a significance level of 1% both prior to and subsequent to the merger. As in this table the impact of moving average of 30 days and 20 days on stock price after merger is examined. Similarly, in the next table the impact of moving average of 5 days and relative strength index of 30 days on stock price after merger is analyzed.

Table 4.4.7 -Impact of Moving Average and Relative Strength Index on Value of the Firm After Merger

	Dependent variable:			
	lp			
	(1)	(2)	(3)	(4)
ma_5d	1.037***	1.143***		
	(0.009)	(0.035)		
rsi_30d			3.339***	3.261***
			(0.153)	(0.152)
Constant	−0.118***		−3.482***	
	(0.022)		(0.271)	
Observations	250	250	239	239
R^2	0.980	0.853	0.679	0.724
Adjusted R^2	0.980	0.804	0.678	0.624
F Statistic	12,180.470***	1,081.538*** (df = 1; 186)	473.878***	458.169*** (df = 1; 175)
Note:				*p<0.1; **p<0.05; ***p<0.01

Source: *Compiled by Author from R output sheet*

Table 4.4.7 displays the findings of both random effect and fixed effect regression. The coefficients for random effect variables are represented by (1) and (3), whereas the coefficients for fixed effect variables are represented by (2) and (4). Prior to the merger, the 5-day moving average coefficient is 0.999 under random effect and 0.932 under fixed effect. After the merger, it increased to 1.037 and 1.143 under the random and fixed effect model respectively. This shows that a change in the 5-day moving average under both models will have a higher impact on the company's stock price after the merger. Similarly, the relative strength index has a bigger impact on the relative strength index of 30 days after the merger, as the coefficient of the relative strength index of 30 days is 2.663 under random effect and 2.610 under fixed effect before the merger which has increased to 3.339 and 3.261 under random and fixed effect model respectively. At the 1% level, the coefficient values of the 5-day moving average and the relative strength index of 30 days have a substantial effect before and after the merger. Further, in table 4.4.8 the impact of total assets on the value of the firm after the merger is analyzed.

Table 4.4.8 -Impact of Total Assets on Value of the Firm After Merger

	Dependent variable:	
	lp	
	(1)	(2)
ta	0.0005	0.001
	(0.002)	(0.002)
Constant	2.210***	
	(0.086)	
Observations	252	252
R^2	0.0004	0.001
Adjusted R^2	−0.004	−0.334
F Statistic	0.094	0.119 (df = 1; 188)
Note:	*p<0.1; **p<0.05; ***p<0.01	

Source: *Compiled by Author from R output sheet*

Table 4.4.8 presents the outcomes obtained from conducting random effect and fixed effect regression analyses. The first equation (1) denotes the coefficients associated with random effect variables, whereas the second equation (2) represents the coefficients associated with fixed effect variables. The coefficient of total assets for both the random and fixed effects is 0.001 prior to the merger. Following the merger, the coefficient exhibits an increase to 0.0005 under the random effect model and 0.001 under the fixed effect model. Based on the analysis of both models, it can be concluded that the company's stock price experiences a positive effect as a result of the merger, primarily due to the increase in overall assets. The coefficient values pertaining to total assets do not exhibit a statistically significant influence both prior to and subsequent to the merger. The regression results of the value of the firm after the merger are reported in Table 4.4.9 on the basis of the Hausman test.

On the basis of the results of the Hausman test, Table 4.4.9 displays the regression results that include either random or fixed effects. Specifically, fixed effects are employed if the p-value is less than 0.05, whereas random effects are employed if the p-value is greater than 0.05. In this table, the p-value of the moving average of 30 days, 20 days, and 5 days as well as the relative strength index of 30 days coefficient is less than 0.05, so their fixed values are taken. However, the p-value of total assets is greater than 0.05, so its random values are taken. Before the merger, most of the coefficients were random which became fixed after the merger thereby indicating a positive impact on the stock prices after the merger. Except for total assets, all other variables are

Table 4.4.9 -Regression Results of Value of the Firm After Merger

	Dependent variable:				
	lp				
	(1)	(2)	(3)	(4)	(5)
ma_30d	0.662***				
	(0.139)				
ma_20d		0.893***			
		(0.091)			
ma_5d			1.143***		
			(0.035)		
rsi_30d				3.261***	
				(0.152)	
ta					0.0005
					(0.002)
Constant					2.210***
					(0.086)
Observations	240	245	250	239	252
R^2	0.114	0.348	0.853	0.724	0.0004
Adjusted R^2	−0.203	0.121	0.804	0.624	−0.004
F Statistic	22.697***	96.601***	1,081.538***	458.169***	0.094
Degree of Freedom	(df = 1; 176)	(df = 1; 181)	(df = 1; 186)	(df = 1; 175)	
Note:			*p<0.1; **p<0.05; ***p<0.01		

Source: *Compiled by Author from R output sheet*

statistically significant at 1%, before and after the merger. In the above tables, the impact of moving averages, relative strength index, and total assets on the value of the firm is analyzed in pre- and post-merger. Now, the same is analyzed in the year of the merger in the next table.

The outcomes of both random effect and fixed effect regression analyses are displayed in Table 4.4.10. The values (1) and (3) represent the coefficients for random effect variables, while (2) and (4) represent the coefficients for fixed effect variables. The coefficient of the 30-day moving average was found to be 1.046 under the random effect model and 1.057 under the fixed effect model prior to consolidation. Throughout the year, the coefficient of ma_30d under random effect is 0.963, and under fixed effect, it is 0.720. After the merger, the coefficient of the 30-day moving average (ma_30d) is observed to be 1.112 under random effect and 0.662 under fixed effect. This suggests that, when random effects are considered, the increase in the 30-day moving average following a merger will have a greater impact on the post-merger stock price of the

Table 4.4.10 -Impact of Moving Averages on the Value of the Firm During Merger

	Dependent variable:			
	lp			
	(1)	(2)	(3)	(4)
ma_30d	0.963***	0.720***		
	(0.025)	(0.139)		
ma_20d			0.986***	0.653***
			(0.019)	(0.123)
Constant	0.188***		0.100**	
	(0.055)		(0.042)	
Observations	101	101	108	108
R^2	0.937	0.353	0.962	0.360
Adjusted R^2	0.936	−0.321	0.962	−0.369
F Statistic	1,465.047***	26.724*** (df = 1; 49)	2,713.362***	28.154*** (df = 1; 50)
Note:				*p<0.1; **p<0.05; ***p<0.01

Source: *Compiled by Author from R output sheet*

company. In accordance with the fixed effect model, the 30-day moving average of the stock price was higher prior to the merger. This indicates a diminishing impact on the stock price after the merger under the fixed effect model.

Prior to the merger, the 20-day moving average coefficient is 1.022 under the random effect model and 0.990 under the fixed effect model. Throughout the year, the coefficient of ma_20d under random effect is 0.986, and under fixed effect, it is 0.653. The coefficient has increased to 1.085 under the random effect model and to 0.893 under the fixed effect model as a result of the merger. This result indicates that the application of a random effect model demonstrates a significant impact of a 20-day moving average on the stock prices of companies following a merger, with a greater degree of influence. Under fixed effect, however, the coefficient of ma_20d is highest prior to the merger. Prior to, during, and after the merger, the coefficient values associated with the 30-day and 20-day moving averages exhibit a statistically significant impact at a significance level of 1%. Further, in the next table, the impact of the moving average and relative strength index on the value of the firm during the merger is examined.

The results of both random effect and fixed effect regression are displayed in Table

Table 4.4.11 -Impact of Moving Average and Relative Strength Index on Value of the Firm During Merger

	Dependent variable:			
	lp			
	(1)	(2)	(3)	(4)
ma_5d	1.018***	0.783***		
	(0.011)	(0.058)		
rsi_30d			2.467***	2.201***
			(0.337)	(0.352)
Constant	−0.040		−2.129***	
	(0.025)		(0.600)	
Observations	117	117	101	101
R^2	0.987	0.763	0.359	0.444
Adjusted R^2	0.987	0.509	0.353	−0.134
F Statistic	8,848.584***	180.067*** (df = 1; 56)	53.646***	39.155*** (df = 1; 49)
Note:				*p<0.1; **p<0.05; ***p<0.01

Source: *Compiled by Author from R output sheet*

4.4.11. Coefficients for random effect variables are (1) and (3), while coefficients for fixed effect variables are (2) and (4). Prior to the merger, the 5-day moving average coefficient has a random effect value of 0.999 and a fixed effect value of 0.932. Under random and fixed effect models, it has increased to 1.018 and decreased to 0.783 over the course of the year. It has increased to 1.037 and 1.143 under the random and fixed effect models, respectively, after the merger. This indicates that a change in the 5-day moving average under both models will have a greater impact on the stock price of the company following the merger. Similarly, rsi_30d has a greater impact on the relative strength index of 30 days following the merger, as the coefficient of the relative strength index of 30 days, which was 2.663 under random effect and 2.610 under fixed effect prior to the merger, has increased to 3.339 and 3.261 under the random and fixed effect models, respectively. During the merger, the coefficient is 2.467 under a random effect model and 2.201 under a fixed effect model. Before, during, and after a merger, the coefficient values of the 5-day moving average and the 30-day relative strength index have a significant impact at the 1% level. The impact of total assets on the value of the firm during the merger is analyzed in Table 4.4.12.

The results of random effect and fixed effect regression analyses are summarised in

Table 4.4.12 -Impact of Total Assets on Value of the Firm During Merger

	Dependent variable:	
	lp	
	(1)	(2)
ta	0.008	0.011
	(0.010)	(0.010)
Constant	2.253***	
	(0.070)	
Observations	118	118
R^2	0.068	0.018
Adjusted R^2	0.060	−1.015
F Statistic	0.581	1.071 (df = 1; 57)
Note:	*p<0.1; **p<0.05; ***p<0.01	

Source: *Compiled by Author from R output sheet*

Table 4.4.12. The first equation (1) represents random effect variable coefficients, while the second equation (2) represents fixed effect variable coefficients. Prior to the merger, the coefficient of total assets for both random and fixed effects is 0.001. During the year of the merger, the coefficient for total assets is 0.008 for random effect and 0.011 for fixed effect. Following the merger, the coefficient is 0.0005 under the random effect model and 0.001 under the fixed effect model. Based on the analysis of both models, it can be concluded that the merger has a positive impact on the stock price of the company, primarily due to the increase in total assets compared to pre-merger levels. Nonetheless, the coefficient is greatest in the year of the merger, indicating that the total assets have the greatest influence on the stock price of the companies during that year. Prior to, during, and after the merger, the coefficient values pertaining to total assets do not exhibit a statistically significant influence. The regression results of the value of the firm during the merger are reported in Table 4.4.13 on the basis of the Hausman test. On the basis of the results of the Hausman test, Table 4.4.13 displays the regression results that include either random or fixed effects. Specifically, fixed effects are employed if the p-value is less than 0.05, whereas random effects are employed if the p-value is greater than 0.05. In this table, the p-value of the moving average of 20 days, 5 days, relative strength index of 30 days, and total assets coefficient is less than 0.05, so their fixed values are taken. However, the p-value of the moving average of 30 days is greater than 0.05, so its random values are taken. Before the merger, most of the

Table 4.4.13 -Regression Results of Value of the Firm During Merger

	Dependent variable:				
	lp				
	(1)	(2)	(3)	(4)	(5)
ma_30d	0.963***				
	(0.025)				
ma_20d		0.653***			
		(0.123)			
ma_5d			0.783***		
			(0.058)		
rsi_30d				2.201***	
				(0.352)	
ta					0.011
					(0.010)
Constant	0.188***				
	(0.055)				
Observations	101	108	117	101	118
R^2	0.937	0.360	0.763	0.444	0.018
Adjusted R^2	0.936	−0.369	0.509	−0.134	−1.015
F Statistic	1,465.047***	28.154***	180.067***	39.155***	1.071
Degree of Freedom		(df = 1; 50)	(df = 1; 56)	(df = 1; 49)	(df = 1; 57)
Note:			*p<0.1; **p<0.05; ***p<0.01		

Source: *Compiled by Author from R output sheet*

coefficients were random which has become fixed after the merger thereby indicating a positive impact on the stock prices during as well as after the merger. Except for total assets, all other variables are statistically significant at 1%, before, during, and after the merger. In the next table, the impact of moving averages on the value of the firm considering the overall merger.

The results of both random effects and fixed effects regression analyses are presented in Table 4.4.14. The coefficients for random effect variables are represented by values

(1) and (3), whereas the coefficients for fixed effect variables are represented by values (2) and (4). The coefficient of the 30-day moving average was determined to be 1.046 in the random effect model and 1.057 in the fixed effect model before consolidation. Over the course of the year, the coefficient of ma_30d exhibits a value of 0.963 when subjected to random effects, while it demonstrates a value of 0.720 when subjected to fixed effects. Following the merger, it has been observed that the coefficient of the 30-day moving average (ma_30d) is 1.112 under the random effect model and 0.662 under

Table 4.4.14 -Impact of Moving Averages on the Value of the Firm Considering Overall Merger

	Dependent variable:			
	lp			
	(1)	(2)	(3)	(4)
ma_30d	1.029***	0.844***		
	(0.016)	(0.034)		
ma_20d			1.028***	0.910***
			(0.012)	(0.027)
Constant	−0.030		−0.042	
	(0.035)		(0.026)	
Observations	538	538	551	551
R^2	0.884	0.571	0.931	0.703
Adjusted R^2	0.884	0.515	0.931	0.664
F Statistic	4,035.694***	632.165*** (df = 1; 474)	7,439.196***	1,152.155*** (df = 1; 487)
Note:				*p<0.1; **p<0.05; ***p<0.01

Source: *Compiled by Author from R output sheet*

the fixed effect model. In the event of a comprehensive merger, the coefficient is 1.029 under the random effect model and 0.844 under the fixed effect model. This implies that the incorporation of random effects will result in a more pronounced influence of the rise in the 30-day moving average on the post-merger stock price of the company. Based on the fixed effect model, it can be observed that the stock price exhibited a higher 30-day moving average prior to the merger. The findings suggest that the merger has a declining influence on the stock price, as observed within the framework of a fixed effect model.

Before the merger took place, the 20-day moving average coefficient was observed to be 1.022 under the random effect model and 0.990 under the fixed effect model. Over the course of the year, the coefficient of ma_20d exhibits a value of 0.986 when considering random effects, while it demonstrates a value of 0.653 when considering fixed effects. As a consequence of the merger, the coefficient has risen to 1.085 in the random effect model and to 0.893 in the fixed effect model. When considering a comprehensive merger, the coefficient values are 1.028 and 0.910 for the random effect and fixed effect models, respectively. The findings suggest that the use of a random effect model reveals a statistically significant influence of a 20-day moving average on the stock prices of companies subsequent to a merger, exhibiting a higher level of impact. In the context of fixed effects, it is observed that the coefficient of ma_20d exhibits its highest value prior to the occurrence of the merger. The coefficient values linked to the 30-day and 20-day moving averages demonstrate a statistically significant impact at a significance level of 1% throughout the entire process of the merger, including the periods before, during, and after the merger. Further, in Table 4.4.15 the impact of the moving average of 5 days and relative strength index of 30 days on the value of the firm considering the overall merger.

Table 4.4.15 -Impact of Moving Average and Relative Strength Index on the Value of the Firm Considering Overall Merger

	Dependent variable:			
	lp			
	(1)	(2)	(3)	(4)
ma_5d	1.013***	0.983***		
	(0.005)	(0.012)		
rsi_30d			2.337***	2.208***
			(0.150)	(0.151)
Constant	−0.037***		−1.881***	
	(0.012)		(0.265)	
Observations	569	569	537	537
R^2	0.984	0.927	0.377	0.313
Adjusted R^2	0.984	0.917	0.375	0.221
F Statistic	34,481.180***	6,373.746*** (df = 1; 505)	241.249***	215.037*** (df = 1; 473)
Note:				*p<0.1; **p<0.05; ***p<0.01

Source: *Compiled by Author from R output sheet*

The results of both random effect and fixed effect regression are displayed in Table 4.4.15. Coefficients for random effect variables are (1) and (3), while coefficients for fixed effect variables are (2) and (4). Prior to the merger, the 5-day moving average coefficient has a random effect value of 0.999 and a fixed effect value of 0.932. Under random and fixed effect models, it has increased to 1.018 and decreased to 0.783 over the course of the year. It has increased to 1.037 and 1.143 under the random and fixed effect models, respectively, after the merger. In the case of an overall merger, the coefficient of the 5-day moving average is 1.013 and 0.983 under the random and fixed effect model respectively. This indicates that a change in the 5-day moving average under both models will have a greater impact on the stock price of the company following the merger.

Similarly, rsi_30d has a greater impact on the relative strength index of 30 days following the merger, as the coefficient of the relative strength index of 30 days, which was 2.663 under random effect and 2.610 under fixed effect prior to the merger, has increased to 3.339 and 3.261 under the random and fixed effect models, respectively. During the merger, the coefficient is 2.467 under a random effect model and 2.201 under a fixed effect model. In the case of an overall merger, the coefficient is 2.337 and 2.208 under the random and fixed effect models respectively. Before, during, after, and overall merger, the coefficient values of the 5-day moving average and the 30-day relative strength index have a significant impact at the 1% level. In the next table, the impact of total assets on the value of the firm considering the overall merger is examined.

Table 4.4.16 -Impact of Total Assets on the Value of the Firm Considering Overall Merger

	Dependent variable:	
	lp	
	(1)	(2)
ta	0.001	0.001
	(0.001)	(0.001)
Constant	2.124***	
	(0.077)	
Observations	576	576
R^2	0.034	0.0005
Adjusted R^2	0.032	−0.122
F Statistic	0.173	0.253 (df = 1; 512)
Note:	*p<0.1; **p<0.05; ***p<0.01	

Source: *Compiled by Author from R output sheet*

Table 4.4.16 summarises the results of random effect and fixed effect regression analyses. The first equation (1) represents variable coefficients with random effect, while the second equation (2) represents variable coefficients with fixed effect. Prior to the merger, the total asset coefficient for both random and fixed effects is 0.001. The coefficient for total assets during the year of the merger is 0.008 for random effect and 0.011 for fixed effect. Following the merger, the coefficient under the random effect model is 0.0005 and the coefficient under the fixed effect model is 0.001. In the event of an overall merger, the total asset coefficient is 0.001 for both random and fixed effects. Based on the analysis of both models, it can be concluded that the merger has a positive effect on the company's stock price, primarily due to the increase in total assets relative to pre-merger levels. In spite of this, the coefficient is greatest in the year of the merger, indicating that the total assets have the greatest impact on the stock prices of the companies during that year. Prior to, during, after, and the overall merger has no statistically significant effect on the total asset coefficient values. Further, in Table 4.4.17 the regression results of the value of the firm considering the overall merger are analyzed.

Table 4.4.17 -Regression Results of Value of the Firm Considering Overall Merger

	Dependent variable:				
	lp				
	(1)	(2)	(3)	(4)	(5)
ma_30d	0.844***				
	(0.034)				
ma_20d		0.910***			
		(0.027)			
ma_5d			0.983***		
			(0.012)		
rsi_30d				2.208***	
				(0.151)	
ta					0.001
					(0.001)
Constant					2.124***
					(0.077)
Observations	538	551	569	537	576
R^2	0.571	0.703	0.927	0.313	0.034
Adjusted R^2	0.515	0.664	0.917	0.221	0.032
F Statistic	632.165***	1,152.155***	6,373.746***	215.037***	0.173
Degree of Freedom	(df = 1; 474)	(df = 1; 487)	(df = 1; 505)	(df = 1; 473)	
Note:					*p<0.1; **p<0.05; ***p<0.01

Source: *Compiled by Author from R output sheet*

Based on the results of the Hausman test, Table 4.4.17 displays the regression results for random and fixed effects. In particular, fixed effects are used if the p-value is less than 0.05, while random effects are used if the p-value is greater than 0.05. In this table, the coefficients for the 30-day moving average, 20-day moving average, 5-day moving average, and 30-day relative strength index have p values less than 0.05, so their values are fixed. However, the p-value of total assets is greater than 0.05, so their random values are selected. Before the merger, the majority of coefficients were random, but after the merger they have become fixed, indicating a positive effect on stock prices during, after, and overall merger. With the exception of total assets, all other variables are statistically significant at the 1% level before, during, after, and overall merger. The correlation matrix of the value of the firm in case of the merger is presented in Table 4.4.18.

Table 4.4.18 -Correlation Matrix of Value of the Firm- Merger

	ma_30d	ma_20d	ma_5d	rsi_30d	lp	ta
ma_30d	1					
ma_20d	0.994	1				
ma_5d	0.967	0.983	1			
rsi_30d	0.417	0.476	0.573	1		
lp	0.946	0.966	0.992	0.614	1	
ta	-0.055	-0.053	-0.053	-0.023	-0.046	1

Source: *Compiled by Author from R output sheet*

The correlation between the variables in the case of a merger is displayed in Table 4.4.18. The relationship between the moving average of 30 days, 20 days, 5 days and the relative strength index of 30 days as well as the last price are positively correlated. However, the relationship of these variables with total assets is negatively correlated. Further, in the next table, the average abnormal returns and cumulative average abnormal returns are analyzed in case of merger.

Table 4.4.19 represents the average abnormal return and cumulative average abnormal return in the case of a merger. In this case, 30 days before the merger and 30 days after the merger is considered. For few days, the CAAR is negative, however the same is positive after the merger thereby indicating a positive impact on the shareholder's wealth after the merger. Further, in the next table, descriptive statistics of the value of

Table 4.4.19 -Analysis of AAR and CAAR - Merger

Days	CAAR	AAR	Mean	St.Error	Standard Dev.	Kurtosis	Skewness
-30	-0.0373	-0.0373	-0.0004	0.0045	0.0244	-0.2549	0.5376
-29	-0.0700	-0.0327	0.0046	0.0043	0.0229	0.0942	-0.6048
-28	-0.0433	0.0267	0.0637	0.0450	0.2505	12.5896	3.7024
-27	-0.0761	-0.0329	0.0045	0.0054	0.0287	2.9389	1.4695
-26	-0.0164	0.0597	0.1033	0.0578	0.3111	5.8358	2.7128
-25	0.0203	0.0367	0.0761	0.0462	0.2531	11.7513	3.5672
-24	0.0077	-0.0126	0.0260	0.0350	0.1884	28.2939	5.2891
-23	0.0327	0.0250	0.0640	0.0466	0.2551	12.0610	3.6292
-22	0.0187	-0.0140	0.0230	0.0327	0.1820	30.5078	5.5030
-21	-0.0131	-0.0318	0.0054	0.0038	0.0204	0.5110	0.1979
-20	0.0165	0.0296	0.0736	0.0496	0.2625	10.9979	3.4803
-19	0.0781	0.0616	0.1053	0.0575	0.3098	5.9067	2.7325
-18	0.1157	0.0376	0.0745	0.0445	0.2479	12.4972	3.6836
-17	0.0792	-0.0365	0.0004	0.0043	0.0232	1.6178	0.5153
-16	0.1049	0.0257	0.0626	0.0450	0.2506	12.6298	3.7103
-15	0.0648	-0.0400	-0.0033	0.0032	0.0174	0.6148	0.1678
-14	0.0950	0.0301	0.0693	0.0463	0.2538	12.0198	3.6215
-13	0.1011	0.0061	0.0430	0.0323	0.1799	29.2700	5.3470
-12	0.0681	-0.0330	0.0041	0.0033	0.0183	-0.4276	-0.1821
-11	0.0621	-0.0060	0.0320	0.0337	0.1847	28.6676	5.3067
-10	0.0592	-0.0029	0.0363	0.0350	0.1882	27.0684	5.1294
-9	0.0882	0.0290	0.0730	0.0497	0.2628	10.9609	3.4729
-8	0.1475	0.0594	0.1066	0.0597	0.3160	5.5228	2.6603
-7	0.2045	0.0569	0.1039	0.0599	0.3171	5.5089	2.6560
-6	0.2639	0.0594	0.1029	0.0577	0.3106	5.9048	2.7319
-5	0.2935	0.0296	0.0666	0.0450	0.2504	12.4085	3.6654
-4	0.2551	-0.0384	-0.0014	0.0035	0.0197	0.6570	-0.3014
-3	0.2174	-0.0377	-0.0008	0.0064	0.0348	3.6924	-0.1874
-2	0.2177	0.0003	0.0412	0.0357	0.1889	27.3667	5.2052
-1	0.2823	0.0646	0.1124	0.0593	0.3139	5.5247	2.6606
0	0.3456	0.0634	0.1003	0.0542	0.3015	6.3782	2.7945
1	0.3151	-0.0305	0.0066	0.0086	0.0471	2.4864	0.9768
2	0.3049	-0.0102	0.0267	0.0328	0.1829	29.3559	5.3478
3	0.2701	-0.0348	0.0022	0.0050	0.0272	1.4423	-0.1879
4	0.2523	-0.0179	0.0190	0.0330	0.1835	29.9130	5.4227
5	0.2140	-0.0383	-0.0015	0.0045	0.0241	1.3617	-0.4604
6	0.2087	-0.0052	0.0351	0.0359	0.1900	27.4187	5.2120
7	0.2696	0.0609	0.1045	0.0577	0.3106	5.8478	2.7151
8	0.2962	0.0266	0.0635	0.0450	0.2506	12.5697	3.6980
9	0.2562	-0.0399	-0.0032	0.0035	0.0190	0.1952	0.1559
10	0.2828	0.0265	0.0656	0.0466	0.2553	11.9027	3.5970
11	0.2798	-0.0030	0.0363	0.0346	0.1863	28.3782	5.3009
12	0.3019	0.0221	0.0590	0.0453	0.2520	12.5169	3.6872
13	0.2609	-0.0410	-0.0041	0.0035	0.0192	-0.2977	-0.0729
14	0.2261	-0.0348	0.0022	0.0034	0.0184	2.7073	0.5712
15	0.2245	-0.0016	0.0365	0.0336	0.1839	28.6635	5.3020
16	0.2167	-0.0078	0.0291	0.0326	0.1817	29.8966	5.4171
17	0.1754	-0.0413	-0.0044	0.0028	0.0158	1.2669	0.3699
18	0.1400	-0.0353	0.0017	0.0036	0.0192	2.3943	1.0779
19	0.1084	-0.0316	0.0061	0.0036	0.0185	1.5361	-0.0644
20	0.1999	0.0915	0.1372	0.0653	0.3515	3.1009	2.2078
21	0.2228	0.0229	0.0618	0.0467	0.2559	11.9907	3.6162
22	0.2171	-0.0057	0.0334	0.0347	0.1868	28.3730	5.2994
23	0.2483	0.0312	0.0754	0.0498	0.2637	10.6296	3.4095
24	0.3094	0.0611	0.1013	0.0557	0.3052	6.2411	2.7904
25	0.3036	-0.0059	0.0321	0.0336	0.1842	29.0314	5.3524
26	0.2985	-0.0050	0.0330	0.0337	0.1847	28.5336	5.2842
27	0.2935	-0.0050	0.0319	0.0325	0.1810	30.0263	5.4411
28	0.2556	-0.0379	-0.0010	0.0051	0.0283	4.9366	0.1682
29	0.2125	-0.0431	-0.0069	0.0042	0.0220	0.9264	-0.8652
30	0.2752	0.0627	0.1103	0.0599	0.3171	5.2716	2.5858

Source: *Compiled by Author from Excel output sheet*

the firm in case of an acquisition are presented.

Table 4.4.20 -Descriptive Statistics of Value of the Firm -Acquisition

Statistic	N	Mean	St. Dev.	Min	Max
PR_MA_30D	1268	1.692411	0.733773	-1.686133	3.707542
PR_MA_20D	1268	1.696376	0.75999	-2.259637	3.74991
PR_MA_5D	1268	1.700442	0.813246	-3.221849	3.789581
PR_RSI_30D	1268	1.698531	0.138349	0.441617	1.97456
PR_LP	1268	1.706892	0.819798	-3.20412	3.752048
PR_TA	1268	-2.106547	87.996684	-3041.180715	419.467709
PO_MA_30D	1268	1.944462	0.847269	-3.30103	5.209426
PO_MA_20D	1268	1.910326	0.908725	-3.30103	5.196245
PO_MA_5D	1268	1.900263	0.948827	-3.30103	5.233504
PO_RSI_30D	1268	1.686595	0.129229	0.489832	1.966642
PO_LP	1268	1.8635	0.968096	-3.39794	5.267172
PO_TA	1268	0.210437	5.926495	-135.180368	57.517183

Source: *Compiled by Author from R output sheet*

Table 4.4.20 illustrates the descriptive statistics of the dependent and independent variables used in this study for the pre-acquisition and post-acquisition cases, respectively. Before the acquisition, the moving average of 30 days, the moving average of 20 days, and the moving average of 5 days had respective means of 1.692411, 1.696376, and 1.700442 which increased to 1.944462, 1.910326, and 1.900263 after the acquisition. Only the mean of these variables has increased post-acquisition, indicating a positive impact on the stock price. Before the acquisition, the average total assets were negative, but after it they became positive. Therefore, suggesting a favorable effect on the stock prices of the merged companies. In this case, only the standard deviation of the 30-day relative strength index and total assets is reduced after the acquisition, whereas the standard deviation of all other variables is increased. Next, in Table 4.4.21 the impact of moving averages on the value of the firm before the acquisition is analyzed.

Table 4.4.21 presents the outcomes of both random effect and fixed effect regression analyses. The coefficients for random effect variables are denoted by values (1) and (3), while values (2) and (4) reflect the coefficients for fixed effect variables. Prior to the acquisition, the coefficient of the 30-day moving average was observed to be 1.038 under the random effect model and 0.989 under the fixed effect model. This suggests that the fluctuation in the 30-day moving average when influenced by random effects,

Table 4.4.21 -Impact of Moving Averages on Value of the Firm Before Acquisition

	Dependent variable:			
	lp			
	(1)	(2)	(3)	(4)
ma_30d	1.038***	0.989***		
	(0.011)	(0.045)		
ma_20d			1.025***	0.940***
			(0.008)	(0.034)
Constant	−0.024		−0.016	
	(0.021)		(0.016)	
Observations	939	939	952	952
R^2	0.898	0.412	0.940	0.522
Adjusted R^2	0.898	0.211	0.940	0.359
F Statistic	8,322.957***	490.430*** (df = 1; 699)	15,022.400***	773.991*** (df = 1; 710)
Note:				*p<0.1; **p<0.05; ***p<0.01

Source: *Compiled by Author from R output sheet*

will exert a more significant influence on the company's stock price. The influence of the 20-day moving average is observed to be stronger under random effects, with a value of 1.025, compared to a coefficient of 0.940 under fixed effects. The coefficient values associated with the 30-day and 20-day moving averages exhibit a statistically significant impact at a significance level of 1% prior to the occurrence of an acquisition. In the next table, the impact of the moving average of 5 days and the relative strength index of 30 days on the value of the firm before acquisition is analyzed.

Table 4.4.22 -Impact of Moving Average and Relative Strength Index on Value of the Firm Before Acquisition

	Dependent variable:			
	lp			
	(1)	(2)	(3)	(4)
ma_5d	1.003***	0.941***		
	(0.004)	(0.017)		
rsi_30d			2.376***	2.366***
			(0.091)	(0.094)
Constant	0.004		−2.271***	
	(0.007)		(0.160)	
Observations	982	982	910	910
R^2	0.986	0.817	0.429	0.482
Adjusted R^2	0.986	0.751	0.428	0.304
F Statistic	69,253.640***	3,214.291*** (df = 1; 721)	683.545***	630.035*** (df = 1; 676)
Note:				*p<0.1; **p<0.05; ***p<0.01

Source: *Compiled by Author from R output sheet*

Table 4.4.22 displays the findings of both random effect and fixed effect regression. Coefficients for random effect variables are (1) and (3), while coefficients for fixed effect variables are (2) and (4). Prior to the acquisition, the 5-day moving average coefficient has a random effect value of 1.003 and a fixed effect value of 0.941. This indicates that a change in the 5-day moving average under random effect will have a greater effect on the stock price of the company. Similarly, the random effect has a greater impact on the relative strength index of 30 days, as the coefficient of the relative strength index of 30 days under random effect is 2.376, and under fixed effect, it is 2.366. The coefficient values of the 5-day moving average and the 30-day relative strength index have a substantial impact at the 1% level. In the next table, the impact of total assets on the value of the firm before acquisition is analyzed.

Table 4.4.23 -Impact of Total Assets on Value of the Firm Considering Before Acquisition

	Dependent variable:	
	lp	
	(1)	(2)
ta	−0.0001	−0.0001
	(0.0004)	(0.0004)
Constant	1.709***	
	(0.049)	
Observations	991	991
R^2	0.026	0.0001
Adjusted R^2	0.025	−0.369
F Statistic	0.071	0.085 (df = 1; 723)
Note:	*p<0.1; **p<0.05; ***p<0.01	

Source: *Compiled by Author from R output sheet*

Table 4.4.23 displays the findings of both random effect and fixed effect regression. The coefficients for random effect variables are represented by (1), whereas the coefficients for fixed effect variables are represented by (2). Prior to the acquisition, the total asset coefficient is 0.0001 for both the random and fixed effects. Prior to acquisition, total assets had a negative impact on the company's stock price, according to both models. The coefficient values of total assets have no significant influence. In Table 4.4.24, the regression results are reported on the basis of the Hausman test.

On the basis of the results of the Hausman test, Table 4.4.24 displays the regression results that include either random or fixed effects. Specifically, fixed effects are

Table 4.4.24 - Regression Results of Value of the Firm Before Acquisition

	Dependent variable:				
	lp				
	(1)	(2)	(3)	(4)	(5)
ma_30d	1.038*** (0.011)				
ma_20d		0.940*** (0.034)			
ma_5d			0.941*** (0.017)		
rsi_30d				2.376*** (0.091)	
ta					−0.0001 (0.0004)
Constant	−0.024 (0.021)			−2.271*** (0.160)	1.709*** (0.049)
Observations	939	952	982	910	991
R^2	0.898	0.522	0.817	0.429	0.026
Adjusted R^2	0.898	0.359	0.751	0.428	0.025
F Statistic	8,322.957***	773.991*** (df=1; 710)	3,214.291*** (df=1; 721)	683.545***	0.071
Note:					*p<0.1; **p<0.05; ***p<0.01

Source: *Compiled by Author from R output sheet*

employed if the p-value is less than 0.05, whereas random effects are employed if the p-value is greater than 0.05. In this table, the p-value of the moving average of 20 days and 5 days coefficient is less than 0.05, so its value is fixed. However, the p-value of all other variables is greater than 0.05, so their random values are taken. Except for total assets, all other variables are statistically significant at 1%, before acquisition. Now, in the next table the impact of moving averages on the value of the firm after the acquisition is analyzed.

The results of both random effect and fixed effect regression analysis are displayed in Table 4.4.25. The coefficients pertaining to random effect variables are represented by values (1) and (3), whereas values (2) and (4) correspond to the coefficients associated with fixed effect variables. Before the acquisition took place, the coefficient of the 30-day moving average was determined to be 1.038 according to the random effect model and 0.989 according to the fixed effect model. Following the acquisition, the coefficient has exhibited a decline to 1.005 and 0.590 under the random and fixed effect models, respectively. This implies that the influence of the change in the 30-day moving average is less significant under both models after acquisition as compared to the pre-acquisition period. The study reveals that the impact of the 20-day moving average is more pronounced prior to acquisition, exhibiting a value of 1.025 under random effect and a coefficient of 0.940 under fixed effect before acquisition. After the acquisition, the coefficient values decline to 1.008 and 0.765 under the random and fixed effects,

Table 4.4.25 -Impact of Moving Averages on Value of the Firm After Acquisition

	Dependent variable:			
	lp			
	(1)	(2)	(3)	(4)
ma_30d	1.005***	0.590***		
	(0.016)	(0.045)		
ma_20d			1.008***	0.765***
			(0.011)	(0.033)
Constant	−0.087**		−0.071***	
	(0.034)		(0.024)	
Observations	1,158	1,158	1,194	1,194
R^2	0.781	0.169	0.876	0.373
Adjusted R^2	0.781	−0.128	0.876	0.155
F Statistic	3,986.869***	172.918*** (df = 1; 853)	8,291.625***	526.632*** (df = 1; 885)
Note:				*p<0.1; **p<0.05; ***p<0.01

Source: *Compiled by Author from R output sheet*

respectively. The coefficient values linked to the 30-day and 20-day moving averages demonstrate a statistically significant influence at a significance level of 1% both before and after the acquisition. The impact of the moving average of 5 days and the relative strength index of 30 days on the value of the firm after acquisition is analyzed in Table 4.4.26.

Table 4.4.26 displays the findings of both random effect and fixed effect regression. Coefficients for random effect variables are (1) and (3), while coefficients for fixed effect variables are (2) and (4). Prior to the acquisition, the 5-day moving average coefficient has a random effect value of 1.003 and a fixed effect value of 0.941. After the acquisition, the value of the coefficient is increased to 1.023 and 1.098 under random and fixed effect models respectively. This indicates that a change in the 5-day moving average will have a greater effect on the stock price of the company after acquisition. Similarly, the relative strength index of 30 days after acquisition has a greater impact, as the coefficient of the relative strength index of 30 days under random effect is 2.376, and under fixed effect, it is 2.366 before acquisition which has increased to 3.034 and 2.987 after acquisition. The coefficient values of the 5-day moving average and the 30-day relative strength index have a substantial impact at the 1% level before

Table 4.4.26 -Impact of Moving Average and Relative Strength Index on Value of the Firm After Acquisition

	Dependent variable:			
	lp			
	(1)	(2)	(3)	(4)
ma_5d	1.023***	1.098***		
	(0.006)	(0.014)		
rsi_30d			3.034***	2.987***
			(0.087)	(0.088)
Constant	−0.082***		−3.222***	
	(0.014)		(0.153)	
Observations	1,229	1,229	1,142	1,142
R^2	0.955	0.866	0.527	0.577
Adjusted R^2	0.955	0.820	0.527	0.424
F Statistic	25,560.640***	5,912.038*** (df = 1; 913)	1,224.873***	1,143.185*** (df = 1; 839)
Note:				*p<0.1; **p<0.05; ***p<0.01

Source: *Compiled by Author from R output sheet*

and after the acquisition. In Table 4.4.27, the impact of total assets on the value of the firm after acquisition is examined.

Table 4.4.27 -Impact of Total Assets on Value of the Firm After Acquisition

	Dependent variable:	
	lp	
	(1)	(2)
ta	−0.0005	−0.0003
	(0.002)	(0.002)
Constant	1.866***	
	(0.053)	
Observations	1,235	1,235
R^2	0.005	0.00003
Adjusted R^2	0.004	−0.343
F Statistic	0.078	0.029 (df = 1; 919)
Note:	*p<0.1; **p<0.05; ***p<0.01	

Source: *Compiled by Author from R output sheet*

Table 4.4.27 displays the findings of both random effect and fixed effect regression. The coefficients for random effect variables are represented by (1), whereas the coefficients for fixed effect variables are represented by (2). Prior to the acquisition, the total asset coefficient was 0.0001 for both the random and fixed effects. After the acquisition, the total asset is 0.0005 under random effect and 0.0003 under the fixed effect model. After the acquisition, total assets had increased a negative impact on the company's stock price, according to both models. The coefficient values of total assets have no significant influence before and after acquisition. The regression results of the value of the firm after acquisition are reported in Table 4.4.28 on the basis of the Hausman test.

Table 4.4.28 -Regression Results of Value of the Firm After Acquisition

	Dependent variable:				
	lp				
	(1)	(2)	(3)	(4)	(5)
ma_30d	0.590***				
	(0.045)				
ma_20d		0.765***			
		(0.033)			
ma_5d			1.098***		
			(0.014)		
rsi_30d				2.987***	
				(0.088)	
ta					−0.0005
					(0.002)
Constant					1.866***
					(0.053)
Observations	1,158	1,194	1,229	1,142	1,235
R^2	0.169	0.373	0.866	0.577	0.005
Adjusted R^2	−0.128	0.155	0.820	0.424	0.004
F Statistic	172.918***	526.632***	5,912.038***	1,143.185***	0.078
Degree of Freedom	(df = 1; 853)	(df = 1; 885)	(df = 1; 913)	(df = 1; 839)	
Note:			*p<0.1; **p<0.05; ***p<0.01		

Source: *Compiled by Author from R output sheet*

On the basis of the results of the Hausman test, Table 4.4.28 displays the regression results that include either random or fixed effects. Specifically, fixed effects are employed if the p-value is less than 0.05, whereas random effects are employed if the p-value is greater than 0.05. In this table, the p-value of the moving average of 30 days, 20 days,5 days and the relative strength index of 30 days coefficient is less than 0.05, so their value is fixed. However, the p-value of total assets is greater than 0.05, so their random values are taken. Except for total assets, all other variables are statistically significant at 1%, before and after acquisition. Further, the impact of moving averages on the value of the firm during acquisition is examined in Table 4.4.29.

Table 4.4.29 -Impact of Moving Averages on Value of the Firm During Acquisition

	Dependent variable:			
	lp			
	(1)	(2)	(3)	(4)
ma_30d	1.010***	0.803***		
	(0.016)	(0.077)		
ma_20d			1.008***	0.724***
			(0.013)	(0.061)
Constant	0.036		0.017	
	(0.033)		(0.027)	
Observations	498	498	527	527
R^2	0.890	0.311	0.924	0.359
Adjusted R^2	0.890	−0.427	0.924	−0.332
F Statistic	3,965.007***	108.163*** (df = 1; 240)	6,235.352***	141.881*** (df = 1; 253)
Note:				*p<0.1; **p<0.05; ***p<0.01

Source: *Compiled by Author from R output sheet*

The results of both random effect and fixed effect regression analysis are displayed in Table 4.4.29. The coefficients pertaining to random effect variables are represented by values (1) and (3), whereas values (2) and (4) correspond to the coefficients associated with fixed effect variables. Before the acquisition took place, the coefficient of the 30-day moving average was determined to be 1.038 according to the random effect model and 0.989 according to the fixed effect model. During the acquisition, the coefficient of the moving average of 30 days declined to 1.010 and 0.803 under random and fixed effect models respectively. Further, Following the acquisition, the coefficient has exhibited a decline to 1.005 and 0.590 under the random and fixed effect models, respectively. This implies that the influence of the change in the 30-day moving average is less significant under both models after acquisition as compared to the pre-acquisition period as well as during the year of acquisition.

The study reveals that the impact of the 20-day moving average is more pronounced prior to acquisition, exhibiting a value of 1.025 under random effect and a coefficient of 0.940 under fixed effect before acquisition. During the year of acquisition, the coefficient is 1.008 and 0.724 under random and fixed effect respectively. After the acquisition, the coefficient value is 1.008 and 0.765 under the random and fixed effects, respectively. The coefficient values linked to the 30-day and 20-day moving averages demonstrate a statistically significant influence at a significance level of 1% both before, during, and after the acquisition. Now, in the next table, the impact of the moving average of 5 days and the relative strength index of 30 days on the value of the firm during acquisition is analyzed in Table 4.4.30.

Table 4.4.30 -Impact of Moving Average and Relative Strength Index on Value of the Firm During Acquisition

	Dependent variable:			
	lp			
	(1)	(2)	(3)	(4)
ma_5d	0.995^{***}	0.789^{***}		
	(0.009)	(0.029)		
rsi_30d			2.397^{***}	2.276^{***}
			(0.143)	(0.158)
Constant	−0.005		-2.171^{***}	
	(0.019)		(0.253)	
Observations	565	565	484	484
R^2	0.961	0.733	0.373	0.470
Adjusted R^2	0.961	0.450	0.372	−0.100
F Statistic	$13{,}441.380^{***}$	751.861^{***} (df = 1; 274)	280.045^{***}	206.281^{***} (df = 1; 233)
Note:				*p<0.1; **p<0.05; ***p<0.01

Source: *Compiled by Author from R output sheet*

Table 4.4.30 displays the findings of both random effect and fixed effect regression. Coefficients for random effect variables are (1) and (3), while coefficients for fixed effect variables are (2) and (4). Prior to the acquisition, the 5-day moving average coefficient had a random effect value of 1.003 and a fixed effect value of 0.941. During the year, the value of the coefficient under random effect is 0.995 and the fixed effect is 0.789. After the acquisition, the value of the coefficient is increased to 1.023 and 1.098 under random and fixed effect models respectively. This indicates that a change in the 5-day moving average will have a greater effect on the stock price of the company after acquisition.

Similarly, the relative strength index of 30 days after acquisition has a greater impact, as the coefficient of the relative strength index of 30 days under random effect is 2.376, and under fixed effect it is 2.366 before acquisition which has increased to 3.034 and 2.987 after acquisition. During the year, the coefficient is 2.397 and 2.276 under the random and fixed effect model. The coefficient values of the 5-day moving average and the 30-day relative strength index have a substantial impact at the 1% level before, during, and after the acquisition. Further, in Table 4.4.31 the impact of total assets on the value of the firm during acquisition is analyzed.

Table 4.4.31 -Impact of Total Assets on the Value of the Firm During Acquisition

	Dependent variable:	
	lp	
	(1)	(2)
ta	−0.003*	−0.003*
	(0.002)	(0.002)
Constant	1.989***	
	(0.049)	
Observations	572	572
R^2	0.034	0.011
Adjusted R^2	0.032	−1.030
F Statistic	3.170*	3.221* (df = 1; 278)
Note:	*p<0.1; **p<0.05; ***p<0.01	

Source: *Compiled by Author from R output sheet*

Table 4.4.31 displays the findings of both random effect and fixed effect regression. The coefficients for random effect variables are represented by (1), whereas the coefficients for fixed effect variables are represented by (2). Prior to the acquisition, the total asset coefficient is 0.0001 for both the random and fixed effects. During the year of acquisition the coefficient is 0.003 and 0.003 respectively. After the acquisition, total assets is 0.0005 under random effect and 0.0003 under fixed effect model. After acquisition, total assets had reduced a negative impact on the company's stock price if compared to during the year of acquisition, according to both models. The coefficient values of total assets have no significant influence before and after acquisition. However, it is significant at 10% in the year of acquisition. The regression results of value of the firm during acquisition is reported in table 4.4.32 on the basis of Hausman test.

On the basis of the results of the Hausman test, Table 4.4.32 displays the regression

Table 4.4.32 -Regression Results of Value of the Firm During Acquisition

	Dependent variable:				
	lp				
	(1)	(2)	(3)	(4)	(5)
ma_30d	0.803***				
	(0.077)				
ma_20d		0.724***			
		(0.061)			
ma_5d			0.789***		
			(0.029)		
rsi_30d				2.397***	
				(0.143)	
ta					−0.003*
					(0.002)
Constant				−2.171***	1.989***
				(0.253)	(0.049)
Observations	498	527	565	484	572
R^2	0.311	0.359	0.733	0.373	0.034
Adjusted R^2	−0.427	−0.332	0.450	0.372	0.032
F Statistic	108.163***	141.881***	751.861***	280.045***	3.170*
Degree of Freedom	(df = 1; 240)	(df = 1; 253)	(df = 1; 274)		
Note:			*p<0.1; **p<0.05; ***p<0.01		

Source: *Compiled by Author from R output sheet*

results that include either random or fixed effects. Specifically, fixed effects are employed if the p-value is less than 0.05, whereas random effects are employed if the p-value is greater than 0.05. In this table, the p-value of the moving average of 30 days, 20 days, and 5 days coefficient is less than 0.05, so their value is fixed in the year of acquisition. However, the p-value of total assets and relative strength index of 30 days is greater than 0.05, so their random values are taken. Except for total assets, all other variables are statistically significant at 1%, before and after acquisition. However, during the year of acquisition, the total assets are also significant. The coefficient of total assets is significant at the 10% level. Further, in Table 4.4.33 the impact of moving averages on the value of the firm considering overall acquisition is analyzed.

The results of both random effect and fixed effect regression analysis are displayed in Table 4.4.33. The coefficients pertaining to random effect variables are represented by values (1) and (3), whereas values (2) and (4) correspond to the coefficients associated with fixed effect variables. Before the acquisition took place, the coefficient of the 30-

Table 4.4.33 -Impact of Moving Averages on the Value of the Firm Considering Overall Acquisition

	Dependent variable:			
	lp			
	(1)	(2)	(3)	(4)
ma_30d	1.001***	0.893***		
	(0.010)	(0.018)		
ma_20d			1.007***	0.947***
			(0.007)	(0.014)
Constant	−0.017		−0.023	
	(0.020)		(0.015)	
Observations	2,595	2,595	2,673	2,673
R^2	0.808	0.511	0.882	0.665
Adjusted R^2	0.808	0.446	0.882	0.622
F Statistic	10,356.270***	2,389.907*** (df = 1; 2290)	19,242.410***	4,698.688*** (df = 1; 2364)
Note:				*p<0.1; **p<0.05; ***p<0.01

Source: *Compiled by Author from R output sheet*

day moving average was determined to be 1.038 according to the random effect model and 0.989 according to the fixed effect model. During the acquisition, the coefficient of the moving average of 30 days declined to 1.010 and 0.803 under random and fixed effect models respectively. Further, Following the acquisition, the coefficient has exhibited a decline to 1.005 and 0.590 under the random and fixed effect models, respectively. In the case of overall acquisition, the coefficient is 1.001 and 0.893 under the random and fixed effect model. This implies that the influence of the change in the 30-day moving average is less significant under both models after acquisition as compared to the pre-acquisition period, during the year of acquisition as well as overall acquisition.

The study reveals that the impact of the 20-day moving average is more pronounced under the random effect model prior to acquisition, exhibiting a value of 1.025 under random effect and a coefficient of 0.940 under fixed effect before acquisition. During the year of acquisition, the coefficient is 1.008 and 0.724 under random and fixed effect respectively. After the acquisition, the coefficient value is 1.008 and 0.765 under the random and fixed effects, respectively. In the case of overall acquisition, the coefficient is 1.007 and 0.947 under random and fixed effect models respectively. Under the fixed effect model, the coefficient has the highest impact on overall acquisition. The coefficient values linked to the 30-day and 20-day moving averages demonstrate a statistically significant influence at a significance level of 1% both before, during, after, and overall acquisition. The impact of the moving average of 5 days and the relative strength index of 30 days on the value of the firm considering overall acquisition is analyzed in Table 4.4.34.

Table 4.4.34 -Impact of Moving Average and Relative Strength Index on the Value of the Firm Considering Overall Acquisition

	Dependent variable:			
	lp			
	(1)	(2)	(3)	(4)
ma_5d	1.005***	1.005***		
	(0.004)	(0.006)		
rsi_30d			2.579***	2.551***
			(0.071)	(0.072)
Constant	−0.028***		−2.498***	
	(0.009)		(0.127)	
Observations	2,776	2,776	2,536	2,536
R^2	0.955	0.908	0.362	0.357
Adjusted R^2	0.955	0.896	0.361	0.270
F Statistic	55,627.960***	24,327.860*** (df = 1; 2460)	1,309.591***	1,240.993*** (df = 1; 2233)
Note:				*p<0.1; **p<0.05; ***p<0.01

Source: *Compiled by Author from R output sheet*

The results of both random effect and fixed effect regression are displayed in Table 4.4.34. The coefficients for random effect variables are (1) and (3), whereas the coefficients for variables with a fixed effect are (2) and (4). The 5-day moving average coefficient has a random effect value of 1.003 and a fixed effect value of 0.941 prior to the acquisition. Throughout the year, the coefficient for random effect is 0.995% and the coefficient for fixed effect is 0.789%. Under random and fixed effect models, the coefficient value increases to 1.023 and 1.098, respectively, after acquisition. In the case of total acquisition, the coefficient under both models is 1.005. This suggests that a change in the 5-day moving average will have a larger impact on the stock price of the acquired company.

Similarly, the relative strength index of 30 days after acquisition has a greater impact, as the coefficient of the relative strength index of 30 days under random effect is 2.376, and under fixed effect, it is 2.366 before acquisition which has increased to 3.034 and

2.987 after acquisition. During the year, the coefficient is 2.397 and 2.276 under the random and fixed effect model. In the case of overall acquisition, the coefficient is 2.579 and 2.551 under the random and fixed effect model. The coefficient values of the 5-day moving average and the 30-day relative strength index have a substantial impact at the 1% level before, during, after, and overall acquisition. Next, in Table 4.4.35 the impact of total assets on the value of the firm considering overall acquisition is examined.

Table 4.4.35 -Impact of Total Assets on the Value of the Firm Considering Overall Acquisition

	Dependent variable:	
	lp	
	(1)	(2)
ta	0.001	0.001
	(0.001)	(0.001)
Constant	1.851***	
	(0.047)	
Observations	2,798	2,798
R^2	0.019	0.001
Adjusted R^2	0.019	−0.126
F Statistic	2.090	2.185 (df = 1; 2482)
Note:	*p<0.1; **p<0.05; ***p<0.01	

Source: *Compiled by Author from R output sheet*

Table 4.4.35 displays the findings of both random effect and fixed effect regression. The coefficients for random effect variables are represented by (1), whereas the coefficients for fixed effect variables are represented by (2). Prior to the acquisition, the total asset coefficient was 0.0001 for both the random and fixed effects. During the year of acquisition, the coefficient is 0.003 and 0.003 respectively. After the acquisition, total assets are 0.0005 under random effect and 0.0003 under the fixed effect model. In the case of overall acquisition, the coefficient is positive, it is 0.001 under both the models. Therefore, it can be concluded that the total assets have a significant impact on stock price in the overall acquisition. The coefficient values of total assets have no significant influence before, after, and overall acquisition. However, it is significant at 10% in the year of acquisition. The regression results of the value of the firm considering overall acquisition are presented in Table 4.4.36 on the basis of the Hausman test.

On the basis of the results of the Hausman test, Table 4.4.36 displays the regression results that include either random or fixed effects. Specifically, fixed effects are

Table 4.4.36 - Regression Results of Value of the Firm Considering Overall Acquisition

	Dependent variable:				
	lp				
	(1)	(2)	(3)	(4)	(5)
ma_30d	0.893***				
	(0.018)				
ma_20d		0.947***			
		(0.014)			
ma_5d			1.005***		
			(0.004)		
rsi_30d				2.551***	
				(0.072)	
ta					0.001
					(0.001)
Constant			−0.028***		1.851***
			(0.009)		(0.047)
Observations	2,595	2,673	2,776	2,536	2,798
R^2	0.511	0.665	0.955	0.357	0.019
Adjusted R^2	0.446	0.622	0.955	0.270	0.019
F Statistic	2,389.907***	4,698.688***	55,627.960***	1,240.993***	2.090
Degree of Freedom	(df = 1; 2290)	(df = 1; 2364)		(df = 1; 2233)	
Note:					*p<0.1; **p<0.05; ***p<0.01

Source: *Compiled by Author from R output sheet*

employed if the p-value is less than 0.05, whereas random effects are employed if the p-value is greater than 0.05. In this table, the p-value of the moving average of 30 days, 20 days, and relative strength index of 30 days coefficient is less than 0.05, so their value is fixed in overall acquisition. However, the p-value of total assets and moving average of 5 days is greater than 0.05, so their random values are taken. Except for total assets, all other variables are statistically significant at 1%, before, after, and overall acquisition. However, during the year of acquisition, the total assets are also significant. The coefficient of total assets is significant at the 10% level. The correlation matrix of the value of the firm in case of an acquisition is presented in Table 4.4.37.

The correlation between the variables in the case of an acquisition is displayed in Table 4.4.37. The relationship between the moving average of 30 days, 20 days, 5 days and the relative strength index of 30 days as well as the last price are positively correlated. However, the relationship of these variables with total assets is negatively correlated. In the next table, the analysis of average abnormal return and cumulative average

Table 4.4.37 -Correlation Matrix of Value of the Firm - Acquisition

	ma_30d	ma_20d	ma_5d	rsi_30d	lp	ta
ma_30d	1					
ma_20d	0.994	1				
ma_5d	0.967	0.984	1			
rsi_30d	0.370	0.414	0.485	1		
lp	0.945	0.964	0.988	0.513	1	
ta	-0.002	0.0003	-0.005	-0.013	-0.005	1

Source: *Compiled by Author from R output sheet*

abnormal return is presented.

As Table 4.4.38 shows the result of listed companies, that data has been analyzed to assess the short-run stock price reaction, taken into consideration for evaluation of M&A impact during the last three years. In this regard, the fluctuation of stock prices pre and post-merger is evaluated. As can be observed from the trend shown by AAR before the merger it was slightly negative, however the same has become positive initially post-merger but ultimately leads to negative AAR only. If we see the mean of the company's stock price pre and post-merger a wide gap appears as before the merger the mean was negative on most of the days whereas after the merger it was positive.

Pre and Post analysis:

Data of the listed companies were analysed to consider 61 days i.e. 30 days before the merger and 30 days after the merger. In this objective, any significant change in the stock price of the particular company is taken into consideration for evaluating average abnormal return and cumulative average abnormal return to establish any major reaction in a particular stock. The capital asset pricing model (CAPM) is used to calculate the slope of the companies and NIFTY. The equation is as under:

$$E(R_m) = R_f + \beta (R_m - R_f)$$

Table 4.4.38 -Analysis of AAR and CAR - Acquisition

Days	CAAR	AAR	Mean	St.Error	Standard Dev.	Kurtosis	Skewness
-30	0.0065	0.0065	0.0618	0.0193	0.2377	12.0054	3.6914
-29	0.0215	0.0149	0.0681	0.0194	0.2443	10.9707	3.5582
-28	0.0076	-0.0138	0.0392	0.0144	0.1796	24.6423	5.0455
-27	0.0068	-0.0008	0.0525	0.0178	0.2226	14.5414	4.0074
-26	-0.0037	-0.0105	0.0435	0.0159	0.1963	20.2332	4.6398
-25	0.0094	0.0131	0.0670	0.0197	0.2465	10.7059	3.5186
-24	-0.0003	-0.0097	0.0427	0.0165	0.2078	17.8096	4.3984
-23	-0.0155	-0.0152	0.0375	0.0143	0.1780	25.6112	5.1509
-22	-0.0210	-0.0056	0.0461	0.0163	0.2064	17.6592	4.3505
-21	-0.0589	-0.0378	0.0136	0.0091	0.1150	68.1340	8.0876
-20	-0.0830	-0.0241	0.0283	0.0130	0.1613	32.5031	5.7372
-19	-0.0911	-0.0081	0.0449	0.0167	0.2091	17.3965	4.3451
-18	-0.1037	-0.0126	0.0392	0.0164	0.2073	18.0632	4.4255
-17	-0.1351	-0.0314	0.0208	0.0113	0.1403	45.2872	6.7373
-16	-0.1298	0.0054	0.0594	0.0189	0.2356	12.3754	3.7441
-15	-0.1296	0.0002	0.0553	0.0184	0.2256	14.0026	3.9480
-14	-0.1054	0.0241	0.0796	0.0217	0.2696	8.0229	3.1311
-13	-0.1042	0.0012	0.0547	0.0189	0.2355	12.6182	3.7844
-12	-0.1212	-0.0170	0.0366	0.0160	0.1970	20.5745	4.6921
-11	-0.1034	0.0178	0.0711	0.0204	0.2562	9.5253	3.3555
-10	-0.1295	-0.0261	0.0268	0.0131	0.1618	33.0226	5.8291
-9	-0.1111	0.0184	0.0740	0.0210	0.2598	9.0954	3.2929
-8	-0.1000	0.0112	0.0642	0.0195	0.2452	10.9784	3.5615
-7	-0.1202	-0.0202	0.0331	0.0147	0.1808	25.1290	5.1197
-6	-0.1102	0.0100	0.0642	0.0199	0.2477	10.7006	3.5228
-5	-0.1123	-0.0021	0.0512	0.0178	0.2228	14.5857	4.0163
-4	-0.1168	-0.0045	0.0506	0.0174	0.2126	16.3934	4.2190
-3	-0.0816	0.0352	0.0890	0.0219	0.2751	7.2943	3.0112
-2	-0.0983	-0.0167	0.0355	0.0142	0.1779	25.5687	5.1143
-1	-0.1249	-0.0267	0.0257	0.0130	0.1616	32.6271	5.7492
0	-0.1530	-0.0281	0.0230	0.0123	0.1577	34.7285	5.9285
1	-0.1537	-0.0007	0.0548	0.0185	0.2269	13.7728	3.9094
2	-0.1256	0.0282	0.0850	0.0228	0.2817	6.9290	2.9592
3	-0.1078	0.0178	0.0715	0.0205	0.2572	9.3939	3.3321
4	-0.1267	-0.0189	0.0343	0.0146	0.1804	25.0373	5.0965
5	-0.1259	0.0008	0.0545	0.0179	0.2225	14.5565	4.0183
6	-0.1339	-0.0080	0.0453	0.0169	0.2100	17.1309	4.3060
7	-0.1406	-0.0067	0.0467	0.0168	0.2092	17.3101	4.3374
8	-0.1530	-0.0124	0.0404	0.0155	0.1941	20.9846	4.7253
9	-0.1607	-0.0077	0.0450	0.0167	0.2087	17.4122	4.3385
10	-0.1792	-0.0184	0.0343	0.0143	0.1785	25.8348	5.1880
11	-0.1864	-0.0073	0.0467	0.0171	0.2112	16.8314	4.2683
12	-0.1751	0.0114	0.0674	0.0204	0.2502	10.3461	3.4760
13	-0.1524	0.0227	0.0781	0.0217	0.2697	8.0934	3.1480
14	-0.1485	0.0039	0.0567	0.0186	0.2343	12.6131	3.7681
15	-0.1747	-0.0262	0.0264	0.0131	0.1620	32.3949	5.7368
16	-0.1741	0.0006	0.0540	0.0189	0.2365	12.3917	3.7400
17	-0.1797	-0.0056	0.0482	0.0170	0.2105	16.8456	4.2701
18	-0.1798	-0.0001	0.0530	0.0177	0.2216	14.7159	4.0324
19	-0.1927	-0.0130	0.0391	0.0153	0.1927	21.3532	4.7560
20	-0.2173	-0.0245	0.0283	0.0130	0.1612	33.0643	5.8286
21	-0.2031	0.0141	0.0673	0.0195	0.2447	10.9234	3.5489
22	-0.2228	-0.0196	0.0347	0.0150	0.1827	24.5656	5.0729
23	-0.1858	0.0369	0.0914	0.0229	0.2864	6.4090	2.8694
24	-0.1985	-0.0127	0.0394	0.0153	0.1926	21.3743	4.7598
25	-0.2258	-0.0273	0.0248	0.0130	0.1619	32.2891	5.6599
26	-0.2414	-0.0156	0.0381	0.0160	0.1972	20.3369	4.6529
27	-0.2268	0.0147	0.0696	0.0210	0.2603	9.1580	3.2922
28	-0.2215	0.0052	0.0588	0.0188	0.2351	12.4509	3.7498
29	-0.2374	-0.0159	0.0365	0.0155	0.1943	21.1120	4.7322
30	-0.2540	-0.0165	0.0368	0.0159	0.1967	20.5340	4.6755

Source: *Compiled by Author from Excel output sheet*

Where $E(R_m)$ = expected rate of return , R_f = risk free return, β = beta of the stock , R_m= market rate of return

The fixed Deposit rate offered by the SBI for the specified date or period has been treated as a risk-free return. The beta in the equation is calculated by using the formula i.e. Covariance of stock and market/ Variance of market. The rate of return of stock is calculated by using the change in stock price for the specified dates.

By using the above-mentioned steps we have calculated the expected rate of return. With the help of expected return, we have calculated AAR and CAR to analyze the impact of the stock price on the shareholder's wealth in the short run. It has been observed from the analysis that pre-merger AAR was positive for most of the days whereas after the merger the same is negative for most of the days which shows that the actual return is less than the expected return.

We find that positive correlation on the stock prices of merged companies. However, some of the company's stock prices had a negative correlation. There may be some other factors that influence the stock price due to market capitalization and the volume of a particular stock or capital base.The cumulative abnormal return was negative only before the merger but it is always positive after the merger which indicates that the company is able to fetch more return than expected overall after the merger in the short run, hence ultimately increasing the shareholder's wealth. In this section, we took some key measures in order to find better results for predicting future market prices and compare such results in two time phases, one pre-merger and acquisition, and the other post-merger and acquisition.

In comparison to combined firms, the volume of stock trading was very low prior to merger and acquisition. Following the merger, the acquirer or combined firms have seen a significant increase in volume. The volume of stock trading by corporations has increased, which can be considered helpful to the companies in the current and future circumstances. As a result, the stock trading volume has an impact on the stock prices of the merged firms, and in this case, it had a positive impact after the merger.

In the short run, the standard deviation of stock price comparisons between overall and the difference between pre and post-M&A. The companies' standard deviations were lower before the merger, indicating that the risk was relatively low; but, following the merger, the companies' standard deviations are large, indicating that the risk is relatively high.

Table 4.4.39 -Regression Analysis of Value of the Firm

Null Hypotheses	**Description**	**Accept/Reject**
$Ho_{4.1}$	There is no impact of moving average of 30 days and 20 days on the value of the firm before the merger	Rejected
$Ho_{4.2}$	There is no impact of the moving average of 5 days and relative strength index of 30 days on the value of the firm before the merger	Rejected
$Ho_{4.3}$	There is no impact of total assets on the value of the firm before the merger	Fail to Reject
$Ho_{4.4}$	There is no impact of the moving average of 30 days and 20 days on the value of the firm after the merger	Rejected
$Ho_{4.5}$	There is no impact of the moving average of 5 days and relative strength index of 30 days on the value of the firm after the merger	Rejected
$Ho_{4.6}$	There is no impact of total assets on the value of the firm after the merger	Fail to Reject
$Ho_{4.7}$	There is no impact of moving average of 30 days and 20 days on the value of the firm during the merger	Rejected
$Ho_{4.8}$	There is no impact of the moving average of 5 days and relative strength index of 30 days on the value of the firm during the merger	Rejected
$Ho_{4.9}$	There is no impact of total assets on the value of the firm during the merger	Fail to Reject
$Ho_{4.10}$	There is no impact of moving average of 30 days and 20 days on the value of the firm considering the overall merger	Rejected

Null Hypotheses	Description	Accept/Reject
$Ho_{4.11}$	There is no impact of the moving average of 5 days and relative strength index of 30 days on the value of the firm considering the overall merger	Rejected
$Ho_{4.12}$	There is no impact of total assets on the value of the firm considering the overall merger	Fail to Reject
$Ho_{4.13}$	There is no impact of the moving average of 30 days and 20 days on the value of the firm before acquisition	Rejected
$Ho_{4.14}$	There is no impact of the moving average of 5 days and relative strength index of 30 days on the value of the firm before acquisition	Rejected
$Ho_{4.15}$	There is no impact of total assets on the value of the firm before acquisition	Fail to Reject
$Ho_{4.16}$	There is no impact of moving average of 30 days and 20 days on the value of the firm after acquisition	Rejected
$Ho_{4.17}$	There is no impact of the moving average of 5 days and relative strength index of 30 days on the value of the firm after acquisition	Rejected
$Ho_{4.18}$	There is no impact of total assets on the value of the firm after acquisition	Fail to Reject
$Ho_{4.19}$	There is no impact of moving average of 30 days and 20 days on the value of the firm during acquisition	Rejected
$Ho_{4.20}$	There is no impact of the moving average of 5 days and relative strength index of 30 days on the value of the firm during acquisition	Rejected
$Ho_{4.21}$	There is no impact of total assets on the value of the firm during acquisition	Rejected
$Ho_{4.22}$	There is no impact of moving average of 30 days and 20 days on the value of the firm considering overall acquisition	Rejected

Null Hypotheses	Description	Accept/Reject
$Ho_{4.23}$	There is no impact of the moving average of 5 days and relative strength index of 30 days on the value of the firm considering overall acquisition	Rejected
$Ho_{4.24}$	There is no impact of total assets on the value of the firm considering overall acquisition	Fail to Reject

Source: *Compiled by Author from R output sheet*

It may be concluded that there is no significant impact of total assets on the stock price of the company before, after, during, and overall merger. However, all other variables have a significant impact on the stock price of the company before and after the merger. Similarly in the case of an acquisition, except during the acquisition the total assets do not have a significant impact on the stock price of the company. All other variables have a significant impact on the stock price of the company before and after acquisition.

Table 4.4.40 -Comparison of Pre- and Post-Merger and Acquisition

Variable	Merger		Acquisition	
	Pre	Post	Pre	Post
Objective 1: Financing Pattern				
R squared Sales	0.122	-0.019	0.051	0.045*
Return on Capital Employed	-0.058	-0.064	-0.045	-0.133***
Return with Total Assets	-0.122*	-0.080	-0.073**	-0.131***
Objective 2: Operating Efficiency				
Under Time-varying decay model				
Return on Assets	-0.0355***	0.03173**	-0.01491	0.00506
Operating Return on Assets	0.7676***	0.9427***	0.76152***	0.84611***
Sales	0.0055	0.03421	-0.02812	0.14869***

Variable	Merger		Acquisition	
	Pre	Post	Pre	Post
Five-Year Average Turnover	-0.1129***	0.04196	-0.05652**	-0.01443
Inventory Turnover	-0.0854**	-0.01641	-0.05247**	0.00477
Under Time invariant inefficiency model				
Return on Assets	-0.0334***	0.0342**	-0.01397*	0.00577
Operating Return on Assets	0.7706***	0.9378***	0.75810***	0.84468***
Sales	0.0272	0.0265	-0.00167	0.14283***
Five-Year Average Turnover	-0.1248***	0.03158	-0.07235***	-0.013416
Inventory Turnover	-0.0828**	-0.01936	-0.06573***	0.00122
Under Time-varying decay inefficiency model				
Return on Assets	-0.03574***	0.03173**	-0.01491	0.00506
Operating Return on Assets	0.76623***	0.9427***	0.7615***	0.84611***
Sales	-0.0032	0.0342	-0.0281	0.14869***
Five-Year Average Turnover	-0.0977***	0.04195	-0.0565**	-0.01443
Inventory Turnover	-0.07552**	-0.0164	-0.05246**	0.00477
Objective 3: Financial Performance				
Earnings Before Interest, Taxes, Depreciation and Amortisation	0.579***	0.627***	0.590***	0.605***
Earnings Before Interest and Taxes	0.541***	0.771***	0.581***	0.747***
Return on Assets	0.512***	0.834***	0.671***	0.854***

Variable	Merger		Acquisition	
	Pre	Post	Pre	Post
Return on Capital	0.494***	0.840***	0.549***	0.788***
Return on Capital Employed	0.207***	0.451***	0.345***	0.577***
Financial Leverage	-0.127***	-0.194***	-0.173***	-0.174***
Degree of Financial Leverage	-0.113**	-0.047	-0.121***	-0.184***
Degree of Operating Leverage	0.064	0.113	0.137***	0.281
Cash Flow from Net Income	1.055***	0.870***	1.033***	0.856
Objective 4: Value of the Firm				
Moving Average of 30 days	1.046***	0.662***	1.038***	0.590***
Moving Average of 20 days	1.022***	0.893***	0.940***	0.765***
Moving Average of 5 days	0.932***	1.143***	0.941***	1.098***
Relative Strength Index of 30 days	2.663***	3.261***	2.376***	2.987***
Total Assets	-0.001	0.0005	-0.0001	-0.0005

Note: *p<0.1, **p<0.05, ***p<0.01

This research examines the impact of mergers on a company's bottom line using a time-varying decay model, specifically the truncated-normal model. The study finds that a one percent increase in OROA and a five-year average turnover post-merger results in a slowdown in growth. However, the time-invariant inefficiency model shows that ROA increases from 0.0023184 to 0.0172536 after the acquisition, indicating an improvement in operating performance of around 1.5%.

The post-merger coefficient of EBITDA is 0.624, with a 5% increase under random effects and a 1% increase under fixed effects. The effect of a merger on earnings before interest and taxes (EBIT) becomes more pronounced over time, indicating improved financial performance for the companies after the merger. The Return on Capital Employed (ROCE) variable has a 0.451 and 0.538 coefficient, respectively.

Financial leverage has a downward trend both before and after the merger. The coefficient of FL in a pre-merger scenario is 0.127 in the random effect model and 0.115 in the fixed effect model. The study also examines how companies' use of financial leverage affects their bottom lines after merging. The negative coefficient of DFL has decreased, reducing its effect on the companies' financial performance since the merger.

The post-acquisition coefficient of EBITDA is 0.643, with a larger effect on the bottom line. The relative strength index has a larger impact on the relative strength index 30 days after the merger than before the merger. The coefficient of total assets for both the random and fixed effects models indicates that the merger has a positive impact on the stock price of the combined company, primarily due to the increase in total assets.

***

CHAPTER 5:

FINDINGS, CONCLUSIONS, LIMITATIONS AND IMPLICATIONS

CHAPTER 5: FINDINGS, CONCLUSIONS, LIMITATIONS AND IMPLICATIONS

5.1 Introduction

This is the last chapter, and it discusses the conclusion of the research study, concentrating on the research goals and the empirical results of this research paper. In order to make suggestions on the short-term impact that mergers and acquisitions have on shareholder returns, this section also takes into consideration the recommendations made by the researcher on the basis of the linked literature as well as the theoretical literature and framework. Lastly, the chapter comes to a close by offering some ideas for connected fields that other academics and researchers could find fruitful for future investigation.

5.2 Research Objectives

The following research objectives were set out to be fulfilled in chapter one of this research study:

1. To analyze the financing pattern of the resulting companies pre and post-M & As.

2. To compare the operating efficiency of the merged company on the basis of pre and post-M &As.

3. To study the impact of mergers and acquisitions on the financial performance of resulting listed companies.

4. To analyze the impact of M&As on the shareholder's wealth of the listed companies in the short run.

5.3 Research Conclusions

5.3.1 Results and conclusion of objective one

In this chapter, the study identifies the financing structure (debt vs. equity) in mergers that occurred during the fiscal year 2016-17 and 2017-18 and its impact on the company's debt-equity ratio. The completion time and the acquirers are critical in determining whether the mergers should be financed with restructuring internal money.

By analyzing two data sets from 468 merger deals and acquisition deals that occurred throughout that fiscal year. We analyzed the change in capital structure as well as the performance of resulting companies by using a regression model. Debt equity ratio has been taken as a dependent variable and R squared Sales, Normalized Return on Capital Employed, and Return with Total Assets are taken as independent variables in both pre- and post-merger and acquisition. The study will benefit the investors to analyze the companies more accurately. Previous studies have mainly concentrated on the sources of financing and payment mechanisms to be employed in mergers and acquisitions. So, this study is significant in addition to the available literature.

We have run a regression model in order to see the impact of different variables on the debt-equity ratio of the companies before and after merger and acquisition. Different equations have been used to check this impact. Equations have also been modified by adding or subtracting few of the variables to see how it impacts the debt-equity ratio. The overall impact has also been analyzed pre- and post-merger and acquisition as well as the impact of these variables on the debt-equity ratio in the year of mergers and acquisitions is also checked. Results drawn from these equations are as follows:

- In the case of a regression model with random effects and fixed effects having independent variables as R squared sales, normalized ROCE, ROCE with Total Assets, and dependent variable as total debt to total equity. It has been found that a rise in the R-squared sales value is associated with a reduction of 1.9% and 0.7% in the debt-equity ratio when employing the random effect and fixed effect models, respectively following the merger. R squared sales, normalized ROCE has a greater effect on total debt and total equity than after the merger. The correlation between Return on Capital Employed (ROCE) and Debt-to-Equity Ratio (DER) exhibits a negative association, both prior to and subsequent to the merger.
- Now, the equation is further modified and the independent variable is taken as a return with total assets in case of pre-and post-merger. Following the merger, the coefficient of RWTA exhibits values of 0.080 and 0.138 under the random effect and fixed effect models, respectively. Prior to the occurrence of the merger, the coefficient of RWTA exhibited a value of 0.122 when assessed using the random effect model, and 0.155 under the fixed effect model. This

finding suggests that a decline in a negative trend in the value of RWTA will lead to a corresponding improvement in the debt-equity ratio when considering both the random effect and fixed effect models, respectively. Therefore, the negative impact of RWTA on the DER has reduced after the merger compared to the pre-merger period.

- Further, the variables r squared sales and return on capital employed are analyzed in the case of pre- and post-acquisition. In the case of a regression model with random effects and fixed effects consisting of the independent variables as R squared sales, normalized ROCE, ROCE with Total Assets, and dependent variable as total debt to total equity. It has been found that following the acquisition a rise in the R-squared sales value will increase the DER by 4.5% and 5.7% when employing the random effect and fixed effect models, respectively. Consequently, Prior to the acquisition has had a more pronounced impact on the Debt-to-Equity Ratio (DER) in relation to the R-squared sales under the random effect model and post-acquisition under fixed effect. The correlation between Return on Capital Employed (ROCE) and Debt-to-Equity Ratio (DER) exhibits a negative association, both prior to and subsequent to the acquisition.
- Then we modified the equation and used only the return on capital employed with total assets as an independent variable. Following the acquisition, the coefficient of RWTA exhibits values of 0.131 and 0.143 under the random effect and fixed effect models, respectively. Prior to the occurrence of the acquisition, the coefficient of RWTA exhibited a value of 0.073 when assessed using the random effect model, and 0.097 under the fixed effect model. This finding suggests that an upward trend in the value of RWTA will lead to a corresponding decline in the debt-equity ratio when considering both the random effect and fixed effect models, respectively. There exists a negative correlation between the Return on capital employed with Total Assets (RWTA) and the Debt-to-Equity Ratio (DER) in pre- and post-acquisition.

Hence, overall, the findings are in most cases normalized ROCE and ROCE with total assets are negatively related to the Debt Equity Ratio. However, R-squared sales are still positively related to it in both pre-and post-mergers and acquisitions.

This study has provided a different perspective regarding the financing pattern of merged and acquired companies before and after their merger and acquisition. To the best of our knowledge, most of the studies relate to either source of finance or payment methods, It can be said this is the first study that has considered the impact of financing patterns on the debt-equity ratio of the companies. This study will benefit the investors to analyze the company's financing pattern more accurately.

5.3.2 Results and conclusion of objective two

In this chapter, the study has addressed the objective to compare the operating efficiency of the merged company on the basis of pre and post-M &As. This chapter analyses the operating efficiencies of resulting companies pre- and post-mergers and acquisitions using data from 2013-14 to 2021-22 of Indian companies that were merged during the financial years 2016-17 and 2017-18. The stochastic frontier analysis has been used in order to analyze the operating efficiencies of the resulting companies. This study is conducted in order to check if operating margins are impacted by the operating return on assets, return on assets, inventory turnover, and turnover after resultant companies attributed to synergy between the two companies.

Most of the studies have focused on merger and acquisition deals in a specific sector or industry. However, overall consideration of the merged and acquired companies is not taken to see the impact on operating efficiency of the resulting companies pre- and post-merger and acquisition which has been identified as a gap in this objective. We have used Stochastic Frontier Analysis in this objective to analyze the financial statistics comparable between dependent and independent variables using STATA. The results drawn using this method are as follows:

- Firstly, we analyzed stochastic frontier analysis using a time-varying decay model before and after the merger. Here the independent variables are taken as operating return on assets and five-year average turnover. The coefficient of Mu is used to determine the impact of these variables on the operating efficiency of the company. The value of Mu is 0.9956765 which signifies that a one percent increase in the operating return on assets (OROA) and the five-year average turnover post-merger will lead to an increase in the growth rate.

Nevertheless, the coefficient of Mu exhibited a negative value prior to the occurrence of the merger.

- Next, the same variables are executed in another model i.e., Time Invariant Inefficiency Model. According to this Model, the Coefficient of Operating Return on Assets (OROA) experienced a significant increase from 0.8010874 before the merger to 0.9142983 after the merger. This indicates an approximate improvement of 11 percent in the operating performance subsequent to the merger. The coefficient of the five-year average turnover after the merger is positive, suggesting that the operating performance has improved compared to before the merger when the coefficient was negative.
- Further, the same variables are run using a different model named as time-varying decay inefficiency model. The results drawn are merger has a positive impact on the operating margin, as evidenced by the positive influence of both the operating return on assets (OROA) and the five-year average turnover in the context of time-varying decay inefficiency. However, the only positive aspect in terms of operating return on assets (OROA) was observed prior to the merger. Hence, it can be asserted that both variables have exerted a positive influence on the operational performance of the company's post-merger.
- Next, the stochastic frontier analysis is done for the independent variables' return on assets and inventory turnover. These variables are first examined under a time-varying decay model before and after the merger. The results are drawn on the basis of the coefficient of Mu which is estimated to be 0.0621751. This coefficient indicates that a one percent increase in both the return on assets (ROA) and inventory turnover following a merger will result in a decline of 6.21 percent in the growth rate. Nevertheless, the coefficient exhibited a positive value prior to the merger.
- Further, the same variables are executed through the Time-Invariant Inefficiency Model and it is found that the coefficient of Return on Assets (ROA) after the merger is 0.1545546, compared to 0.00705 before the merger. This suggests that the operating performance has improved by approximately 15 percent after the merger, as indicated by the increased value of the ROA coefficient.

- Again, these variables are run but through another model i.e., a time-varying decay inefficiency model. In this model, the ROA and inventory turnover are positively influencing the operating margin after the merger which was influencing negatively before the merger.
- Now, the variable is modified to sales, and the model taken to analyze is the time-varying decay model where the coefficient of Mu, denoted as 390.0716 after the merger was 0.5563 before the merger. Before the merger, the coefficient was positive which signifies that a one percent increase in turnover will result in a growth rate increase of 55.63 percent. However, it has become negative post-merger which means that a one percent increase in turnover will result in a decline in the growth rate of operating performance.
- Further, the same variable is analyzed through a different model i.e., the time invariant inefficiency model where the Coefficient of Sales is determined to be 0.6695934 post-merger which was 0.1629605 pre-merger. This value suggests that the operating performance of all companies has become better due to the change in the percentage of coefficient of sales by approx. 50% after merger.
- Lastly, the independent variables sales are run through the model called the time-varying decay inefficiency model where it is observed that the turnover has a positive influence on the operating margin post-merger and before the merger.
- The above cases relate to the merger. Now, the variables are run through all three models in case of an acquisition. In this firstly, the variables operating return on assets and five-year average turnover are analyzed through a time-varying decay model where the coefficient of Mu is determined to be 575.1974 after acquisition which was 169.6808 before acquisition. This coefficient signifies that a one percent increase in the operating return on assets (OROA) and the five-year average turnover post-merger will lead to a decline in the growth rate after acquisition.
- Next, the same variables are run through different models i.e., the time-invariant inefficiency model. According to this Model, the Coefficient of Operating Return on Assets (OROA) experienced a significant increase from 0.6858719 before the acquisition to 0.903771 after the acquisition. This indicates an

approximate improvement of 2 percent in the operating performance subsequent to the acquisition.

- Again, the same variables are executed but using a different model i.e., a time-varying decay inefficiency model. The acquisition has a positive impact on the operating margin, as evidenced by the positive influence of both the operating return on assets (OROA) and the five-year average turnover in the context of time-varying decay inefficiency. However, the only positive aspect in terms of operating return on assets (OROA) was observed prior to the acquisition.
- Now, the variables are modified to return on assets and inventory turnover. These variables are executed through firstly time-varying decay model where the coefficient of Mu is estimated to be 0.8008007. This coefficient indicates that a one percent increase in both the return on assets (ROA) and inventory turnover following an acquisition will result in a decline of 80 percent in the growth rate.
- Next, the same variables are executed using another model i.e., time-invariant inefficiency model. According to this Model, the coefficient of Return on Assets (ROA) after the acquisition is 0.0172536, compared to 0.0023184 before the acquisition. This suggests that the operating performance has improved by approximately 1.5 percent after the merger, as indicated by the increased value of the ROA coefficient.
- Not only this, the same variables are analyzed through the time-varying decay inefficiency model. In this model, the ROA and inventory turnover positively influence the operating margin after the acquisition. The coefficients are positive before acquisition as well.
- Further, the variable is modified to sales and it is run through the model called time-varying decay model firstly which indicates that the coefficient of *mu*, denoted as 17.8502 after acquisition was 0.4640823 before acquisition. Before acquisition, the coefficient was positive which signifies that a one percent increase in turnover will result in a growth rate increase of 46.40 percent. However, it has become negative post-acquisition which means that a one percent increase in turnover will result in a decline in the growth rate of operating performance.

- Next, the same variable is run through the time-invariant inefficiency model. According to this model, the Coefficient of Sales is determined to be 0.6006861 post-acquisition which was 0.2991654 pre-acquisition. This value suggests that the operating performance of all companies has become better due to the change in the percentage of coefficient of sales by approx. 30% after acquisition.
- Finally, the variable sales remained the same. However, the model is modified to the time-varying decay inefficiency model where it is observed that the turnover has a positive influence on the operating margin post-acquisition and prior to the acquisition.

  Hence, it can be concluded that turnover has a positive impact on operating efficiency using different models. Return on assets and operating return on assets also have a positive impact after merger and acquisition on operating efficiency.

5.3.3 Results and conclusion of objective three

The chapter addresses the objective to study the impact of mergers and acquisitions on the financial performance of resulting listed companies. Most of the previous studies focused on M&A deals and market-based activities on which valuation and other market capitalization move with that. However, there is a scope for checking the impact of mergers and acquisitions on the financial performance pre- and post-merger and acquisition. In this, we have analyzed the financial performance of the resulting companies after merger and acquisition, for the same we have extracted the data from the Bloomberg database for the period from 2013-14 to 2021-22 of mergers that took place in two financial years 2016-17 and 2017-18. The sample consists of 150 companies from 2013-2022. The regression model is used to analyze the impact on the financial performance of the companies pre- and post-merger and acquisition. The results drawn are as follows:

- Firstly, we run a regression model with random effects as well as fixed effects consisting of independent variables EBITDA and EBIT, and dependent variables as Net Income pre- and post-merger. The results drawn are, that after the merger, the coefficient of EBITDA is observed to be 0.627 under the random effect model and 0.624 under the fixed effect model. The values observed were 0.579 under the random effect model and 0.540 under the fixed effect model prior to the merger. This finding suggests that there is a statistically significant change in EBITDA, with an approximate increase of 5 percent under random effects and 1 percent under fixed effects. This implies that the post-merger EBITDA has had a greater impact on the financial performance. Likewise, it can be observed that Earnings Before Interest and Taxes (EBIT) exhibit a more pronounced effect following a merger in both models, suggesting an enhanced financial performance of the companies subsequent to the merger. The coefficient of EBIT was 0.676 under the random effects model and 0.541 under the fixed effects model prior to the merger. Following the merger, the coefficient of EBIT is 0.771 under the random effects model and 0.729 under the fixed effects model.

- Thereafter the independent variables are changed ROA and ROC whereas the dependent variable is the same. The regression model is run with both fixed effects and random effects. The coefficient of Return on Assets (ROA) is found to be 0.512 under the random effects model and 0.515 under the fixed effects model prior to the merger. Following the merger, the coefficient of ROA is estimated to be 0.769 under the random effects model and 0.834 under the fixed effects model. This suggests that the alteration in Return on Assets (ROA) will have a more pronounced effect on the financial performance in both models after the merger. The financial performance of the companies has demonstrated improvement subsequent to the merger. The coefficient of the ROC is 0.494 in both the random effect and fixed effect models prior to the merger. However, after the merger, the coefficient has increased to 0.773 and 0.840 in the random effect and fixed effect models, respectively.

- Further, the equations are modified and the regression model is used with fixed as well as random effects consisting of the independent variables as ROCE and Financial Leverage pre- and post-merger. The coefficient values for the Return on Capital Employed (ROCE) variable are 0.451 and 0.538 when estimated using the random effects and fixed effects models, respectively. Prior to the merger, the coefficient of Return on Capital Employed (ROCE) was observed to be 0.207 under the random effects model and 0.219 under the fixed effects model. This suggests that the rise in the proportion of Return on Capital Employed (ROCE) subsequent to the merger has enhanced the financial performance of the companies. However, it should be noted that financial leverage exhibits a negative trend both prior to and subsequent to the merger. In the event of a pre-merger scenario, the coefficient of FL was observed to be 0.127 under the random effect and 0.115 under the fixed effect model. Subsequently, this coefficient increased to 0.194 and 0.242 under the random and fixed models, respectively. The financial performance of companies is being adversely impacted by financial leverage, as observed in both the random effect and fixed effect models before and after the merger. However, subsequent to the merger, there has been an increase in this percentage, consequently leading to a detrimental impact of financial leverage on the financial performance of the companies. The coefficient values of Return on Capital Employed (ROCE) exhibit a statistically significant impact at a significance level of 1% in both the pre-merger and post-merger periods.

- Equations are again modified and the independent variables taken are the degree of financial leverage and operating leverage under both random and fixed effect models. The coefficient for the Degree of Financial Leverage (DFL) is 0.113 under the random effects model and 0.135 under the fixed effects model prior to the merger. However, following the merger, the value decreased to 0.047 under the random effect model and 0.106 under the fixed effect model. This suggests that the decrease in the negative coefficient of DFL has mitigated the adverse impact of this variable on the financial performance of the companies following the merger. During the pre-merger period, the coefficient of DOL was observed to be 0.064 under the random effects model and 0.054 under the fixed effects model. Subsequently, there was an increase in the coefficient to 0.113 under the random effects model.

- Lastly, the equation is modified and the regression model is run only on cash flow from net income. The coefficient of cash flow from net income (CFNI) is observed to be 0.870 under the random effect model and 0.898 under the fixed effect model following the merger. Prior to the merger, these coefficients were recorded as 0.988 under the random effect model and 1.055 under the fixed effect model. This suggests that the cash flow from net income has declined following the merger in both models, indicating a decline in financial performance after the merger.

- Similarly, now the regression model is run with random effects as well as fixed effects pre- and post-acquisition. After the acquisition, the coefficient of EBITDA is observed to be 0.605 under the random effect model and 0.643 under the fixed effect model. The values observed were 0.590 under the random effect model and the fixed effect model prior to the acquisition. This finding suggests that there is a minute change in EBITDA, with under-random effects and fixed effects post-acquisition. Still, the post-acquisition EBITDA has had a greater impact on the financial performance. Likewise, it can be observed that Earnings Before Interest and Taxes (EBIT) exhibit a more pronounced effect following an acquisition in both models, suggesting an enhanced financial performance of the companies subsequent to the acquisition. The coefficient of EBIT is 0.615 under the random effects model and 0.581 under the fixed effects model prior to the acquisition. Following the acquisition, the coefficient of EBIT is 0.747 under the random effects model and 0.748 under the fixed effects model.

- Now, the independent variables are changed to ROA and ROC pre- and post-acquisition under both models. The coefficient of Return on Assets (ROA) is found to be 0.645 under the random effects model and 0.671 under the fixed effects model prior to the acquisition. Following the acquisition, the coefficient of ROA is estimated to be 0.766 under the random effects model and 0.854 under the fixed effects model. This suggests that the change in Return on Assets (ROA) will have a more pronounced effect on the financial performance of both models after the acquisition. The coefficient of the ROC is 0.549 under the random effect and 0.567 under fixed effect models prior to the acquisition. However, after the acquisition, the coefficient increased to 0.704 and 0.788 in the random effect and fixed effect models, respectively. This indicates a stronger influence of the ROC post-acquisition.

- Now, the equations are further modified consisting of independent variables as ROCE and FL under both models. The coefficient values for the Return on Capital Employed (ROCE) variable are 0.466 and 0.577 when estimated using the random effects and fixed effects models, respectively. Prior to the acquisition, the coefficient of Return on Capital Employed (ROCE) was observed to be 0.345 under the random effects model and 0.366 under the fixed effects model. This suggests that the rise in the proportion of Return on Capital Employed (ROCE) subsequent to the acquisition has enhanced the financial performance of the companies. However, it should be noted that financial leverage exhibits a negative trend both prior to and subsequent to the acquisition. In the event of a pre-acquisition scenario, the coefficient of FL was observed to be 0.173 under the random effect and 0.164 under the fixed effect model. Subsequently, this coefficient increased to 0.194 and 0.242 under the random and fixed models, respectively. The financial performance of companies is being adversely impacted by financial leverage, as observed in both the random effect and fixed effect models before and after the acquisition.

- The same model is again run with new independent variables i.e., DFL and DOL pre-and post-acquisition. The coefficient for the Degree of Financial Leverage (DFL) is 0.121 under the random effects model and 0.124 under the fixed effects model prior to the acquisition. However, following the acquisition, the value has increased to 0.184 under the random effect model and 0.214 under the fixed effect model. This suggests that the increase in the negative coefficient of DFL has enhanced the adverse impact of this variable on the financial performance of the companies following the acquisition. During the pre-acquisition period, the coefficient of DOL was observed to be 0.137 under the random effects model and 0.157 under the fixed effects model. Subsequently, there was an increase in the coefficient to 0.216 under the random effect model and 0.281 under the fixed effect model. The rise in the proportion of degree of operating leverage (DOL) under both models has resulted in enhanced financial performance among companies.

- Further, the equations are modified where the independent variable is taken as cash flow from net income pre- and post-acquisition. The coefficient of cash flow from net income (CFNI) is observed to be 0.856 under the random effect model and 0.879 under the fixed effect model following the acquisition. Prior to the acquisition, these coefficients were recorded as 0.984 under the random effect model and 1.033 under the fixed effect model. This suggests that the CFNI has decreased following the acquisition in both models, indicating a decline in financial performance after the acquisition.

Hence, it can be concluded that ROCE, EBIT, ROA, and ROC are positively related to financial performance in most of the cases. However, the coefficients of DOL and DFL are negative in most of the cases thereby showing a negative relationship with the financial performance of the companies. Post-merger and acquisition the company's financial performance has been improved. Therefore, synergies have helped in improving the financial performance of the companies making them more viable for investment by the investors.

5.3.4 Results and conclusion of objective four

The values of such firms' shares tend to increase in the short term after their formation. However, the vast majority of corporations have not been successful in accomplishing their goal that was set before M&A. Despite this, firms that have merged with larger ones have been successful thanks to the continued expansion of their acquirers. It has been shown that investor prospective thinking towards hope in the acquiring firms had a significant impact in enhancing the share price of the companies that were amalgamating. However, it has been observed that the overall price change is due to an indication of additional investment by acquirer companies in the target companies following the deals, as well as investor expectations towards specific strong holdings in the stock markets. This was discovered through the use of price correlation analysis. The majority of financial investors concentrate their efforts on selling shares according to liquidity circumstances so that the firm may satisfy its legal and accounting obligations.

Under this objective, we analyze the impact of M&As on the shareholder's wealth of the listed companies in the short run. For this purpose, we run a regression analysis using R studio to see the impact of M&As on shareholders' wealth using different variables in case of merger and acquisition. The results drawn are as follows:

- Firstly, we run a regression model with independent variables moving averages of 30 days and 20 days. It is found that prior to the merger, the coefficient of the 30-day moving average was found to be 1.046 under the random effect model and 1.057 under the fixed effect model. Following the merger, it is observed that the coefficient of the 30-day moving average is 1.112 under random effect, while the coefficient of the 30-day moving average (ma_20d) under fixed effect is 0.662. This suggests that the rise in the 30-day moving average following a merger, when considering random effects, will exert a more significant influence on the post-merger stock price of the company. Further, it is also found that following the merger, the coefficient of moving average of 20 days has increased to 1.085 under the random effect model and decreased to 0.893 under the fixed effect model. This finding indicates that the application of a random effect model demonstrates a significant impact of a 20-day moving average on the stock prices of companies following a merger, with a heightened level of influence.
- Further, the model is run on RSI of 30 days and moving average of 5 days where it is found Prior to the merger, the 5-day moving average coefficient is 0.999 under random effect and 0.932 under fixed effect. After the merger, it increased to 1.037 and 1.143 under random and fixed effect models respectively. This shows that a change in the 5-day moving average under both models will have a higher impact on the company's stock price after the merger. Similarly, the relative strength index has a bigger impact on the relative strength index of 30 days after the merger, as the coefficient of the relative strength index of 30 days is 2.663 under random effect and 2.610 under fixed effect before the merger which has increased to 3.339 and 3.261 under random and fixed effect model respectively.
- The model is then run on total assets being the independent variable under both random and fixed effect models where it is found that the coefficient of total assets

for both the random and fixed effects is 0.001 prior to the merger. Following the merger, the coefficient exhibits an increase to 0.0005 under the random effect model and 0.001 under the fixed effect model. Based on the analysis of both models, it can be concluded that the company's stock price experiences a positive effect as a result of the merger, primarily due to the increase in overall assets.

- In a similar way, the regression model is executed using independent variables consisting of the 30-day and 20-day moving averages in the context of acquisition. Here it is found that before the acquisition took place, the coefficient of the 30-day moving average was determined to be 1.038 according to the random effect model and 0.989 according to the fixed effect model. Following the acquisition, the coefficient has exhibited a decline to 1.005 and 0.590 under the random and fixed effect models, respectively. This implies that the influence of the change in the 30-day moving average is less significant under both models after acquisition as compared to the pre-acquisition period. The study reveals that the impact of the 20-day moving average is more pronounced prior to acquisition, exhibiting a value of 1.025 under random effect and a coefficient of 0.940 under fixed effect before acquisition. After the acquisition, the coefficient values decline to 1.008 and 0.765 under the random and fixed effects, respectively.
- Next, the same model is executed on moving averages of 5 days and relative strength index of 30 days where it is found that prior to the acquisition, the 5-day moving average coefficient has a random effect value of 1.003 and a fixed effect value of 0.941. After the acquisition, the value of the coefficient is increased to 1.023 and 1.098 under random and fixed effect models respectively. This indicates that a change in the 5-day moving average will have a greater effect on the stock price of the company after acquisition. Similarly, the relative strength index of 30 days after acquisition has a greater impact, as the coefficient of the relative strength index of 30 days under random effect is 2.376, and under fixed effect, it is 2.366 before acquisition which has increased to 3.034 and 2.987 after acquisition.
- Finally, the model is executed on total assets as well where the results showed that Prior to the acquisition, the total asset coefficient is 0.0001 for both the random and fixed effects. After the acquisition, total assets are 0.0005 under random effect and 0.0003 under the fixed effect model. After the acquisition, total assets had increased a negative impact on the company's stock price, according to both models.

The data has also been analyzed using average abnormal return on stock price before and after merger and acquisition. In this regard, the fluctuation of stock prices pre- and post-merger is evaluated. For few days, the CAAR is negative, however the same is positive after the merger thereby indicating a positive impact on the shareholder's wealth after the merger. If we see the mean of the company's stock price pre- and post-merger a wide gap appears as before the merger the mean was negative on most of the days whereas after the merger it was positive.

The AAR i.e., average abnormal returns are also calculated to analyze the impact of the stock price on the shareholder's wealth in the short run. It is observed that the cumulative abnormal return was negative before the merger as well as after the merger which indicates that the company is unable to fetch more return than expected overall after the merger in the short run, hence ultimately increasing the shareholder's wealth.

5.4 Research Recommendations

Future research can consider more specific variables for example: discounted cashflows, and method of payment of M&A deals, and reverse the variable of this study with a comparison of new developments. In academia, it will remain a burning topic in the coming time and influence the industry to grow and expand the business. In considering the analytical part M&A research has established its area or field of the subject in the financial market. M&A comprises various components such as accounting, law, taxation, and corporate policy these days due to this it is treated as a one specialized subject of study. Some of the corporates establish separate departments to deal with merger and acquisition activities. It can be said that it is a continuous process in businesses these days, and that's why there is always a need to research and update it mainly for academia, policymakers, industrialists, corporate professionals, merchant bankers, banks, etc. Furthermore, in the coming decades, data may be available for exploring other aspects and providing better solutions for deeper, complex, strategic problems.

Based on the time it can be explored as explanatory research, event study, cluster study, geographical-based study, etc. As we have explored the financing pattern of resulting companies in our study this can be further expanded beyond debt and equity ratio by taking new variables. As we have analyzed the operating efficiencies of the listed companies pre- and post-merger this can be further analyzed by taking a new time frame and a specific set of industry. Big corporate players who are most of the time in the news of mergers and acquisitions can be compared to see the impact of their synergies pre- and post-merger and acquisition. Analysis of Mergers and acquisitions deals is important to see the reasons behind their growth operational efficiencies or overall financial performance. This study also categorizes the value of the firm as a special or important part of merger and acquisition analysis. Market capitalization is also an important aspect for investors to value their investments. Accordingly, they invest their money into a particular business. Further, the researcher can explore the four broad areas of M&A in their future research.

5.5 Limitations to the Study

This research study was restricted to Indian companies that were listed on the stock market and were active in mergers and acquisitions. It was equivalent from both perspectives, both in terms of efficiency and the funding arrangement. For the purpose of this research, I analyzed a large dataset to come up with an overall perspective on the effectiveness of mergers and acquisitions and the effects they have. In addition, research may be conducted on the payment method of M&A agreements, as well as industry-specific factors, etc., in the context of India. Because our analysis only looked at publicly traded corporations, imagining a wider range of mergers and acquisitions was challenging, expensive, and time-consuming. Due to the fact that other sorts of data were not available, the author chose not to use them. These data are susceptible to rigorous procedures, which the author was unable to envision.

This study is majorly comprised of four areas such as financing structure, operating efficiency, financial performance, and shareholder's wealth which means it can be further extended with different perspectives in order to show how it impacts the financial growth of the company. The cross-border mergers and acquisitions can also be studied keeping the same objectives as used by the author in this study to analyse the impact on the growth of such resulting companies. This study is limited to India only. Hence, data from other developed countries can also be taken to analyze the impact of mergers and acquisitions deals over there. The data taken in this study belongs to the mergers and acquisitions deals that took place between 2016-17 and 2017-18 which can be posed as a limitation. Further, researchers can take recent data for their study for the analysis of merger and acquisition deals taking place.

The variables taken for the purpose of analysis are also limited which can be either modified or extended for further research. The researchers can take different financial ratios or averages for the purpose of their research work. This study has used a regression model, stochastic frontier analysis, and event study which can be further extended by the researcher by using new methodologies. Continuous and more research is required. With the ongoing growth of mergers and acquisitions in the companies, research must keep up.

5.6 Implications

- The findings of this research may be useful to the management of the companies and companies who are in the process of merger and acquisition or who are planning to go for merger and acquisition. This study will help them to understand the various financial aspects as well as the power of synergy. This study shows how the financing pattern can influence the growth of the company.
- The factors which influence operating efficiency, and financial performance can be used by management to analyze their own financial statements pre-and post-merger and acquisition. The impact of mergers and acquisitions on the growth of the company can be easily investigated with the help of the findings of this study.
- The shareholders are the most important stakeholders in any company. So this study is useful for the investors as well to make a decision before investing their funds in the merged or acquired company. The economic impact can be analyzed by them before making any investment.
- This study is also useful for the policymakers/lawmakers as with the changing environment the policies or laws also need to be amended in order to make the merger and acquisition more convenient for the companies to grow together. Policymakers must strive for a balance between encouraging innovation and

increasing competition, as well as a commitment to less restricted policies related to it as well as investor protection, financial stability, and integrity.

- The researchers can also find this study very useful in order to enhance their vision and focus on the upcoming changes in mergers and acquisitions. This study can be further extended by taking the data from the current years or cross-country data for the purpose of analysis.
- Mergers and acquisitions provide numerous advantages to entrepreneurs all over the globe. It has made it easier for companies to expand into global markets rather than just domestic ones.
- Mergers and acquisitions have a bright future as it is now treated as a separate subject of study as it involves various components such as accounting, taxation, law, corporate policy, etc. Hence, this study is important for corporate professionals in order to enhance their knowledge on the topic of mergers and acquisitions.
- This study is useful to the government in order to impose any tax or any changes in taxation laws or impose or reduce any restriction to protect the interest of shareholders/ consumers.
- This study is important for the different regulatory as well as SEBI in order to protect the interest of the shareholders of the companies.

***

REFERENCES

Abdou, H. A., Agbeyo, O. O., Jones, K., Sorour, K., & Abdou, H. (2016). The impact of M&A on the Nigerian financial market: a pre-post analysis. In *Investment Management and Financial Innovation* (Vol. 13, Issue 1). http://ssrn.com/abstract=2756768Electroniccopyavailableat:https://ssrn.com/abstract=2756768Electroniccopyavailableat:http://ssrn.com/abstract=2756768

Acero, I., & Alcalde, N. (2021). Institutional context as a moderator of the relationship between board structure and acquirer returns. *Research in International Business and Finance*, *57*. https://doi.org/10.1016/j.ribaf.2021.101420

Adler, H. S., & Sneath, C. G. (1987). Acquiring Companies in the USA. *Long Range Planning*, *20*(2), 42-50.

Ahluwalia, S., & Kassicieh, S. (2022). Effect of financial clusters on startup mergers and acquisitions. *International Journal of Financial Studies*, *10*(1). https://doi.org/10.3390/ijfs10010001

Akpan, M. N. U., Aik, N. C., Wanke, P. F., & Chau, W. H. (2018). Exploring the long-term trade-off between efficiency and value creation in horizontal M&As: Evidence from Nigeria. *African Journal of Economic and Management Studies*, *9*(2), 130–147. https://doi.org/10.1108/AJEMS-06-2017-0139

Alcalde, N., & Powell, R. (2022). Government intervention in European mergers and acquisitions. *North American Journal of Economics and Finance*, *61*. https://doi.org/10.1016/j.najef.2022.101689

Antoniou, A., Petmezas, D., & Zhao, H. (2007). Bidder gains and losses of firms involved in many acquisitions. *Journal of Business Finance and Accounting*, *34*(7–8), 1221–1244. https://doi.org/10.1111/j.1468-5957.2007.02012.x

Anwar, R., Abidin, S. Z., & Hassan, O. H. (2015). Function means analysis for ablution concept solution. *The Turkish Online Journal of Educational Technology*, *2015*(Special Issue for INTE), 224-231

Aureli, S. (2015). Performance of unlisted Italian companies acquired by multinationals from emerging markets: The case of Indian acquisitions. *Journal of Organizational Change Management*, *28*(5), 895–924. https://doi.org/10.1108/ JOCM-12-2014-0233

Balasubramanian, V., & Bhattacharyya, S. (1986). Database structure and system design of an online acquisition system. *Information processing & management*, *22*(6), 503-509.

Barros, V., Verga Matos, P., Miranda Sarmento, J., & Rino Vieira, P. (2022). M&A activity as a driver for better ESG performance. *Technological Forecasting and Social Change*, *175*. https://doi.org/10.1016/j.techfore.2021.121338

Barth, J. R., Lin, D., & Yost, K. (2011). Small and Medium Enterprise Financing in Transition Economies. *Atlantic Economic Journal*, *39*(1), 19–38. https://doi.org/10.1007/s11293-010-9260-0

Barnhart, G. (1987). Common critical success factors for integrating mergers and acquisitions. *Journal of Management in Engineering*, *3*(1), 38-46.

Basnet, A., Davis, F., Walker, T., & Zhao, K. (2021). The effect of securities class action lawsuits on mergers and acquisitions. *Global Finance Journal*, *48*. https://doi.org/10.1016/j.gfj.2020.100556

Battese, G. E., & Coelli, T. J. (1988). Prediction of firm-level technical efficiencies with a generalized frontier production function and panel data. *Journal of econometrics*, *38*(3), 387-399.

Battese, G. E., & Coelli, T. J. (1992). Frontier production functions, technical efficiency and panel data: with application to paddy farmers in India. *Journal of productivity analysis*, *3*, 153-169.

Bathelt, H., & Henn, S. (2021). Knowledge exchanges, trust, and secretive geographies in merger and acquisition processes. *Environment and Planning A*, *53*(6), 1435–1453. https://doi.org/10.1177/0308518X211013360

Bauer, F., Friesl, M., & Dao, M. A. (2022). Run or hide: changes in acquisition behaviour during the COVID-19 pandemic. *Journal of Strategy and Management*, *15*(1), 38–53. https://doi.org/10.1108/JSMA-02-2021-0046

Bens, D. A., Goodman, T. H., & Neamtiu, M. (2012). Does investment-related pressure lead to misreporting? an analysis of reporting following M&A transactions. *Accounting Review*, *87*(3), 839–865. https://doi.org/10.2308/accr-10210

Bernad, C., Fuentelsaz, L., & Gómez, J. (2010). The effect of mergers and acquisitions on productivity: An empirical application to Spanish banking. *Omega (United Kingdom)*, *38*(5), 283–293. https://doi.org/10.1016/j.omega.2009.07.005

Bernad, C., Fuentelsaz, L., & Gomez, J. (2013). The consequences of mergers on the profitability of Spanish savings banks. *Service Industries Journal*, *33*(2), 266–278. https://doi.org/10.1080/02642069.2011.601295

Bhasin, N., Soni, A., & Kar, R. N. (2021). Do Institutional and Macroeconomic Factors Matter in IT companies M&As? Evidence from India. *Business Perspectives and Research*, *9*(2), 286–305. https://doi.org/10.1177/2278533720964927

Blanco-Oliver, A. (2021). Banking reforms and bank efficiency: Evidence for the collapse of Spanish savings banks. *International Review of Economics and Finance*, *74*, 334–347. https://doi.org/10.1016/j.iref.2021.03.015

Boo, C., & Kim, C. (2022). What drives acquirers' myopic marketing management? *Applied Economics Letters*, *29*(7), 640–643. https://doi.org/10.1080/13504851.2021.1883520

Borodin, A., Ziyadin, S., Islyam, G., & Panaedova, G. (2020). Impact of mergers and acquisitions on companies' financial performance. *Journal of International Studies*, *13*(2), 34–47. https://doi.org/10.14254/2071-8330.2020/13-2/3

Bradley, M., Desai, A., & Kim, E. H. (1983). The rationale behind interfirm tender offers: Information or synergy? *Journal of financial economics*, *11*(1-4), 183-206.

Brookes, B. C. (1977). Theory of the Bradford law. *Journal of documentation*, *33*(3), 180-209.

Bugeja, M., Lu, M., Shan, Y., & To, T. (2021). The probability of informed trading and mergers and acquisitions. *Accounting and Finance*, *61*(1), 169–203. https://doi.org/10.1111/acfi.12562

Burns, N., Minnick, K., & Smith, A. H. (2021). The role of directors with related supply chain industry experience in corporate acquisition decisions. In *Journal of Corporate Finance* (Vol. 67). Elsevier B.V. https://doi.org/10.1016/j.jcorpfin.2021.101911

Caiazza, S., Galloppo, G., & Paimanova, V. (2021). The role of sustainability performance after merger and acquisition deals in short and long-term. *Journal of Cleaner Production*, *314*. https://doi.org/10.1016/j.jclepro.2021.127982

Calcagno, R., de Bodt, E., & Demidova, I. (2021). Takeover duration and negotiation process. *European Financial Management*, *27*(4), 589–619. https://doi.org/10.1111/eufm.12331

Carline, N. F., & Gogineni, S. (2021). Antitakeover provisions and investment in mergers and acquisitions: A causal reevaluation. *Journal of Corporate Finance*, *69*. https://doi.org/10.1016/j.jcorpfin.2021.101962

Chakrabarti, A. K. (1990). Organizational factors in post-acquisition performance. *IEEE transactions on engineering management*, *37*(4), 259-268.

Chan, J. M. L., & Zheng, H. (2022). FDI on the move: cross-border M&A and migrant networks. *Review of World Economics*, *158*(3), 947–985. https://doi.org/10.1007/s10290-021-00450-1

Chatterjee, S., Hasan, I., John, K., & Yan, A. (2021). Stock liquidity, empire building, and valuation. *Journal of Corporate Finance*, *70*. https://doi.org/10.1016/j.jcorpfin.2021.102051

Chatterjee, S., Lubatkin, M. H., Schweiger, D. M., & Weber, Y. (1992). Cultural differences and shareholder value in related mergers: Linking equity and human capital. *Strategic management journal*, *13*(5), 319-334.

Chen, C., Lu, W., & Liu, M. (2022). Corporate social responsibility learning in mergers and acquisitions. *Asia-Pacific Journal of Accounting and Economics*, *29*(1), 53–76. https://doi.org/10.1080/16081625.2019.1680297

Chen, J. L. (2012). The synergistic effects of IT-enabled resources on organizational capabilities and firm performance. *Information and Management*, *49*(3–4), 142–150. https://doi.org/10.1016/j.im.2012.01.005

Ching-Yick Tse, E., & Crawford-Welch, S. (2015). *AN ANALYSIS OF MERGER AND ACQUISITION ACTIVITY IN THE HOSPITALITY INDUSTRY FOR THE PERIOD 1970-1988*.

Cho, S. Y., Arthurs, J. D., Townsend, D. M., Miller, D. R., & Barden, J. Q. (2016). Performance deviations and acquisition premiums: The impact of CEO celebrity on managerial risk-taking. *Strategic Management Journal*, *37*(13), 2677–2694. https://doi.org/10.1002/smj.2468

Choi, J., Shin, N., & Chang, Y. S. (2021). Strategic investment decisions for emerging technology fields in the health care sector based on m&a analysis. *Sustainability (Switzerland)*, *13*(7). https://doi.org/10.3390/su13073644

Chu, Y., Chu, J., & Liu, H. (2021). The impact of mergers and acquisitions on brand equity: A structural analysis. *International Journal of Research in Marketing*, *38*(3), 615–638. https://doi.org/10.1016/j.ijresmar.2020.11.006

Chudamani, K. S., & Shalini, R. (1983). Journal acquisition—cost effectiveness of models. *Information processing & management*, *19*(5), 307-311.

Cipollina, M., Pietrovito, F., & Pozzolo, A. F. (2021). Do cross-border mergers and acquisitions reflect participations into global value chains? *World Economy*, *44*(11), 3168–3201. https://doi.org/10.1111/twec.13135

Cotei, C., Farhat, J., & Khurana, I. (2022). The impact of policy uncertainty on the M&A exit of startup firms. *Journal of Economics and Finance*, *46*(1), 99–120. https://doi.org/10.1007/s12197-021-09553-9

da Costa, R. L., Miguel, J., Dias, Á., Pereira, L., & Santos, J. (2021). Exploring the Cultural, Managerial and Organizational Implications on Mergers and Acquisitions Outcomes. *Organizacija*, *54*(1), 18–35. https://doi.org/10.2478/orga-2021-0002

Datta, D. K., & Yu, P. L. (1991). Corporate acquisitions: the merging of habitual domains. *Human Systems Management*, *10*(1), 47-60.

Datta, D. K., Pinches, G. E., & Narayanan, V. K. (1992). Factors influencing wealth creation from mergers and acquisitions: A meta-analysis. *Strategic management journal*, *13*(1), 67-84.

de Sousa Barros, T., Cárdenas, J., & Mendes-Da-Silva, W. (2021). The effect of interlocking directorates on mergers and acquisitions in Brazil. *Journal of Management and Governance*, *25*(3), 811–839. https://doi.org/10.1007/ s10997-020-09529-7

Delaney, F. T., & Wamuziri, S. C. (2004). The impact of mergers and acquisitions on shareholder wealth in the UK construction industry. *Engineering, Construction and Architectural Management, 11*(1), 65–73. https://doi.org/10.1108/ 09699980410512674

Dennis, S. A., Wang, S., & Zhang, Y. (2021). Debt Issues around Mergers & Acquisitions. *Research in International Business and Finance, 58*. https://doi.org/10.1016 /j.ribaf.2021.101446

Desyllas, P., & Hughes, A. (2009). The revealed preferences of high technology acquirers: An analysis of the innovation characteristics of their targets. *Cambridge Journal of Economics, 33*(6), 1089–1111. https://doi.org/10.1093/ cje/bep004

Du, J., Leten, B., & Vanhaverbeke, W. (2014). Managing open innovation projects with science-based and market-based partners. *Research Policy, 43*(5), 828–840. https://doi.org/10.1016/j.respol.2013.12.008

Duan, Y., Deng, Z., Liu, H., Yang, M., Liu, M., & Wang, X. (2022). Exploring the mediating effect of managerial ability on knowledge diversity and innovation performance in reverse cross-border M&As: Evidence from Chinese manufacturing corporations. *International Journal of Production Economics, 247*. https://doi.org/10.1016/j.ijpe.2022.108434

Evripidou, L. (2012). M&As in the airline industry: Motives and systematic risk. *International Journal of Organizational Analysis, 20*(4), 435–446. https://doi.org/10.1108/19348831211268625

Fang, T. J., Han, J., He, J., & Shi, J. (2021). Property rights protection and mergers and acquisitions. *Pacific Basin Finance Journal, 68*. https://doi.org/10.1016/ j.pacfin.2021.101593

Fernald, K., Pennings, E., & Claassen, E. (2015). Biotechnology Commercialization Strategies: Risk and Return in Interfirm Cooperation. *Journal of Product Innovation Management, 32*(6), 971–996. https://doi.org/10.1111/jpim.12218

Ferris, S. P., & Sainani, S. (2021a). Do CFOs matter? Evidence from the M&A process. *Journal of Corporate Finance, 67*. https://doi.org/10.1016/j.jcorpfin.2020. 101856

Ferris, S. P., & Sainani, S. (2021b). Do CFOs matter? Evidence from the M&A process. *Journal of Corporate Finance, 67*. https://doi.org/10.1016/j.jcorpfin. 2020.101856

Filip, A., Lobo, G. J., Paugam, L., & Stolowy, H. (2022). Disclosures About Key Value Drivers in M&A Announcement Press Releases: An Exploratory Study. *Abacus, 58*(1), 62–104. https://doi.org/10.1111/abac.12234

Foster Jr, J. D. (1986, April). Impact of Petroleum Industry Recapitalization Upon Integral Material Suppliers. In *SPE Symposium on Energy, Finance, and Taxation Policies* (pp. SPE-14640). SPE.

Francoeur, C. (2006). The long-run performance of cross-border mergers and acquisitions: Evidence to support the internalization theory. *Corporate Ownership and Control, 4*(2 C), 312–324. https://doi.org/10.22495/ cocv4i2c2p8

Gada, V. P., Goyal, L., & Popli, M. (2021). Earnouts in M&A deal structuring: The impact of CEO prevention focus. *Journal of International Management*, *27*(1). https://doi.org/10.1016/j.intman.2021.100825

Gao, N., Hua, C., & Khurshed, A. (2021). Loan price in mergers and acquisitions. *Journal of Corporate Finance*, *67*. https://doi.org/10.1016/j.jcorpfin.2020. 101754

Gao, Q., Zhang, Z., Li, Z., Li, Y., & Shao, X. (2022). Strategic green marketing and cross-border merger and acquisition completion: The role of corporate social responsibility and green patent development. *Journal of Cleaner Production*, *343*. https://doi.org/10.1016/j.jclepro.2022.130961

Gorton, G., Kahl, M., & Rosen, R. J. (2009). Eat or be eaten: A theory of mergers and firm size. *The Journal of Finance*, *64*(3), 1291-1344.

Gregori, W. D., & Nardo, M. (2021). The effect of restrictive measures on cross-border investment in the European Union. *World Economy*, *44*(7), 1914–1943. https://doi.org/10.1111/twec.13104

Gregoriou, A., Nguyen, B. D., Nguyen, T. D., Le, H., & Hudson, R. (2021). Economic policy uncertainty and cross-border mergers and acquisitions. *International Review of Financial Analysis*, *78*. https://doi.org/10.1016/j.irfa.2021.101911

Gu, Y., Ben, S., & Lv, J. (2022). Peer Effect in Merger and Acquisition Activities and Its Impact on Corporate Sustainable Development: Evidence from China. *Sustainability (Switzerland)*, *14*(7). https://doi.org/10.3390/su14073891

Halkos, G. E., & Tzeremes, N. G. (2013). Estimating the degree of operating efficiency gains from a potential bank merger and acquisition: A DEA bootstrapped approach. *Journal of Banking and Finance*, *37*(5), 1658–1668. https://doi.org/10.1016/j.jbankfin.2012.12.009

Ho, T., Brownen-Trinh, R., & Xu, F. (2021). The information content of target price forecasts: Evidence from mergers and acquisitions. *Journal of Business Finance and Accounting*, *48*(5–6), 1134–1171. https://doi.org/10.1111/jbfa.12521

Hong, X., Lin, X., Fang, L., Gao, Y., & Li, R. (2022). Application of Machine Learning Models for Predictions on Cross-Border Merger and Acquisition Decisions with ESG Characteristics from an Ecosystem and Sustainable Development Perspective. *Sustainability (Switzerland)*, *14*(5). https://doi.org/10.3390/su14052838

Hsu, J., Yang, T. H., & Tsai, Y. C. (2021). The long-run performance of cross-border acquirers: An analysis of synergy sources. *Journal of Multinational Financial Management*, *60*. https://doi.org/10.1016/j.mulfin.2021.100694

Hsu, P. H., Huang, P., Humphery-Jenner, M., & Powell, R. (2021). Cross-border mergers and acquisitions for innovation. *Journal of International Money and Finance*, *112*. https://doi.org/10.1016/j.jimonfin.2020.102320

Hu, H., Platt, K., & Su, C. H. (2022). Strategic Announcement Sequencing: Earnings and M&A Announcements. *Journal of Behavioral Finance*, *23*(2), 132–149. https://doi.org/10.1080/15427560.2020.1864734

Huang, C., Ozkan, N., & Xu, F. (2022). Shareholder Litigation Risk and Firms' Choice of External Growth. *Journal of Financial and Quantitative Analysis*. https://doi.org/10.1017/S0022109022000187

Huang, Y. L., Chen, Y. R., & Chen, B. S. (2021). Executive Stock Options, Corporate Cash Holdings and M&A Decisions. *NTU Management Review*, *31*(1), 71–115. https://doi.org/10.6226/NTUMR.202104_31(1).0003

Huian, M. C. (2011). Post M & A accounting performance of romanian banks. *Creating Global Competitive Economies: A 360-Degree Approach - Proceedings of the 17th International Business Information Management Association Conference, IBIMA 2011*, *4*, 2399–2414. https://doi.org/10.5171/2012.184557

Irwin, K., Gilstrap, C., Drnevich, P., & Sunny, M. (2022). The acquisition of capabilities: How firms use dynamic and ordinary capabilities to manage uncertainty. *Journal of Management and Organization*. https://doi.org/10.1017/jmo.2022.23

Jang, Y., & Yehuda, N. (2021). Resource Adjustment Costs, Cost Stickiness, and Value Creation in Mergers and Acquisitions*. *Contemporary Accounting Research*, *38*(3), 2264–2301. https://doi.org/10.1111/1911-3846.12668

Jensen, Michael C., and Meckling, William H. 1976. Theory of the firm: managerial behavior, agency costs and ownership structure. *Journal of Financial Economics no.4 (October): 305-60*

Jordan, M. I., & Rumelhart, D. E. (1992). Forward models: Supervised learning with a distal teacher. *Cognitive science*, *16*(3), 307-354.

Ju, B. K., Yoo, S. H., & Baek, C. (2022). Economies of Scale in City Gas Sector in Seoul, South Korea: Evidence from an Empirical Investigation. *Sustainability (Switzerland)*, *14*(9). https://doi.org/10.3390/su14095371

Kang, J. K. (1993). The international market for corporate control: Mergers and acquisitions of US firms by Japanese firms. *Journal of financial economics*, *34*(3), 345-371.

Kaplan, S. (1989). The effects of management buyouts on operating performance and value. *Journal of financial economics*, *24*(2), 217-254.

Kaplan, S. N. (1994). Top executive rewards and firm performance: A comparison of Japan and the United States. *Journal of political Economy*, *102*(3), 510-546.

Karamustafa-Köse, G., Schneider, S. C., & Davis, J. D. (2022). Unpacking the dynamics in acquisition of capabilities: the role of identities during postmerger integration. *Journal of Organizational Change Management*, *35*(8), 13–38. https://doi.org/10.1108/JOCM-02-2021-0053

Kiisk, V., & Rungi, M. (2020). Knowledge cannibalism in the European ICT sector. *Learning Organization*, *27*(4), 305–319. https://doi.org/10.1108/TLO-01-2019-0003

Kim, M., Ge, Q., & Kim, D. (2021). Mergers and labor market outcomes in the US airline industry. *Contemporary Economic Policy*, *39*(4), 849–866. https://doi.org/10.1111/coep.12520

Kirjavainen, J., Makinen, S. J., Saari, U. A., & Risikko, K. (2021, May 17). Using mergers and acquisitions to prepare for disruption. *2021 IEEE Technology and Engineering Management Conference - Europe, TEMSCON-EUR 2021*. https://doi.org/10.1109/TEMSCON-EUR52034.2021.9488637

Kiselakova, D., & Sofrankova, B. (2015). Effects and risks of mergers and acquisitions on entrepreneurship in banking and finance: Empirical study from Slovakia. *Review of European Studies*, *7*(7), 23–35. https://doi.org/10.5539/res.v7n7p23

Klitzka, M., He, J., & Schiereck, D. (2022). The rationality of M&A targets in the choice of payment methods. In *Review of Managerial Science* (Vol. 16, Issue 4, pp. 933–967). Springer Science and Business Media Deutschland GmbH. https://doi.org/10.1007/s11846-021-00469-6

Kolari, J. W., Pynnonen, S., & Tuncez, A. M. (2021). Further evidence on long-run abnormal returns after corporate events. *Quarterly Review of Economics and Finance*, *81*, 421–439. https://doi.org/10.1016/j.qref.2020.10.011

Korzeb, Z., Samaniego-Medina, R., & Giráldez-Puig, P. (2022). Cultural differences and cross-border investment project performance: an analysis of the Polish banking sector. *Economic Research-Ekonomska Istrazivanja*, *35*(1), 6579–6600. https://doi.org/10.1080/1331677X.2022.2052332

Krishna, V., & Jain, S. K. (2022). Modes of collaboration in open innovation practice of pharmaceutical firms in India: the analysis of survey and patent data. *Journal of Intellectual Capital*, *23*(2), 222–248. https://doi.org/10.1108/JIC-04-2020-0113

Krishnamurti, C., Shams, S., & Chowdhury, H. (2021). Evidence on the trade-off between corporate social responsibility and mergers and acquisitions investment. *Australian Journal of Management*, *46*(3), 466–498. https://doi.org/10.1177/0312896220950394

Kumar, R. (2009). Post-merger corporate performance: An Indian perspective. *Management Research News*, *32*(2), 145–157. https://doi.org/10.1108/01409170910927604

Kumaraswamy, S., Ebrahim, R., & Nasser, H. (2019). Impact of corporate restructuring on the financial performance of gulf cooperation council firms. *Polish Journal of Management Studies*, *19*(2), 262–272. https://doi.org/10.17512/pjms.2019.19.2.22

Kumbhakar, S. C. (1987). The specification of technical and allocative inefficiency in stochastic production and profit frontiers. *Journal of econometrics*, *34*(3), 335-348.

Kumbhakar, S. C. (1990). Production frontiers, panel data, and time-varying technical inefficiency. *Journal of econometrics*, *46*(1-2), 201-211.

Kumbhakar, S. C., & Wang, H. J. (2005). Estimation of growth convergence using a stochastic production frontier approach. *Economics Letters*, *88*(3), 300-305.

Lang, X. (2021). Evaluating the Potential Efficiency from Virtual Mergers and Acquisitions of Chinese Banks. *Proceedings - 2nd International Conference on E-Commerce and Internet Technology, ECIT 2021*, 167–170. https://doi.org/10.1109/ECIT52743.2021.00045

Lee, H. S., Degtereva, E. A., & Zobov, A. M. (2021). The impact of the COVID-19 pandemic on cross-border mergers and acquisitions' determinants: New empirical evidence from quasi-poisson and negative binomial regression models. *Economies*, *9*(4). https://doi.org/10.3390/economies9040184

Lee, Y., and Schmidt, P. (1993), "A Production Frontier Model with Flexible Temporal Variation in Technical Efficiency," in H. Fried, K. Lovell and S. Schmidt (Eds.), The Measurement of Productive Efficiency. Oxford: Oxford University Press.

Leschik, D., Rossberger, R., & Oczkowski, E. (2022). M&As in Germany: measuring success for the pharma and biotech industries. *Journal of Business Strategy*, *43*(2), 87–95. https://doi.org/10.1108/JBS-07-2020-0153

Levine, O., & Wu, Y. (2021). Asset volatility and capital structure: Evidence from corporate mergers. *Management Science*, *67*(5), 2773–2798. https://doi.org/10.1287/mnsc.2020.3607

Li, C., Li, H., & Zhao, Z. (2022). Geographic proximity and M&As: Evidence from China. In *Emerging Markets Review* (Vol. 51). Elsevier B.V. https://doi.org/10.1016/j.ememar.2022.100892

Li, J., Wang, P., Tao, X., & Wen, Y. (2021). Productivity Analysis for Banks' Merger and Acquisition Using Two-Stage DEA: Evidence from China. *Journal of Systems Science and Information*, *9*(6), 627–659. https://doi.org/10.21078/ JSSI-2021-627-33

Li, S., Ang, J. S., Wu, C., & Yang, S. (2021). Valuing technological synergies in mergers. *North American Journal of Economics and Finance*, *58*. https://doi.org/10.1016/j.najef.2021.101464

Li, S., Liu, C., & Peng, X. (2022). The Impact of Financialization on Mergers and acquisitions:Evidence from Chinese Manufacturing Listed Firms. *Emerging Markets Finance and Trade*, *58*(11), 3152–3163. https://doi.org/10.1080/1540496X.2022.2031969

Li, W., Su, Y., & Wang, K. (2022). How does economic policy uncertainty affect cross-border M&A: Evidence from Chinese firms. *Emerging Markets Review*, *52*. https://doi.org/10.1016/j.ememar.2022.100908

Li, Y., & Singal, M. (2021). Deal characteristics and M&A performance: How do hospitality firms fare? *International Journal of Hospitality Management, 96.* https://doi.org/10.1016/j.ijhm.2021.102947

Liu, K., Wu, S., Guo, N., & Fang, Q. (2021). Host Country's carbon emission and cross-border M&A performance: Evidence from listed enterprises in China. *Journal of Cleaner Production, 314.* https://doi.org/10.1016/j.jclepro.2021.127977

Liu, T., Lu, Z. (Gene), Shu, T., & Wei, F. (2022). Unique bidder-target relatedness and synergies creation in mergers and acquisitions. *Journal of Corporate Finance, 73.* https://doi.org/10.1016/j.jcorpfin.2022.102196

Loureiro, G., & Silva, S. (2021). The impact of securities regulation on the information environment around stock-financed acquisitions. *Journal of International Financial Markets, Institutions and Money, 73.* https://doi.org/10.1016/j.intfin.2021.101374

Lv, J., Xiong, Y., & Zheng, Y. (2022). Determinants of outward foreign direct investment entry mode choice: evidence from Chinese-listed companies. *Chinese Management Studies, 16*(1), 231–243. https://doi.org/10.1108/CMS-08-2020-0347

Ma, Y., & Xu, J. (2020). Segmentally aware: know when to merge and when to purge. *Journal of Organizational Change Management, 33*(1), 196–214. https://doi.org/10.1108/JOCM-06-2019-0201

Majumdar, S. K., Yaylacicegi, U., & Moussawi, R. (2012). Mergers and synergy: Lessons from contemporary telecommunications history. *Telecommunications Policy, 36*(2), 140–154. https://doi.org/10.1016/j.telpol.2011.11.010

Maroof, Z., & Jawad, M. (2019). Merger & acquisition: A comparative integration analysis of third world country. *FEMIB 2019 - 1st International Conference on Finance, Economics, Management and IT Business*, 78–85. https://doi.org/10.5220/0007761000780085

Maroof, Z., & Shah, S. M. A. (2017). DOES VERTICAL INTEGRATION STRATEGY FOR MERGER & ACQUISITIONS A FRUITFUL DECISION? AN EVIDENCE FROM PAKISTANI MERGER MARKET. In *Academy of Accounting and Financial Studies Journal* (Vol. 21, Issue 2).

Mei, B., & Sun, C. (2008). Event analysis of the impact of mergers and acquisitions on the financial performance of the U.S. forest products industry. *Forest Policy and Economics, 10*(5), 286–294. https://doi.org/10.1016/j.forpol.2007.11.005

Mihaiu, D. M. (2018). Financial Synergies of Mergers and Acquisitions: Between Intentions and Achievements. *Springer Proceedings in Business and Economics*, 237–252. https://doi.org/10.1007/978-3-319-71876-7_22

Mingwei, Z., Jiachun, Y., Yuju, L., & Yitao, M. (2020). A Study of MA Performance Based on Enterprise Capability Measurement Model: Taking Shanghai RAAS

Serial MA in 2014 as an Example. *Proceedings - 2020 16th Dahe Fortune China Forum and Chinese High-Educational Management Annual Academic Conference, DFHMC 2020*, 189–193. https://doi.org/10.1109/DFHMC52214.2020.00044

Mishra, P. (2018). Are Mergers and Acquisitions Necessarily Anti-competitive? Empirical Evidence from India's Manufacturing Sector. *Margin, 12*(3), 276–307. https://doi.org/10.1177/0973801018768987

Mishra, P., & Jaiswal, N. (2017). Impact of Mergers and Acquisitions on Firms' Export Competitiveness: Experience of Indian Pharmaceutical Industry. *South Asia Economic Journal, 18*(1), 1–20. https://doi.org/10.1177/1391561416661625

Moatti, V., Ren, C. R., Anand, J., & Dussauge, P. (2015). Disentangling the performance effects of efficiency and bargaining power in horizontal growth strategies: An empirical investigation in the global retail industry. *Strategic Management Journal, 36*(5), 745–757. https://doi.org/10.1002/smj.2244

Monteiro, R., & Silva, S. (2022). The impact of securities regulation in the European Union on M&A: does it compensate to go beyond borders? *Journal of Financial Regulation and Compliance, 30*(3), 282–311. https://doi.org/10.1108/JFRC-08-2021-0066

Motis, J. (2007). Mergers and acquisitions motives. *Toulouse School of Economics, University of Crete*, 1-31.

Nguyen, G., & Vu, L. (2021). Does venture capital syndication affect mergers and acquisitions? *Journal of Corporate Finance, 67*. https://doi.org/10.1016/j.jcorpfin.2020.101851

Niederman, F., & Baker, E. W. (2022). The "case to theory transformation method" for initiating is theory: the process and an illustration using is integration following mergers and acquisitions. *Information Technology and People*. https://doi.org/10.1108/ITP-10-2020-0696

Noles, M. J. (n.d.). *Rural Hospital Mergers and Acquisitions: Which Hospitals Are Being Acquired and How Are They Performing Afterward?*

Ocieszak, M. (2020). Determinants of Companies' Financial Performance following M&A Transactions in Poland. *Central European Management Journal, 28*(4), 51–66. https://doi.org/10.7206/cemj.2658-0845.34

Olden, R. E. (1992). Introduction to ownership and transition. ii: Succession and firm valuation. *Journal of Management in Engineering, 8*(4), 376-383.

O'Shaughnessy, K. C., & Flanagan, D. J. (1998). Determinants of layoff announcements following M&As: An empirical investigation. *Strategic Management Journal, 19*(10), 989–999. https://doi.org/10.1002/(SICI)1097-0266(199810)19:10<989::AID-SMJ994>3.0.CO;2-3

Øyna, S., Almor, T., Elango, B., & Tarba, S. Y. (2018). Maturing born globals and their acquisitive behaviour. *International Business Review*, *27*(3), 714–725. https://doi.org/10.1016/j.ibusrev.2017.12.002

Palmer, N., Tanner, S., Detrick, C., & Wagner, I. (2007). For top insurance companies, customer focus and merger mastery produce superior results. *Strategy and Leadership*, *35*(2), 39–45. https://doi.org/10.1108/10878570710734525

Pereira, G. I., Niesten, E., & Pinkse, J. (2022). Sustainable energy systems in the making: A study on business model adaptation in incumbent utilities. *Technological Forecasting and Social Change*, *174*. https://doi.org/10.1016/j.techfore.2021.121207

Pitt, M. M., & Lee, L. F. (1981). The measurement and sources of technical inefficiency in the Indonesian weaving industry. *Journal of development economics*, *9*(1), 43-64.

Rahman, M., Lambkin, M., & Hussain, D. (2016). Value creation and appropriation following M&A: A data envelopment analysis. *Journal of Business Research*, *69*(12), 5628–5635. https://doi.org/10.1016/j.jbusres.2016.03.070

Raithatha, M., & Ladkani, R. (2022). Do board characteristics play a moderating role in M&A decisions of family firms? *International Journal of Emerging Markets*. https://doi.org/10.1108/IJOEM-07-2021-1068

Rashid, A., & Naeem, N. (2017). Effects of mergers on corporate performance: An empirical evaluation using OLS and the empirical Bayesian methods. *Borsa Istanbul Review*, *17*(1), 10–24. https://doi.org/10.1016/j.bir.2016.09.004

Reddy, R. K., Park, S. J., & Mooty, S. (2022). Emerging market firm investments in advanced markets: A country of origin perspective. *Journal of Multinational Financial Management*, *65*. https://doi.org/10.1016/j.mulfin.2022.100748

Renneboog, L., & Vansteenkiste, C. (2019). Failure and success in mergers and acquisitions. *Journal of Corporate Finance*, *58*, 650-699.

R.H. Coase (1937), *The nature of the firm, Reprinted from Economica, in A.E.A Readings in Price Theory,* edited by G.J. Stigler and K.E. Boulding. Homewood, IL: Richard D. Irwin (1952).

Richards, T. J., & Manfredo, M. R. (2003). *Post-Merger Performance of Agricultural Cooperatives*.

Sahu, S. K., & Agarwal, N. (2017). Inter-firm differences in mergers and acquisitions: a study of the pharmaceutical sector in India. *Journal of Economic Studies*, *44*(5), 861–878. https://doi.org/10.1108/JES-12-2015-0239

Schweizer, D., & Wu, G. (2021). Law Firm expertise and shareholder wealth. *Financial Markets, Institutions and Instruments*, *30*(4), 129–163. https://doi.org/10.1111/fmii.12152

Schweizer, L., Wang, L., Koscher, E., & Michaelis, B. (2022). Experiential learning, M&A performance, and post-acquisition integration strategy: A meta-analysis. *Long Range Planning*. https://doi.org/10.1016/j.lrp.2022.102212

Shafique, M., & Hagedoorn, J. (2022). Look at U: Technological scope of the acquirer, technological complementarity with the target, and post-acquisition R&D output. *Technovation, 115*. https://doi.org/10.1016/j.technovation.2022.102533

Shao, B., Asatani, K., Sasaki, H., & Sakata, I. (2021). Categorization of mergers and acquisitions using transaction network features. *Research in International Business and Finance, 57*. https://doi.org/10.1016/j.ribaf.2021.101421

Shen, H., Liang, Y., Li, H., Liu, J., & Lu, G. (2021). Does geopolitical risk promote mergers and acquisitions of listed companies in energy and electric power industries. *Energy Economics, 95*. https://doi.org/10.1016/j.eneco.2021.105115

Shi, J., Yu, C., & Li, Y. (2022). Beyond Linear: The Relationship between Corporate Social Responsibility and Market Reactions to Cross-Border Mergers and Acquisitions. *Emerging Markets Finance and Trade, 58*(3), 638–654. https://doi.org/10.1080/1540496X.2020.1829409

Shim, J. (2011). Mergers and acquisitions, Diversification and performance in the U.S. Property-liability insurance industry. *Journal of Financial Services Research, 39*(3), 119–144. https://doi.org/10.1007/s10693-010-0094-3

Siegel, D. S., & Simons, K. L. (2010). Research notes and commentaries assessing the effects of mergers and acquisitions on firm performance, plant productivity, and workers: New evidence from matched employer-employee data. In *Strategic Management Journal* (Vol. 31, Issue 8, pp. 903–916). https://doi.org/10.1002/smj.843

Smimou, K. (2015). Regional equity market conditions and cross-border mergers and acquisitions (M&A): Evidence from the BRIC, Eastern Europe, and Africa. *International Journal of Emerging Markets, 10*(3), 535–559. https://doi.org/10.1108/IJoEM-09-2013-0157

Srinivasa Reddy, K., Nangia, V. K., & Agrawal, R. (2013). Corporate mergers and financial performance: a new assessment of Indian cases. *Nankai Business Review International, 4*(2), 107–129. https://doi.org/10.1108/204087413113 23326

Stefko, R., Heckova, J., Gavurova, B., Valentiny, T., Chapcakova, A., & Ratnayake Kascakova, D. (2022). An analysis of the impact of economic context of selected determinants of cross-border mergers and acquisitions in the EU. *Economic Research-Ekonomska Istraživanja*, 1–18. https://doi.org/10.1080/1331677x.2022.2048200

Syukur, M., & Bungkilo, D.-A. (2020). The aermaths of acquisition in Indonesia Cite this paper The aftermaths of acquisition in Indonesia. In *Int. J. Monetary Economics and Finance* (Vol. 13, Issue 1). http://www.kppu.go.id/id/merger-dan-akuisisi/

Tampakoudis, I., Nerantzidis, M., Eweje, G., & Leventis, S. (2022). The impact of gender diversity on shareholder wealth: Evidence from European bank M&A. *Journal of Financial Stability*, *60*. https://doi.org/10.1016/j.jfs.2022.101020

Tavares Lehmann, A. T., & Lehmann, F. (2017). Outward direct investment by Chinese state-owned enterprises: Can host country policy act as a country-specific advantage? *Competitiveness Review*, *27*(3), 231–252. https://doi.org/10.1108/CR-08-2016-0052

Trejo-Pech, C. J. O., Gunderson, M. A., & Lambert, D. M. (2021). Mergers and acquisitions in the U.S. agribusiness sector, 1990–2017. *Agribusiness*, *37*(4), 713–730. https://doi.org/10.1002/agr.21695

Todd, D. (1984). Strategies of growth, diversification and rationalization in the evolution of concentration in British shipbuilding. *Regional studies*, *18*(1), 55-67.

Tripathi, V., & Lamba, A. (2015). What drives cross-border mergers and acquisitions?: A study of Indian multinational enterprises. *Journal of Strategy and Management*, *8*(4), 384–414. https://doi.org/10.1108/JSMA-05-2015-0040

Tse, E. C. Y., & Crawford-Welch, S. (1989). An analysis of merger and acquisition activity in the hospitality industry for the period 1970-1988. *Hospitality Education and Research Journal*, *13*(3), 1-13.

Umashankar, N., Bahadir, S. C., & Bharadwaj, S. (2022). Despite Efficiencies, Mergers and Acquisitions Reduce Firm Value by Hurting Customer Satisfaction. *Journal of Marketing*, *86*(2), 66–86. https://doi.org/10.1177/00222429211024255

Wan, L., Ren, L., Lin, B., & Xu, X. (2021). Does investment banker human capital matter in acquisitions? Evidence from China. *Journal of Corporate Finance*, *70*. https://doi.org/10.1016/j.jcorpfin.2021.102048

Wang, K. T., Wu, Y., & Sun, A. (2021). Acquisitions and the cost of debt: Evidence from China. *International Review of Financial Analysis*, *78*. https://doi.org/10.1016/j.irfa.2021.101925

Wang, W. (2005). An evaluation of the Balanced Scorecard® in equity valuation. The case of exchange ratio in the M&As of Taiwan's financial industry. *Journal of Intellectual Capital*, *6*(2), 206–221. https://doi.org/10.1108/146919305105 92807

Wang, Z., Lu, W., & Liu, M. (2021). Corporate social responsibility overinvestment in mergers and acquisitions. *International Review of Financial Analysis*, *78*. https://doi.org/10.1016/j.irfa.2021.101944

Weston, J.F., Mitchel, M.L., Mulherin, J.H. and Salwan, P. (2010). Takeovers, restructuring, and corporate governance. *Fourth ed. Delhi: Pearson Education*

Woody, C. (1924). A survey of educational research in 1923. *The Journal of Educational Research*, *9*(5), 357-381.

Wójcik, D., Keenan, L., Pažitka, V., Urban, M., & Wu, W. (2022). The Changing Landscape of International Financial Centers in the Twenty-First Century: Cross-border Mergers and Acquisitions in the Global Financial Network. *Economic Geography*, *98*(2), 97–118. https://doi.org/10.1080/00130095.2021. 2010535

Yang, H., Zhang, Q., Zhao, X., & Wang, Z. (2022). Does political corruption affect mergers and acquisitions decisions? Evidence from China. *International Review of Economics and Finance*, *78*, 248–266. https://doi.org/10.1016/j.iref.2021. 12.003

Yang, J., & Gon Kim, W. (2010). Post-merger stock performance of acquiring hospitality firms. In *Tourism Economics* (Vol. 16, Issue 1).

Yang, N., Zhang, Y., Yu, L., Wang, J., & Liu, X. (2022). Cross-border mergers and acquisitions, regional cultural diversity and acquirers' corporate social responsibility: Evidence from China listed companies. *International Review of Economics and Finance*, *79*, 565–578. https://doi.org/10.1016/j.iref.2022. 02.041

Yang, S., & Wu, C. (2021). Do Chinese managers listen to the media?: Evidence from mergers and acquisitions. *Research in International Business and Finance*, *58*. https://doi.org/10.1016/j.ribaf.2021.101458

Yang, Y. (2019). Effects of the size of acquisition on a hotel group's financial performance. *Journal of Hospitality Financial Management*, *27*(1), 49–54. https://doi.org/10.7275/kpvx-q091

Yen, T. Y., & André, P. (2019). Market reaction to the effect of corporate social responsibility on mergers and acquisitions: Evidence on emerging markets. *Quarterly Review of Economics and Finance*, *71*, 114–131. https://doi.org/10.1016/j.qref.2018.07.003

Zaraa Boubaker, F., Naoui, K., Boubaker, F., & Naoui, K. (2020). A post-merger performance of acquiring firms: evidence from French stock market. In *Int. J. Entrepreneurship and Small Business* (Vol. 39, Issue 2).

Zheng, D., Yuan, Z., Ding, S., & Cui, T. (2021). Enhancing environmental sustainability through corporate governance: the merger and acquisition perspective. *Energy, Sustainability and Society*, *11*(1). https://doi.org/10.1186/ s13705-021-00318-0

Zhu, B., Xia, X., & Zheng, X. (2021). One way out of the share pledging quagmire: Evidence from mergers and acquisitions. *Journal of Corporate Finance*, *71*. https://doi.org/10.1016/j.jcorpfin.2021.102120

Zhu, D. H., & Westphal, J. D. (2021). Structural power, corporate strategy, and performance. *Strategic Management Journal*, *42*(3), 624–651. https://doi.org/ 10.1002/smj.3239

Zhu, Z., Huang, W., Shen, W., & Ding, Y. (2017). Why financial performance of the technology-based merger and acquisition is counterproductive to its market reaction: A study based on the listed Chinese pharmaceutical companies. *PICMET 2016 - Portland International Conference on Management of Engineering and Technology: Technology Management For Social Innovation, Proceedings*, 2363–2367. https://doi.org/10.1109/PICMET.2016.7806604